The Sky Between
the Leaves

Film reviews, essays & interviews
1992–2012

David Walsh

Published by Mehring Books
P.O. Box 48377
Oak Park, MI 48237
Printed in the United States of America
© 2013 Mehring Books
All rights reserved.

Library of Congress Cataloging-in-Publication Data

Walsh, David, 1949-
The sky between the leaves : film reviews, essays & interviews, 1992-2012 / David Walsh.
    pages cm
Includes index.
ISBN 978-1-893638-27-3 (pbk. : alk. paper) -- ISBN 1-893638-27-8 (pbk. : alk. paper) -- ISBN 978-1-893638-38-9 (ebook) -- ISBN 1-893638-38-3 (ebook)
1. Motion pictures--Reviews. 2. Motion picture producers and directors--Interviews. 3. Motion picture actors and actresses--Interviews 4. Film critics--Interviews. 5. Motion picture industry--United States--History--20th century. 6. Motion picture industry--United States--History--21st century. 7. Marxist criticism. I. Title.
PN1995.W35 2013
791.43'75--dc23
                              2013014302

For Joanne

Contents

Film Festivals

Interviews

Essays & Film History

Index

Introduction

"A protest against reality, either conscious or unconscious, active or passive, optimistic or pessimistic, always forms part of a really creative piece of work." – Trotsky

I

The majority of the film reviews, interviews and essays in this book appeared originally in the World Socialist Web Site (wsws.org), the Internet-based publication launched by the Trotskyist International Committee of the Fourth International (ICFI) in February 1998. A number of items in this collection, which predate the founding of the WSWS, appeared in newspapers published by the Workers League and its successor organization, the Socialist Equality Party. The earliest pieces (1992–93) were written in New York City. I moved to the Detroit area in late 1993, almost simultaneously with the transformation of the *Bulletin* into the *International Workers Bulletin* (IWB), where the next selection of reviews and other material appeared (1994–96).

Tracing the provenance of these reviews and essays in terms of their general attitude toward art and culture, leaving aside for the moment questions of personal history and opinion, involves a discussion of both critical world events and the evolution of the Trotskyist movement, to which I have adhered for 40 years. The development within the International Committee of systematic work on problems of culture and art, and my own participation in this process, was the outcome of the ICFI's response to the dissolution of the Soviet Union in December 1991.

At its twelfth Plenum in March 1992, the International Committee examined the historic significance and political implications of that event. It clearly marked a fundamental turning point in the history of the international workers movement. Since the October Revolution of 1917, when the Russian working class, led by the Bolshevik Party, overthrew the bourgeois Provisional Government and established the first workers state in history, the social, political, intellectual and cultural development of the international working class was inextricably linked to this central event of modern world history.

As the Fourth International had foreseen, the policies of the anti-Marxist and nationalist Stalinist bureaucracy had destroyed the USSR. The international working class had suffered a major defeat. The question was thus posed: upon what basis would a new mass revolutionary socialist movement emerge? Notwithstanding the triumphalism of the ruling elites and the demoralization of legions of petty-bourgeois radicals, who were anxious to affix the preface "ex-" to their earlier and varied leftish political identities, the International Committee insisted that the fundamental *objective* contradictions of the capitalist system had not been resolved. Indeed, the global integration of capitalist production and the vast worldwide expansion of the working class were leading, more or less rapidly, to the intensification of economic, political and social contradictions that would find expression in a new upsurge of the international class struggle.

But what of the *subjective* prerequisites for socialist revolution? Through what process would the objective impulses for the overthrow of capitalism find subjective expression in the consciousness of the working class? In his report to the twelfth Plenum, David North, a leading member of the ICFI, sought to answer these critical questions through an examination of the history of the international workers movement, and, in particular, its development in the decades prior to the 1917 October Revolution.

The conquest of power by the Bolshevik Party was not a historical accident, the product of a chance interaction between an especially severe crisis of a bourgeois government and the determined action of a revolutionary party that just happened to be at the right place at the right time. No, the October Revolution was the outcome of a massive growth in the political consciousness of the international working class in the decades that followed the publication of the *Communist Manifesto* in 1848 and, especially, in the aftermath of the suppression of the Paris Commune in May 1871. The forty six years separating the Commune in Paris from the Soviet in Petrograd witnessed an immense development of the political consciousness of the working class, whose most advanced expression was the founding of the Second International in 1889 and the emergence of socialist parties throughout the world, including the mass SPD in Germany.

The growth of socialist consciousness was not only the product of the struggle for specific economic and political demands. The development of art and culture—through the work of writers, painters, musicians (often, but not always, partial to socialism) and the Marxist critics who appraised their efforts—played an immense role in shaping and broadening the outlook of the working class; of sharpening its awareness of the injustices of capitalism; strengthening and refining the workers' outrage and willingness to sacrifice; and making more ardent their belief and confidence in the possibility of realizing socialism and building a society based on genuine social equality and solidarity.

Socialism required a cultural awakening among a significant section of the working class, for such an awakening is essential to the development of a conscious, revolutionary critical attitude toward capitalist society. This awakening, however, did not occur independently of the efforts of the revolutionary party. Rather, it is the party—the most conscious section of the working class—that leads the fight for this development. The intellectual essence of socialist consciousness is a critical revolutionary attitude to the existing social relations and everyday political assumptions and concepts as they emerge and find "spontaneous" expression in bourgeois society. Thus, the development of the work of the party in the sphere of art and culture had to be an essential component of the struggle for revolutionary socialist consciousness.

The intellectual-political project outlined by the International Committee in 1992 was to have a profound effect on my life and work, and that of my companion Joanne Laurier, within the Trotskyist movement. In 1993 we met with David North in New York City. By this time, I had been working full-time on the *Bulletin* and the *International Workers Bulletin* for two years. He discussed the plans for a substantial expansion of the ICFI's coverage of the arts. Would we agree, he asked, to relocate to Detroit, where I would join the staff of the IWB as its arts editor? We readily accepted the invitation, packed our belongings and arrived in Detroit in late November 1993. There, amidst comrades and friends, we enjoyed a collaborative environment ideal for the development of serious and sustained intellectual work.

Over the years that followed, the international discussion and coordination of political and cultural work within the Trotskyist movement made great strides, a process accelerated by various technological advances, including the Internet. Since 1998, the project of the World Socialist Web Site has been sustained by an extraordinary global political-intellectual collaboration of revolutionary Marxists.

In the course of this work, a remarkable group of commentators on film, music and art has emerged, including Joanne Laurier and Fred Mazelis in the US, Paul Bond in Britain, Sybille Fuchs and Stefan Steinberg in Germany, Richard Philips in Australia and the late Piyaseeli Wijetungasinghe in Sri Lanka, to name only a few of the comrades who have made significant contributions to the development of the cultural work of the WSWS.

The results recorded in the articles posted on our web site testify to the intellectual vitality and democratic spirit of the political and cultural life of the international Trotskyist movement out of which this work emerged. The integration of cultural work into the daily political life of the ICFI represents an extraordinary achievement, whose political consequences will become increasingly clear as dramatic political events unfold within the United States and internationally.

II

In writing about the global film industry, there is always the temptation to see its difficulties and failings in largely subjective terms. That is certainly how the industry generally sees itself. Given the quality of the products, the personalities and the vast sums of money involved, there is much to complain about. However, in the end, the narrowness and even perfidy of studio executives, the general turn to the right by a significant portion of the intelligentsia, the artistic weaknesses and failings of the filmmakers themselves, the prominence of various scoundrels and charlatans—while all of them genuine factors in the current problems—are subjective expressions of an objective process.

We seek to trace out the conditions and character of cinema in our time from the conditions and character of the world in our time. The evolution of filmmaking is embedded in social development. One of the critical tasks, in our view, paraphrasing the Russian Marxist Georgi Plekhanov (and the nineteenth century Russian critic V.G. Belinsky), is to define at what point on the social path the film writers and directors found humanity. Cinema, a mass art form, is especially sensitive to the level of the class struggle, to the political and social activity and consciousness of the working class. Filmmakers have been nourished by social movements and, conversely, starved by their absence.

A number of essays in this volume point to the influence of the upsurge in the American working class, as well as the Russian Revolution and social upheavals in Germany, Hungary and elsewhere, on Hollywood films of the 1930s and 1940s in particular. Many writers, directors and actors gravitated to the left, for the most part toward the Communist Party. That specific history has its ultimately tragic dimensions, but the ability of American movies to reflect life and entertain masses of people was indisputably bound up with this radicalization.

Charlie Chaplin, Orson Welles and John Ford, three of the greatest figures of the era, were all considered artists of the left in the late 1930s and early 1940s. In reality, there were many in Hollywood, US-born and émigrés alike, prepared to criticize important features of American capitalist life, as a series of films in the postwar world demonstrates (*Ruthless, The Lady from Shanghai, Force of Evil, Body and Soul, The Best Years of Our Lives, Caught, Flamingo Road, Key Largo* and others).

The launching of the film industry blacklist in 1947 and the crude, brutal hearings of the House Committee on Un-American Activities (HUAC) in 1947 and 1951–52 were not paranoid fishing expeditions. The possibility of a mass audience being exposed to radical views represented a genuine ideological threat to the US ruling elite that had to be dealt with.

The emergence of the United States as the leading imperialist power, signaled by the mass exterminations in Hiroshima and Nagasaki, and the anticommunist poisoning of the political and intellectual atmosphere shattered the illusion that a more egalitarian, even socialistic society was on the agenda in America.

The left-wing elements in Hollywood, the New York theater and elsewhere were entirely unprepared and ill equipped for the McCarthyite witch-hunts and, ultimately, the political retreat of the working class in the postwar period.

Miseducated and intellectually disarmed by Stalinism, these layers were working off a false reading of the critical experiences of the 1930s and 1940s. They had been all too easily convinced that Franklin Roosevelt and the Democratic Party, resolute defenders of capitalism, could lead the population out of the social misery of the Depression, something only accomplished by the outbreak of a new imperialist war.

Then, once the Soviet Union was invaded in June 1941, the artists in and around the Communist Party threw themselves into supporting the war and, in the process, helped to disorient a considerable portion of the

American population. The American left, in the thrall of the Communist Party's pro-Roosevelt "Popular Frontism," was to a great extent indifferent or even hostile to the great questions of historic and political principles raised by Trotsky's fight against the Stalinist betrayal of the 1917 October Revolution. (Of course, there were honorable exceptions to this stance among actors and writers. The names of Edward G. Robinson, James T. Farrell, Edmund Wilson and Mary McCarthy come immediately to mind).

The outright purging of left-wing film artists and the cowing of so many others had a devastating and long-term impact, whose consequences we still live with today. Nonetheless, the emergence of the explosive struggle for Civil Rights in the 1950s, the growth of popular and cultural opposition to the Vietnam War and the general state of rebelliousness of the late 1960s and 1970s, including the major urban uprisings in Los Angeles, Newark and Detroit, continued to sustain the filmmakers, although in a politically more amorphous and diminished fashion.

The "New Hollywood" of the late 1960s and 1970s (Penn, Altman, Scorsese, Coppola, Kubrick, Cassavetes, Ashby, Cimino, Malick, Allen, Lumet, Pollack, Benton, Peckinpah, Nichols, Polanski et al.) produced some fresh and innovative work, which at times took a searching look at official American institutions and mythologies. However, even the most nonconformist films suffered from a diluted interest in the concrete conditions and life of the working class, as well as a profound lack of awareness about the events that had shaped the previous half-century and therefore their own times.

These weaknesses were essential ingredients, more generally, of the middle class protest politics of the day. As we have noted a number of times, the "New Left" rejected a socialist orientation to the working class and avoided a historical reckoning—above all—with the Russian Revolution and the nature of Stalinism, either because the issues were too complex or because they hit a little too close to home.

Contrary to the shallow notion that circulates in the media and the universities, the most important feature of the period 1968–75 was not the "counterculture" or even the student revolt. In a number of countries (France, Italy, Portugal, Argentina, Chile and others), genuinely pre-revolutionary conditions arose, which threatened the existence of the capitalist social order—and which could have altered the course of modern history. However, the Stalinists, social democrats and centrists were able to destroy the revolutionary potential in each circumstance and preserve bourgeois rule.

III

The severe decline of filmmaking in the last several decades has co-incided with a period of social reaction. The militant working class move-ment in the US, not based on conscious opposition to capitalism and re-maining under the political aegis of the Democratic Party, found itself in a blind alley. The American ruling elite, from the late 1970s onward, ral-lied and organized a counteroffensive, first under Jimmy Carter and then, more systematically, under Ronald Reagan, George H.W. Bush, Bill Clinton, George W. Bush and, most recently, Barack Obama.

The processes of global economic integration dealt lethal blows to all the national-opportunist labor organizations and Stalinist regimes, and the resulting re-integration of Russia and especially China provided imperialism with a breathing space. Workers found themselves on the defensive and the ballyhoo about the "end of socialism," as noted above, had a significant impact on those leftists and intellectuals who were al-ready half-looking, in any case, for a means of climbing back "on board." The stock market and real estate boom, and the money to be made in the media and entertainment industry, provided even more compelling incentives.

In its modern history, the US has never known a period of social quies-cence like the 1990s and 2000s—the product of the forcible and artificial suppression of the class struggle. No improvement in the social circum-stances of wide layers of the population—the material basis for the politi-cal (and intellectual) conformism and conservatism of the early 1950s—was occurring. Quite the contrary, those circumstances were deteriorating sharply and social inequality was growing like a cancer.

However, a combination of economic and ideological processes, in-cluding the worthlessness of the old trade unions and protest movements, left the working class temporarily paralyzed. It is here, in this confluence of social developments, that we have to locate the fundamental source of the decline of American filmmaking in the last third of a century. Under these conditions, the more principled and astute artists became discouraged, en-tered into crisis and either fell silent or went "with the flow"; the trivial, the self-absorbed, the socially disoriented came to the fore.

The already eroded state of historical and social consciousness, the product of decades of anticommunist propaganda and the campaign against socially oriented art, as well as the rejection by the anti-Marxist "left"

(Frankfurt School, existentialism, postmodernism) of the concepts of objective truth, reason and progress, rendered the artists especially vulnerable.

Plekhanov once referred to "periods of social indifferentism" that "correspond to the stage of social development when the given ruling class is preparing to leave the historical stage, but has not yet done so because the class which is to put an end to its rule has not yet fully matured." In such periods, he wrote, the artists' "souls fall into a 'cold slumber,' their moral level sinks very low. They do not then ask themselves whether the cause is right or whether the order that they are serving with their talent is a good one. They seek only rich patrons, concern themselves only with the profitable sale of their works."[1]

The revival of art and culture is dependent today on the revival of the class struggle and the workers movement on a new socialist and internationalist basis. Art cannot save itself, as Trotsky noted, "It will rot away inevitably ... unless present-day society is able to rebuild itself. This task is essentially revolutionary in character."[2]

The resurgence of widespread and tumultuous opposition to the profit system will help scatter the "clouds of skepticism and of pessimism which cover the horizon of mankind,"[3] including the artists' horizon.

IV

The International Committee of the Fourth International has been alone in taking on "Western Marxism," the Frankfurt School and other reactionary "left" tendencies and subjecting them to criticism. The pseudo-left organizations wash their hands of the responsibility of examining artistic trends altogether, encourage banal protest or identity politics "agitprop," leave the field open for the likes of various "left" academics, or do a combination of all three.

The lingering prominence of these "left" intellectuals, whose activity and thought are rooted in a rejection of the revolutionary role of the working class and hostility to Trotsky's perspective of world socialist revolution, is a consequence of the protracted decline in the influence of classical Marxism. The genocide of socialists carried out by Stalin and the persecutions of the

---

[1] Georgi Plekhanov, "V.G. Belinsky's Literary Views," *Selected Philosophical Works*, vol. 5 (Moscow: Progress Publishers, 1981), 204.

[2] Leon Trotsky, "Art and Politics in Our Epoch," *Leon Trotsky on Literature and Art*, ed. Paul N. Siegel (New York: Pathfinder, 1970), 106.

[3] Ibid., 114.

fascist regimes devastated an entire generation of Marxists. The most direct impact of this immeasurable loss was a terrible lowering of the political and cultural level of the international workers movement.

Paradoxically, the dissolution of the Soviet Union provided objective conditions for the renewal of the culture of classical Marxism within the international working class. But this renewal could not develop as an automatic process. The International Committee of the Fourth International understood the historical significance and political implications of the breakdown of the USSR and devised an intellectually creative response to this event.

In developing its cultural work, the ICFI could draw upon the tradition and example of the Trotskyist movement's engagement in this sphere. One of the opening shots in the conflict with the incipient Stalinist bureaucracy in the Soviet Union was Trotsky's *Literature and Revolution* (1923–24), aimed at the cultural backwardness within which the national-bureaucratic caste flourished. Published a decade and a half later, the "Manifesto for an Independent Revolutionary Art" (1938), co-authored by Trotsky and French writer André Breton, and signed by Mexican painter Diego Rivera, which argued that "true art is unable not to be revolutionary," remains one of the strongest statements ever produced in defense of art and intellectual freedom.

The title of this book comes from Breton's poem "In the beautiful half-light of 1934," which I interpret as a reference to the attempt to see through the immediate obstructions to a brighter and broader reality.

These reviews and essays begin from the notion that art is a means of knowing and orienting oneself in the world, that the significant artist strives to make his or her work correspond to the actual nature of things and that work accomplishing this has an *objectively* true and enduring value. "Art points through and beyond itself," in Hegel's phrase, toward essential truths about the wider world of society, human relationships and psychology.

Art brings to our attention the greatest human concerns not in the form of scientific or philosophical reasoning, but in pictorial and sensuous form, in concrete images, which please or move or trouble, or do all three. The artist does not *prove* the truth of his or her conceptions, but *shows* it. "The true artist, like the true scientist, *always adds to what existed before him.*"[4] However, this theoretical distinction between different modes of the cognition of objective truth—the scientific and artistic—must be understood dialectically.

---

[4] Aleksandr Voronsky, "On Art," *Art as the Cognition of Life* (Oak Park: Mehring Books, 1998), 214.

The artistic search for emotional truth is not a license for indifference to historical, social and political context. Or, as Marx once aptly remarked, "Ignorance never helped anyone!"

Moreover, whatever the level of the theoretical and social consciousness of a given artist, the critic has no right whatever to base evaluations of artistic work on nothing more than his or her own unresolved and intuitive emotional responses. The critic never simply "feels." He or she also must think. The critic must not indulge either the artist or himself. His or her thoughtful apprehension of the work at hand, bringing to bear not only an aesthetic sensibility but also historical knowledge and social insight, is essential to its evaluation and appreciation.

The claim that Marxist criticism consists of nothing more than a formulaic identification of the "class standpoint" of one or another artist, writer, filmmaker, or architect is—like most anti-Marxist shibboleths—a vulgar slander. Insofar as there are tendencies in the academic "left" that see their task as unmasking artwork as mere forms of bourgeois manipulation and the artist as nothing more than a "social construct," they represent a thoroughgoing repudiation of scientific socialism.

Marxism, which has inspired the most sophisticated works of criticism, has polemicized relentlessly against the sort of tendentiousness that reduces art to the level of propaganda. Art has to be judged by its authenticity, depth, sincerity and beauty. These qualities depend, however, upon the artist's capacity to express with honesty and fearlessness some critical aspect of the "ensemble of social relations" of which reality consists.

The class struggle, capitalism, exploitation, poverty, imperialism and war are not merely propagandistic terms. They are the objective categories, properties and elements of objective reality in which modern social life is embedded. And the fact that this is insufficiently acknowledged, ignored and even denied by so many would-be artists and "opinion makers" is a major symptom of the crisis of contemporary culture. Those who believe that it is possible to reveal "emotional truth" without shedding light mercilessly on social reality are deceiving their audiences and lying to themselves.

We have now entered a period of upheavals in which a new mass movement against capitalism will emerge. The resurgence of the class struggle will inspire a new generation of artists and suggest new creative paths and possibilities. In this process the struggle of the revolutionary party for the development of socialist consciousness within the working class will play a critical and indispensable role.

This volume is a contribution to the efforts of the ICFI over the past two decades to direct the attention of workers and young people to the state of artistic and cultural life, to raise their understanding and sensitivity and broaden their outlook. The aim of this book is to raise the consciousness of the working class and youth, by shedding light on the general problems of culture in our time, by calling attention to the most telling artistic successes and failures and by encouraging viewers, critics and artists alike to adopt a more searching attitude toward filmmaking and to see and feel the world in a new way.

At the same time, we certainly seek to influence artists attempting to climb out of the mire of the present culture. We are confident that from among the young, the unknown, those subsisting on little or nothing at present, will emerge filmmakers, writers, painters, who will put artistic truth before everything else.

In conclusion, permit me to express my gratitude to all the comrades whose counsel was essential to the working out of the ideas that find expression in this book. The writings in this volume developed through the dialectic of close intellectual collaboration involving the continuous exchange of drafts, rewrites, discussion, disagreements, conflicts and reconciliations. I consider myself fortunate to be part of a world community of revolutionary internationalists whose conceptions of art are inseparably bound up with the struggle for the socialist liberation of the working class and all humanity.

*   *   *   *   *

Note: The editors have made every effort to track down the original sources of the various comments by critics and filmmakers cited, and, for the most part, have succeeded. However, given the sometimes ephemeral character of information and even publications in the digital age, certain sources have apparently been lost in the mists of time.

October 7, 2013

Reviews

The Return of Robert Altman: *The Player*

Bulletin; May 1, 1992

Directed by Robert Altman;
written by Michael Tolkin and based on a novel by Tolkin

The appearance of a new film by Robert Altman is an event of significance. The director of a number of commercial and artistic successes in the 1970s, Altman, now 67, has lived in self-imposed exile from Hollywood for some years, venturing occasionally into theater or television. *The Player* marks his return to the world of large-scale film production and distribution. Whatever the weaknesses of the film, his return is welcome.

The Player is a film about the film industry, or in Altman's words, it is "about itself ... a movie of a movie that's about movies." The central figure is a young studio executive, Griffin Mill (well played by Tim Robbins), who inhabits a universe that has transcended amorality. The only law of the industry portrayed in *The Player* is the "quick kill." Memory, in regard to any individual, extends to the box office receipts of his or her last project. Mill is continually besieged by screenwriters who "pitch" him films—"It's *Ghost* meets *Manchurian Candidate*"—which almost always include parts for Julia Roberts and Bruce Willis, this month's bankable stars.

Business is conducted everywhere, in offices, restaurants, parties, boardrooms, automobiles via car phones, fax machines and other state-of-the-art paraphernalia. Every item of clothing and furnishing must be the best, must be "seen" to be the best. Only the highest-level position and the largest office count for anything, and the nearer you are to the top, the nearer you are to dismissal, failure and ignominy. Mill keeps demanding of everyone in authority he meets, "Should I clean out my office?" In a piece of unnecessary irony, the film's script has Mill delivering a banquet speech, declaring that movies are art, "now more than ever."

Paranoia, treachery, self-abasement—the morals of Caligula's Rome—these are the features of present-day Hollywood, according to the film's makers. Mill's existence is without any certainty or permanence. He is young and nasty. He is threatened by the younger and nastier, in particular by one Larry Levy (Peter Gallagher), who haunts his existence. At the same time, Mill is receiving threatening postcards from a spurned screenwriter, one of the many he has promised "to get back to." When the death threats become too much for him, he tracks down the writer he believes responsible, mistakenly, and kills him in the parking lot of an art-film house that is showing *The Bicycle Thief.*

Mill becomes involved with the writer's former girlfriend, June (Greta Scacchi), an Icelandic painter of icy, blue canvases, and, through her acceptance, comes to terms with his crime. She proves to have less of a conscience than he. At the luxurious desert spa Mill takes her to, she asks, in awe, "Do places like this exist?" He responds, "Only in movies."

By film's end, Mill and June are an expectant couple, he is now head of the studio and the film pitched to him as a hard-hitting piece of social reality with "no stars" and "no happy ending" has been transformed, inevitably, into a Julia Roberts–Bruce Willis vehicle with a predictable conclusion. Only one dark cloud remains on the horizon—the original postcard-writer. But Mill has a strategy to deal with that.

The film, which Altman described to the *New York Times* as an "essay on morality,"[5] is amusing and sharp in a number of ways. In a nice touch, the head of the studio whom Mill eventually replaces is played by a character actor (Brion James) who normally plays thugs and killers. The scene—in which Mill's nemesis, Levy, suggests that the studio could do without writers altogether, and Mill adds that if they only could do away with writers and directors too they might be on to something—is a pointed reminder about the principles that guide the industry.

But the film's "strength," its "knowing" quality, its closeness to the Hollywood scene, its utilization of dozens of stars, its insider jokes, is also its weakness. Hollywood's big crime is not that it "kills" writers and creativity in general. It is not a private club whose activities only affect the "players" immediately involved.

---

[5] Bernard Weinraub, "When Hollywood Is a Killer" *New York Times*, April 5, 1992. Available: http://www.nytimes.com/1992/04/05/movies/film-when-hollywood-is-a-killer.html?pagewanted=all&src=pm

Film is a powerful medium. Under the profit system, this form, with all its great technological weaponry, remains in private hands, in the hands of a few mediocre cutthroats. Their "vision" of the world, or the vision they pay their hirelings to come up with, is transmitted in thousands of movie theaters. What *The Player* completely loses sight of is the impact of the distorted and outright false views that emerge from the big studio productions.

The primary "victims" of the private ownership of film production are not the writers and directors who get excluded from the process, as legitimate as some of their complaints may be, but the tens of millions of viewers who are consistently lied to and who absorb the film industry's manipulated dreams, to one extent or another, on a daily basis. In other words, *The Player* speaks for the "outsiders" within Hollywood, not for those with little or nothing who are outside of Hollywood.

It would be unfair to assert that *The Player* is less a devastating critique of the Hollywood studios than a "peace offering," but the film is unquestionably "soft" on its subject. One could say that Altman is saddled with an inadequate script, but he is responsible for the ultimate product. There is little question that Altman has a secret or not-so-secret respect and admiration for his central character, for his ability to "get away with murder."

A brief examination of Altman's life and career might explain his ambivalent attitude toward Mill and the film industry as a whole.

Altman was born in Kansas City five years after the birth in the same city of perhaps the greatest of all American improvisers, Charlie Parker. Unlike Parker, however, Altman was born into a well-to-do family, the son of one of the "most successful life insurance salesmen in the world" and "an inveterate gambler,"[6] according to one biographer.

Altman is also a gambler. He told an interviewer from *Playboy* in the 1970s, "Year before last, I won about $26,000, but I never stop while I'm winning. I may bet $500 or $1,000 on a game, but you always lose in the long run because of the percentages."

Discharged from the army in 1947, Altman attended the University of Missouri and then began making industrial films for a company in Kansas City. He co-authored a film script in 1948, and in 1955 he directed a film called *The Delinquents*, which was eventually released by United Artists.

---

[6] Judith M. Kass, *Robert Altman: American Innovator* (New York: Popular Library, 1978), 9.

After making a documentary on the life of James Dean in 1957, Altman became a successful director in television for the next eight years or so, often coming into conflict with his bosses. One of the most consistent bones of contention was his insistence on having more than one voice on the sound track at the same time. The "bath" of sound, in which tone and expression are more important than complete lines and sentences, is characteristic of Altman's work.

He had his first serious commercial success with the antiwar comedy *M*A*S*H* (1970), which struck a responsive chord with audiences at the height of the Vietnam War. This was followed over the next eight years by *Brewster McCloud* (1970), *McCabe and Mrs. Miller* (1971), *Images* (1972), *The Long Goodbye* (1973), *Thieves Like Us* (1974), *California Split* (1974), *Nashville* (1975), *Buffalo Bill and the Indians* (1976), *Three Women* (1977) and *A Wedding* (1978).

Altman's eccentric, semi-anarchistic, improvisational conceptions and methods found favor to a certain extent under conditions of the radicalization of the 1969–75 period. His films and his outlook fell out of favor over the subsequent years. His tactlessness in dealing with studio chiefs—including a reported fistfight with one executive who wanted to cut *Nashville*—was no longer tolerated when his films ceased to make money. Problems in the making of *Popeye* in 1980, which went over budget, were the last straw in the eyes of the studios. Altman went into exile in Paris, directing the occasional theater or television piece, including the recent *Vincent and Theo*. He now lives in New York City.

It is not inappropriate that a filmmaker whose central theme is instability, the loss of certitude and the collapse of identity should have become one of the most significant figures in the post-studio system insecurity of Hollywood in the 1970s.

Robin Wood has described Altman's "recurrent pattern" in the following words: "The protagonist, initially confident of his ability to cope with what he undertakes, gradually discovers that his control is an illusion; he has involved himself in a process of which his understanding is far from complete and which will probably culminate in his destruction."[7]

To repeat, Altman is a gambler and the son of an insurance salesman. He has said: "To be a gambler, the risk has to be devastating. If you're a

[7] Robin Wood, "Robert Altman," *Cinema: A Critical Dictionary* (New York: The Viking Press, 1980), 26.

gambler, what you have to lose is your total security. Money represents security ... and there's a certain joie de vivre when you get close to danger,
your body sets up for it ... but for a gambler that's dangerous, because the
risks have to keep escalating."[8]

Unpredictability, instability, the working of chance, spontaneity, arbitrariness, the lack of logic in the universe—these make up Altman's sensibility. They also influence his method of directing the acting. He often looks
to his actors to contribute lines and entire blocks of dialogue. He rewrites
scenes at the last moment. "I prefer to get up early in the morning to write
the final dialogue for that day's scenes. It's not improvisation. It's just a
technique for keeping the working process as spontaneous as possible."[9]

At his best, Altman has a feeling for the tragedy of the man or woman in
over his or her head, those self-deluded petty-bourgeois who "always lose
in the long run because of the percentages." *California Split*, a film about
gamblers, *The Long Goodbye*, a version of the Raymond Chandler novel, and
Thieves Like Us, the story of small-time bandits during the Depression, are
perhaps his most accomplished films. They exude a sympathy and compassion for those who always lose in America. In fact, they represent a kind of
celebration of losing. *Nashville*, an overambitious but occasionally fascinating study of the country and western music industry as a metaphor for
the American political structure, and *Buffalo Bill*, an account of the famous
"Indian fighter," both make sharp attacks on hucksterism, patriotism and
lies of all kinds.

Altman is unquestionably an extraordinary director of actors. He has
demonstrated the greatest sensitivity, the test of any artist, to the women
in his films. He has brought out enduring performances from actresses as
disparate as Julie Christie, Lily Tomlin, Gwen Welles, Barbara Harris, Ann
Prentiss and Ronee Blakley. *Three Women*, a mysterious film that Altman
said was based on a dream, contains extraordinary performances from
Shelley Duvall, Sissy Spacek and Janice Rule. A critic who referred to the
"sustained lyricism of Altman's ... contemplative and ever-moving camera"
in *Three Women*, commented that the director "wants his audience above all
to remain restless and unsettled. He is the sworn enemy of happy endings
and comforting morals."[10] At his best, Altman convincingly and artistically

---

[8] Kass, 33.

[9] Ibid., 18.

[10] Andrew Sarris in the *Village Voice*, cited in Kass, 244–45.

conveys his own outrage about the state of personal and social relations, an outrage that provokes the viewer to consider how the world ought to be changed.

The Player cannot be considered as Altman "at his best." The inadequacy of Altman's conceptions, his unmistakable sympathy not for Mill as an executive, but for Mill as a risk-taker, combined with a script that is too neat, clever and pleased with itself, make *The Player* far less than the slashing attack its reviews have claimed it to be. Nonetheless. the film has enough moments of fun and subversion, enough outrage, enough intelligence to make a viewing worthwhile.

Riff Raff and the Films of Ken Loach
Bulletin; February 19, 1993

The opening of Ken Loach's *Riff Raff* in New York City, as well as the recent retrospective of his films at the Film Society of Lincoln Center, are providing audiences in this country the rare opportunity of viewing and judging the work of this British filmmaker.

The Lincoln Center tribute, which included the screening of twelve of his film and television works, in particular, makes an overall assessment of Loach's thirty-year career possible.

The films, including *Riff Raff*, reveal a sensitivity and an intelligence, combined with a genuine sympathy for the working class and the most oppressed layers of society. Loach has, over more than a quarter of a century, remained true to his essential principles and continues to tell stories of working class life at a time when movie screens in general are dominated by the self-absorption of the most depraved and ignorant sections of the middle class. His films have, on a number of occasions, been subject to state censorship, and he finds it always a struggle to raise the funds for new films. These are his strengths, and they are not insignificant ones.

At the same time, these strengths cannot be allowed to obscure the serious weaknesses that prevent the films from influencing their audiences at the most profound levels. The weaknesses are of two kinds: the artistic limitations of the British "neorealist" school, and those bound up with problems in the objective situation and the development of the working class and socialist movement in Britain and internationally.

Loach was born in Warwickshire in 1936, attended Oxford University from 1957 to 1960, and performed as an actor for two years before becoming assistant director of a repertory theater. He gained experience, beginning in 1963, working at the BBC as a trainee director in the drama department and on the popular police series *Z-Cars*. Loach won recognition for his work with producer Tony Garnett on a number of productions for the BBC's Wednesday Play series, which began in 1964.

The television productions *Up the Junction* (1965), *Cathy Come Home* (1966) and his first feature, *Poor Cow* (1967), all starring Carol White, made clear Loach's sympathies and concerns. All three dealt with working class London and its problems—housing, jobs, crime, love and sexuality amid poverty. These three works created controversy, and his television work, in particular, drew a considerable popular audience.

Loach's first commercial success came in 1969 with *Kes*, the story of a 15-year-old schoolboy in a Yorkshire mining town. The boy lives with his mother and thick-skinned half-brother who works as a miner. His life derives its only pleasure and meaning from his relationship with an untamed kestrel, a hunting bird. In the end, the bird is killed by his brother, suggesting the way in which both the working class turns its violence on itself and all of the boy's options are snuffed out.

In 1971, Loach made *Family Life* (also shown as *Wednesday's Child*), from a script by David Mercer and based on the work of radical psychiatrist R.D. Laing. The film attempted to show that the central character's "schizophrenia" was a product of social and family relations.

By the late 1960s, Loach, along with an entire layer of artists and intellectuals, had come into contact with the Trotskyists of the Socialist Labour League (later the Workers Revolutionary Party).[11] This relationship undoubtedly turned Loach quite directly toward the problems of working class leadership: the betrayals of the Labour Party and trade union bureaucrats and the struggle for a revolutionary alternative.

---

[11] The Socialist Labour League, which became the Workers Revolutionary Party in 1973, was the British section of the International Committee of the Fourth International (ICFI), whose leading figures included Gerry Healy, Michael Banda and Cliff Slaughter. The WRP underwent a political degeneration in the 1970s and early 1980s, leading to a conflict in the ICFI, beginning in 1982, and a split in 1985–86. At that time, the International Committee rearmed itself on Trotskyist principles and broke definitively with the national-opportunist elements in the former WRP leadership.

The Big Flame (1969), which dealt with an occupation of the Liverpool docks, *Rank and File* (1971), a dramatized version of the Pilkington glass strike of 1970, and *Days of Hope* (1975), which traced the years between the end of World War I and the betrayal of the 1926 British General Strike, were all efforts directed at addressing these questions. In regard to *Days of Hope*, Loach has said, "The big issue which we tried to make plain to ordinary folk was that the Labour leadership had betrayed them fifty years ago, and were about to do so again."[12]

Loach returned to directing feature films only at the end of the 1970s with *Black Jack* (1979), an adaptation of a children's book, *The Gamekeeper* (1980) and *Looks and Smiles* (1981), the story of a couple of working class teenagers from Sheffield.

In 1986, Loach filmed the story of an anti-Stalinist and anti-capitalist East German dissident singer who leaves for the West (*Singing the Blues in Red*), and, in 1990, he made a film exposing the role of the British intelligence service in Ulster (*Hidden Agenda*).

Several of Loach's projects—*Questions of Leadership* (1983), dealing with the British trade union leaders' treachery, *Which Side Are You On?* (1984), a compilation of miners' songs and poems, and the anti-Zionist play *Perdition* (1987)—have been banned for political reasons.

Riff Raff, from a script by Bill Jesse, as much as any of the other works, demonstrates Loach's strengths and weaknesses. At the center of the film is Stevie (Robert Carlyle), a young Glasgow native just out of prison, who comes down to London and gets a job on a non-union building site. The job has brought together a disparate group of itinerant laborers from all parts of the country, as well as a number of immigrant workers.

The central figure in the group is Larry (played by former building worker Ricky Tomlinson, framed up along with Des Warren in a notorious victimization case in 1972). It is he who demonstrates the highest degree of class-consciousness, denouncing the capitalist system and attempting to organize the workers on the site itself. Socialism for him (and perhaps Loach) is not a program for changing the world, but a kind of personal moral code.

Stevie stumbles into a relationship with Susan (Emer McCourt), an aspiring singer. She has no voice and no hope of a successful career, but she lives on pathetic illusions. Susan is susceptible to trying a variety of remedies for her desperation: health food, the I Ching, consultations with

---

[12]   Available: http://www.filmreference.com/Directors-Ku-Lu/Loach-Ken.html

a psychic. Eventually succumbing to her pain and fear, she becomes an addict. Her relationship with Stevie founders.

In response to the low pay, firings, brutal conditions and, finally, a near-fatal accident, Stevie and another worker return to the building site one night and set the place on fire. It is with this image that the film ends.

Considering Loach's political background and the subject matter of the film, it is reasonable to criticize *Riff Raff* for its outlook. Its apparent suggestion, in the wake of the calamitous collapse of all the traditional labor and Stalinist bureaucracies over the past few years, that the working class can solve any of its problems simply through the building of trade unions or by the use of Luddite-type violence is patently absurd.

The filmmaker is not obliged to advance the "correct" solution to any problem, but he should certainly steer clear of obviously false ones. It is a genuine political evasion on Loach's part to imply that all the complex questions associated with the betrayals of the British and international working class can be sidestepped, in favor of a kind of old-fashioned militant syndicalism.

In a comment to an interviewer, which did him no credit, Loach responded, "I was once close to having a Trotskyist stand, and I am still an anti-Stalinist, but I find the label revolutionary to be rather embarrassing."

Riff Raff, which won the International Critics Prize at the Cannes Festival in 1991 and was subsequently named European Film of the Year, has been almost universally praised in the press. And for understandable reasons. It stands in sharp contrast to most of the film industry's offerings today: bland, impersonal efforts, made with neither feeling nor principles.

There is no question that Loach's vivid presentation of the life of the working class merits an audience.

Loach makes his point of view quite clear. "Another thing was that as Britain emerged from the spell Thatcher put on it in the eighties," he recently told an interviewer. "Myself and one or two of the writers that I worked with felt dissatisfied with ourselves because we hadn't really put on the screen the appalling cost in human misery that aggressive Thatcherite policies had wrought on everybody. The last few years have been an attempt to remedy that."[13]

It would be possible to leave the matter at that, to join in the general applause, the serious political weaknesses notwithstanding, except for one

---

[13]   Graham Fuller, *Loach on Loach* (London: Faber and Faber, 1998), 111.

nagging fact: *Riff Raff* is not, at a certain level, especially convincing, nor is it enormously moving. And a viewing of a number of Loach's films reveals the same unfortunate problem: the universal absence of a dramatic story that penetrates to the innermost core of the viewer. What we see instead are social problems given material form. That is not the same thing as the highest form of art. It would be the most serious error to leave in the mind of the moviegoer that this is the best that a socialist-minded artist can do.

How is this weakness to be accounted for?

This is how Loach describes his approach to film directing: "I want to make films which are real, which correspond faithfully to experience; to describe what is going on between people; to be authentic about the world."[14] In a recent lecture at the National Film Theatre in London, he remarked: "All I hope, when people see my films, is that they say, 'Yes, that's how things are.' And if that's how things are, then shouldn't we try to change it?"

To be sensitive to how people live together, to be authentic in relation to the details of their lives and struggles—these are not unworthy aims. But is an aim, in any field, the same as the final result?

In 1982, when asked how he felt about people discussing the merits of his cinematic techniques, Loach replied, "I'm very happy that people should be discussing these issues, but I'd rather they were discussing the role of the trade union leaders. These are issues which it seems to me are very much more important than the role of naturalism in film—that's quite interesting but marginal."

Trevor Griffiths, the playwright and screenwriter, has commented, "If Loach could make a film without a camera he would. He wants the actors to just be themselves so that everything looks as though it has just happened."[15]

If Loach is reacting against the tendency to emphasize form as a thing in itself, one can sympathize with his concerns. It is perfectly true, of course, that form is subordinate to content, that the purpose of a film is to generate a consideration of objective reality. But precisely *how* that is accomplished is hardly a marginal matter; it is the central task of an artist.

Is the apparent reproduction of everyday life, a kind of "photographic realism," the most effective way of getting at the essential? For Loach and

---

[14] Jonathan Hacker and David Price, *Take Ten: Contemporary British Film Directors* (New York: Oxford University Press, 1991), 302.

[15] Available: http://www.lrb.co.uk/v24/n21/ryan-gilbey/ putting-the-manifesto-before-the-movie

most of the members of his generation of British filmmakers this never even arose as a question. They took various forms of "neorealism" or documentary-style drama as their unconsidered starting point.

Objections to these approaches are not simply a matter of taste. The understanding that art rearranges and fractures surface reality in order to make its truth reveal itself, and that this rearrangement can be carried out consciously, has been an objective conquest of artistic thought and practice in the twentieth century. It is not necessary to subscribe to the solutions of any particular artist or school, but to turn one's back on the entire problem of form or narrative structure reveals a deeply ingrained nationalism and provincialism. This is, of course, an objective problem and not simply Loach's weakness.

One of the ideological crimes of the leadership of the Socialist Labour League was its refusal to take up any kind of struggle against the parochialism that dominated the circles of artists it attracted. This was in its own way an adaptation to British nationalism. The inability of Loach and other artists to solve complex political and artistic questions is intimately bound up with the degeneration of the SLL-WRP leadership (see footnote 7 on page 9).

If a filmmaker concentrates so thoroughly on the reproduction of everyday life, a number of problems arise, which reveal themselves in *Riff Raff*. First of all, the film and script present the building workers as friendly, loyal and fun-loving—a bit like Robin Hood's merry men. Tomlinson has commented: "I know conditions [can be] terrible, with the rats and all, but there was also that little bit of humor and that comradeship ..." The film runs the risk of making the present so delightful, and glorifying the working class *as it is* to such an extent, that the spectator is drawn to the life presented. If life under these conditions offers so many charms, what burning need is there to change it?

Second, there is the problem of "particularism." Loach says: "*Riff Raff* is about building workers in London. I know absolutely nothing about building workers in America." An extraordinary remark. Then why should a construction worker in America or anyone else watch the film? As a travelogue, as an exercise in the exotic? Simply for laughs? The emphasis on dialect, on getting every detail right, becomes itself a diversion. More than that, it reduces the film to something the moviegoer can reject, simply because he or she does not speak the dialect or live the particular life the film depicts. Artificiality offers the possibility, on the other hand, of giving a wide spectrum of moviegoers access to the specific world of an artistic work.

Third, if you are pretending that what the viewer is seeing is "authentic," is experience itself, then how do you introduce broad themes? In "real life," an emotional or social problem may reveal itself only over a course of years, and then only partially, confusingly. A drama abstracts, maximizes, exaggerates and concentrates in order to make the truth appear. Loach rejects, in principle, such "artificial" methods. So his films generally fall into two contradictory parts: stretches of "everyday life," punctuated by "dramatic" confrontations, or set pieces in which the film's fundamental concerns are introduced (like lumps in dough).

The results are not deeply convincing. The intellect is engaged, but not the heart and soul. And the stories do not remain with the viewer in the form of powerful images. They fade, and what one recalls are Loach's sincerity and principle.

This sharp criticism, of course, must be seen in its historical context. Loach has continued to fight for his films, in relative isolation, over the past two decades under extremely adverse conditions, in the face of a stagnant, reactionary climate. Many of his contemporaries, some of them with a considerable history in the revolutionary movement, have turned into the most wretched careerists.

Riff Raff is unquestionably a film that deserves to be seen. That there has been a considerable response in this country, even within the cynical fraternity of film critics, is an indication that a hunger for something substantial exists. For provoking that reaction, for raising the questions of working class solidarity and the necessity of a struggle against capitalism, Loach deserves full credit. It is simply unfortunate that the expectation aroused in the viewer is not, so to speak, matched by a dramatic story told in the most powerful fashion. It would be wrong to suggest that this is asking too much.

Jane Campion's *The Piano*: A Sensitive Touch to a Fairly Selfish Theme

International Workers Bulletin; January 17, 1994

Written and directed by Jane Campion

In Jane Campion's film *The Piano*, mute Scottish widow Ada McGrath (Holly Hunter) and her child take themselves off to New Zealand in 1852 to start a new life. Ada and her stuffy, but earnest, new husband Stewart (Sam Neill) do not hit it off. She does, however, strike up a relationship with her husband's overseer, Baines (Harvey Keitel), an illiterate who paints his face in the style of the aboriginal Maoris. Through a somewhat circuitous route, he has ended up the owner of her piano. Baines proposes to sell her back the instrument one black key at a time, in exchange for music lessons. The lessons turn into erotic encounters. All this leads to jealousy and violence.

Campion was born in Waikanae, New Zealand, and attended the Australian Film, Television and Radio School. She has a television movie, *Two Friends* (1985), and two other feature films to her credit: *Sweetie* (1989), a portrait of a disturbed girl and her family, and *An Angel at My Table* (1990), based on the novels of Janet Frame.

The Piano has been praised on many sides for its "sensuality" and its "visionary brilliance." It is a great success.

The director, in her production notes, made the following comment: "I feel a kinship between the kind of romance Emily Brontë portrayed in *Wuthering Heights* and this film. Hers is not the notion of romance that we've come to use; it's very harsh and extreme, a Gothic exploration of the romantic impulse."[16]

This is quite significant and deserves some consideration. If I make the point that *The Piano* as a work of art stands in almost direct opposition to *Wuthering Heights*, it is not in order to attack Campion as an individual or deny her talent (which is genuine). The problem is a thornier and, at heart, objective one: the disorientation of the artist under the prevailing ideological conditions, and, to speak directly to the matter, the truly pernicious influence of contemporary feminism on many women (and men) artists.

Self-pity is a very poor foundation on which to construct a work of art, or much anything else for that matter.

An unstated assumption underlies *The Piano* (an assumption undoubtedly shared by much of its potential viewing audience), to wit: sensitive middle class women are special, abused, silenced (Ada is mute by choice, she has been traumatized by life somehow) and deserve better from the world. The film takes as a starting point much of what it actually needs to establish *dramatically*, but cannot, because of the essential hollowness of its outlook.

A certain tone is set in one of its first sequences. A crew of sailors unloads Ada's belongings in the surf. Mother and daughter, somewhat dazed from the journey and the rude landing, appear vulnerable and frail. The seamen, on the other hand, are crude, uncouth and careless. They clearly

---

[16]   Cited in Caryn James, "A Distinctive Shade of Darkness," November 28, 1993, *New York Times.* Available: http://www.nytimes.com/1993/11/28/movies/a-distinctive-shade-of-darkness.html?pagewanted=all&src=pm

have no appreciation of the significance of the piano. To them, it is simply something heavy to lug around.

When asked if there is anything further she needs or wants, Ada, through her daughter, replies that she has had enough of the stinking ship and they can all go to hell. (One thinks of the Manhattan lady advertising executive or up-and-coming lawyer upbraiding a subway conductor when there has been a delay in train service.) The audience members titter in sympathy with the poor woman. They know straight away to whom this film is addressed and to whom it is not.

Campion has failed, frankly, to bring to life a plausible, mid-nineteenth-century Scottish widow. She has created a middle class professional woman from one of the large urban centers of western Europe, North America or Australia/New Zealand, 1993 model, and transported her back in time.

The film as a whole is filled with implausibilities. How is it that Baines, the illiterate backwoodsman, turns out to be such a tame, understanding and articulate creature? After sending for her thousands of miles, why is Stewart so easily put off by Ada? And how does she dare, isolated and friendless in a new country, to enter so rapidly and willingly into a liaison with Baines?

It is not a question of demanding naturalistic detail, but, once the film-maker herself has created a certain framework, expecting some kind of coherence. The film is not essentially an effort to grasp the truth about the world, *but to shape the world according to a particular sensibility*.

In a peculiar way, Campion both reveals her own orientation, and fundamental complacency, and underestimates the pressures that women, including many in the middle classes, do in fact confront. *The Piano* presents someone who has, presumably of her own accord, come halfway around the world to marry a new husband. And yet she refuses, from the very outset, to make the slightest effort, on principle, to ingratiate herself with him. Is that likely? Isn't it far more tragic that many women accommodate themselves to intolerable situations from fear of destitution, loneliness, etc.?

Emily Brontë approached things in a different manner. The lives of Emily and her two novelist sisters, Charlotte (1816–55, the author of *Jane Eyre*) and Anne (1820–49, a lesser talent), are fabled. They spent almost their entire short existences at an isolated moorland parsonage in Haworth, Yorkshire, in the north of England.

The times they lived in were bleak and desperate. This was the era of the rapid growth of London, Manchester, Liverpool, Glasgow and the new manufacturing centers of the Midlands, whose populations lived in physical wretchedness. The threat of the hated workhouse, depicted in the novels of Charles Dickens, hung over the head of every laborer.

This was the age of Chartism, the first independent movement of the working class. As one commentator put it, during the "Hungry Forties," "two fears were ever present in the minds of the prosperous classes: terror of pestilence and terror of a rising of the 'mob.'"

In art, we associate the period with the last phase of Romanticism, a movement characterized by an infatuation with emotion, imagination and individualism. As one historian puts it, "The longing that haunted it [Romanticism] was for the lost unity of man and nature. The bourgeois world [of 1830–48] was a profoundly and deliberately asocial one. ... Three sources assuaged this thirst for the lost harmony of man in the world: the Middle Ages, primitive man (or, what could amount to the same thing, exoticism and the 'folk'), and the French Revolution."[17]

Out of all this—the intense, claustrophobic family life, the harsh social climate, the stormy effusions of Romanticism—Emily Brontë created one extraordinary novel at the age of 27, *Wuthering Heights*, three years before her death. The story of the ill-fated love of Heathcliff and Catherine Earnshaw, and of his revenge, is saturated with a passionate hatred of polite society and all forms of restraint. Catherine's mystical vision in the book was no doubt Emily Brontë's: "I see a repose which neither earth nor hell can break ... where life is boundless in its duration, and love in its sympathy, and joy in its fullness."[18]

We referred above to one of the opening sequences of *The Piano*. In her novel, Brontë introduces Heathcliff in an altogether different fashion. Catherine's father goes off on business from their isolated rural estate and returns with a "gypsy brat" and "a tale of his seeing it starving, and houseless, and as good as dumb, in the streets of Liverpool."[19] Heathcliff emerges as a kind of demonic force, in keeping with the Byronic view of the dual nature—half-revolutionary, half-malevolent—of the great Romantic myth-heroes and literary creations (Satan, Napoleon, Don Juan, Faustus) in general. But, in any event, Brontë's work burns with protest against the conditions of Heathcliff's early life, against abuse, against injustice.

---

[17]   Eric Hobsbawm, *The Age of Revolution: 1789–1848* (Cleveland, The World Publishing Co., 1962), 263–64.

[18]   Emily Brontë, *Wuthering Heights* (USA: Barnes & Noble, 1993), 142.

[19]   Ibid., 31.

One commentator has noted that while Marx and Engels repudiated the idealization of the aesthetics of the Middle Ages indulged in by Romanticism, "That movement also contained Byron and Shelley, for whom [they] held great respect. There is little doubt that they made a distinction between 'Philistine' Romanticism and a plebeian and folklore-oriented Romanticism."[20] Marx, in 1854, included Charlotte Brontë (Emily had died by then), along with Elizabeth Gaskell, William Makepeace Thackeray and Dickens, in the "present splendid brotherhood of fiction writers in England, whose graphic and eloquent pages have issued to the world more political and social truths than have been uttered by all the professional politicians, publicists and moralists put together."[21]

In all honesty, why does Campion think her film makes a point of contact with *Wuthering Heights*, which burst out of Brontë as a condemnation of everything corrupt and inhuman that existed? Because her character goes "beyond the bounds," so to speak? Because of the film's emphasis on the intuitive, the sensual? But these elements are quite unconvincing in the film and the characters' motivations seem petty. Romanticism as a movement wasn't simply concerned with self-expression. On the part of its most heroic representatives, it was a doomed, but inspired, attempt to regenerate and remake bourgeois society emotionally and intellectually, to make it "live up to" the great democratic ideals of the French Revolution. The outcome of the 1848 struggles demonstrated to nearly everyone, artists included, the hopelessness of such an effort.

Objectively, *The Piano* and *Wuthering Heights* have almost nothing of substance in common, but Campion is no doubt sincere in thinking that they do. What is the problem? Artists (and not only artists) have difficulty, because their entire framework for looking at social problems is so warped. It is as if people were looking at objects under water. Campion no doubt considers herself a radical and a critic of society. The fault lies with the absence of any mass movement against capitalism that might provide a social compass, on the one hand, and the dominance, on the other, of petty-bourgeois protest movements and a general atmosphere that nourishes self-pity and self-absorption.

---

[20] Stefan Morawski, introduction, *Karl Marx and Frederick Engels on Literature and Art*, eds., Lee Baxandall and Stefan Morawski, (New York: International General, 1973), 44.

[21] Karl Marx and Frederick Engels, "The English Middle Class," *Collected Works*, Vol. 13, 1854–55 (New York: International Publishers, 1980), 664.

A balance sheet could be drawn up. Movements such as feminism, black nationalism and gay rights have not helped anyone to see the world and its most fundamental social relationships more clearly; they have had precisely the opposite, narrowing effect. They have objectively damaged artistic and intellectual work.

The film's great popularity stems from the fact that it applies a sensitive veneer to a fairly selfish and comforting theme: the "specialness" of the petty-bourgeois individual and his or her inalienable right to find personal fulfillment and be protected against the more brutish side of existence. This is a message many still want to hear.

Naked Truth: Mike Leigh's *Naked*

International Workers Bulletin; January 24, 1994

Written and directed by Mike Leigh

Mike Leigh, the director and "writer" (each of his scripts actually takes shape through weeks of improvisation and rehearsal) of *Naked*, told an interviewer: "I think it's about the chaos of the nineties, about the disintegration of things. There is a chaos, an anarchy, a disorder in the world, a confusion underpinning things ... That's what I tried to show."

In many respects, he has succeeded brilliantly.

Johnny (David Thewlis) steals a car and flees Manchester to escape a beating. In London, he shows up at the house of an old girlfriend, Louise (Lesley Sharp) and becomes briefly involved with her roommate, Sophie (Katrin Carlidge). When that relationship threatens to close in on him, he takes off and spends two nights on the streets of London, encountering a series of lost souls. In the end, after an unprovoked beating by a gang of youth, Johnny returns to Louise's place. The household has meanwhile been invaded by Jeremy (Greg Cruttwell), a champagne-swilling sadist driving a Porsche—the boyfriend of an absent roommate—whom the women take to be the landlord. After the arrival of the third flatmate, Sandra (Claire Skinner), and Jeremy's departure, Louise announces her intention to return to Manchester. Johnny agrees to accompany her. She heads off for the office to hand in her notice. But there won't be any happy ending. After pocketing some cash, Johnny hobbles off into the streets of London on his injured leg.

The first and last sequences, those that take place in Louise's flat, are the weakest in the film. She is a little too solid and wholesome, while both Jeremy—except in one sequence in which he screams into his cellular phone at a business associate in horrible French—and Sandra are too cartoonish to fully engage the viewer. This has always been a weakness of Leigh's films (*High Hopes* [1988], *Life Is Sweet* [1991], along with many plays for British television). Despite their obvious seriousness, each has been marred by the presence of characters so grotesque as to weaken the viewer's interest in their fate.

The sequences on the streets of London, however, are devastating. No artist in recent memory has presented despair and anomie so powerfully. "Thatcherism" is more than a phrase here. We feel sensuously what has been done to people, and what they do to each other as a result.

In the middle of the night, in the middle of nowhere Johnny runs into a young kid shouting his girlfriend's name into the chilly darkness. He's come down from Scotland, obviously penniless, after nearly killing his father in an argument. He's foul-mouthed and violent. Johnny promises to stay on the corner and should the girl come along, he'll keep her there. The girl eventually does show up. The brief sequence that follows is extraordinary. The condescending or even contemptuous attitude that Leigh too often adopts vis-à-vis his characters here truly falls away in the face of the depth of the pain and misery.

In another sequence, also at night, Johnny has seated himself on the pavement outside the glass doors of a large office building. He is reading the Book of Revelations. The security guard engages him in a conversation. It turns out that the building is unoccupied; he's guarding empty space. The guard tells Johnny he can come in, as long as he keeps out of sight. A philosophical discussion ensues. Johnny sees it as his mission—John the Baptist?—to tell all who will listen that God is vicious and cruel: "the monkey with the beard and the crap ideas." The human race has had it, he tells the night watchman: "The end of the world is nigh, Bri; the game is up."

Johnny has charm; he's not boring. Lonely people invite him in everywhere, although it usually doesn't do them or him any good. In perhaps the most memorable sequence of the film, a shy waitress takes him home. She is obviously subletting or keeping the house for its owner. The sitting room is full of art objects and books, many of them associated with ancient Greece. They have nothing to do with the girl. She hasn't read the *Iliad*; she doesn't have the slightest knowledge of Greek civilization. All she can do is ask Johnny, to his disgust, what she knows are utterly banal questions: Did you ever have a dog? What did you do for Christmas? Do you have a picture of your mum?

The grotesque contrast between the culture embodied in the books and objects and the girl's ignorance—no fault of her own—becomes painfully aware to her. Johnny is a reminder of her own sense of herself as insignificant, a human zero. She drinks too much and throws Johnny out into the cold.

There are constant references, physical and social, to the evolution of the human species. The implicit question seems to be: How has all that history come down to this wretchedness and cultural poverty?

The overall picture is a devastating one.

Some Marxists make the mistake of thinking that "negative" and bleak artistic works are more than a little suspicious. (Although anyone who is simply in need of being cheered up is perhaps not cut out for Marxism.) But there's bleak and there's bleak. There are works, of course, which are simply cold and cynical and self-serving, covert or not so covert apologies for what exists. Such works usually put forward the view, in one fashion or other, that if any social change were to come about, things would be just as bad or worse than before.

But there is artistic "pessimism" that closely approaches the most critical and radical attitude. Trotsky's laudatory review of Louis-Ferdinand Céline's *Journey to the End of the Night*—one of the darkest novels ever written—discusses this sort of outlook.

The task of the artist is to tell the truth as he or she perceives and feels it. The revolution takes place off-screen, off-stage. In the case of a dramatic film or novel, a conscious artist may depict the disasters encountered by his or her characters precisely in order that the viewer or reader will be better equipped *to avoid them*. The artist says: "Look, this is what will happen to you if you go on like you have been doing. Wake up. The situation is hopeless, unless ... " This has nothing to do with fatalism.

In any event, any work of art that is simply the materialization of a preconceived notion is limited, some would say worthless. The element of spontaneity, of actively and creatively attacking the material world, is decisive here. *Naked* is frankly worth fifty films by those left directors in Britain who, in the final analysis, want to paint pretty or optimistic or sentimental pictures about an imaginary working class. The dramatic presentation—i.e., not simply an intellectual description—of *"just how bad things really are"* can only play the most positive role in the present circumstances.

A Poor Man Pursues Love:
Through the Olive Trees

International Workers Bulletin; October 10, 1994

Written and directed by Abbas Kiarostami

Whether anyone chooses to acknowledge it or not, Iranian director Abbas Kiarostami (born in 1940) is one of the world's important filmmakers, one of the very few.

When he says, "I think that technique for technique's sake is a big lie, as it doesn't answer real feelings and real needs," he effectively reduces the great majority of contemporary directors to insignificance.

Of course, good intentions are not at all the same thing as art. But Kiarostami is not simply an intelligent or compassionate man: he has an extraordinary film sense. *Through the Olive Trees* is beautiful, as well as full of feeling and social insight.

The story is both simple and complex: A film crew is in a village in northern Iran that has been destroyed by an earthquake. Much of the population lives by the highway in makeshift housing. Apparently, the government is unwilling or unable to relieve their suffering. The name of the film the crew is shooting is *And Life Goes On …* —in actuality the name of Kiarostami's previous film set in the same village.

In the opening scene, the director (Mohamad Ali Keshavarz) is wading through a crowd of girls, speaking to this one and that one. He's looking for his leading actress. His assistant (Zarifeh Shiva) takes down a few names. From the crowd one girl (Tahereh Ladania) begins to give him a hard time: his last film hadn't even been shown in the region; wasn't it all a waste of time? She gets the part. As Kiarostami said in an interview about his own method of choosing his performers, "my choice depends on the person's self-confidence. And the closeness of the person to the character."

Hossein (Hossein Rezai), a young bricklayer, is eventually cast as the film husband of Tahereh, whom he has been pursuing in "real life" without success. Her family disapproves of him because he is illiterate and has no house. Hossein takes advantage of the time between shots to woo the girl. He argues that due to the earthquake, now everyone is homeless like him. He persists in his suit, in the face of her absolute silence.

As Kiarostami suggests, "In Iran resources are very scarce. Persistence becomes a trait."

In the last sequence of the film, Hossein follows the girl along a dirt road, through an olive grove and across a field, arguing against her possible objections the entire time. He tells her that wealth and literacy aren't the only qualities, "intelligence and understanding are important too. Old women [like the girl's grandmother] only think about rich men who own houses and factories."

The final shot of the film, which lasts several minutes, is taken from the top of a hill. The camera observes the couple far off in the distance. Due to the length of the shot and the distance of the figures, the viewer's own state of mind begins to waver between consciousness and unconsciousness. We enter something of a dream world. Does the girl finally turn and speak to Hossein? Does he run across the field out of joy or unbearable sorrow? The questions are not important. The real point is what happens off-screen, that life is changed "to fit our dreams."

The treatment of social difference and the weight of longstanding traditions, the careful but unequivocal protest against the conditions of life, the simplicity of the narrative and dialogue, the clarity of the acting—this is the stuff of classical filmmaking. We are in the presence of an extraordinary talent.

How a Worker's Life Is Used Up: *A Borrowed Life*

International Workers Bulletin; November 7, 1994

Written and directed by Wu Nienjen

A Borrowed Life is another remarkable film from Taiwan, by veteran screenwriter Wu Nienjen. Born in 1952, Wu began writing scripts for the Central Motion Picture Corporation in 1978. He has worked with most of the directors responsible for the resurgence of Taiwanese cinema—Hou Hsiao-hsien, Edward Yang, Chang Yi, Wang Tong and Ke Yi-cheng, among others. He has written more than seventy screenplays. *A Borrowed Life* is his first film as director.

One can learn a great deal from this film, both about life and about how to present its truth in artistic form.

This is an autobiographical work; Wu has made a film about his father. Sega (Tsai Chen-nan) has come to Chioufen in northern Taiwan to marry into a somewhat more prosperous family than his own. Chioufen is comparatively well off because it is a mining village, enjoying a boom in the early 1950s. Sega goes to work in the gold mines.

He and his wife (Tsai Chiou-fong) have three children. Sega likes to leave his oldest son in the movie theater and go off to drink with his friends and the hostesses. There is scant pleasure in the lives of any of the miners or their families.

Sega looks back nostalgically to the period when the Japanese ruled Taiwan—until 1945—and longs to make the trip to the imperial palace in Tokyo and to Mount Fuji. He insists that his family call him "Do-san," an approximation of the Japanese To-san (father).

The film has several decisive moments at which painful truths are revealed in an understated but powerful fashion. In one sequence, Sega, his wife and children travel to his family's home to see off his younger brother, who has joined the army. The celebration goes off smoothly, all obligations are met, no one says a word about why the brother is enlisting or what it might mean. But as he is going out the front gate, followed by Sega, their father shouts, off-camera: "All my life I've raised sons who were used by others!"

The gold mines are becoming exhausted. Sega is laid off. He goes to the pawnshop to sell off family heirlooms. More and more people are leaving the village. Eventually, after an extended period of unemployment, he goes to work in the coal mines. He and his son, Wen-jian, quarrel about his gambling at mahjongg.

In one memorable scene, Wen-jian goes to the coal mine to meet his father. Sega comes out of the mine, pushing a car full of coal along a railroad track. He is black with dust, his ankle is bleeding. The son offers to help push the car up a hill. The pair move away from the camera. The father simply says to Wen-jian: "Study hard." What took Claude Berri tens of millions of dollars and several hours to establish in *Germinal* is more than summed up in a minute or two by Wu.

The film is called *A Borrowed Life*. A "stolen life" might be more appropriate. Sega's life is first of all stolen by the mines—he becomes stricken with emphysema; by all sorts of civic and family obligations that are essentially meaningless; and by his own fantasies about Japan and the emperor.

He retires from the coal mines at 55; his pension goes to help his younger son set up a business. When he is 59, he is diagnosed as a diabetic.

By this time, he is obliged to carry an oxygen tank wherever he goes. He quarrels with his wife and family. His only consolation is his grandson, but he regrets that the boy does not speak Japanese.

In 1990, he is admitted to an intensive care unit, hardly able to breathe. After a final visit with Wen-jian, he pulls the IV from his arm and jumps out of the hospital window. He dies shortly afterward.

Here is a film about a working class life that does not strain to convince, or hammer or pull at our heartstrings. It movingly sets out the essential facts and relationships and leaves the viewer free to draw his or her own conclusions. It is heartening to know that such a film has been made—and in the 1990s.

Four Films from Taiwan and China

International Workers Bulletin; November 6, 1995

Good Men, Good Women: directed by Hou Hsiao-hsien; *Heartbreak Island*: directed by Hsu Hsiao-ming; *The Postman*: written and directed by He Jianjun; *Lonely Hearts Club*: written and directed by Yee Chin-yen

In an oft-quoted remark reportedly made to a young Romanian poet in a Zurich restaurant during World War I, Lenin is supposed to have said, in part, "One can never be radical enough; that is, one must always try to be as radical as reality itself."

Taiwan's Hou Hsiao-hsien, born in 1947 in Guangdong Province, China, is one of the world's leading filmmakers. His own films include *A Time to Live and a Time to Die* (1985), *A City of Sadness* (1989) and *The Puppetmaster* (1993). Hou has also served as producer on Edward Yang's *Taipei Story* (1985), Zhang Yimou's *Raise the Red Lantern* (1991), Hsu Hsiao-ming's *Dust of Angels* (1992) and *Heartbreak Island* (1995), Wu Nienjen's *A Borrowed Life* (1994) and Chen Kuo-fu's *Treasure Island* (1993).

Good Men, Good Women is a complicated film that demands concentration and thought on the part of the viewer. It takes place in three different time periods. In present-day Taiwan, a distraught and depressed actress, Liang Ching (Annie Shizuka Inoh), starts receiving pages of her stolen diary faxed to her by an anonymous caller.

These bring back to her a period in the 1980s when she worked as a bar hostess, hooked on drugs, and had an affair with a small-time gangster.

Following his murder, she accepted a payoff from his killers, which she is still living on.

Liang, in the present, is rehearsing for a film. She will play the part of Chiang Bi-yu, a member of the anti-Japanese resistance in China and a left-wing activist in Taiwan in the late 1940s. The story of Chiang Bi-yu (also Inoh) and her husband, Chung Hao-tung (Lim Giong), who is eventually executed in the anticommunist terror of the early 1950s, is the third strand of the film.

Hou contrasts the life-and-death struggles of the 1940s and 1950s with the efforts of Liang Ching to stay afloat in the 1990s. He says his theme is to show what remains constant, "the true color and energies of men and women." The viewer may not draw the same conclusion, but the film brings two eras and their particular problems to life.

The varying images in *Good Men, Good Women* are extraordinarily distinct and beautiful because they are so purposeful. The film is dedicated to "all the political victims of the fifties." Where else today, except in Taiwan, are such films being made?

Heartbreak Island also involves political repression in Taiwan and its consequences. Chen Lin-ling (Vicky Wei) is released from prison after more than ten years for her participation in antigovernment terrorism. In a flashback, we see Lin-ling's teacher, Wah Rong (King Jieh-wen), take her under his wing and introduce her to political life. After his arrest, convinced that he faces death in prison, Lin-ling turns to bomb-making.

Freed from jail more than a decade later, she discovers that her erstwhile comrades, including Wah Rong, have become complacent petty bourgeois. Her former lover, for example, owns a coffee shop that also serves as a meeting place for students of New Age mysticism. Lin-ling is driven to despair and madness.

Without a trace of sarcasm or misplaced irony, Hsu Hsiao-ming describes with great acuteness the transformation of a generation. Many of those involved in the real-life incident that forms the historical basis for the film are now members of the bourgeois opposition party, the DPP. The director commented in an interview: "I tend to feel contemptuous of those who turned their back on their own ideals."

The Postman is the second film by He Jianjun, a member of Chinese filmmaking's "sixth generation." Born in 1960, He has worked in various capacities on films by Chen Kaige (*Farewell My Concubine*) and Zhang Yimou. *The Postman* is a devastating portrait of life in a shabby Beijing neighborhood known as the "Happiness District." A damp grey and yellow fog envelops the run-down housing blocks and their inhabitants.

Xian Dou (Fang Yuanzheng), a young postman, lives with his sister in a shabby house—the only remaining link to their parents, who died when they were young. He is brought in to replace the former postman, who has confessed to stealing and reading letters. A post office colleague plays guessing games about the mail as she frenetically and relentlessly stamps the stack of daily mail. Xian, emotionally cut off from the world, soon starts opening and reading letters.

He becomes involved in the lives of the correspondents: a prostitute, the family of a young suicide victim, a homosexual couple. At the same time, his sister's marriage throws him into an emotional crisis—with shattering consequences.

Twice in the film he tells a simple story about being in a peach orchard with his sister and being chased out. It is at once enigmatic, dreamlike, terrifying. The second telling of the little story, as a voice-over, over the image of his sister's traumatized face, is unforgettable.

The film is a brutal account of psychological damage produced by a repressive and stifling social system. He Jianjun has now been banned from making films by the Chinese authorities.

Lonely Hearts Club is the first feature film by Taiwan's Yee Chin-yen. It lacks the intensity of the other three discussed here, but it is a perceptive study of quiet desperation and boredom. A woman in her forties, Chen (Pai Yueh-O), works at a dull job in an office. Her marriage to an unfaithful husband seems loveless. One day a new office boy, Lone (Hsieh Hsien-tang), appears. She develops a crush on him. She doesn't know he is gay, a participant in a bar scene that also proves chilly and unsatisfying.

Lone's theft of a wallet sets off a chain of events, involving Chen as well, which leads to semicomic-semitragic consequences. In the final analysis, all the efforts of the film's nine characters to make contact with other people fail ignominiously.

Good Men, Good Women, Heartbreak Island and *The Postman*, although quite different, share certain characteristics. They each discuss with great frankness and honesty a devastating sequence of events. While advancing an obvious anti-establishment view, none of the directors shies away from the most painful or disturbing revelations. The films contain precise imagery; sure, thoughtful and convincing acting; a certain coolness, even serenity, in the examination of the most terrible difficulties. The films proceed slowly, quietly, rigorously, making no concession to the short attention span of today's average moviegoer, conditioned by television commercials and tabloid journalism.

These are films that at least attempt to begin with life and not certain precepts about life. They don't exist to enhance the images and reputations of their makers. Nor are they swept along by the current wave of intellectual and social reaction. Nor do they draw pretty pictures of this or that segment of the population in accordance with the dictates of "radical" politics.

It's a shame that very few people in North America and Europe will ever see these works. They are, in this reviewer's opinion, the closest thing at this point to films that are "as radical as reality itself."

Titanic as a Social Phenomenon

World Socialist Web Site; February 25, 1998

Written and directed by James Cameron

James Cameron's *Titanic* is a massive global success. The film is taking in millions of dollars a week, on its way apparently to the $1 billion mark. Even Cameron claims to be "a little bit mystified." What is behind this remarkable phenomenon?

The first possibility that suggests itself is that the film possesses that relatively rare combination of artistic merit and mass popular appeal. One thinks, for example, of many of Chaplin's films, or perhaps certain of Alfred Hitchcock's. A critical viewing of *Titanic*, however, is enough to dispel that notion. Cameron's film is, in this writer's view, a mediocre and predictable work, with caricatures instead of characters, and dialogue worthy of television soap operas.

The following exchange between the two central protagonists—the supposedly devil-may-care artist, Jack Dawson (Leonardo DiCaprio), and the unhappy socialite, Rose DeWitt Bukater (Kate Winslet)—is fairly typical:

JACK: Rose, you're no picnic ... You're a spoiled little brat even, but under that you're a strong, pure heart, and you're the most amazingly astounding girl I've ever known and—

ROSE: Jack, I—

JACK: No wait. Let me try to get this out. You're amazing ... and I know I have nothing to offer you, Rose. I know that. But I'm involved now. You jump, I jump, remember? I can't turn away without knowin' that you're goin' to be alright.

[Rose feels the tears coming to her eyes. Jack is so open and real ... not like anyone she has ever known.]

ROSE: You're making this very hard. I'll be fine. Really.

JACK: I don't think so. They've got you in a glass jar like some butterfly, and you're goin' to die if you don't break out. Maybe not right away, 'cause you're strong. But sooner or later the fire in you is goin' to go out.

ROSE: It's not up to you to save me, Jack.

JACK: You're right. Only you can do that.

Naturally, dialogue and plot are not everything in the cinema. There is a definite tradition in Hollywood filmmaking of directors transcending second-rate screenplays or worse (even sometimes their own) through either irony, visual audacity or the suggestion of emotional and intellectual depths going far beyond the limits of the immediate story line.

This is not the case here. Cameron does nothing to overcome his own trite script, displays no remarkable visual sense and hints at nothing beyond the banalities we see and hear. In fact, he is apparently quite proud of the lack of contradictions in his film and its characters. David Ansen in *Newsweek* writes: "The thing about Jack Dawson ... is that he doesn't have a dark side. DiCaprio had never played a character without demons. 'How do you do that?' DiCaprio says. 'I was asking Jim [Cameron]: "Can't we add some dark things to this character?" And he was like, "No, Leo, you can't."'"[22]

Cameron is, we have suggested before, a competent craftsman, not a significant artist. His own account, in an interview, of his initial interest in filmmaking is revealing: "I used to go down to the USC [University of

---

[22] David Ansen, *Newsweek,* 131.8 (February 23, 1998), 58–64.

Southern California] library and read everything. I'd Xerox stuff. I made my own reference library of doctoral dissertations on optical printing and all that. I really studied technical stuff formally."[23]

The director's taste in films is also revelatory. "A film that affected me a lot when I was eighteen or nineteen was [British director David Lean's] *Dr. Zhivago*."[24] At a time—the early 1970s—when many film students or young people interested in the field would have been studying and discussing the work of, say, Jean-Luc Godard, Luis Buñuel, Joseph Losey or Erich Rohmer, Cameron admired one of the most stolid and least challenging directors of the day. *Doctor Zhivago*, in particular, was described by one critic as "a work with more commercial than critical success, a work also of the most impeccable impersonality"[25]

If *Titanic*'s success cannot be explained by artistic excellence, then what does account for it?

A significant factor is no doubt the general decline in the level of Hollywood filmmaking and, inevitably, popular taste. When individuals between the ages of 15 and 30 declare that *Titanic* is the "best film they have ever seen," to what are they comparing it: *Jurassic Park* (1993), *Forrest Gump* (1994), *Return of the Jedi* (1983), *Home Alone* (1990), *Batman* (1989), *Independence Day* (1996), *Ghost* (1990) or *Men in Black* (1997)? All these films, made within the last decade and a half, can be found on the list of the top twenty all-time box-office successes.

The problem is not simply that bombastic market-driven films have been reaching large audiences (although they have become, it seems, blander and more bombastic than ever); to a certain extent that has always been the case. But the world's cinemas have never before been so monopolized by these would-be blockbusters, to the exclusion of more interesting American and international films. The artistic judgments of the general public, through no fault of its own, are inevitably circumscribed and stunted under these conditions. Movie audiences have been increasingly deprived of intelligent entertainment by an industry, dominated by a few conglomerates, that has run out of nearly every idea except how to turn a profit.

---

23   Available: http://www.industrycentral.net/director_interviews/JC01.HTM

24   Ibid.

25   Andrew Sarris, *The American Cinema—Directors and Directions: 1929–1968* (New York: E.P. Dutton, 1968), 160.

This elementary understanding provides a framework within which one can begin to make sense of the *Titanic* phenomenon—but only a framework.

The response to *Titanic* is so great and so out of proportion to the quality of the film itself that one is forced to view its success as a social phenomenon worthy of analysis. This is not simply a film—it is virtually *a cause*. Its admirers defend it with fervor and admit no challenges and no criticisms—it is not simply a "good" film, or a "wonderful" film, it must be acknowledged as "the greatest film of all time."

(If the film were truly "great," as its admirers claim, it would be impossible for *anyone*, of any age, to see it five, ten or even more times. A great film, by definition, is a demanding film. One cannot rush back to see such a work; one needs to recover from the experience and assimilate its contents.)

To account for the *Titanic* phenomenon, the media suggest several factors—above all, the increased buying power of young women and, especially, teenage girls. This does not explain very much. In the first place, girls do not by any means make up the film's entire audience (nearly forty percent of the audience, male and female, is *over twenty-five*), although they may make up a disproportionate percentage of those who are seeing it repeatedly and in groups. And even if it were true that only one segment of the population was flocking to the film in massive numbers, one would still have to look for answers as to why. The attractive features of Leonardo DiCaprio can only go so far by way of explanation.

Even many of the film's admirers admit that *Titanic* is dramatically inept—so why can't they help themselves? What set of social circumstances would impel broad layers of the population to identify *so strongly* with such a *weak* piece of work, and invest it, as their many comments have demonstrated, with qualities that it does not begin to possess?

One of the predominant characteristics of the present day is the sense of the general worthlessness of the old institutions and the beliefs or shibboleths bound up with them, institutions and beliefs that many *feel*, even if they are not conscious of it, to be merely left over, by some kind of inertia, from a previous epoch when they may have had meaning. It is a widespread and unstated assumption that nothing is to be expected from the existing political parties, parliaments, business groups, the mass media, churches, trade unions—only corruption and lies.

New perspectives and new causes, however, have not to this point gripped masses of people. The population remains largely uncommitted, politically and intellectually. Young people in particular are restless, uncertain, aquiver. They don't even ask yet, in large numbers, "Which way?"—to ask that one must already know that a worthy destination exists.

Yet there is a widely felt yearning for commitment, for purpose. One sees this in many distorted and even reactionary forms, from the Promise Keepers to the Million Man March.[26]

Under these conditions the very fact of its initial popularity (aided by media manipulation) helps a film like *Titanic* to become *immensely* popular. "It is attractive to me precisely because it is attractive to others; I have to see something extraordinary and tragic in the film because others have seen it." This is not so much conformism, although that enters into it, as the desire for affiliation, for some unifying element, when the new social affiliation and the new basis for unifying humanity have not appeared to the vast majority.

In voicing their support for the film, young people are responding to what they perceive to be *Titanic*'s theme: the need to break from conventions and experience, at no matter what cost, freedom and love. This is no doubt in part a response to the prevailing climate of conformism and cynicism. But this genuine, if confused, sentiment is being directed toward a work that is fundamentally false and shallow.

There is no trace of genuine revolt in Cameron's film. It is a thoroughly self-satisfied piece of work. There is not, after all, anything necessary, anything that flows from the conflict between Winslet's character and her family and fiancé, in the ultimate tragedy. Jack and Rose find happiness together relatively easily; they simply happen to be on board a sinking ship. Presumably, had the *Titanic* not struck an iceberg, they would have lived happily ever after.

One of the difficulties in the situation is that the same low cultural level that has produced the film has, to a large extent, produced the public reaction to it.

It might be best perhaps to describe *Titanic* as a sort of lowest common denominator. The film contains certain minimums necessary to draw an audience—attractive leading actors, a "tragic love story," expensive special effects, a

---

[26] Promise Keepers is a right-wing Christian organization for men, founded in 1990. The Million Man March was a rally organized by the Nation of Islam in October 1995 on a pro-capitalist program of African American "self-help" and economic "self-defense."

mild dose of social criticism, a fascinating historical event, media support—but its very blandness, in combination with these elements, accounts for its great success. *Titanic* is, in effect, a blank screen onto which a great many people are projecting vague, *but very powerful*, longings—about life, love, society—which they cannot yet formulate in more concrete and focused terms.

There is nothing "mystifying" about such a relatively vacuous film winning tremendous popularity. On the contrary, no other film would fill this particular bill. It is *Titanic*'s emptiness that allows the audience to invent a film, and a world, for itself in the course of those three-and-a-quarter hours or as many viewings as it takes.

Orson Welles's *Touch of Evil*: That Ticking Noise in Our Heads

World Socialist Web Site; October 20, 1998

Orson Welles directed the filming of *Touch of Evil*, his seventh feature, in early 1957. He got the assignment from Universal Studios in part due to the urging of the film's leading actor, Charlton Heston. It was Welles's first Hollywood film in a decade, and his only one of the 1950s. He had garnered a reputation for prodigality, for being difficult, for being "artistic." He brought in *Touch of Evil*, much of it filmed in the Los Angeles suburb of Venice, on schedule and on budget.

During postproduction, however, Welles and Universal executives had a falling out. The studio objected to the manner in which Welles, in his proposed version, had organized the various strands of the narrative. He began a scene, cut to another, returned and concluded the first scene, then cut to the last part of the second. Universal re-edited the film and added a few sequences, against Welles's wishes, to give it a smoother, more continuous feel and to "help" the exposition in certain spots. The director more or less disowned the version released in May 1958, which went virtually unnoticed in the US. It was Welles's last American picture.

Based on a recently found fifty-eight-page memo, sent by Welles to studio executives at the time, efforts have been made to restore the film so that it conforms more closely to the director's conception. This new version of *Touch of Evil*, which restores much of the cross-cutting, is currently showing in movie theaters in the US.

The film, based on the pulp novel *Badge of Evil* by Whit Masterson, tells the story of an investigation into the death of a local big shot, Rudy Linnekar, killed by a bomb planted in the trunk of his car, in a seedy American town on the Mexican border. A Mexican narcotics investigator, Miguel "Mike" Vargas (Heston), honeymooning with his wife Susan (Janet Leigh), becomes involved because he happens to witness the explosion. Meanwhile, the couple faces threats and violence because Heston's character is in the midst of prosecuting a drug case against a crime family, the Grandis, that operates on both sides of the border.

Vargas, an honest man, comes up against the efforts of a policeman on the American side, Hank Quinlan (Welles), to railroad the Mexican son-in-law of the murdered man. Infuriated and threatened by Vargas, Quinlan joins forces with "Uncle Joe" Grandi (Akim Tamiroff) to discredit the Mexican official by framing his wife on drug charges and accusing them both of being drug addicts. The scheme unravels primarily because Quinlan's trusted assistant, Sgt. Pete Menzies (Joseph Calleia), becomes disgusted with the methods of his longtime friend and mentor.

Touch of Evil is justly famous for a number of things. First of all, its opening crane shot, lasting several minutes, which follows both the convertible carrying the time bomb and the married pair as they all proceed toward the US border on the Mexican side. Following their progress, the camera reveals a tawdry, impoverished town. At the border checkpoint, the newlyweds are waved through after a few routine questions. The blonde woman in the convertible, the rich man's mistress, anxiously tells the border guards and her companion, "I've got this ticking noise in my head." What a line! As the camera returns to Heston and Leigh, who embrace, the bomb explodes. Welles accomplishes more in one shot than most directors do in two hours.

The shot is more than a technical tour de force. The use of one extended take, which visually unifies so many elements, suggests a single, indivisible universe and it is a universe in which a layer of corruption coats virtually everyone and everything.

Touch of Evil is also famed for its look. Critic Manny Farber noted: "Welles's storm tunnel has always the sense of a black prankster in control of the melodrama, using a low-angle camera, quack types as repulsive as Fellini's, and high-contrast night light to create a dank, shadowy, nightmare space."[27] Farber described Calleia's Menzies, "scared out of his wits ... a grey little bureaucrat

---

[27] Manny Farber, *Negative Space* (New York: Praeger Publishers, 1971), 6.

fitted perfectly into *Touch of Evil* with the sinister lighting and tilted scenes in which he's found, buglike at the end of hallways and rooms."[28]

There are the acting performances. Even the often wooden Heston is good in this film; Leigh, Welles himself, Calleia; Ray Collins as the opportunist district attorney; Joseph Cotten as an aging police official; Tamiroff, chewing up the scenery with his ridiculous toupee; Dennis Weaver as a nervous, twitching motel clerk fascinated and terrified by Leigh's presence; Mort Mills as Schwartz, the only American who helps Vargas out; Mercedes McCambridge (out of *Johnny Guitar*) as a lesbian gang leader who says, "Let me stay. I wanna watch," as Leigh is held down on a motel bed and seems threatened with a gang rape; and, of course, Marlene Dietrich. Dietrich, whom Welles called up one night out of the blue and asked to come work on his film the next day, is Quinlan's old flame, a brothel keeper and fortune-teller of some vague description.

She gets to comment on Quinlan when the policeman shows up at her door, perhaps echoing some in Hollywood who hadn't seen Welles in person—the once-dashing actor-director who now weighed nearly 300 pounds—in nearly a decade. "I didn't recognize you. You should lay off those candy bars. ... You're a mess, honey." Later, she proclaims his imminent doom when he asks her to read his fortune: "You haven't got any. ... Your future is all used up." And she gets the final word, as Quinlan lies dying in a dirty, polluted canal: "He was some kind of a man. What does it matter what you say about people?"

Touch of Evil is about racism and American chauvinism, and the haves and have-nots. Within the film's universe, there are two "interracial" marriages: Leigh and her Mexican husband, Linnekar's daughter and hers; the latter marriage also crosses class barriers. Both unions are commented on. The border guards are surprised to discover this white woman married to a Mexican man, even a prominent one. When she is pointed out to Quinlan as Vargas's wife, he comments nastily, "She don't look Mexican either." During the interrogation of Sanchez (Victor Millan), the husband of Linnekar's daughter, Quinlan observes that he doubts the slain man wanted to have a "Mexican shoe clerk for a son-in-law."

Although she's married to Vargas, Susan is capable of sneering at Mexico and Mexicans. When she's accosted by a young man in the street, unbeknownst to her one of the Grandi gang, she disdainfully calls him

---

[28]   Ibid., 8.

"Pancho." Later, Uncle Joe asks her why she called his nephew Pancho. She doesn't know. "Just for laughs, I guess," is the best she can do.

The film is also about the police, police corruption, police terror and the abuse of power. This film was made, after all, in the wake of the McCarthyite witch-hunts. Welles was never blacklisted, but he might as well have been. (He certainly was denounced as a Communist sympathizer by the Hearst press.)[29] It can't be considered an accident that he didn't direct a film in the US between 1947 and 1957. His ideas weren't welcome, and he didn't feel comfortable in the atmosphere that prevailed. By 1957, the civil rights movement had begun in earnest; Quinlan, from a certain point of view, fits one's picture of a Southern redneck sheriff.

Vargas stands up to Welles's character, who has "solved" the case by planting dynamite in Sanchez's apartment. They later have this exchange:

Quinlan: Our friend Vargas has some very special ideas about police procedure. He seems to think it don't matter whether killers hang or not so long as we obey the fine print.

Vargas: Captain, I don't think a policeman should work like a dog catcher in putting criminals behind bars. No! In any free country, a policeman is supposed to enforce the law, and the law protects the guilty as well as the innocent.

Quinlan: Our job is tough enough.

Vargas: It's supposed to be. A policeman's job is only easy in a police state.

Touch of Evil is about sex, sexual fear and frustration, impotence, voyeurism, exhibitionism. Poor Janet Leigh, a blonde goddess, is peered at, leered at, spied on, drugged, stripped and violated metaphorically on a number of occasions. Sexuality is associated with a bombing, a strangling,

---

[29] In fact, as Joseph McBride argues persuasively in *What Ever Happened to Orson Welles? A Portrait of an Independent Career* (Lexington: University Press of Kentucky, 2006), Welles was, in fact, blacklisted. McBride points to "unmistakable evidence, hidden in plain sight, that Welles's political and cultural activities had caused him to be blacklisted during the postwar era. His decision to leave the country in 1947, just as the Hollywood blacklist was being imposed, and his reinvention of himself as a wandering European filmmaker, largely out of necessity, hastened his already strong bent toward independence from the commercial system." (xvii)

a mock gang rape. But then, no sexual relationship is ever consummated in the film. Every time Heston and Leigh start to kiss, they're disturbed. Even their intimate conversations on the phone are interrupted, usually by Vargas's being called off to duty. Repression—what doesn't take place, what isn't allowed, what isn't completed—dominates.

Both married couples, in fact, are separated the entire film. For their part, Linnekar and his stripper girlfriend are blown up in the first scene. No one has a mate. Quinlan's wife has been murdered years before; Dietrich has no use for him. He has aged badly and is so overweight. She casts doubt on his sexual capability. He suggests, "Well, when this case is over, I'll come around some night and sample some of your chili." She says drily, "Better be careful. Maybe too hot for you." The strongest feelings are expressed by Menzies for Quinlan. When Dietrich is asked, at the end, if she liked Quinlan, she replies: "The cop did. The one who killed him. He loved him."

Much of the film's power comes from the complicated relationship of Welles to his character. The director/actor explicitly denied any such complexity: "It's a mistake to think I approve of Quinlan at all. To me he's hateful; there is no ambiguity in his character. He's more than a little ordinary cop, but that does not stop him being hateful."[30] The film's images suggest a less simple reality.

A purely sociological reading of *Touch of Evil*, or any serious work, will never prove satisfying. There is far from a one-to-one relationship between the nightmarish world of the film and American social reality of the 1950s, although clearly the former speaks to and illuminates the latter in significant ways. A viewer content simply to ask him- or herself, Are these accurate portrayals of cops, politicians and hoodlums, or of the relations between them, or of the milieus they inhabit? will derive something from the film, but he or she will avoid its richest and most suggestive ingredients. *Touch of Evil*, looked at closely, includes virtually nothing "realistic." The somewhat banal story grasps at certain essential qualities of immediate reality, but if the film did not represent a relatively autonomous intellectual and moral arena in which Welles worked at the themes and problems that obsessed him from an early age, it would have little enduring value.

---

30 André Bazin, Charles Bitsch, Jean Domarchi, "Cahiers du Cinema" (June 27, 1958), Mark W. Estrin, *Orson Welles: Interviews* (Jackson: University Press of Mississippi, 2002), 50.

Farber identified Welles's "career-long theme," and this is something of a commonplace, as "the corruption of the not-so-innocent Everyman through wealth and power."[31] Complementing this, Andrew Sarris has observed that "every Welles film is designed around the massive presence of the artist as autobiographer. Call him Hearst or Falstaff, Macbeth or Othello, Quinlan or Arkadin, he is always at least partly himself, ironic, bombastic, pathetic and, above all, presumptuous."[32]

These points are no doubt true, but I think they miss something essential. If Welles were simply an egoist who despised corruption, even one with a remarkable flair for drama, I'm not certain his film work would continue to resonate as it does. Exposés of police misdeeds are not uncommon, even in contemporary American cinema. The quantity of evildoing by cops recounted in *L.A. Confidential*, a shallow and forgettable work, far outdoes anything in *Touch of Evil*. And it is not even the sense that corruption is all-pervasive that distinguishes Welles's films. On the contrary, many modern films paint a far bleaker picture.

To a certain extent this is the point. Welles, it seems to me, brings out both the necessity of corruption, its inevitability given the nature of contemporary society, and at the same time, its *non-necessity*. (People are *touched* by evil and corruption; it is not something essential to their being.) He is fascinated above all by the human personality and its almost infinite capacities. His concern with his own personality, although not untouched by self-aggrandizement, is of a relatively objective character. He studies himself, his responses to people and events, his progress, even his own degeneration, as a scientist-artist-autobiographer, and presents his results in the form of the characters he creates.

I think Welles, like an Oscar Wilde, was not so much enamored of his own powers as he was deeply concerned by the problem of *engendering such powers in others*, so that the general public could "make itself artistic." There is a deeply democratic streak in his work. He believed that everyone could feel what he felt, see what he saw. (His efforts to produce classic works in an innovative style for mass audiences in the late 1930s provide an obvious reference point.) And he knew or intuited enough about life to understand that what prevented people from living as they could was fundamentally social in character.

---

[31] Farber, 6.

[32] Andrew Sarris, *The American Cinema—Directors and Directions: 1929–1968* (New York: E.P. Dutton, 1968), 79.

The affinity for Shakespeare, which Welles felt from boyhood (his first reading primer was *A Midsummer Night's Dream*), was natural. Here were the world-historical, monumental individuals, some tormented, others grotesque, in whom he found the confirmation of his own feelings about himself and others. Figures not "larger than life," as they are often rather thoughtlessly described, but the norm, at least potentially, in a future in which the average human type will rise to the heights of an Aristotle, a Goethe, or a Marx, and beyond.

But that is the future. In the present, personality presents a problem. I think Welles was deeply disturbed and intrigued by the degree to which breadth of personality tends to be bound up in the present social order with corruption and moral depravity. So many of his works seem to involve a tragic acceptance that one can't be grand and ambitious in this world without doing evil.

"The less you are, the less you express your own life, the more you *have,* i.e., the greater is your *alienated* life, the greater is the store of your estranged being."[33] This is Marx on Welles's characters, or it might as well have been. For all of his protagonists—Kane, Arkadin, Quinlan—the piling up of success or power at one pole inevitably involves a psychic and sexual shriveling up at the other.

Welles is not moralizing. It's the human cost, *the waste* that drives him crazy. It's the disproportion between the capacities of his heroes and the pettiness of their actual pursuits and accomplishments—accumulating money, power, fame—that wounds him to the quick.

(If we think of his work as semi-autobiographical, there seems to be an element of harsh self-evaluation in this. Aren't we being encouraged, in his later films, to think of Welles as an artist who was seduced by the film industry, who squandered his talents, who completed only a fraction of the work he set out to do? Whether this self-criticism is entirely just is another question.)

This discrepancy holds true for Quinlan, the corrupt small-town policeman, too. His entrance is prepared, like Henry V's. We hear about him before we see him. He is legendary, "our local police celebrity." His car tears up to the scene of the crime. We first view him from below as he struggles to pull himself out of the back seat. He immediately exhibits his intuitive genius. He *is* a great detective. (The man he tries to frame up proves to be guilty.)

---

[33] Karl Marx, *Economic and Philosophic Manuscripts of 1844* (Moscow: Progress Publishers, 1977), 111.

More than that, he dominates every scene. Vargas is upright, but he never has the impact of Quinlan. Half the time Vargas runs around like a chicken with its head cut off. He neglects his wife and places her in danger. He pursues Quinlan, but without the help of Menzies (who says, "I am what I am because of him [Quinlan]"), he never would have exposed the detective.

And yet Quinlan is filthy, a monster, a murderer. Welles has made himself toadlike, bloated, malevolent. But, even so, his end is tragic. People shouldn't become what he becomes, or die like he dies, a big, fat ridiculous animal floating away in a pool of dark, oily, garbage-filled water. To make such a horrible man a tragic figure and to make an audience feel his tragedy, without sentimentality, even as it despises him, is the mark of a great artist.

A Horrible State of War:
The Thin Red Line

World Socialist Web Site; January 23, 1999

Written and directed by Terrence Malick; based on the novel by James Jones

I hope a great many people will see Terrence Malick's *The Thin Red Line* and be moved by it, as I was. I can think of few, if any, American films made in the past number of years as compassionate as this one.

The film, adapted from James Jones's 1962 novel, follows US forces attempting to seize control of the Japanese-occupied island of Guadalcanal in the South Pacific in 1942. The men of Charlie Company, an army rifle unit, land without encountering opposition, but they suffer heavy casualties when they attempt to scale and capture a strategically significant hill. A Japanese bunker built at the top of the slope gives their forces a commanding position; a daring raid destroys it. The American troops vanquish the Japanese in a battle, overrun their encampment and take a sizable number of prisoners. The company is rewarded with a week's rest. Upon their return to the battle-front, another skirmish with the enemy leads to more death and sadness. The film ends with the company's departure from the island.

Malick conscientiously depicts the course and outcome of the military operations. But his film is principally focused on a handful of men and the ways in which they grapple with the moral problems posed by war.

Pvt. Witt (Jim Caviezel), a Southerner, is entranced by the natural beauty of the Solomon Islands and the life led by its Melanesian population. He has deserted his unit more than once to live on one or another of the islands. Pvt. Bell (Ben Chaplin) survives by idealizing his wife. In the midst of the horror, he remembers or imagines this slim, pure figure. First Sgt. Edward Welsh (Sean Penn) is battle-hardened, but perhaps insufficiently. His dilemma is that he continues, despite everything, to feel sympathy for his fellow creatures. Captain James Staros (Elias Koteas) is in charge of the company. Determined to keep his men alive, he refuses at one point to launch a suicidal assault on the Japanese position. Lt. Col. Gordon Tall (Nick Nolte), Staros's superior, is a career officer. He views the fighting on Guadalcanal as his opportunity, after years of being passed over, to make a name for himself and win advancement.

The film's characters advance conflicting notions about Man and Nature, Man's Nature, Man *in* Nature. Attempting to justify his own harsh commands, Col. Tall argues that nature itself is "cruel" and merciless. Staros, you sense, views life as sacred and all men as God's children. For Bell, everything is redeemed or apparently redeemed by human love and passion. In Melanesian society Witt sees what he takes to be the elementary harmony of humanity and nature. He wonders what gave rise to war and violence. Man is nothing, Welsh tells Witt, and any attempt to alter the present terrible state of things is like "running into a burning house where nobody can be saved."

Unhappily, because these men tend to speak and act as the embodiment of particular ideologies or spiritual principles, rather than as spontaneously acting human beings, a good deal of the dialogue and voice-over commentary has a stilted and somewhat contrived feel to it. Large issues are under discussion, but they too often remain undigested in the body of the film. "The director," as a critic once wrote about another filmmaker, "is always trying to say more than his technique can express."[34] Moreover, Malick has a tendency to rely on clear images to make up for amorphous or undeveloped ideas.

The characters are not given equal weight or voice. The film begins and ends with Witt, and you assume that his view of things counts for something out of the ordinary. While he has seen "another world" on the islands, he is neither a deserter nor a pacifist. He expresses love for

---

[34] Andrew Sarris, *The American Cinema—Directors and Directions: 1929–1968* (New York: E.P. Dutton, 1968), 200.

the men of his unit—"They're my people"—and volunteers for danger-ous missions. To Witt, all men are one, possessing one face and one soul. Again and again, he asks himself: how did humanity's essential goodness, which he experiences firsthand in "primitive" communities, give way to its present debased and degenerate condition within "civilized" society? "This great evil," he asks, "where does it come from? How did it steal into the world? What root did it grow from? Who's doing this? Who killing us? Robbing us of life and light? Mocking us with the sight of what we might have known?"

Sgt. Welsh perhaps offers a clue, in a line that is almost thrown away, when he angrily tells his captain that the war is about "property. The whole fucking thing's about property." The film's overall sensibility brings to mind the outlook of Jean-Jacques Rousseau. In his *Discourse on Inequality* (1755), the great French philosopher asserted that property brought hu-manity's communal existence, with its primitive simplicity and nobility, to an end; inequality, slavery and misery had arisen. "The new-born state of society thus gave rise to a horrible state of war."[35]

This is all very interesting and perhaps potentially profound, but if that's all there were to the film—these sorts of musings—it would fade relatively quickly from memory. It doesn't, because Malick came across a crueler and more difficult situation than he found in the circumstances of even the most interesting of his American characters.

A brief digression: Malick is what's popularly called a "cult figure." An unhappy fate! According to Ephraim Katz's film encyclopedia, Malick was born in Ottawa, Illinois, in November 1943. The son of an oil company exec-utive, he was raised in Texas and Oklahoma. After graduating from Harvard and attending Oxford as a Rhodes scholar, he went to work as a journalist for *Newsweek*, *Life* and the *New Yorker* and also taught philosophy at MIT. Deciding upon a career in filmmaking, he enrolled in the American Film Institute's Center for Advanced Film Studies.

Malick worked on a number of screenplays before he got his first op-portunity to direct a film, *Badlands* —about a young couple on a murder spree—in 1973. He made his second and, until *The Thin Red Line*, only other film in 1978, *Days of Heaven* —the story of a tragic love triangle set at the turn of the century. In Katz's words, "Discouraged by the poor box-office

---

[35] Cited in Frederick Copleston, *A History of Philosophy*, Vol. 6 (Garden City: Image Books, 1964), 84–85.

response to the latter film, the reclusive director withdrew from sight. In subsequent years he divided his time between Paris and Texas."[36] The reputation of his films and his artistic abilities grew as the years went by, and there was no public sign of the director.

In fact, I am not an ardent admirer of Malick's first two works. While they are attractive and made with obvious care, both films, it seems to me, suffer from a certain self-consciousness and coldness and a supercilious attitude toward their primarily working class characters. I always felt Malick's supposed sympathy for and understanding of his unfortunate protagonists was problematic, more posturing than genuinely felt or, at any rate, conveyed.

He has reemerged as a far more substantial artist, with one of the few antiwar films in the recent period that's worthy of the term. War, he shows, is madness and chaos and filth and death and noise and cruelty. "War doesn't ennoble men," a narrator says. "It makes them small, mean, ferocious; it poisons the soul." The viewer is reminded and *feels strongly* that war, even the most noble and just—and this was not—is destructive to all its participants.

I would make a further and greater claim for *The Thin Red Line*. The film shows what happens to the American soldiers, the figures we identify with, in the course of the fighting. Some suffer wounds or die; some who escape physically unharmed are driven to the brink of insanity or beyond. All this is powerful and legitimate. But then Malick shows us what only art or perhaps only the cinema has the power to let us see—the human face of the "enemy."

The Japanese are more or less invisible until the Americans overrun the machine gun bunker; they are simply silhouettes against the sky for the most part. No faces, no features. Then we see a group of them, taken prisoner, huddled on the bunker floor—half-naked, shivering, terrified, mostly young. Some of them have been brutalized by the victors. What's more, the prisoners in many ways resemble their captors. Why are these people killing each other? The Japanese actors, whose names I don't know, are brilliant. No other US filmmaker in recent years that I can think of has showed such concern for the vanquished, the humiliated, the beaten.

And later, after the Japanese encampment in the jungle is taken, another and even more devastating scene: wailing, inconsolable and half-mad prisoners, others shell-shocked and benumbed. One kisses a dead comrade;

---

[36] Ephraim Katz, *The Film Encyclopedia* (New York: Harper Resource, 1994), 886.

another holds himself rigid, leaning forward into space, his body like a tombstone. And in the midst of this, an American soldier who extracts teeth from dead Japanese soldiers for souvenirs, tells an uncomprehending captive, "What are you to me? Nothing." Disturbing and unforgettable images.

In my view, the film hinges on these relatively brief scenes. After sitting through them, you feel that everything up to that point has merely been preparatory, that all the previous action has been rushing toward this moment, is only truly meaningful because of it. Did the director plan things this way? Or did the force and truth of these scenes emerge only when he saw the footage in the editing process? I have no way of knowing. Nick Nolte told an interviewer, in the context of discussions he had with Malick during the shooting, "The real question of the film is: Does compassion have any place in war?" In any event, the filmmaker correctly chose to organize the entire film around these painful sequences. They form its moral and emotional and dramatic center.

In replying to a letter from a reader who disagreed with our negative assessment of Steven Spielberg's *Saving Private Ryan* last year, we made the following point: "What does the phrase 'anti-war' imply? Not simply that you are opposed to what is done to you and your country's army, but that you are opposed to what is done to the enemy *and what you yourself do to the enemy.*"[37]

Malick has grasped this fact and dramatized it. The scenes of the Japanese prisoners are extraordinary; I don't know of any equivalents in the American cinema. Embodied here, I have to believe, are not simply deep feelings about the character of the Second World War, but also bitterness and shame over US conduct around the globe in the past several decades. This is not the sort of thing that is likely to win a director an Academy Award. None of the critics I've read, even those who admire the film, as much as mention these sequences.

Some critics who praised *Saving Private Ryan* now claim that *The Thin Red Line* complements Spielberg's work. Any serious analysis would suggest that Malick's film essentially refutes the earlier work. It throws into relief the banality and mendacity of Spielberg's film, made with an eye to currying favor with the establishment and, with any luck, obtaining an invitation to the White House.

Many things may go into a serious artistic work. And such a work has many possible points of departure. Critics and commentators, some more

---

[37]   Available: http://wsws.org/en/articles/1998/09/ryan-s01.html

perceptively than others, wrack their brains over such things. But is there anyone cynical or irresponsible enough to believe, at this point in history, that profound compassion for the suffering of others is not one of the critical components and starting points of art?

Cast Adrift: Sam Raimi's *A Simple Plan*

World Socialist Web Site; January 27, 1999

Directed by Sam Raimi; adapted by Scott B. Smith from his own novel

Dreiser asserted somewhere that he wrote *An American Tragedy* in part because he had observed the appearance around the turn of the century of a new social type, someone who would do anything, including commit murder, to gain entrance into the golden world of wealth and glamour.

Sam Raimi's *A Simple Plan* is most admirable for its concreteness. What interests me about this film are the connections it draws between diminished economic expectations, a hollow or merely perfunctory moral outlook and irrational behavior.

The story is this: on New Year's Eve, three men find a duffel bag full of money at the site of a small plane that has crashed in the snow. The three are Hank Mitchell (Bill Paxton), college educated and gainfully employed, his childlike brother, Jacob (Billy Bob Thornton), and Jacob's friend, Lou (Brent Briscoe), a loudmouth and a drinker. At first, Hank wants to turn the money over to the police. Lou, unemployed and in debt, easily convinces him otherwise. Hank agrees on condition that they wait until spring and if no one comes for it by then, divide it between themselves at that time. He also insists on holding the cash. When he tells his wife, Sarah (Bridget Fonda), she too resists at first. Give it back, she says. He pours the dozens of packets of hundred dollar bills on their living room table. This has an effect. Later, in bed, she proposes the first of her schemes to improve their chances of holding on to the money.

Naturally, with this auspicious beginning, everything goes wrong—as it always does when small, desperate people try to get clever about large sums of money, something they're not used to being around. They get nervous, exude anxiety, make mistakes, mistrust each other. Every one of

Sarah's plans proves disastrous. Hank finds himself capable of extraordinary acts of violence.

It's interesting—and sometimes exhilarating and sometimes frustrating—to observe how an artist's work rises above, sinks below, but never coincides with his or her conscious outlook. In their published comments about the film, the director, screenwriter, producer and actors speak rather generally about the destructive role of money. In *A Simple Plan*, someone comments, "Money becomes a contagious disease, a disease that once touched, marks you forever." It's perfectly true that in America and elsewhere people have been capable for a long time of doing all sorts of things for money. Lots of films, good and bad, have been made on that theme.

I suppose what's significant about this film is that the pivotal figures, Hank and Sarah, aren't provided with the typical motives for desperate acts—poverty or innate corruption and neurosis. (Nor are they simply the victims of misfortune. They act with their eyes more or less wide open.) The pair are articulate, attractive and reasonably comfortable. They own a pleasant home. They have a beautiful new baby. But I think Raimi establishes the narrowness of their lives. Hank, despite his college education, works as a clerk in a feed store; Sarah shelves books in a library. In two brief but telling sequences we see that their employers give them little room to breathe. Hank's father, we learn, was a farmer unable to hold on to his property, who eventually killed himself. The film takes *as a given* that economic advancement is no longer a serious possibility for such people. It's the specificity of this background that gives life and interest to the not very unusual melodrama that takes place.

Of course, a life of diminished expectations does not necessarily lead to mayhem. The viewer also feels the thinness of whatever moral code it is that has held these respectable, law-abiding people back from behaving reprehensibly. What would hold them back? The inertia provided by church, political party, allegiance to country, fear of public opinion, a sense of responsibility to an employer, and so forth. Not much of that is in evidence here. The film is perhaps most effective in this. You sense that this snowbound town has been cast adrift: it might as well be in the middle of the ocean. Life there has little to do with life in the prosperous centers. Life there has little to do with life *anywhere else*. Everyone is isolated, on his or her own. Not much is holding anyone back any longer. The impoverished, debased moral climate that has been deliberately cultivated and the growing belief by millions that they will never share in the prosperity they see and hear so much—isn't that a volatile, unstable mix?

Raimi, best known for a series of stylish, cartoonish horror films (*The Evil Dead* [1981], *Army of Darkness* [1992], etc.), is obviously talented. He wanted to make a more serious film this time, and he has. It is uniformly well acted. Raimi has worked with the Coen brothers, but I think *A Simple Plan* is considerably superior to the relentlessly snide *Fargo* (1996). Ironically, his film falls short in the end because it suffers somewhat from the same failing it criticizes: a tendency to take shortcuts.

You don't feel, frankly, that the screenwriter and director have made the intellectual investment necessary. They pose a genuine dilemma, but don't quite have the resources to convincingly and compellingly resolve it. At the time of Hank's first act of violence, for example, there is no visual equivalent of the voice in Clyde Griffiths' ear: "But will you now, and when you need not ... once more plunge yourself in the horror of that defeat and failure which has so tortured you and from which this now releases you?"[38] What a Dreiser does, and this film does not, is patiently and re-morselessly build up a set of circumstances from which the protagonist, given who and what he is, can find no logical escape except through a horrible act.

Hank's action comes too easily and *too soon*. The process through which we would develop a grasp and even a sympathy for his situation, through which we would become *complicit* and potentially at least consider our own lives in the light of his difficulties, is cut short. And there are other similar instances: psychological plausibility sacrificed to the supposed obligations of the genre. Indeed, novelist and screenwriter Smith explains that "the book is more in the thriller camp than it is a literary-psychological novel. Whenever it became a question of exploring some moral dimension or driving the plot on, I went with the latter."[39] I wouldn't think this is something to boast about, but we live in such times.

Nonetheless, whatever its shortcomings, here is an honest and absorbing film that tells you something about modern life.

---

[38] Theodore Dreiser, *An American Tragedy* (New York: The Library of America, 2003), 565.

[39] Rosellen Brown, "Choosing Evil," *New York Times*, September 19, 1993. Available: http://www.nytimes.com/1993/09/19/books/choosing-evil

The Unhappiness of Youth:
Boys Don't Cry

World Socialist Web Site; November 8, 1999

Directed by Kimberly Peirce; written by Peirce and Andy Bienen

Boys Don't Cry is a fictionalized account of a tragic series of events that took place in rural Nebraska in December 1993. Teena Brandon, a young woman of 20, moved to Falls City (a farming community of 5,200 people) from Lincoln, dressing and passing herself off as a young man, Brandon Teena. She befriended a number of people, including several local girls. When her secret was exposed, two erstwhile friends, John Lotter and Tom Nissen, beat and raped her. When local police failed to arrest them despite Brandon's identification, the two men shot and killed her and two potential witnesses a week later. In court, Nissen testified against Lotter, and received three consecutive life sentences; Lotter is currently on death row.

Kimberly Peirce (co-screenwriter and director) and Andy Bienen (co-screenwriter) have done a remarkably sensitive job, by and large, of dramatizing this terrible story. It is always astonishing in America these days, given the official ignorance and reaction, to encounter a work that somehow gets things right, or even mostly right. From watching the mass media you would draw the conclusion that nobody in the US understands why anyone lives or dies, or does anything.

Boys Don't Cry is about young people in America; that is to say, it is about unhappiness. Unhappiness, and the various desperate attempts to overcome it, and the ways in which those attempts are suppressed or crushed. Teena/ Brandon (Hilary Swank) dresses like a boy and goes off to Falls City because she is tired of being called a "dyke" in Lincoln. She thinks that in a new place where no one knows her, she will be happier. Lana Tisdel (Chloë Sevigny), with whom Brandon falls in love, works in a factory weighing spinach, lives with her mother who drinks too much, and dreams of being a professional karaoke singer. She falls for Brandon because he treats her better than the other boys. She wants to go anywhere that's outside Falls City.

John (Peter Sarsgaard) and Tom (Brendan Sexton III) have little or nothing going for them. No jobs, no future. They've already spent time in the penitentiary. John used to go out with Lana and still feels something for her. They adopt Brandon as their pal. When "he" turns out to be a woman, they go crazy with humiliation and jealousy. But there is something satisfying in the discovery too. For these two, very near the bottom of society, here is someone apparently even lower.

Many things in *Boys Don't Cry* are wonderfully done. The despair is captured. Some of the early scenes with Sevigny's Lana are particularly acute. She first meets Brandon in a bar where she and a couple of friends get up and sing about "The Bluest Eyes in Texas." Sevigny has these sleepy eyes and a manner that combines arrogance and self-effacement in equal measure. "Who are you?" she throws out insolently as she passes Brandon for the first time. The next time they meet, Lana is wandering around a convenience store, wasted, trying to convince the storeowner to sell her some beer.

The fashion in which the relationship between Lana and Brandon begins is handled well. They feel something for each other, and gender doesn't matter very much. Lana is provided with ample evidence that Brandon is a female, but chooses to ignore it. This seems believable.

In its own way, the story points to how scrambled social, family and sexual relations have become in the US. The world these young people live in has little to do with America as it officially presents itself. They live a kind of anarchistic existence, cut off from the direct influence of all the official institutions—parties, churches, unions—that carry on mostly out of inertia. It's hardly a utopia, this life of dead-end jobs, drinking, drugs, minor and not so minor scrapes with the law. But Peirce and Bienen show that there is something else here too, or the desire for something else.

Some commentators write about these characters as though they represent an exotic life form. In respectable publications, critics write with contempt about "trailer trash." In fact, tens of millions of people live in circumstances not too dissimilar to these. They are not participating in the stock market boom, therefore they don't count.

Another way of avoiding the social issue is to write about "homophobia in the heartland." Of course, antigay prejudice is a poison that needs to be specifically combated. But no one has the right to be astonished by the fact that conditions of such hopelessness and lack of culture breed backwardness. Outrage at the fates of Teena Brandon and Matthew Shepard[40] is

---

[40] Matthew Wayne Shepard (December 1, 1976–October 12, 1998) was a gay student at the University of Wyoming who was tortured and murdered near Laramie, Wyoming, in October 1998.

somewhat hollow if it is not accompanied by outrage at the wretchedness that helped produced the tragedies.

I don't know the immediate motives of the film's creators. Peirce obviously felt strongly about the tragedy. It took her five years to raise the money and assemble the cast of *Boys Don't Cry*. She told an interviewer: "My whole point was that I fell in love with Brandon. I felt his story needed to be told. The media coverage was very sensational from the beginning. Nobody got inside the character. No one ever really knew about the love story. My whole point was to honor him. My whole point was to explore the mechanics of hatred so that this stuff didn't happen again."

Whatever the limitations of her outlook, Peirce was honest enough to take a hard look at the set of circumstances surrounding Brandon's death. One might say that through her artistic integrity she stumbled on the general tragedy surrounding the individual tragedy.

I think the filmmakers, however, must have been made nervous at a certain point by the kind of film they found themselves making. If they had maintained their course and made the story of Teena Brandon's fate into a wholehearted indictment of American life, which of course is what it naturally tends toward being, the work would not have been well received in their own milieu or by the media. Unfortunately, the filmmakers "came to their senses" a little too soon.

So *Boys Don't Cry* loses its way as it approaches its denouement in Brandon's rape and murder. Or, rather, the film finds its way back to a somewhat predictable and well-trodden path, the story of saintly versus monstrous individuals. Whereas before we had bad, brazen Lana, stumbling around malls in a stupor, now she sobers up and has the stereotyped look of "a woman in love." This is not necessarily progress. Swank as Brandon loses her edge. Tom and John become cardboard cutouts, mere villains. Everything in the film clogs up, slows down.

One example: Brandon and Lana have decided to run away together. Then Lana, not surprisingly, has second thoughts. When Brandon shows up in her room, she lets her and the audience know that she has reservations with body language, a grimace, monosyllabic responses. Why are we being handed the information on a plate all of a sudden? The film loses subtlety as it narrows its focus, as it turns its back on the bigger and more terrifying picture. This can be explained. As long as their understanding and intuition about the present state of affairs guide the filmmakers, events and dialogue flow organically, lightly, under their own steam. As soon as Peirce and Bienen begin to worry about fulfilling their own and other people's expectations for the film, when they limit themselves to exposing the mechanisms of a "hate crime," *Boys Don't Cry* loses its power.

The rape and murder are presented in extended and graphic detail. Again, this suggests that the filmmakers don't quite know how to end their story or what to emphasize, so they take the less demanding way out and simply horrify their audience. That's not so difficult to do. There are always plenty of things to horrify people with. Unfortunately, some viewers may take the easy way out too, and choose to remember the violence while forgetting the relatively clear-eyed portrait that came before of a segment of the population so brutalized and alienated that the ultimate explosion seems almost an inevitable consequence. In any event, there is enough here of a sober and accurate accounting to make this one of the better American films of the year.

The Rise and Fall and Rise Again of John Waters: *Cecil B. Demented*

World Socialist Web Site; August 23, 2000

Written and directed by John Waters

This is the best American film I've seen this year, and probably the only one that does something to advance the pleasure principle.

John Waters has been making films for thirty years or more. A native of Baltimore, born in 1946, Waters made his name with *Pink Flamingos* (1972) and *Female Trouble* (1975), two genuinely tasteless and remarkable films, which managed to embrace the grotesque in working class and lower middle class and suburban American life, without slipping into condescension or prettification. They were disturbing films, deliberately ugly and absurd, but among the few that gave the viewer something of the look and feel of the way millions and millions of people—almost entirely excluded from artistic representation—in the US were living and continue to live: thrashing about wildly in confusion, desire and anxiety.

Waters's films of the 1980s seemed less interesting to me. There are amusing and clever bits in *Hairspray* (1988) and *Cry-Baby* (1988), but, all in all, they seemed to represent a falling off, perhaps an (unconscious) accommodation to an unfavorable climate. That may be a little unfair, or at least incomplete. There was also an aesthetic problem: how was Waters to maintain the crude and "badly made" quality of his earlier films, which gave them some of their vitality, as he developed his technique and had far greater resources to work with? It's a problem that in one way or another confronts every serious filmmaker. In any event, with *Pecker* (1998) and *Cecil B. Demented*, in my view, Waters has returned more or less to form.

In the new film, Cecil B. Demented is the leader of a band of cinema guerrillas who capture Hollywood star Honey Whitlock, in Baltimore on a publicity tour for her newest effort, *Some Kind of Happiness* ("A screwball romantic comedy, life-affirming ... Couldn't we use a little optimism in the movies?"), and force her to play the leading role in their own no-budget film, *Raving Beauty*. Demented, who tends to speak in slogans, is intent on leading "a revolution to destroy mainstream cinema." Among his rallying cries: "Power to the people who punish bad cinema!"

The first sequence in which Demented directs Honey, on a slightly haphazard film set built inside a deserted movie theater, takes place at an art cinema showing a "Pasolini festival." Lyle, a drug addict, and Cherish, a former porn star, apparently play the owners of the cinema, with Honey the latter's mother. The dialogue goes something like this:

Cherish: We didn't sell one ticket.

Lyle: Pasolini is playing and we have an empty theater.

Honey: It's that multiplex theater.

Lyle: Not for the *Flintstones* sequel!

After that, Demented decides to take his film crew out in the streets, for "real life ... and real terror." Eventually, Honey comes to appreciate the virtues of underground cinema and throws herself into the project. In the course of making their film, the group invades and disrupts a number of events, beginning with a showing of *Patch Adams—the Director's Cut* (at which the entire audience is sobbing) in a suburban mall. Then comes a press and industry party hosted by the Maryland Film Commission, whose guests are guzzling oysters. The group members confront the film industry types about their rotten films and corrupt lives. "I was only following studio orders," whimpers one of the latter. Another, who directed an inferior remake of a foreign film, asserts in self-defense, "American audiences won't watch subtitles." A third, the "vice president of creative affairs," says, "I don't go to the movies." The head of the film commission promises one of Demented's band, if she'll release him, "We'll go to Sundance together!"

Next, the group takes upon itself to close down the filming of *Gump Again* (the remake of *Forrest Gump*, 1994), taking place on a set composed of fake grass in front of a fake city skyline. The director and the cameraman, Jean-Pierre, are complacent hacks. "Nobody can stop the popularity of Forrest Gump!" the former indignantly tells the invaders of his set. The star of the remake, Kevin Nealon, lamely puts in, "I only take the roles I'm offered." When all hell breaks loose, the director's voice can be heard loudly proclaiming that the disruption is costing "a thousand dollars a second!"

In the course of their struggle, Demented, Honey and the others also pass through cinemas showing karate and porno marathons. A battle erupts at one point between the karate fans and the "family film" crowd and, later, another between Teamsters members and porn lovers. Confrontations between the guerrillas and the authorities become more and more violent, and fatal. The film's fiery denouement takes place during a Honey Whitlock triple-bill and look-alike contest organized at a drive-in.

Waters and his performers manage to establish the precisely correct tone. The extravagance and silliness are played with absolute earnestness. Cecil (Stephen Dorff), looking a little like Lou Castel in Fassbinder's *Beware of a Holy Whore* (1971), is a wild-eyed martinet with "Otto Preminger" (a legendary dictator on the set) tattooed on his arm. He's forbidden his cast and crew to find any sexual release during shooting, demanding "celibacy for celluloid" and calling on them to "save your sexual energy for the screen."

Melanie Griffith too has the role of her career as Honey, a bit dimwitted, selfish, with that little-girl voice, but capable, like so many actors in real life, of extraordinary self-sacrifice and dedication and going far "beyond themselves" when it comes to roles and projects they believe in.

Waters has made a work that says what practically no one else will admit out loud: that Hollywood is turning out bland and conformist films and that the movie studios, dominated by large financial interests, are operated by philistines and cowards. "I'm a prophet against profit," declares Cecil. "One day you'll thank me for saving you from your bad career," he tells Honey. "Technique is nothing more than failed style" is another of his proclamations. Honey, once she's gotten into the swing of things, tells a hostile crowd that "'family' is just a dirty word for censorship," and later, announces, "Bad movies must be avenged!"

All in all, the film is a joy, a sensual argument for "cinema unrest," as Waters calls it, and a liberating experience because, for a change, one has the sense that the director is speaking honestly with his own voice. Moreover, virtually every target of the film is legitimate and deserving of scorn and derision. Of course, the film is one prolonged joke, but, behind the humor is the notion that art is not about financial success, but a serious and urgent activity, with consequences, and worth making enormous sacrifices for. And that no cinema without those qualities is worth considering. Waters makes fun of Demented and his cronies, but the mockery is tempered with sympathy, even envy.

The critical response has generally been favorable, but in a number of relatively prestigious publications, one encounters this sort of attitude: "It's a bit trite," "This is of course a simplification," and even, in French, "Pas très drôle" [not very funny]. I'm suspicious of those who respond in this manner. Frankly, anyone in and around the film industry to whom this work is not a pleasure has a vested interest in the status quo. I'm inclined to agree with Cecil: "Death [or at the very least, ignominy] to those who support mainstream cinema!"

Children in the Mountains:
A Time for Drunken Horses
World Socialist Web Site; October 5, 2000

Written and directed by Bahman Ghobadi

I first encountered Iranian Kurdish filmmaker Bahman Ghobadi's work in a surprising manner. A short film of his, *Life in Fog* (1999), turned up uncredited on a videotape of another Iranian filmmaker's work last year at the San Francisco film festival.

The twenty-eight minute film caught my attention. It was more or less a documentary about four kids living in terribly hard conditions, apparently on their own, in the mountains. Their reality seemed to be composed of fog, snow, rain, cold, earth and stones.

A Time for Drunken Horses takes up these same children and works their story into a feature-length fiction. It's a very painful, very beautiful film, made with extraordinary intensity and sincerity.

The children are Kurds, a stateless people, whose population of more than 20 million is divided up among four countries in the region. Their mother is dead, their smuggler father's away. In fact, everyone smuggles here on the border between Iran and Iraq. The two nations fought a bloody war here for nearly ten years. Mines are buried everywhere; border patrols and god knows who else lie in ambush. It's hard to imagine a harsher existence. One wouldn't want to.

In the middle of all this, the children act toward one another with the greatest love and devotion. Ayoub, the eldest boy, has to work night and day to keep food in all their mouths. His sister Ameneh goes to school; maybe she'll make something of herself. Madi, 15, is deformed. He needs constant treatment. A doctor tells the children that he'll die if he doesn't have an operation, and, at that, the operation will only prolong his life by several months.

Ayoub works even harder, but there is too much going against him. He can't raise the money to pay the hospital on the Iraqi side of the border. Rojin, the eldest sister, agrees to marry an Iraqi Kurd on condition that the family pay for her brother's operation. When the girl arrives, the other family reneges; they want nothing to do with the crippled boy. The mother-in-law: "I don't want him. I sent for a bride." Instead, they offer a mule in compensation. But Rojin must go through with the marriage. It's hard to bear.

Ayoub, planning to sell the mule in Iraq to raise the money for the operation, joins a group of smugglers crossing the border. Nothing will stop him. The smugglers are attacked. They need to flee, but their animals have been given vodka to keep them warm (hence the film's title) and can't get to their feet. It's a terrifying, chaotic moment. Ayoub, despite everything, continues. When we last see him he's picking his way over barbed wire.

You remember the faces of these young people, above all, against a remorseless landscape. You would imagine that a tiny, isolated rural community, nearly cut off from the modern world, must generally produce a hothouse atmosphere: all the energy of its inhabitants expended in a small space and applied to a limited number of tasks. The external pressure exerted on the Kurds and their sense that they have no friends in the world only intensifies those internal bonds, almost to the point of madness. The persistence and loyalty and love are so intense, it's almost difficult to watch.

Ghobadi may be the only Kurdish filmmaker presently working. Conditions in Iran, which are slightly better for the Kurds, make that possible. He doesn't see himself as an Iranian director, or, at any rate, sees his work as different from theirs, but clearly the influence of Iranian cinema, if only in making it aesthetically and intellectually possible to treat such realities, is considerable.

In conversation, Ghobadi is a charming and friendly man. He's made what is in certain ways a brilliant film. Yet I found myself disagreeing with a number of things he said. He repeated to us that these children were happy, that their harsh conditions were the only ones they knew, that they found nothing wrong with their lives because they had nothing to compare it to, and so forth. The film suggests something different. It shows poverty and misery, children nearly destroying themselves or nearly being destroyed by their circumstances. They don't look happy about it for an instant.

To watch Rojin as she sells herself in marriage—for a mule!—and Ayoub as he watches in agony as his sister goes to her wretched fate ... If Ghobadi is not registering a protest here, then what is he doing?

In any event, even in the most isolated region there are class differences, those who live even in relative luxury and those who don't. I don't believe there's a human being alive who can't tell when he's being beat up by the world around him. (Whether he thinks there are any prospects of doing anything about it is, of course, another matter.) The film is a devastating critique of social life in the region and the conditions masses of children face in many parts of this unhappy globe. Ghobadi the filmmaker is more advanced than Ghobadi the social commentator.

In any event, *A Time for Drunken Horses* exists, and we're fortunate that it does.

Independent Filmmaking That Is Genuinely Independent: *Platform* and *Yi Yi*

World Socialist Web Site; October 12, 2000

Written and directed by Jia Zhangke, Edward Yang

Jia Zhangke's *Platform*

Platform (*Zhantai*) was apparently a Chinese pop song in the 1980s. In an interview, director Jia Zhangke explained that the song—whose title refers to a railway platform—contains the line, "We are waiting, our whole hearts are waiting, waiting forever ..." He observed: "It's because we're still 'waiting' that I decided to name the film after the song."

Jia is an independent Chinese filmmaker, who works without obtaining the approval of the Beijing regime. This is his second work, following the masterful *Xiao Wu* (1997), about a young pickpocket in a provincial town.

Platform considers the economic changes that occurred in China in the 1980s, the promotion of capitalist relations, and their social and personal consequences. It follows, over the course of three hours, the fate of a number of young people. They're members at first of the Peasant Culture Group from Fenyang, obliged to perform the immortal "Train Heading for Shaoshan"—Shaoshan being Mao Zedong's birthplace. A repressive atmosphere predominates. Wearing bell-bottoms is considered a sign of antisocial behavior. One youth is told, "You sound more like a capitalist roader." He tells a girl her father is "like a KGB man." Simplicity, poverty and naiveté: another girl asks, "Is it true that kissing makes you pregnant?"

In the spring of 1980, the leader of the performance group announces: "From now on, Western-style music will be included in our shows." One thing leads to another. The government cuts its subsidies, and the Peasant Culture Group transforms itself into the "All-Star Rock and Breakdown Electronic Band." Allegiances and ties within the group loosen and even dissolve. In the end, a consumerist society has been produced. Bourgeois domesticity is now the norm.

The director is a rarity in that he criticizes the Mao era, without reducing people, including local party officials and others, to caricatures. He suggests that there were those who believed they were sacrificing to bring into being a new type of society. He criticizes the Deng Xiaoping era, without cynicism and without exhibiting the slightest nostalgia for the earlier period. He shows, however, that the majority of the population is "still waiting" for the benefits of "reform" promised them, and how painful and difficult that is. He leaves the audience free to draw its own conclusions about this history.

Jia works slowly and patiently, treating complex social and emotional problems with extraordinary confidence and pictorial skill. A conversation in a cramped bedroom or on the city's battlements is allowed to take its natural course. He has a penchant for scenes of couples sitting uncomfortably on couches or beds under windows. One remembers the awkward silences as much as the spoken words. The filmmaker's raw material is provincial life and its cast of somewhat inarticulate, diffident, even alienated characters. With that unglamorous material, he paints a picture of elemental human striving—for love and companionship, for kindness, for a freer existence—and the obstacles it comes up against. Perhaps this is what Jia means when he writes that he wants "to explore and exhibit progressive power hidden among people." It is difficult to conceive of such an artist emerging entirely apart from the development of a generally more critical atmosphere, in China and elsewhere. He is a major filmmaker.

An issue that was discussed in the first part of this series [From the 2000 Toronto International Film Festival] initially arose following a viewing of *Platform*. Jia depicts two realities, both harsh and unsatisfying. His own approach to life—his humanity and compassion and lyricism—suggests a third reality, something that still needs to be created. This may say something significant about the role of art. When I asked Jia about it, I was afraid from his response that something—literally—had been lost in the translation. Later, on rereading his comments, I think he did understand the point. He spoke about the need for a "more forgiving" way of living. I was moved by the film and our conversation (also present was actress Zhao Tao), as brief as it was.

Edward Yang's *Yi Yi*

Edward Yang, born in Shanghai in 1947, was one of the founding members of the new Taiwanese cinema. He gained a reputation with such films as *Taipei Story* (1985), *A Brighter Summer Day* (1991) and *A Confucian Confusion* (1994). He is known for his consideration of contemporary Taiwanese manners and morals. *Yi Yi* is his most recent work.

I'm told that "Yi Yi" means "one-one" and can also mean "individually." This apparently refers to the distinct ways in which the characters respond to life and society.

A great many things go on, again during the course of three hours, involving "NJ" Jian and his extended family. The marriage of his idiotic brother-in-law is disrupted by the appearance of a jilted girlfriend. NJ's mother-in-law suffers a stroke and enters into a coma. His daughter, who feels responsible for the old woman's condition, begins a tentative romance. His wife takes stock of her life and finds it wanting: "I have so little? How can it be so little? I live a blank. ... What am I doing every day?" She goes off to a Buddhist retreat on a mountain and returns with her Master, who accepts checks. Her young son faces his own crisis, bullied by girls and isolated from those around him. He seems on his way to becoming an artist; he photographs the backs of people's heads to help them see themselves more fully.

NJ encounters an old girlfriend, Sherry. He's sufficiently unhappy or distracted to pursue the possibilities in the situation. Years before, he'd disappeared from her life, without a word. "Why didn't you come that day? I never got over it." Sent by his apparently failing computer company on a business mission to Japan, NJ arranges to spend some time there with Sherry. She tells him again, "That day, I waited and waited. I was so angry." He says, lamely: "You pushed me to be an engineer. You can't run someone's life." In the end, he can't go through with the affair and rushes out of the hotel room. "Why do I always make the same mistake?"

NJ's partners betray him, refusing to sign with a Japanese computer genius and instead opting for a cheap imitation. "Where is our dignity?" he asks. "What's that got to do with business?" one of his associates responds.

There are truly remarkable and compelling moments in *Yi Yi*, but it feels driven by distinct and at times mutually exclusive impulses. Indeed this problem manifests itself in the structure of the work: the various strands of the narrative feel driven by distinct impulses and produce quite different responses in a viewer. Those elements of the film bound up with NJ and his business partners and his wife and her Buddhism have something unsettling and authentic about them. One feels in the presence of individuals trapped or who have trapped themselves in impossible circumstances: material wealth and moral emptiness.

On the other hand, in my view, the stories of the son and daughter seem animated by a rather complacent desire to trace "interpersonal relations" and the "rhythms of life" in an abstract and not terribly interesting manner. It's all rather neatly packaged. The relationship between the daughter and her grandmother seems stale, as does the Sherry episode. Perhaps in an instinctive response to the tameness of too much of the film, Yang has provided a "dramatic" denouement (a shooting), which merely strikes one as extraneous and contrived.

The greatest strength of the film, in my view, is the character of NJ. He is a substantial figure, a principled and tormented man in an unprincipled and self-satisfied milieu. I was pleased to discover that the "actor" playing the part is the veteran screenwriter and director Wu Nien-jen (hence "NJ"?). Wu, born in 1952, authored the scripts for Hou Hsiao-hsien's *Dust in the Wind* (1986), *A City of Sadness* (1989) and *The Puppetmaster* (1993), as well as Yang's *That Day, on the Beach* (1983). He also directed the remarkable *A Borrowed Life* (1994), about his father, which I thought one of the best films of the past decade. I give full credit to Yang for casting him. Whatever contradictory impulses may be at work, the role of NJ is a significant contribution and Wu is continuously riveting.

Whither the Coen Brothers?
O Brother, Where Art Thou?

World Socialist Web Site; February 10, 2001

Directed by Joel Coen; written by Ethan Coen and Joel Coen

Joel and Ethan Coen have collaborated on eight films since 1984, the former writing and the latter directing. By no stretch of the imagination could any of the films be considered entirely or even largely successful. Nearly every work has been marred by bursts of mean-spiritedness and cynicism, an inappropriate jokiness, that tend to undercut and detract from the more truthful or compelling moments. Yet virtually every one of the films has had a feature or the hint of a feature that suggested that the Coens might be on to something, or might at least be capable of being on to something.

Raising Arizona (1987), their second feature—following the overheated gothic *film noir Blood Simple* (1984)—was often genuinely funny, and *Miller's*

Crossing (1990), an interesting reworking of Dashiell Hammett's *Red Harvest* (1929). *Barton Fink* (1991), with its cartoon leftist writer in Hollywood during the 1930s, coming into contact with the "real America," in the form of a psychopathic salesman, represented a low point. *Fargo* (1996), despite its caricatures and its bloody subject matter, had a certain humanity to it, principally due to the performance of Frances McDormand.

The Coens' latest film, *O Brother, Where Art Thou?*, is not a great leap forward, but still … one can see something, far away on the horizon perhaps, that might represent an insight or an attempt to gain one.

The film is threaded with conceits. The title to begin with, a reference to Preston Sturges's remarkable *Sullivan's Travels* (1941), in which a director of Hollywood comedies suddenly decides to make a "serious" film with the proposed title of *O Brother, Where Art Thou?* Then there is the straight-faced assertion in the credits that the film is "based upon" Homer's *The Odyssey*. (*Sullivan's Travels* was itself a reference to another classic, *Gulliver's Travels* [1726] by Jonathan Swift.) Of course, that the film is itself the creation of two brothers gives the title another twist. Our leg is being pulled in various directions at once.

In a quasi-mythical Mississippi of the 1930s, Ulysses Everett McGill (George Clooney) escapes from a prison farm with two companions, Pete (John Turturro) and Delmar (Tim Blake Nelson). Ulysses' tortuous effort to make his way home to his wife, Penny (Holly Hunter) and his batch of daughters—a journey he dupes his two fellow escapees into undertaking by promises of a hidden fortune—forms the substance of the film. Along the way the three encounter a modern Cyclops (a vicious one-eyed Bible salesman), a trio of Sirens (seductresses washing clothes—and singing of course—by a stream) and a corrupt politician whose given name is Menelaus (nicknamed "Pappy"), in addition to a blues man who claims to have sold his soul to the devil (*à la* blues legend Robert Johnson [1911–1938]), the manic-depressive gangster Baby Face Nelson, a terrifying lawman hot in pursuit and a gathering of Ku Klux Klansmen. They also, unbeknownst to themselves, become hit recording artists, a fact that helps save their bacon in the long run.

Our heroes undergo setbacks and minor triumphs, disasters and near-disasters, even scrapes with death—one thing after another. Through it all, they manage, more or less, to sustain their essential naiveté, goofiness and optimism. Everything is larger than life and not intended to be particularly convincing. Clooney's character, a self-styled "pater familias" and, in his own mind, the only one of the three capable of "abstract thought," sticks in the memory as a pretty likable and attractive character.

I think the most pleasant surprise, however, is the relative absence of malice in the film. I feared the worst, as the denouement approached and all the possibilities of the townsfolk turning into some monstrous mob of "rednecks" loomed. It doesn't work out that way. Indeed, the Coens go out of their way to provide a rather softhearted (and somewhat contrived and simplistic) ending, with the Klan chief ridden out of town on a rail. Popular culture saves the day! In it, somehow, America proves to be at its best.

Any film that treats the Depression, chain gangs, farm foreclosures, the Klan, lynchings, corrupt politicians, hypocritical Bible salesmen, etc., etc., is worth looking into. If only in the vaguest sense, there must be a sensibility in operation that has at least done preliminary work.

Equally, any film that pays tribute to such extraordinary music must also bear examination. The Coens, with famed producer T-Bone Burnett in charge, have included gospel, country and bluegrass tunes, some of them in original versions, some newly recorded. Among those asked to participate in the making of the soundtrack included Ralph Stanley, Gillian Welch, John Hartford, Alison Krauss, Emmylou Harris, the Fairfield Four and Norman Blake.

Something is up here. The Coens are trying to figure out, it would seem, what makes America tick; why, at almost the same instant, it can be so backward and so sublime, so reactionary and so democratic, so mad and so sane.

Unfortunately, they haven't gotten terribly far with their deliberations. As soon as one expresses support for the appealing elements in the films, all its weaknesses come leaping out. There is still far too much contempt expressed for the filmmakers' own creations—Turturro's moronic Pete is insufferable for most of the film, and Nelson's Delmar is not all that much better. The Coens pick and choose, indicating their own dramatic unclarity as well as their susceptibility to the pressure of liberal public opinion. Only Southern whites are permitted to be idiotic, the blacks are more or less saintly or iconic. And there is no internal coherence to the caricaturing. Ulysses, Pete and Delmar ham it up outrageously when they record and later perform their version of "Man of Constant Sorrow." Other groups, singing country or gospel, are treated respectfully. Since characterization has no logic, much of the more extreme behavior loses its edge; it simply seems arbitrary, quirky.

The truth is, I suspect, that the director and writer themselves don't know what to make of an area that has produced so much beauty and so much horror. By juxtaposing the two qualities, by playing and juggling with them, they hope something will come out of it. Occasionally it does, but not often and not consistently enough. To the love of the music, to a feeling for the region's crazy-quilt character, to intuition about the social and emotional possibilities that lie beneath the surface, needs to be added, I think, a deeper understanding of all the historical experiences, especially since the Civil War, that produced the explosive and complex set of social contradictions making up the South.

Homer's Odysseus (Ulysses in Latin) was up against the fate ordained for him by the gods on Mount Olympus. What's the thread linking the obstacles in Ulysses Everett McGill's path? There really isn't one, except insofar as they each represent one of the Coens' gags. The various confrontations form a series of disconnected set pieces. Because of that they lose strength, even become tedious, repetitive. At times the obstacles take on a social dimension: the fiendish lawman/pursuer, the Bible salesman, the Klansmen. At other times, they have no particular content. The Sirens' sequence, although pretty, seems entirely gratuitous. One feels the brothers simply filling up space and killing time.

The real difficulty, I suspect, and it's bound up with the current state of artistic affairs, is that the Coens still feel the need to keep at a distance a coherent social critique. That would be unfashionable. After all, one serious look at the South in the 1930s, under conditions where such an ideological prejudice was not at work, would surely convince anyone as bright as these filmmakers that the central problem was the existing social order in all its dimensions: banks, sheriffs, racists, politicians, and so forth. It certainly would have been possible to have retained the chaos and yet have infused it with more of an organized sense of the world and more of a protest. The narrative—which one is continually hoping will cohere and fully come to life, and never does—would have been something more than merely *potentially* delightful. As it is, the film is made up of fragments, some convincing, but too many that are irritating.

In praising the film in his December 22, 2000, review ("Hail, Ulysses, Escaped Convict"[41]), *New York Times* critic A.O. Scott points out the presence in early twentieth century American folk music of "the longing for

---

[41] Available: http://www.nytimes.com/2000/12/22/movies/film-review-hail-ulysses-escaped-convict.html

another world." The reviewer notes intriguingly that "The Big Rock Candy Mountain," the song that is heard over the threesome's initial escape from the prison farm, "expresses a weary, heartfelt longing for a life free of toil and injustice. 'O Brother, Where Art Thou?' similarly offers a fairy-tale view of an America in which the real brutalities of poverty and racism are magically dissolved by the power of song."

This may in part be wishful thinking. It doesn't seem to me the film has that consistently visionary quality; it too often loses track of itself, gets derailed, finds itself at dead ends, and even when it does aspire to that quality, too often *O Brother, Where Art Thou?* falls back on somewhat facile means of resolving the characters' dilemmas. Nonetheless, it would be interesting to see what the director and writer might produce if they decided once and for all not to take the line of least resistance.

The Limitations of Ed Harris's *Pollock*

World Socialist Web Site; March 31, 2001

Directed by Ed Harris; screenplay by Barbara Turner and Susan Emshwiller; based on the book *Jackson Pollock: An American Saga*, by Steven Naifeh and Gregory White Smith

Pollock, directed by actor Ed Harris, who also plays the lead role, treats the last fifteen years of American painter Jackson Pollock's life, from his encounter with fellow painter Lee Krasner (whom he was to marry) in New York City in 1941 until his death in an automobile accident on Long Island in 1956 at the age of 44.

The film uses material from a number of sources, especially the biography, *Jackson Pollock: An American Saga*, by Steven Naifeh and Gregory White Smith, first published in 1989.

Pollock begins in 1950. The artist is approached by a woman clutching a copy of *Life* magazine, which had done a spread on him, asking for an autograph. He looks off, anxious, wondering. The film goes back nine years in his life. Pollock is a struggling artist, cursing Picasso and living with his brother, Sande, and his wife. He is obviously a troubled soul, prone to bursts of violence, depression, drunkenness.

Pollock encounters Krasner. She is enthralled by his paintings. Over the course of a number of years, she sacrifices some part of her own career to further his fortunes in the art world. She also provides him some degree of emotional stability. He meets legendary art patroness Peggy Guggenheim and in 1943 has his first one-man show, where he also encounters art critic Clement Greenberg, later to be his champion.

Krasner and Pollock move to Long Island, where she isolates him from old friends and he tries to stop drinking. Accidentally, while working on a canvas on his studio floor, he invents his famous drip technique (paint was allowed to fall from the brush or can on to the canvas) in 1947. The resulting works bring him great success, including the famous *Life* piece two years later. His good fortune, however, does nothing to resolve his personal difficulties. On the contrary, he is haunted by the sense that he's a fraud.

Five years later, Pollock's recent shows have not met with success. Greenberg has more or less deserted him. Pollock is drinking like a fish, having affairs. His relationship with Krasner is at the breaking point. They scream insults at one another. When she is off in Italy, he takes up openly with his girlfriend. One night, particularly drunk, he drives his car, with his mistress and a friend of hers as passengers, off the road at high speed and dies in the crash.

Ed Harris spent years thinking about and preparing this film, apparently since he read the book by Naifeh and Smith soon after it came out. He took up painting in the early 1990s. In the movie's production notes, he explains, "I've been painting and drawing off and on since I became committed to making this film. I had a little studio built so I'd have enough floor space to work on larger canvases." Indeed, Harris is most convincing when he reproduces Pollock's drip technique.

The film has a certain air of seriousness about it. Harris's efforts, one feels, are genuine and sincere. He wanted to communicate something of Pollock's anguish and honesty, and perhaps something of his own, as an actor in the commercial film industry. Marcia Gay Harden is endearing as Lee Krasner—perhaps too endearing—but her performance is an honest one as well. *Pollock* is Harris's first effort at directing a film, after performing in nearly fifty over the past two decades, and he has accomplished the work in an intelligent and straightforward manner.

The difficulty, however, is that film is so narrowly focused and so limited in its approach that the most essential truths about Pollock and his circumstances are permitted to escape. The script by Barbara Turner and Susan Emshwiller assembles a number of biographical details, without ever making profound sense of them. The artist's downward spiral is predictable and predictably presented. Pollock is tortured when we first encounter him, tortured throughout, and this quality is ascribed entirely to personal psychological causes.

Again from the production notes, Harris comments: "A desperate need for approval usually forces one into doing that which is recognizable. ... Pollock's need for approval bordered on the psychopathic and yet his even deeper need to create art that had no hint of the lie about it drove him to make art that had never been made before and was certainly fair game for ridicule and abuse."

This does not take us much closer to the specifics of Pollock's situation, and indeed, the film's script is a bit of a template. Any number of apparently self-tormented painters, composers, writers, and so on, could be made to fit the general characterization Harris provides. We are still left with the question, what was Jackson Pollock's particular dilemma?

The "Problem of Pollock" and, more generally, the "Problem of Abstract Expressionism" and postwar American painting are enormous ones. There is a large body of literature on these issues, much of it confused or deliberately mystifying. At the outset, one should make clear that the fate of Pollock and his fellow painters was *directly* bound up with the most pressing and inescapable political problems of the mid-twentieth century: the growth of Stalinism in the Soviet Union and the Communist parties around the world, the character of Trotsky's opposition to Stalinism and the tragic fate of the socialist revolution in the 1930s and 1940s, as well as the nature of American society as it emerged from World War II.

Jackson Pollock's father, LeRoy, had been a socialist and his son became one, too. As Naifeh and Smith note, "From his first encounter with socialist ideas ... LeRoy responded to their call for fairness and equality." LeRoy Pollock supported socialist labor leaders such as Eugene V. Debs, the radical Industrial Workers of the World and, in 1917, "celebrated at the news that the workers of Russia had taken control of their government. Of his five sons, two would become active in the labor movement and one would join the Communist party. The other two would become artists."[42]

Naifeh and Smith observe that the future painter was introduced at an early age to left-wing ideas, but that it was the city of Los Angeles in the late 1920s "that finally pushed Jackson into the turbulent world of

---

[42] Steven Naifeh and Gregory White Smith, *Jackson Pollock: An American Saga* (New York: Harper, 1989), 29.

radical politics."[43] In 1929, after various confrontations at his high school, Pollock wrote his brothers, "The whole outfit think I am a rotten rebel from Russia."[44]

After moving to New York in 1930, Pollock studied with the American regionalist Thomas Hart Benton (with whom his older brother, Charles, had also studied). The Mexican painters and muralists—José Clemente Orozco, Diego Rivera and David Siqueiros—impressed him from the early 1930s. Rivera had been in the Communist Party, but split with Stalinism and joined the Trotskyists. Siqueiros was a loyal Stalinist and later took part in an assassination attempt against Trotsky. Many of Pollock's friends were in and around the Communist Party. In April 1936, he went to work in Siqueiros's studio in New York, where preparations for May Day were being made, and participated in the May 1 parade along with the float he had helped build.

By the late 1930s, Pablo Picasso, especially his "Guernica," and the surrealists—Joan Miró, Max Ernst and, above all, André Masson—became critically important for Pollock. Many leading surrealists came to the US—and New York City in particular—to escape fascism and war in Europe. Pollock participated in the International Surrealist Exhibition in 1942 held in New York, although he never considered himself a member of the movement.

The influence of Trotsky's ideas within New York intellectual circles was significant, although relatively few understood or cared to grasp their Marxist essence. The wretched character of Soviet "Socialist Realist" painting in particular impelled many into the camp of "anti-Stalinism." Lee Krasner was a sympathizer of Trotsky—or the state capitalist deviation from Trotskyism, the group led by Max Shachtman—as were a number of the future abstract expressionists, including Adolph Gottlieb and Mark Rothko, as well as the three prominent art critics of the postwar period: Greenberg, Harold Rosenberg and Meyer Schapiro. With many, however, reeling under the blows of American democratic-imperialist propaganda and losing confidence, if they ever had it, in the revolutionary capacities of the working class, anti-Stalinism quickly transformed itself into simple anticommunism in the war and postwar years.

Treating the development of the abstract painters in the US as a purely internal affair of art history is absurd. As Trotsky said of the

---

[43]   Ibid., 132.

[44]   Ibid., 145.

poet Mayakovsky and his suicide, "Where could artistic harmony come from in these decades of catastrophe ...?"[45] Ironically, American painting emerged from provincialism and assimilated the most modern technique at a time of extraordinary political tragedy: the betrayal of the October Revolution, the rise of fascism and the threat of another world war. By the time the American painters could speak in mature tones, let's say, they found speaking itself an increasingly painful and even dread-laden prospect.

By the late 1940s, while the media in the US, driven by Cold War imperatives, celebrated the triumph of American painting and the shift of the art world's capital to New York, the painters themselves were horrified by many aspects of postwar American society.

Disappointment, disillusionment, despair—these moods came to predominate. Marxism, or some version of it, gave way to psychoanalysis—and not Freudian psychoanalysis at that, but Jungian, with its reactionary "collective unconscious," mythologizing and universal archetypes. There took place, as one commentator put it, a "rush inward."

As Serge Guilbaut suggested, in his useful but one-sided account, *How New York Stole the Idea of Modern Art*, "They [the painters] were sick of politics and therefore thought they were sick of history as well. By using primitive imagery and myths to cut themselves off from the historical reality of their own time, they hoped to protect themselves from the manipulation and disillusionment they had suffered previously ...[46]

"For them ... the political situation had become hopeless in its complexity and absurdity ... The avant-garde retained traces of political consciousness, but devoid of direction. The political content of their art had been emptied out by the use of myth. Pollock, Rothko, Gottlieb, [Barnett] Newman—the avant-garde painters who talked about their art, did not reject history, because it was there in all its hideous features, snapping at their throats. They did not reject the idea of some kind of action, of some reaction to the social situation. They did not avoid the problems of the age but transformed them into something else; they transformed history into nature. As Roland Barthes has put it, 'By moving from history to nature,

---

[45]   Leon Trotsky, "The Suicide of Vladimir Mayakovsky," *Leon Trotsky on Literature and Art*, ed. Paul N. Siegel (New York: Pathfinder, 1970), 174.

[46]   Serge Guilbaut, *How New York Stole the Idea of Modern Art: Abstract Expressionism, Freedom and the Cold War* (Chicago: University of Chicago Press, 1983), 77.

myth gets rid of something. It does away with the complexity of human actions and bestows upon them the simplicity of essences.'"[47]

There is an entire school of Stalinist or semi-Stalinist commentators who like to blame Trotsky and Trotskyism for the evolution of the New York intellectuals, including that tedious snob Clement Greenberg. Guilbaut in his book at times succumbed to this tendency. This is nonsense. Trotsky opposed Stalinism, reactionary theories of "proletarian culture" and the monstrosity of "Socialist Realism" by insisting (along with André Breton) that true art, which "insists on expressing the inner needs of man and of mankind in its time … is unable *not* to be revolutionary, *not* to aspire to a complete and radical reconstruction of society."[48] Trotsky argued that the highest task of art was to take part in the preparation of the social revolution, but that the artist could only advance that goal when he or she had assimilated its essence into his or her bones and marrow.

It is worth repeating that in the case of the American abstract painters, despair and *a considerable degree of technical maturation* arrived simultaneously. Pollock, Willem de Kooning, Franz Kline, Rothko and others produced certain magnificent paintings. They appear as a rather heroic group, standing up for certain spiritual truths in the midst of conformist, McCarthyite, Cold War America. Although they were not entirely innocents. The State Department and various agencies of the US government began to make use of the New York painters' work, as a sign of the sort of work produced under "democratic" conditions versus the deadly efforts sanctioned by the "totalitarian" USSR, and none of them apparently objected.

In any event, the abstract expressionist effort was a doomed one. This found expression in the personal fates of a number of the painters. Pollock was not the only suicide or semi-suicide. Arshile Gorky had already hanged himself (1948) by the time of Pollock's death. Kline drank himself to death in 1962, David Smith, the sculptor, also died in an automobile accident, in 1965, and Rothko slashed his arms and bled to death in 1970.

Pollock always insisted, as did a number of the New York painters, that his work was not a product of accident, although it came from the unconscious, and that it was not about nothing. He commented in an interview with William Wright in 1950:

---

[47] Ibid., 113.

[48] Leon Trotsky, Diego Rivera, André Breton, "Manifesto: Towards a Free Revolutionary Art," *Leon Trotsky on Literature and Art*, ed. Paul N. Siegel (New York: Pathfinder, 1970), 117.

"Modern art to me is nothing more than the expression of contemporary aims of the age that we're living in ...

"My opinion is that new needs need new techniques. And the modern artists have found new ways and new means of making their statements. It seems to me that the modern painter cannot express this age, the airplane, the atom bomb, the radio, in the old forms of the Renaissance or of any other past culture. Each age finds its own technique."[49]

Can one speak of a subject in Pollock's paintings? The reference to the atom bomb is surely not accidental. Deep anxiety is clearly traceable in every work, as is the impossibility of representing in traditional (rational, articulate, legible) forms the state of things. Something has come to pass that goes beyond the painter's ability to reproduce it; this unreproducibility is itself a subject. Was this legitimate, or a surrender in the face of a difficult, but not incomprehensible and artistically ungraspable reality? Pollock, one senses, struggled with this issue. It seems doubtful that he was ever satisfied with the results he achieved.

Peter Fuller, in his essay "Jackson Pollock," in *Beyond the Crisis in Art*, was perhaps too categorical as to Pollock's failure, but he made some valuable points: "Despite his considerable abilities, however, Pollock *never* developed a convincing historical vision in his own paintings. What prevented him from doing so was, at least in part, history itself: the hopes for a better world and for socialism which, albeit confusedly, he had held since adolescence, were shattered by World War Two. In 1940, he wrote to his brother. 'I have been going thru violent changes the past couple of years. God knows what will come of it all— it's pretty negative stuff so far.' Whatever else it may also have been, it was to remain 'negative' stuff ...

"I am certainly not trying to deny the psychological roots of Pollock's malaise; but I am insisting that ... it had a historical component. Pollock had recognized the inadequacies of Benton's conservative, regionalist world view, and also of the traditional socialist [or Stalinist] vision (epitomized for him by Siqueiros). But he was unable to find any new way of looking at, or imaginatively grasping, his world or himself."[50]

---

[49] B.H. Friedman, *Jackson Pollock: Energy Made Visible* (New York, McGraw-Hill, 1972), 175–76.

[50] Peter Fuller, *Beyond the Crisis in Art* (London: Writers and Readers Publishing Cooperative Society Ltd., 1980), 101.

The historical dimension of Pollock's tragedy, which has such rich artistic possibility, is entirely absent in Ed Harris's film. His Pollock is drawn largely from the psychoanalyst's notebook and perhaps the police blotter. Did the painter's ultimate fate have nothing to do with the larger issues of his day? It is unlikely that the filmmakers consciously concealed Pollock's political history and social aspirations. (Although the decision to begin the film in 1941, with the Krasner encounter, safely gets them beyond the hurdle of having to deal with his radical past.) It probably would not occur to them that such concerns might be the substance of a film. This is one of the difficulties, which needs to be addressed, that still weakens so much of our contemporary art work.

American Madness: *Apocalypse Now Redux*

World Socialist Web Site; August 25, 2001

Directed by Francis Ford Coppola; written by John Milius, Coppola and Michael Herr

Apocalypse Now Redux is a remarkable film. Francis Ford Coppola's indictment of American intervention in Vietnam appeared in its original form in 1979. More than twenty years later, with the entire work reedited from raw footage over a six-month period in 2000 and some fifty minutes added (hence the *Redux*), the film, with all its significant flaws, has perhaps more of a power to disturb the viewer than at the time of its initial release.

In its own way, this is a vindication of the seriousness of the film's critique, however inadequately worked out it may be. If, as apologists of one stripe or another for American capitalism suggest, the Vietnam War was an ugly aberration after which the country ultimately "righted itself," then *Apocalypse Now*, with its picture of a society at the end of its moral tether, would not strike a deep chord. But what has the US experienced since 1979? A continued social and economic unraveling: Reaganism, Iran-Contra, the Persian Gulf War, the impeachment crisis, the bombing of Serbia, the hijacking of a national election and more—all of this taking place in the context of a growing social chasm in the US and a lurch to the right by the entire political establishment. The re-release of the film—entirely apart from

Coppola's immediate motives—and the strong response it has received have an objective, contemporary significance.

In 1969 or so, an army intelligence captain named Willard (Martin Sheen) is ordered by top US military and CIA officials in Saigon to travel up the Nung River into Cambodia and "terminate with extreme prejudice" a Green Beret officer, Kurtz (Marlon Brando), who has apparently become deranged and established an independent fighting force, of Montagnard tribesmen, in his own fiefdom in the jungle.

A patrol boat and its crew are put at Willard's disposal, consisting of Chief Phillips (Albert Hall), a black veteran; Lance Johnson (Sam Bottoms), a renowned surfer; "Chef" (Frederic Forrest), a cook from New Orleans; and "Mr. Clean" (a youthful Laurence Fishburne), a black teenager. After a nightmarish voyage, which costs most of the crew members their lives, Willard reaches Kurtz's compound in a ruined temple and attempts to accomplish his mission.

This is nothing if not an ambitious and audacious work. The opening shot: a line of palm trees, green and lush, a trace of sand or dust blown about by helicopter blades, the helicopters themselves, the trees bursting into flames. The beauty, clarity and menace of the sequence are exhilarating, riveting.

The atmosphere of menace prevails throughout. Those directing this war are obviously capable of any crime, and nearly everyone has been infected. Willard, drunk and bleeding in his hotel room, asks the two soldiers who knock on his door (they are merely delivering a message from the higher-ups) what he's being charged with. We learn that he's already carried out assassinations. He receives his murderous instructions from two officers and a sinister civilian (a CIA man presumably) over a pleasant lunch of roast beef.

The film grapples with the volatile combination of arrogance, ignorance, brutality and "good intentions" that characterizes every American military adventure. The figure of Lieutenant Colonel Bill Kilgore (Robert Duvall) suggests some of these qualities. In a justly famed sequence, Kilgore organizes a helicopter raid (to Wagner's "The Ride of the Valkyries") and subsequently the napalming of a section of coastline both to facilitate Willard's access to the mouth of the river and make possible a surfing excursion. It is Kilgore who gets to proclaim, "I love the smell of napalm in the morning." And it is the same Kilgore who, after organizing the firing on frightened and fleeing villagers, helps one of his victims with her wounded baby. Willard later thinks to himself, "If that's the way Kilgore fought the war, I began to wonder what they had against Kurtz."

The men accompanying Willard are painted in generally sympathetic colors, although they are capable, caught up in the collective lunacy, of terrible acts (such as the panicked machine-gunning of an innocent Vietnamese family aboard a sampan). After a scare in the jungle, Chef wails that all he wanted in life was to be a cook, nothing more; the 17-year-old "Clean" receives a tape from his mother, relating the latest family news; Phillips is a no-nonsense veteran; Lance, more eccentric and remote to begin with, proves most adaptable to the conflict's more insane requirements.

The crew stumbles on a USO show in the middle of the jungle. Three Playboy "Playmates" perform a titillating routine before a crowd of restless and sex-starved enlisted men, precipitating a small riot and a near-mass rape. Later, in one of the newly restored sequences, Willard encounters the Playmates and their agent at a dismal encampment where the latter have been grounded for lack of helicopter fuel. He offers two barrels of the latter if the women will sexually entertain his crew. This scene doesn't contribute much.

Shortly after "Clean" is killed by a brief burst of gunfire from the riverbank, Willard and his crew come upon a French family and its private army at a remote rubber plantation. This scene, which Coppola eliminated in the 1979 version from fear that it slowed down the boat journey (although it had taken weeks to shoot), now seems quite dramatically and ideologically critical. Willard and his hosts sit down for an elegant meal. The head of the family (Christian Marquand) provides his version of Vietnamese history. He denounces the US for helping to create the Vietminh (forerunner of the "Vietcong,") at the end of World War II and, after cursing the "communist traitors" at home, asserts that French families like his have a reason for staying. "We stay because this is ours. You Americans are fighting for the biggest nothing in history." The embittered monologue, written by Coppola, points in its fashion to one of the contradictions of US foreign policy in Vietnam and elsewhere: the insistence that America's actions are not motivated by economic interest or geopolitics, but by the desire to see democracy and freedom prevail.

The final scenes at Kurtz's encampment are, in general, the film's least convincing. Brando is charismatic, but his character's philosophizing (some of it improvised) about freedom, violence and the absurdity of existence adds up to relatively little. Dennis Hopper is simply irritating as a burned-out photojournalist and Kurtz admirer. The strongest moment comes when Brando sits in the doorway among a group of local children and reads to Willard (at the time his prisoner) from *Time* magazine, exposing the mendacity of the administration in Washington. This scene was also newly added.

Apocalypse Now conveys less the "insanity of the war in Vietnam," which one has heard so much about, than the degree to which the violence endemic in American society was projected into Vietnam. There are scarcely any Vietnamese in the film. America largely supplies the insanity in Vietnam. It supplies Kilgore, his napalm, his Wagner and his surfboard. It supplies "Death from above" and "I love the smell of napalm in the morning" and "Terminate with extreme prejudice." There is madness in the behavior, in the very relationships of the Americans. The havoc arises organically from a psychotic state of society. When the chief insists that the sampan must be searched, a bureaucratic formality, Willard objects. It will delay his mission, but also he senses that it will not end well—as it does not. One has an uneasy feeling that every time a group of Americans forms, violence will erupt. And Kurtz is the crowning figure in this universal mayhem.

In inflicting itself on Vietnam, American capitalism at the same time projected its crisis and failure as a society on a screen in such a fashion that they became visible to the entire world. And the war not only embodied that crisis and failure, it deepened them. This is another truth that radiates from *Apocalypse Now* like a beam of light—no country, one realizes, could ever possibly be the same after an experience like this. "Peace" and "normalcy" may return, for the time being, but this is a society heading for disaster.

The weakness of the Kurtz sequence, largely an anticlimax, is bound up with the intellectual dichotomy at the heart of his film, which Coppola never resolved or even seriously addressed. At its most valuable, *Apocalypse Now* —in any of its versions—is a concrete and passionate condemnation of American conduct in Vietnam and, by extension, a devastating picture of the society capable of perpetrating such a monstrous series of crimes. At its murkiest and least coherent, the film is a trite meditation, worthy of a third-year English major, on the supposedly bifurcated human soul.

The latter notion is introduced early in the film by the deceptively soft-spoken general (G.D. Spradlin, a wonderful "character" actor) who presides over the meeting at which Willard receives his orders. He pontificates about the "conflict in every human heart between the rational and the irrational, between good and evil." The French patriarch's widowed daughter-in-law (Aurore Clément), who takes Willard to bed, tells him: "There are two of you. One that loves and one that kills." The theme is returned to a number of times.

Some of this is inherited from Joseph Conrad's *Heart of Darkness* (1902), the novella that served loosely as an inspiration for John Milius's screenplay (Coppola, as noted, and Michael Herr also had a hand in the final script). In Conrad's work, Kurtz is a Belgian ivory trader who journeys to the depths of the Congolese jungle and "reverts" to a state of savagery, succumbing to the basest temptations. In fact, one is encouraged to believe, he has discovered the beast that lies just beneath the civilized veneer. Marlow, the narrator, recognizes an aspect of himself in Kurtz and, at the same time, the possibility of controlling his own "heart of darkness."

A corollary perhaps of Social Darwinism, this type of argument, taken to its logical conclusion, functions as an apology for the abuses and cruelties of the existing social order. After all, the reasoning goes, brutality corresponds to the "natural" human state. Each man or woman is a killer or potential killer at heart.

Milius, a notorious anticommunist (*Red Dawn* [1984]) and proponent of manly individualism (*Conan the Barbarian* [1982]) no doubt contributed his own confusion to the mix. As Willard examines Kurtz's record and writings en route to the jungle stronghold, we are led to believe that the Green Beret officer has certain insights into the nature of the US war effort. But of what sort? Initially at least, the filmmakers paint Kurtz as a "hard-line" military man, disgusted by the refusal of his superiors back in Saigon ("four-star clowns") to wage a total war. At moments, the film seems to suggest that the US might have prevailed if only its forces had had more determined and ruthless leadership. This is the "we were stabbed in the back by the liberals" argument of the paranoid right wing. (Milius is currently a member of the board of directors of the National Rifle Association!) Brando in person seems to steer the character in another, although not all that clear-cut, direction.

A lack of intellectual clarity lies at the root of many of the film's problems. Coppola can be taken to task (and has been) for a number of sins. There is a good deal in *Apocalypse Now* that is pretentious or banal (including virtually the entire narration), and much that is unrealized. And frankly, the drama that was made of the legendary difficulties involved in shooting the film (Martin Sheen's heart attack, the typhoon that stalled filming, various episodes of drug-taking, love affairs, Brando's supposed antics, a budget that climbed from $13 to $30 million as filming lasted 238 days instead of 150, etc.) was not merely tiresome, it seemed to function as a means of diverting attention from the essential muddiness of the filmmaker's conceptions.

There is, for example, the question of the film's "literary" and classical references. On the one hand, journeying by river is legitimately resonant of motifs in American literature (Mark Twain's *Huckleberry Finn* and *Life on the Mississippi*, in particular). Indeed, there is something almost comforting in the story's *structure*: the crew, a haven of relative stability, encountering and leaving behind a succession of mostly unhinged characters on its voyage upstream. On the other hand, however, the effort to fashion the film's narrative into some sort of archetypal warrior's quest (a "philosophic inquiry into the mythology of war," Coppola calls it today) is merely a distraction, in my view, or worse. There are echoes of *The Odyssey* (the three "Siren"-Playmates, and so on), Norse mythology (the Valkyries) and the Arthurian legends ("Lance," as in Lancelot; "Mr. Clean," who dies a virgin like Sir Galahad), among others. Kurtz (himself a character out of a work of fiction) is shown to be reading J.G. Frazer's *The Golden Bough* (1890), the comparative study of magic, folklore and religion that demonstrated parallel beliefs in primitive and Christian cultures. The simultaneous ritual slaughters of Kurtz and an ox, as well as the subsequent behavior of the "natives" toward Willard (he who kills a god becomes a god), presumably refer to certain of Frazer's anthropological findings.

The latter sort of abstract and empty "universalizing" (universals without content) would also tend to dissolve the elements of social and political critique if it were wholeheartedly pursued. After all, these two perspectives work at cross-purposes. If Willard's activity (and the activity of all involved) accords with the ineluctable in human destiny, a voyage that "every man must make," so to speak, then how can a distinct, identifiable group of officials in the US government and the ruling social stratum more generally be held responsible for their actions?

Fortunately, this element of the work is not wholeheartedly pursued. Other—more mundane and intellectually healthier—concerns are also in operation (although the inability to fully reconcile the two arguments, reflected in Coppola's failure to come up with a satisfactory ending, nearly wrecked the project). In a director's statement concerning the new version of *Apocalypse Now*, Coppola observes that virtually every war film is an "antiwar" film and continues: "My film is more of an 'anti-lie' film, in that the fact that a culture can lie about what's really going on in warfare, that people are being brutalized, tortured, maimed and killed, and somehow present this as moral is what horrifies me, and perpetuates the possibility of war." This element, that US policy in Vietnam was based on a great lie, retains its force.

Coppola began to work on the film in 1975, the year of the South Vietnamese forces' final defeat at the hands of the National Liberation Front and the North Vietnamese army (shooting took place in 1976). *Apocalypse Now* carries with it, however transformed and transmuted, something of the hatred then felt by wide layers of the US population for the war. Three million Vietnamese were dead. Tens of thousands of mostly working class American young men had died, millions in the US had been cruelly affected by the conflict. For many young people in particular, hostility to the bloody war in Southeast Asia, as well as the lies, hypocrisy and brutality of successive Democratic and Republican administrations, had become the starting point for a wholesale rejection of capitalist society. The general mood of opposition nourishing Coppola and his colleagues (cinematographer Vittorio Storaro, production designer Dean Tavoularis and the others) and their overall artistic honesty propelled the work forward beyond the filmmakers' own limited and often half-baked conceptions.

Apocalypse Now represented perhaps the high-water mark of 1970s radicalized, critical filmmaking in the US. By the time it reached movie theaters, to considerable success, other trends were at work. Against a background of growing political reaction, American cinema was about to enter a sharp decline from which it has not yet emerged.

It must be said that while Coppola deserves full credit for the strengths of *Apocalypse Now*, the lack of clear historical perspective reflected in its weaknesses did not permit him to weather the storm to come, the Reagan years and beyond. He did not turn out to be another Orson Welles, after all. His filmmaking deteriorated, for the most part, along with the rest (*One from the Heart, The Cotton Club, Peggy Sue Got Married, Tucker*). *Apocalypse Now* stands as a rebuke to its own director based on his recent work, as well, of course, as it does to the vast majority of contemporary American filmmakers.

Gangs of New York: Misanthropy and Contemporary American Filmmaking

World Socialist Web Site; January 16, 2003

Directed by Martin Scorsese; written by Jay Cocks, Steven Zaillian and Kenneth Lonergan

Gangs of New York is a dreadful film, poorly constructed, unconvincing and deeply misanthropic. It has been highly praised by a number of prominent critics in the US, including some who should know better. A.O. Scott of the *New York Times* called it "a near-great movie," which "over time ... will make up the distance."[51] According to the *Chicago Tribune*'s Michael Wilmington, "It's a movie of grand, reckless ambition ... burning with creative passion, overreaching, magnificently wild."[52] Todd McCarthy in *Variety* writes that *Gangs of New York* "bears all the earmarks of a magnum opus for [director] Martin Scorsese."[53] In *Time*, Richard Corliss terms the work a "film epic" and argues that its failings do not "erase the sordid splendor of Scorsese's congested, conflicted, entrancing achievement."[54] David Edelstein of *Slate* writes: "Whatever its fate at the box office, it's a magnificent achievement."[55]

Scorsese's film purports to treat ethnic and gang violence in New York City in the mid-nineteenth century and, according to its admirers, the birth of modern American society. The film begins in 1846, with a vicious battle

---

[51]   A.O. Scott, "To Feel a City Seethe," *The New York Times*, December 20, 2002. Available: http://www.nytimes.com/2002/12/20/movies/film-review-to-feel-a-city-seethe.html

[52]   Michael Wilmington, "Scorsese's 'Gangs' explodes into a near-masterpiece epic of bloodshed and crime," *Chicago Tribune*, December 20, 2002. Available: http://articles.chicagotribune.com/2002-12-20/entertainment/0212200370_1_draft-riots-gangs-of-new-york-leonardo-dicaprio

[53]   Todd McCarthy, "Gangs of New York," *Variety*, December 5, 2002. Available: http://variety.com/2002/film/reviews/gangs-of-new-york-3-1200544486/.

[54]   Richard Corliss, "The Gangs of New York," *Time*, December 20, 2002. Available: http://www.time.com/time/magazine/article/0,9171,400004,00.html

[55]   David Edelstein, "Let It Bleed: Gangs of New York is too damned short," *Slate*, December 20, 2002. Available: http://www.slate.com/articles/arts/movies/2002/12/let_it_bleed.html

between a collection of Irish gangs and their "Nativist" enemies, led by Bill "The Butcher" Cutting (played by Daniel Day-Lewis). Cutting strikes down his chief opponent, Priest Vallon (Liam Neeson), and the latter's young son is taken into custody. Sixteen years later, released from a reformatory, Amsterdam Vallon (Leonardo DiCaprio) sets out to exact vengeance against his father's killer.

The youth works his way into the Butcher's gang, which now rules the crime-ridden Five Points neighborhood (in lower Manhattan), in an uneasy alliance with Boss Tweed (Jim Broadbent) of the Democratic Party's notoriously corrupt Tammany Hall. Amsterdam makes himself invaluable to Cutting and, along the way, falls in love with a female pickpocket, Jenny (Cameron Diaz). His first attempt at dispatching Butcher Bill by treachery having failed, nearly costing his life, Amsterdam decides to openly declare his identity and aims, resurrecting the name of his father's old gang. The final showdown between the two camps is interrupted by the bloody draft riots of July 13–16, 1863 (in which a section of the city's Irish immigrant population in particular rose up against Civil War conscription), and the Union army's attempts to suppress them. Amsterdam, however, manages to deliver a fatal blow.

From the opening images, Scorsese depicts an animalistic world of cruelty and mayhem. Vallon and Cutting are portrayed as barbarian warlords, adhering to some semi-medieval code of honor. After the film has jumped forward to the 1860s, it lovingly and all-too-painstakingly introduces the various ethnic-based gangs, categories of crime, species of criminal and prostitute, and so forth. Indeed, one might be forgiven for concluding that Scorsese, as he did in *The Age of Innocence*, has paid far more attention to decor and physical detail than to narrative and characterization. The banal plot is rather loosely and extraneously hung on this framework of alleged historical fact.

Certainly, the drama is extremely weak. Scorsese has always seemed to adhere to the conviction, misguidedly drawn perhaps from his attraction to the French New Wave and other schools, that he was under no obligation to develop and sustain a coherent story. His work has never risen above, at its best, a cinema of strong characterizations, startling confrontations, no-holds-barred violence. One would be hard-pressed to bring to mind the sequence of events in *Taxi Driver*, *Raging Bull*, *Goodfellas* or *Casino*, for example, much less any enduring themes elaborated in those films.

In *Gangs of New York*, the characters are tritely, predictably drawn and the events contrived. Despite all its furious goings-on, the film is almost entirely lacking in the spontaneity of real life. It is a giant, over-wrought contrivance, a vehicle for communicating the filmmakers' murky and unappealing musings about society and human beings. There are moments in the film so removed from any basis in social or psycho-logical reality, so arbitrary, either so *subjective* or so *malicious* (the open-ing images underground, the celebration marking the gang's victory over Priest Vallon, the clash between the volunteer fire companies) that one wonders which portion of the world and mankind the filmmakers imagine they are representing. Even the look and feel of the film is false and unreal—an unpleasant yellowish glow stays in one's memory—and appears designed to emphasize the essential filthiness of humanity. This is reality organized to correspond to a preconceived notion, and an un-healthy one at that.

The lack of spontaneity reaches its high point in the figure of Bill the Butcher and the performance of Day-Lewis. Cutting is loaded down with significant attributes (handlebar moustache, top hat, glass eye in the shape of an eagle, proto-New York accent—all in all, a comic book appearance), but he is essentially an empty abstraction, a walking conglomeration of what the screenwriters apparently take to be "native" American character-istics: brutality, stubbornness, racism and xenophobia, an abiding sense of honor, indefatigable energy, etc.

Amsterdam (a terrible name!) and Jenny are taken from templates: the rebellious, seething youth and the fiery whore with a golden heart, respec-tively. Outside of the clichés, there is almost nothing to them. Their romance is perfunctory and incidental and leaves one thoroughly unmoved.

The narrative in *Gangs of New York* simply does not hold together in any meaningful fashion. Why does Amsterdam Vallon, for example, work his way into Bill Cutting's good graces in the first place? Not to be in a posi-tion to murder him, because he bribes a Chinese waiter to do that, and he could just as easily have bribed the man without having had anything to do with Cutting's gang. If he is drawn to Cutting, or the filmmakers are, then that needs to be explained. Why should Vallon be attracted to this sadistic and racist thug, his father's killer, and why should we?

The character is based on a real-life figure, Bill "The Butcher" Poole (who operated on behalf of the "Nativist" Know-Nothing Party and died in 1855), a notorious and bloodthirsty gang leader whose specialty, accord-ing to one commentator, "seems to have been gutting rivals with carving knives." For their own reasons, the filmmakers choose to turn Cutting into something of a philosopher-king, providing this sociopath as well with a deep sense of honor. In his most significant speech, draped in an American flag, he tells Amsterdam how much he admired the latter's father, concluding, "He was the only man I ever killed worth remembering. I never had a son. Civilization is crumbling. God bless you." The scene is absurd.

The initial murder plot hatched by Amsterdam against the Butcher is treated only in passing, and its failure is thoroughly anticlimactic. Why should Cutting let Amsterdam off so easily after the attempt on his life? He then claims he will permanently maim the younger man—one fears the worst—but, in fact, does no such thing.

Much is made in the opening scenes of Priest Vallon's associates, who turn up sixteen years later as a cohort of Cutting's, a policeman and a barber. One is led to expect that they will be confronted in some manner by Amsterdam and made to recognize or deny their betrayal of the Irish cause. Only one of them, Monk (Brendan Gleeson), even becomes aware of Amsterdam's true identity, and he, along with the rest, plays no role in the film's denouement. Their presence is simply one of the film's many red herrings.

And what of the peculiar denouement itself, the overshadowing and eventual disruption of the great gang battle by the draft riots? Scorsese sets himself the task of staging two full-scale bloody confrontations, which creates confusion more than anything else. Presumably, he is making a point here, that modern industrial America, in the form of the mass warfare of the Civil War, is putting an end to the individualistic, warlord epoch, but the juxtaposition of events is incomprehensible. The relationship between the gang wars and the riots is never intelligibly established, nor is the attitude of Amsterdam and his associates toward the outburst—not a small matter.

Beyond the failings of the drama, moreover, there is the issue of the accuracy of the historical and social detail, which does not seem to have troubled any of the critics. The first thing that ought to strike any viewer is that no neighborhood like the one depicted in *Gangs of New York* has ever existed—that is to say, a bottomless cesspool of crime and degradation, in which daily life is made up of nothing but a stream of violent atrocities. That such a view should pass uncriticized has a great deal to do with how a section of the middle class intelligentsia views the contemporary inner-city population. Moreover, no doubt filmmakers and critics alike are guided by the conception that the fouler and more degraded the material, the closer one is to "reality."

One loses track of the sordid violence in the film, between the organized criminality of Bill the Butcher and the assorted thieves and cutthroats in the neighborhood, the "spectator sports" (bare-knuckle boxing and a gruesome fight between rats and a dog) and the everyday, random violence (including the clash between the two volunteer fire companies, who allow a home to burn to the ground while they dispute the right to put it out—the house is meanwhile ransacked by local residents).

Scorsese's film was inspired by journalist Herbert Asbury's *The Gangs of New York*, published in the 1920s. Indeed, the filmmaker claims to have been "obsessed" with the book since he first read it in 1970. Novelist Kevin Baker, who has written a novel based on the draft riots (*Paradise Alley*), has commented: "Was the Five Points really so bad? Those who know it at all today know it chiefly through *The Gangs of New York*, Herbert Asbury's 1927 collection of rollicking, hair-raising (and often fanciful) tales of old New York, or through the superb, impressionistic sketches in Luc Sante's *Low Life*. Both works have considerable merit, yet neither goes to much trouble to sort out Five Points lore from hard, historical fact."[56]

Asbury's book is a mixture of fact, anecdote and tall tale. He asserts, for example, that the most notorious of the Bowery Boys gang stood "eight feet tall" with hands "as large as the hams of a Virginia hog," wore a hat that measured "more than two feet across" and "during the hot months ... went about with a great fifty gallon keg of ale dangling from his belt in lieu of a canteen." And this is not the only "fanciful" passage in the work.

In other words, a considerable portion of the material in the book on which Scorsese relied so heavily is apocryphal, a fact that he clearly knew. There is the element here of deliberate falsehood and misrepresentation.

Recent archaeological evidence (readily available to Scorsese) has increased the quantity of "hard, historical fact." Some 850,000 artifacts were unearthed in a block of the old Five Points neighborhood when it was selected as the site of a new courthouse in the early 1990s. After examining the objects, as well as combing through census records, city directories and insurance company data, a team of historians and scientists—according to a 1996 *Village Voice* article by J.A. Lobbia—reached the conclusion "that Five Points was anything but a depraved quarter populated exclusively by

---

[56]   Kevin Baker, "The First Slum in America," *The New York Times,* September 30, 2001. Available: http://www.nytimes.com/2001/09/30/books/the-first-slum-in-america. html

perps and victims; instead, they say, it was a vibrant community and the birthplace of working-class life."[57]

Lobbia continues, "More at odds with images of Five Points inhabitants as thieves and beggars is information about work life. Census records and the directories show that most Five Points residents worked on the docks or in local factories making carriages, umbrellas, looking glasses, shoes, segar [cigar] boxes, and furniture, or in the fast-developing ready-made clothing industry ... Quantities of buttons, needles, and an array of fabrics are among the artifacts that suggest the prevalence of tailors and home piece workers ... As for personal health and cleanliness—attributes that were supposedly lacking in Five Points—there are medicine bottles, syringes used for hygiene, hair combs, and toothbrushes, including one with a handle inscribed 'Extra Fine Paris France.'"[58] (The lives and fates of factory workers, it should be noted, have never aroused the slightest interest in Scorsese. On the other hand, his fixation with gangsters and psychopaths is unwavering, and more than a little disturbing.)

In any event, even if the historical veracity of every incident in *Gangs of New York* were to be established, there is still the matter of the filmmaker's attitude. He has adopted the right-wing tabloid journalist's approach to urban life: sensational, vulgar and heavily weighted toward blaming the poor for their wickedness. The emphasis in the film is not on the social conditions in the neighborhood, on the level of exploitation, on the poverty, but on the almost gleeful and willful viciousness of the residents. As Lobbia notes, "Personal corruption did not account for poverty; depressions, low wages [the average monthly wage for men was $38; women and children made far less], seasonal layoffs, and outlandish rents did. Epidemics of cholera did not erupt because the souls of Five Points tenants were lacking; they erupted because city sanitation was inadequate."[59]

Scorsese's treatment of the draft riots is no more satisfying. The bloody outburst of violence had both economic and political roots. Conscription was enacted by Congress in March 1863. It was vehemently attacked by the Democratic Party, the section of the American bourgeoisie that opposed a resolute struggle against slavery. According to Civil War historian James McPherson, in *Battle Cry of Freedom*, "Democratic newspapers hammered

---

[57] J.A. Lobbia, "Slum Lore," *Village Voice*, January 2, 1996: 34–36.

[58] Ibid.

[59] Ibid.

at the theme that the draft would force white working men to fight for the freedom of blacks who would come north and take away their jobs."[60]

The recently arrived Irish immigrants in New York were particularly susceptible to the Democrats' propaganda, to which they were directly and continuously subjected. The Irish were at the bottom rung of the social ladder in New York and other cities, having largely pushed out black labor by accepting lower wages. Indeed, they were sometimes treated worse than free blacks, with employers noting in their job advertisements "any country or color except Irish." The great economic anxiety that this condition engendered (many had fled from the terrible potato famines in Ireland) was deliberately whipped up and played upon by demagogues. McPherson also notes that "Numerous strikes had left a bitter legacy, none more than a longshoreman's walkout in June 1863 when black stevedores under police protection took the place of striking Irishmen."[61]

The ability of individuals to buy their way out of the draft for $300 (equivalent to a year's wages) encouraged the Democrats and their supporters to denounce the struggle against the Confederacy as a "rich man's fight, but a poor man's war." This argument is repeated uncritically in *Gangs of New York*. However, McPherson points out that the claim is not supported by the facts. Studies of conscription in New York and Ohio, for instance, "have found virtually no correlation between wealth and commutation."[62] In regard to the social backgrounds of white Union soldiers as a whole, he writes, "it seems likely that the only category significantly under-represented would be unskilled workers."[63] The struggle against slavery attracted self-sacrificing layers from every social class and ethnic group, including the Irish immigrants themselves, of whom some 150,000 joined the Union army.

Scorsese's film portrays the draft riots as the quasi-legitimate expression of popular discontent (the director likens them in interviews to the anti-Vietnam war protest movement!), albeit colored by racism, rather than as an outburst of political reaction, the product of economic misery and appeals to the basest sentiments. This is a dishonest, reactionary populism, which sets aside the small matter of the revolutionary, world-historical

---

[60] James McPherson, *Battle Cry of Freedom* (Oxford: Oxford University Press, 1988), 609.

[61] Ibid.

[62] Ibid., 603.

[63] Ibid., 608.

dimensions of the Civil War. For all intents and purposes, the film is hostile to the Northern cause. (When Bill the Butcher, a brute, but a "man of principle," shoots at a portrait of Lincoln, this might be interpreted as an act of legitimate social protest.)

One would be led by the film to believe that "class consciousness" and political protest are associated with bestial behavior. In fact, the principal target of the New York rioters was not the rich *per se*, but draft offices and federal property, black people and those who employed them, Republican newspapers and the homes of leading Republicans and abolitionists—i.e., the most progressive political forces. Eleven blacks were lynched or otherwise murdered during the riots; at least eighty-four rioters were eventually killed by the Union troops called in to quell the uprising. (Interestingly, McPherson observes in *The Struggle for Equality* that "A more kindly spirit toward colored people began to manifest itself in New York in the weeks and months after the draft riots,"[64] and that one consequence was the integration of the entire public transportation system in the city.)

Gangs of New York is a disgraceful film from every point of view. Scorsese has been considering violence in American life for 30 years, a subject about which he no doubt feels strongly. However, in the absence of a historical and social perspective, he has not shed much light on the problem. Scorsese has identified brutality over and over again, sometimes realistically, sometimes not, and graphically portrayed it at length, but he has never investigated its roots in social relations, in class society. The filmmaker, whose early ambition it was to become a Catholic priest, seems satisfied to view violence as embedded in human nature. His response to the phenomenon seems equal parts horror and fascination.

For a film director of a certain type, one with both artistic and "popular" ambitions, a consequence of feeling deeply about man's inhumanity to man and yet considering it inherent in the human condition might be a continual shift between a kind of forced cheerfulness, making desperate efforts to treat violence as the "colorful" stuff of life, and a profound misanthropy, exhibiting only disgust for this degraded species. Both moods seem present in *Gangs of New York*, with the latter inevitably predominant.

Just as pernicious is the conception, advanced by some of the film's admirers, that Scorsese's work accurately portrays the emergence of modern

---

[64] James McPherson, *The Struggle for Equality* (Princeton: Princeton University Press, 1992), 232.

America. Scott in the *Times* writes, "It is not the usual triumphalist story of moral progress and enlightenment, but rather a blood-soaked revenger's tale, in which the modern world arrives in the form of a line of soldiers firing into a crowd. ... Like the old order, the new one is riven by class resentment, racism and political hypocrisy, attributes that change their form at every stage of history but that seem to be as embedded in human nature as the capacity for decency, solidarity and courage."[65] *Slate's* Edelstein asserts that the film "mixes elemental stories of love and revenge with a vision of the larger historical forces that shaped the capitalist society we know today."[66] Roger Ebert, in the *Chicago Sun-Times*, observes that "It is instructive to be reminded that modern America was forged not in quiet rooms by great men in wigs, but in the streets, in the clash of immigrant groups, in a bloody Darwinian struggle."[67]

The notion that American society emerged out of mindless violence and squalor, "in the streets," is a reactionary and anti-intellectual distortion of history. In fact, the US experienced what is now referred to as its Renaissance during the 1840s and 1850s, when figures such as Hawthorne, Poe, Melville, Emerson, Thoreau, Longfellow, Dickinson, Whitman and Stowe all produced their most influential works. This list alone, notwithstanding the fact that many of these writers did not know success at the time (or even, in Dickinson's case, make her work public), testifies to a high level of culture and literacy. It was within this remarkable culture, influenced by the Enlightenment thinkers, German philosophy and utopian socialism, that many of the ideological foundations of the Union cause in the Civil War, the second American Revolution, were laid down.

American society in the pre-revolutionary 1850s was extraordinarily susceptible to progressive thought. As James McPherson has noted, in *For Cause and Comrades*, "Civil War soldiers lived in the world's most politicized and democratic country in the mid-nineteenth century. They had

---

[65]   A.O. Scott, "To Feel a City Seethe," *The New York Times,* December 20, 2002. Available: http://www.nytimes.com/2002/12/20/movies/film-review-to-feel-a-city-seethe.html

[66]   David Edelstein, "Let It Bleed: Gangs of New York is too damned short," *Slate,* December 20, 2002. Available: http://www.slate.com/articles/arts/movies/2002/12/let_it_bleed.html.

[67]   Roger Ebert, "Gangs of New York," *Chicago Sun-Times,* December 20, 2002. Available: http://www.rogerebert.com/reviews/gangs-of-new-york-2002

come of age in the 1850s when highly charged partisan and ideological debates consumed the American polity. A majority of them had voted in the election of 1860, the most heated and momentous election in American history. When they enlisted, many of them did so for patriotic and ideological reasons—to shoot as they had voted, so to speak."[68]

Furthermore, the chatter about "class resentment" and the "larger historical forces that shaped the capitalist society we know today," when applied to *Gangs of New York* is quite "left" sounding, but entirely muddled and misleading. This tacit endorsement of Scorsese's fascination with corruption and filth is bound up with the notion, so prevalent today in certain quarters, that to be "radical" is to have the bleakest possible notion of humanity and society, to ascribe to human beings under any and all historical conditions the worst possible motives. This is sometimes described as exploring the "dark side," or "the underbelly" of American life, as being "unsparing" and "challenging conventional wisdom." In fact, it is no such thing.

The real implication of this view is that the selfishness, greed and racism of humanity as a whole (including its suffering portion), not definite, *capitalist* socioeconomic relations, have brought about the current state of affairs, that people are essentially unworthy and one has no obligation to struggle against existing conditions because they are, after all, inherent in the human condition. This cynical stance is known as justifying today's swinishness by yesterday's swinishness.

The various critics, thanks in part to Scorsese's skewed vision of history, have the events turned on their head. The draft riots did not usher in the modern era or symbolize its birth. Rather they embodied everything that was backward and selfish in the population, inevitably encouraged and sanctioned by the Democratic Party (whose association with the American working class has ever had tragic and disastrous consequences).

In reality, the modern era in the US was brought into being by a social-revolutionary struggle, the Civil War, a titanic blow for equality and democracy. That the war and its outcome never went beyond the bounds of bourgeois property relations was historically inevitable, but the liberating conflict was a moment in that revolutionary continuum that includes the Paris Commune of 1871 and the Russian Revolutions of 1905 and 1917, struggles waged consciously by the working class against the

---

[68] James McPherson, *For Cause and Comrades: Why Men Fought in the Civil War* (Oxford: Oxford University Press, 1997), 92.

bourgeoisie. After the freeing of the slaves and the dismantling of the slavocracy, Marx proclaimed: "*Never* has such a gigantic transformation taken place so rapidly."[69]

A Union victory over the Confederacy would have been far more difficult, almost unthinkable, following Scorsese's line of reasoning: that the war was thoroughly unpopular and the population in the Northern states widely uninterested or hostile to the ending of slavery. The more farsighted elements in the Union army (and in the Northern population as a whole) were conscious, to varying degrees, that the eradication of chattel slavery corresponded to the general interests of human progress and were willing to pay the ultimate price in that cause. How else can one explain the 80 percent vote among Union soldiers for Lincoln in the presidential election of 1864, following the Emancipation Proclamation and following four years of bloody conflict, with all the misleadership, incompetence and outright treachery exhibited by sections of the Northern high command? The notion that *ideas* played a material role in enabling the Union army to overcome adversity and persevere is entirely foreign to Scorsese and the majority of critics.

In the general media celebration of *Gangs of New York* there are various elements. Intellectual corruption plays a role, as the relationship between the film studios and certain media outlets becomes more and more intimate. It may be virtually impossible at present, for example, for a major New York film critic to suggest that a work by Scorsese, produced by Harvey Weinstein and Miramax at a cost of $115 million, is a travesty. Too much is at stake for all concerned.

There is also an element of wishful thinking. To acknowledge that Scorsese—whose film's release is one of the major events of the year in the American cinema—is not a master filmmaker, that he is not even a competent one, that his ideas are regressive and third-rate, that his own work has degenerated from its levels in the 1970s, would be to admit to a cultural crisis whose implications certain critics do not care to contemplate.

Still others celebrate the Scorsese work because it reflects their own self-serving and fashionably contemptuous view of humankind and the American people in particular. The filthiness they see, however, is not in impoverished neighborhoods, but in their own mirrors.

---

[69] Karl Marx, *On America and the Civil War*, trans. Saul K. Padover (New York: McGraw Hill, 1972), 272 (from the *Springfield Republican*, September 24, 1862).

In any event, both the film and its critical reception express a level of extraordinary social and intellectual disorientation that ought not to go unnoticed or unanswered. Other voices and views, we are convinced, will emerge under conditions of a maturing social crisis.

A Convenient Vagueness: *Elephant*

World Socialist Web Site; November 12, 2003

Written and directed by Gus Van Sant

Elephant's general subject matter is the massacre that occurred at Columbine High School in Littleton, Colorado, in April 1999, in which fifteen people were killed and twenty-three wounded, and other school shootings in the US over the past several years. Filmed in an Oregon high school, Gus Van Sant's work follows several students whose paths cross on a fateful and tragic day. The film considers some of the same brief and ordinary encounters from a number of points of view.

Arbitrariness and banality rule the film. John, forced to take the car keys from his drunken father in the middle of the day, arrives late for school and receives detention for it. Another student with an enthusiasm for photography, Elias, snaps pictures of his schoolmates. The film returns several times to the encounter between Elias and John in a school hallway. A handsome athlete, Nathan, is followed by the camera for some time down sterile corridors, past a group of three admiring girls, until he meets his girlfriend, Carrie. Those same three girls chat, eat lunch in the cafeteria and retreat to the restroom to vomit up its contents. A group of students discuss homosexuality with their adviser. An awkward girl who seems something of an outcast, Michelle, is reproached by her gym teacher for not wearing shorts. She works in the library.

One of the eventual killers, Alex, is the target of spitballs in class. At home, he plays Beethoven on the piano. His cohort, Eric, arrives and plays a violent video game. They watch a documentary on television about Hitler. A large box is delivered containing an automatic weapon. They try it out in the garage against a pile of logs. Dressed like commandos and armed to the teeth, they set off for school and begin their killing spree.

The "elephant" in the title has two possible meanings. Van Sant borrowed it from another film he admired, Alan Clarke's *Elephant* (1989), about killings in Northern Ireland, in the mistaken belief that the title of that work referred to the parable about the blind men who are asked to describe the animal by touching various parts of it; each draws quite distinct conclusions about the elephant as a whole based on his partial knowledge. In fact, Clarke's title referred to the "elephant in the living room" that cannot be ignored.

A criticism of Van Sant's film for its failure to present any historical or social context for the Columbine mass murder; indeed, the work's failure to advance any coherent explanation whatsoever for the tragedy is not rendered beside the point by the fact that the director has proceeded quite consciously.

Naturally, this quality has been widely praised. Roger Ebert in the *Chicago Sun-Times* writes: "It [*Elephant*] offers no explanation for the tragedy, no insights into the psyches of the killers, no theories about teenagers or society or guns or psychopathic behavior. It simply looks at the day as it unfolds, and that is a brave and radical act; it refuses to supply reasons and assign cures, so that we can close the case and move on."[70]

Ebert continues: "'I want the audience to make its own observations and draw its own conclusions,' Van Sant told me at Cannes. 'Who knows why those boys acted as they did?' He is honest enough to admit that he does not. Of course a movie about a tragedy that does not explain the tragedy—that provides no personal or social 'reasons' and offers no 'solutions'—is almost against the law in the American entertainment industry. When it comes to tragedy, Hollywood is in the catharsis business."

Jonathan Rosenbaum in the *Chicago Reader* comments: "[I]t's important to know that Van Sant has no better notion of why the Columbine massacre occurred than anyone else. All he has are a few wild guesses—some more plausible than others, none remotely conclusive—and most of the film's flaws can be traced back to those guesses, which take up far more of our attention than they deserve."[71]

What does it mean to explain the Columbine tragedy? Naturally, no one will ever know precisely what went through the minds of its perpetrators

---

[70] Roger Ebert, "Elephant," *Chicago Sun-Times*, November 7, 2003. Available: http://www.rogerebert.com/reviews/elephant-2003

[71] Jonathan Rosenbaum, "Blindsided," *Chicago Reader*, November 6, 2003. Available: http://www.chicagoreader.com/chicago/blindsided/Content?oid=913712

in the days leading up to the event. Nor can anyone point conclusively to this or that trauma or slight as the straw that broke the camel's back. There are individually specific and inexplicable elements in such mad acts. And no doubt the attempts by the American mass media, insofar as they made such, to grapple with the event were predictably shallow and empty.

But why must "explanation" equal "simplistic explanation"? It is impossible to calculate with mathematical exactness why this adolescent as opposed to that one collapses, mentally and morally, in the face of certain socio-psychological pressures. If it is an equally unmanageable task, however, to build up a picture of the social, political and cultural atmosphere in which such irrational acts committed by *some* disoriented youth become a near inevitability, then what is the use of our art or our social science? After all, the Columbine shooting was not an aberration; it came in the midst of a wave of anti-social violence, which has continued in one form or another to the present moment in America. To argue that none of this can be rationally explained is a commentary of its own.

An artistic "explanation" would naturally differ from a social-scientific one. But the "building up of a picture of the social, political and cultural atmosphere" is very much one of the responsibilities of art, although few at present seem to think so.

Ebert describes Van Sant's conscious failure to offer a serious explanation as "a brave and radical act." The sole alternative apparently is to "close the case and move on." This is entirely wrongheaded. The genuinely brave and radical act, which Van Sant did not set himself, would be to locate the source of the tragedy in the diseased and dysfunctional state of American society and deliver a stinging slap to the face of official public opinion.

A general explanation of the phenomenon is possible. A number of pieces appeared on the World Socialist Web Site contributing to such an understanding. In one of them, headlined, "The Columbine High School massacre: American Pastoral ... American Berserk," David North commented in part:

"Consider, for a moment, the social outlook of these two youth. They were admirers of Adolf Hitler, fascinated by fascism's racism, its cult of sadistic violence and death, and its general contempt for humanity. And yet, there was nothing particularly Germanic about the views of [Eric] Harris and [Dylan] Klebold. In a statement that he posted on his web site, Harris wrote: 'I am the law, if you don't like it you die. If I don't like you or I don't like what you want me to do, you die.' These sentiments, expressed with a little more polish, sum up the approach of the American government to the rest of the world. 'Do what we want or we'll destroy you.'"[72]

It has been noted by numerous commentators, including Michael Moore in *Bowling for Columbine*, that the Littleton massacre occurred the same day as the heaviest bombing of Serbia by US-led NATO forces.

Further on, North wrote: "The concentration on individual warning signs will be of little help in preventing further tragedies. Attention should be focused, rather, on the social warning signs, that is, the indications and indices of social and political dysfunction which create the climate that produces events like the Columbine HS massacre. Vital indicators of impending disaster might include: growing polarization between wealth and poverty; atomization of working people and the suppression of their class identity; the glorification of militarism and war; the absence of serious social commentary and political debate; the debased state of popular culture; the worship of the stock exchange; the unrestrained celebration of individual success and personal wealth; the denigration of the ideals of social progress and equality."

The argument that a work of art can seriously treat a phenomenon without discussing its origins or causes is an absurdity, an unfortunate by-product of a reactionary intellectual climate. In fact, insofar as Van Sant is an honest and sensitive individual, he must hint at certain contributing factors, contradicting his own arguments and those of his admirers. If he has no idea why "those boys acted as they did," then why include references to violent video games, to guns and their easy availability, to Nazi Germany, to bullies and bullying, to parental irresponsibility or neglect, to adolescent self-loathing, and not to other alleged factors—for example, the absence of religious teaching in public schools, promiscuous and "decadent" lifestyles, Satanism, MTV, Bill Clinton's immorality, contemporary "ultra-nihilism," and so forth? There is nothing "naturalistic" or spontaneous about *Elephant*. The events of the day do not simply "unfold." The film is as contrived and purposeful as any other work of art.

Indeed, Van Sant told an interviewer from *eye weekly*, "As for resolution or answers or ways to fix the problem, those things exist within the film, but they do have to be arrived at by the viewer." He told *FilmForce*, "The things that inform student culture are created and controlled by the

---

[72]   David North, "The Columbine High School massacre: American Pastoral ... American Berserk," World Socialist Web Site, April 27, 1999. Available: http://www. wsws.org/articles/1999/apr1999/colo-a27.shtml

unseen culture, the sociological aspects of our climbing culture, our 'me' generation, our yuppie culture, our SUVs, or, you know, shopping culture, our war culture."

The problem is not that Van Sant has no explanation for the Columbine killings, but that his explanation or explanations are merely intuitive and impressionistic. And the repetition of various incidents, presumably allowing us to see more detail each time, do not in and of themselves strengthen his film, if no underlying grasp of the social realities is present. Vague and insubstantial, Van Sant's explanation of the event does not rise to the level of a serious social or historical perspective.

This vagueness and insubstantiality is bound up with the director's artistic-intellectual outlook and methods. The question as to which came first, an approach to art that values surface, elusiveness and ephemera or a sympathy for the philosophical notion that no distinction exists between appearance and essence, that both are the same, since everything exists on the exterior, is perhaps an academic one.

Van Sant's admiration for artist Andy Warhol is well known. The filmmaker has commented, "I want art to be like food—when you see a tomato in a store, it's a thing, you understand it, you know what it is. It's part of life. And art should be like that, it should be organic, something that isn't rarefied."

Art *should* be part of life, but life, in fact, is complicated. Social life is not transparent. Its truth does not lie on the exterior. If it were, the oppressed would have far less difficulty in ending their oppression. Nor is the truth about Columbine lying about for everyone to see. It cannot be extrapolated, contrary to Van Sant, simply from images of soulless high school corridors or even certain mini-dramas that occur within its confines. The source of the Columbine shooting does not lie within that particular high school, no matter how closely or sensitively examined, but in the complex state of American social relations and the psychic reverberations it sets off.

One admiring critic suggests that what Van Sant "wants us to do" is "to see what is really present." But that is precisely what we *cannot do* merely on the basis of these slight images! Making a virtue out of the lack of context and depth, no matter what the artist's intentions, will have no positive results.

If the truth be told, the film presents a series of recognizable high school "types," albeit cleverly done "types": the athlete, the misfit, the budding artist, etc. Van Sant admits as much: "There are stereotypes within the movie, but they're played by real kids. So even though they're 'types,' the stereotype goes somewhere." Not very far, actually. The most one can say is that the film avoids certain pitfalls of American studio production: cheap sentimentality, "heartwarming" characters, a crowd-pleasing catharsis, etc. That's all to the good, but it's not the same as establishing the truth about a critical social event or, for that matter, about the life of a single human being.

In fact, Van Sant's aesthetic vagueness coincides with or conceals (no doubt unwittingly) an inability to illuminate deeply either the characters or the episode itself. It is obvious to any viewer that the casual facts and incidents presented do not logically "lead up to" the eventual murderous outcome. The argument will be made: they are not intended to. Clearly. The work deliberately and self-consciously creates a discontinuity between the banal episodes and the terrible climax. This is its claim to fame, so to speak. In part, this is what fascinates the critics, what strikes them as so formally innovative.

But hold on a moment. There is not a complete discontinuity—the film alludes to certain well-known aspects of the case: the complaints about being picked upon, the fascination with guns and Hitler, etc. So what then? Is there a link between the early episodes and the conclusion, or is there not? Or is it not rather the case that the elliptical and "cool" style attempts to bridge the gap, substitutes itself conveniently for the convincing explanation the filmmaker unfortunately cannot provide?

Van Sant is intelligent and perceptive, and endowed with a social conscience. He recently told an interviewer from *The Film Journal* that the current "insane Republican administration is very much like the McCarthy witch-hunts" of the early 1950s. He described the Bush government as very "reactionary," and suggested that it is eager to find "scapegoats to blame things on."[73]

I suggested in 1998, at the time of his nearly shot-by-shot remake of *Psycho*, that Van Sant seemed "too much of a chameleon." How is one to reconcile the memorable *Drugstore Cowboy* and *My Own Private Idaho* (in parts), the dreadful *Even Cowgirls Get the Blues*, the market products *Good Will Hunting* and *Finding Forrester* and now the "experimental" *Gerry* and *Elephant*, which he claims to be making under the influence of European art directors like Chantal Akerman and (the vastly overrated) Bela Tarr?

---

[73] Available: http://www.thefilmjournal.com/issue5/vansant.html

The term "flexibility" or even "eclecticism" does not do justice to this disparate body of work. Something elemental is missing, some intellectual and social anchor.

From the point of view of its ability to shed light on a vital and tragic event, *Elephant* is an intellectual and artistic failure.

Why Has *The Passion of the Christ* Evoked Such a Popular Response in America?

World Socialist Web Site; March 5, 2004

Directed by Mel Gibson; screenplay by Gibson and Benedict Fitzgerald

Mel Gibson's *The Passion of the Christ* is a deeply repugnant film, but not an insignificant one. While offering no contribution to our understanding of Jesus' life or his teachings, or the relation of religion to modern life (even from the point of view of a believer), it does provide insight into a certain contemporary American mentality and mood. In that sense, Gibson's film is far less a work of theology, much less a serious artistic effort, than a revealing, quasi-autobiographical *cri de coeur*—and deserves to be treated as such.

The Passion of the Christ opened to great fanfare in the US last week and has attracted a large audience, especially among the fundamentalist Christian faithful. By and large, the American media have treated the film with great respect. Rupert Murdoch's tabloid *New York Post* dedicated its front page to the film, as did the *New York Daily News*. It has made front page headlines in every major newspaper and received wide play on television. The film has also come under criticism in some quarters, particularly from liberal and Jewish commentators.

The essential facts of *The Passion*'s production are now widely known. Gibson, a leading man in numerous action and dramatic films over the past two decades, belongs to a traditionalist Catholic splinter group, one of the many sects that reject the reforms of the Second Vatican Council of 1962–65. His father, Hutton Gibson, is a Holocaust denier who has railed against the Church hierarchy for decades. Gibson senior describes the Second Vatican Council, which, among other things, officially absolved the Jewish people of responsibility for Christ's death, as "a Masonic plot backed by the Jews."[74]

The movie actor privately financed *The Passion of the Christ*, filmed in Italy in Latin and Aramaic. Its lead performer, James Caviezel (*The Thin Red Line*), is another devout Catholic, who announced on the Christian talk show "The 700 Club," in late February, "I believe I was called to play this role." Gibson first screened a rough cut of his film last year for Christian fundamentalists and other right-wing political and media figures, while excluding potentially critical voices.

The film treats the last twelve hours of Jesus' life, as recounted in the four New Testament Gospels and other, later embellishments, particularly the version of the Passion set down by the German Augustinian nun Anne Catherine Emmerich (1774–1824), a mystic and anti-Semite. Emmerich's *The Dolorous Passion of Our Lord Jesus Christ* adds sadistic details to the Gospel accounts and is filled with references to the "Jewish mob," depicted as "cruel," "wicked" and "hard-hearted."

Gibson's film is disgustingly brutal, perhaps unlike any other widely distributed film before it. For two hours, virtually nonstop, a man is beaten, punched, spit upon, whipped, scourged, tortured and finally nailed to a cross. All the bloody, horrifying details are lovingly filmed. *The Passion of the Christ* is also profoundly anti-Semitic in its imagery and narrative thrust. The entire frenzied, violent work is oddly unaffecting.

The filmmaker asserts that he has limited himself to the last half-day of Jesus' existence on earth to emphasize the "enormity of the sacrifice." Other possible motivations suggest themselves. The narrow scope of *The Passion of the Christ* renders impossible any serious discussion of Jesus' religious and social message. It also excludes the fact of his popularity with wide layers of the Jewish population in Jerusalem. After all, only a few days before his death, according to the Gospels, Jesus was welcomed to the city by jubilant crowds. Most accounts of the Passion begin with this triumphant entry.

Gibson's work, on the other hand, opens with Jesus' internal struggle the night before the crucifixion in the Garden of Gethsemane. Foreseeing what is to come, he asks God that the chalice might pass from him, adding,

---

[74] Christopher Noxon, "Is the Pope Catholic ... Enough?" *New York Times Magazine,* March 9, 2003. Available: http://www.nytimes.com/2003/03/09/magazine/09GIBSON.html

however, "your will be done." A sinister, androgynous Satan tempts and taunts him (he/she reappears throughout the film).

Jesus is arrested, through the treachery of his erstwhile disciple, Judas. Why do the armed men sent by the Jewish high priests take Jesus into custody at night? Gibson's film never addresses the question, because a serious answer would have to take into account the officialdom's fear that the charismatic prophet's detention might lead to popular protest.

The extreme brutality begins almost immediately upon Jesus' arrest. Dramatizing one of Emmerich's additions, Gibson has his captors hang Jesus over the railing of a bridge at the end of his chains, to the point of nearly killing him.

Brought before the Jewish high priests, led by Caiaphas, Jesus is condemned as a heretic and blasphemer. They demand to know if he claims to be the son of God. "I am," he replies. Jesus is spit upon and further abused. "Death!" shriek the offended Jews.

Writing of Gibson's approach to the leading Jewish officials, the *New Republic*'s Leon Wieseltier notes justly: "The figure of Caiaphas, played with disgusting relish by an actor named Mattia Sbragia, is straight out of Oberammergau [location of the medieval German Passion play that depicted the Jews as 'Christ-killers']. Like his fellow priests, he has a graying rabbinical beard and speaks with a gravelly sneer and moves cunningly beneath a *tallit*-like shawl streaked with threads the color of money. He is gold and cold. All he does is demand an execution." These are, as Wieseltier observes, "classically anti-Semitic images."[75]

While Pontius Pilate and the other Roman officials vacillate, seeking to avoid imposing a death sentence on Jesus, the Jewish leaders are utterly relentless. They become ever more enraged and bloodthirsty. Gibson follows the spirit of the Emmerich ravings: "[T]he sight of [Jesus'] sufferings, far from exciting a feeling of compassion in the hard-hearted Jews, simply filled them with disgust, and increased their rage. Pity was, indeed, a feeling unknown in their cruel breasts."

Caiaphas and the "Jewish mob" demand Jesus' death, but Pilate promises only to "chastise" him. A group of brutish Roman soldiers sets gleefully to work whipping, beating, scourging Jesus. The scene, which

---

[75] Leon Wieseltier, "Mel Gibson's Lethal Weapon: The Worship of Blood," *The New Republic,* February 26, 2004. Available: http://work.colum.edu/~amiller/tnr-wieseltier.htm

lasts more than half an hour, is one of the most repellent in the film. The brutish soldiers first beat Jesus with rods, then whips, then a kind of cat-o'-nine-tails whose various strands are tipped with metal. The latter is first tested on a wooden table, where it tears out chunks of wood. When it is used on Jesus' back, bits of flesh and skin fly through the air. By the end of the beating, which no human being could endure, Jesus' body is a mass of striated, bloody flesh. The placement of the crown of thorns on Christ's head is an occasion for additional torture and streams of blood.

Still unsatisfied when the flayed and nearly unconscious Jesus is brought before them, the Jewish mob demands his death. Fearful of mass unrest, Pilate gives in to their demands and authorizes the crucifixion. Jesus is obliged to bear the massive wooden cross up Calvary (in three of the Gospels, another man carries it, and, historically, criminals were only obliged to carry a cross-beam). The driving of the nails into Jesus' hands and feet is another horrific sequence, with the drunken Roman soldiers inflicting unbearable pain on their victim. Stuck on his cross, Jesus begs forgiveness for those persecuting him, and dies. When a centurion sticks a spear in the dead Jesus' side, a shower of blood pours out. In an epilogue, as it were, Jesus rises from the dead, unmarked except for the holes in the palms of his hands.

What is one to make of all this?

Gibson is not without talent. He has obvious skills as an actor. His *Hamlet* (Franco Zeffirelli), while not brilliant, was competent and sometimes moving. Alongside the superviolent *Mad Max* and *Lethal Weapon* series, the American-born, Australian-raised Gibson appeared in a number of films produced by the "new wave" of Australian directors who emerged in the late 1970s (Peter Weir and Gillian Armstrong). He could give relatively straightforward performances in works like *Tequila Sunrise* and *The River*. His persona (and something of his real personality may find expression here) has suggested equal parts genuine amiability, bewilderment and death-defying recklessness.

Even as a director (*The Man Without a Face* and *Braveheart*), Gibson has his moments. His treatment of Pontius Pilate in *The Passion*, perhaps the only character allowed to exhibit genuine contradiction in the film, reveals a certain sensitivity. Pilate is someone he bends over backward to understand. Ideology has apparently prevented Gibson from treating the Jewish leaders in the same fashion.

The characterizations in general are cartoonish. One becomes inured to the bloodletting or averts one's eyes. The overall result is tedium, monotony. This is not a compelling artistic or intellectual experience. Furthermore, although a few miracles are duly recorded, the film does nothing to explore the sacred, the mythic and the epic elements in religion and religious belief. The entire affair is rather banal and cold, and—aside from the extreme level of violence—thoroughly forgettable.

The destruction before one's eyes of a passive, virtually inert human body is a horrifying spectacle, but not necessarily a deeply moving one. To feel the significance of Jesus' death, one must have some grasp of the significance of his life. For all Gibson's assertions about the depth of his faith, his is a largely soulless Jesus Christ, a nonentity. His mother Mary, Mary Magdalene and his supporters are reduced to horrified spectators. Activity and life lie almost entirely with the tormentors and oppressors. A peculiar state of affairs. It's difficult to see how this film might convince the skeptic or waverer about the truth of Jesus' doctrines.

Again, one must insist that Gibson's treatment of Jesus has relatively little to do with traditional Catholic or Christian faith or its artistic iconography. The Passion takes up three or four chapters of each Gospel (in Matthew, 26–28; in Mark, 14–16; in Luke, 22–24; and in John, 18–21). Mark simply says, "And it was the third hour, and they crucified him." The emphasis in the Gospels is on Jesus' teachings, not his horrifying death.

A Canadian Catholic priest, Gérald Caron, writes in the *Toronto Globe and Mail*, "[T]o make such a spectacle of Jesus' passion and death totally disconnected from his message and life mission is theologically flawed. It is not the quantity of blood and suffering that has redeemed us, but Jesus' death—crowning a life of 'service' as Mark says in 10:45. It was the price He had to pay, not to God, but to remain faithful to the call and mission of His life. It was His vision of God's reign that led Him to the cross—not the other way round."

Western art, from Giotto in the late 1200s and early 1300s until the age of the great secular Dutch painters of the seventeenth century, is inconceivable without images of Jesus and the Passion in particular. Hardly a great name is missing from the list of those painters who took up the suffering and death of Christ: Bellini, Mantegna, El Greco, Bosch, Dürer, Caravaggio, Van Dyck, Piero della Francesca, Fra Angelico, Grünewald, Titian, Correggio, Rembrandt, Leonardo ("The Last Supper"), Michelangelo, Raphael, Tintoretto, Botticelli, Van Eyck, Cranach, Rubens, Velasquez and many more.

While the contemporary museum-goer may weary of the religious imagery, it clearly had great collective spiritual meaning to the artists and the viewing public of the time. Christianity's "double bookkeeping," as Trotsky referred to it, did not make the ills of this life disappear, it merely solved them fictitiously.[76] Society, through the medium of the Church, handed out a promissory note, which the oppressed masses were to redeem in the next world. Nonetheless, artists and viewers alike drew real consolation from the death and resurrection of Jesus, a God-in-Man who felt deeply for their suffering, who had died for them, whose return held out the promise of a paradise on earth.

Gibson's *The Passion of the Christ* is a work from which love and compassion for humanity, everything "Christlike" in the best sense of the word, are largely absent.

The postwar Biblical epics (*Quo Vadis, The Robe, Demetrius and the Gladiators, Ben Hur, King of Kings, Barabbas, The Greatest Story Ever Told*), for all their clumsiness and sometimes downright foolishness, nonetheless pursued certain themes: tolerance, forgiveness, opposition to official repression and cruelty. Particularly in the aftermath of the Holocaust and the slaughterhouse of two world wars, filmmakers felt that the message of universal brotherhood and resistance to tyranny would find a receptive audience.

Many remember the scene from William Wyler's *Ben Hur* (1959) in which Jesus gives a thirsty slave a drink of water, angering a Roman soldier, who proceeds to threaten Christ. Jesus simply stands there, the epitome of compassion, looking at the soldier and the latter backs away, awed.

Each generation creates a Jesus in its own image, so to speak. Pier Paolo Pasolini's *The Gospel According to St. Matthew* (1964) belongs loosely to the radicalized era of "liberation theology." Pasolini's work, which is not above suspicion of political opportunism, coming as it did in part as a byproduct of the Catholic-Communist Party rapprochement in Italy in the early 1960s, is nonetheless breathtaking at times. Pasolini's Christ violently ejects the moneylenders from the temple, orders his disciples to surrender their possessions and break from their families, and expresses his preference for the poor and the meek.

Gibson has something else in mind. The actor/filmmaker may not have a specific political agenda, but he is no naïf. To have screened his rough cut last summer for the likes of the *Wall Street Journal*'s Peggy Noonan, the *National Review*'s Kate O'Beirne, syndicated columnist and *Fox News*

---

[76] Leon Trotsky, *Literature and Revolution* (London: RedWords, 1991), 270.

Channel analyst Linda Chavez, and David Kuo, the deputy director of the Bush administration's "faith-based initiative"—right-wing scoundrels all—provides some indication of his general orientation.

The traditionalist Catholic strain has been inextricably linked to right-wing politics. Michael Cuneo, in his *The Smoke of Satan*, wrote that its practitioners "would like nothing more than to be transported back to Louis XIV's France or Franco's Spain, where Catholicism enjoyed an unrivaled presidency over cultural life and other religions existed entirely at its beneficence."[77] In his *Verdict on Vichy*, Michael Curtis pointed out that Frenchman Archbishop Marcel Lefebvre, one of the founders of the traditionalist movement, and his followers supported an extreme right-wing ideology, imbued with anti-Semitism. For many years, they provided sanctuary to Paul Touvier, who tortured and murdered Jews while serving as a Vichy policeman during World War II.

How could Gibson, linked to such ideas and circles, possibly do justice to the humane and indeed profoundly subversive message of Jesus in the Gospels?

The German philosopher Hegel cites Jesus from the Sermon on the Mount, "Blessed are the pure in heart, for they shall see God," and calls this "a dictum of the noblest simplicity." This "pure heart," Hegel points out, further citing the Sermon, is filled with love for "the peacemakers," for those "persecuted for righteousness' sake," for those who strive to be "perfect, even as your Father which is in heaven is perfect."[78] What remarkable sentiments!

Inevitably, comments Hegel, this exacting doctrine must assume a "polemical" (revolutionary-practical) form. "Whatever might disturb the purity of the soul, should be destroyed," he continues. Further quoting Jesus, "Wilt thou be perfect, go and sell what thou hast, and give it to the poor, so shalt thou have a treasure in heaven, and come, follow me," Hegel adds, "Were this precept directly complied with, a social revolution must take place; the poor would become the rich."[79]

---

[77] Michael Cuneo, *The Smoke of Satan: Conservative and Traditionalist Dissent in Contemporary American Catholicism* (Baltimore: Johns Hopkins University Press, 1999), 117.

[78] Georg Wilhelm Friedrich Hegel, *The Philosophy of History* (New York: Dover Publications, 1956), 326–27.

[79] Ibid., 327.

Socialists have often noted the resemblance between early Christianity and the socialist working class movement. Both originated as movements of the oppressed, Christianity as a movement of slaves and freed slaves, of poor people deprived of all rights. Both movements preach and predict a future liberation from bondage and misery, Christianity placing salvation in the afterlife, socialism struggling for the transformation of conditions on earth. Both movements were subject to cruel persecution, outlawed at various points, declared to be enemies of the existing social order.

This subversive, socialistic content, which at least found passing reference in nearly all the Biblical epics of the past, is missing from Gibson's *Passion*. What takes its place, as the film's real positive content?

Critics like Wieseltier and others are capable of scoring points at the film's expense. They may even express outrage. Richard Cohen in the *Washington Post* legitimately points to the cult of violence in Gibson's work and calls it "fascistic." But none of these liberal or erstwhile liberal critics hints at the possibility that *The Passion of the Christ* tells us anything about contemporary America and its discontents.

Gibson is clearly a political right-winger of one variety or another, but the film cannot simply be reduced to those dimensions, although it has undoubtedly become an element in the Bush campaign, even a plank in the Republican election platform, one could say.

The film bears witness to a more general socio-psychological process. What emerges most strongly is the bitterness, resentment and even self-pity of definite social layers.

In the traditional depiction of the Passion, the Roman soldiers and the Jewish bystanders represent *us*, general humanity, including the artist him- or herself. The death of Jesus brings out human capacities for wickedness, for indifference, for nobility. It is intended to set these qualities in relief and permit us to examine ourselves, the degree to which we are "pure in heart." For Gibson, this is not of any great interest. Such considerations are largely brushed aside.

Rather, I sense a semi-autobiographical impulse at work in Gibson's film. And I am not referring to his individual psychological state. The actor/director may very well see himself as a man who has been persecuted, wronged, even (metaphorically) scourged, and no doubt personal demons play a role here, but the mix of aggression and passivity in Gibson's psyche is secondary.

I am speaking of an embittered, troubled social type. The political tendency (in the broadest sense) he represents, which has relatively deep roots in the US and has become more pronounced in recent years, is associated with feelings of deep resentment and paranoia.

Such individuals and groupings on the right are deeply convinced that Americans, and Christians in particular, form an endangered species and face an almost universally hostile world. To these forces, the planet is full of enemies, and the events of September 11 only confirmed this fact. This is a social milieu to which Bush's call for a crusade against the "axis of evil" came as both a vindication and a battle cry. These elements are convinced "everyone is out to get" them. Operating with a great deal of self-delusion, and turning the world upside down, they see America—irony of ironies!—as the victim.

Gibson belongs to this class of marginal personalities who feel they and other Christian Americans have been hard done by, ignored, persecuted. For his father, this creates a conspiracy mania, a hatred of the Catholic hierarchy, for the Jews and for all the "traitors" to the true cause. One should recall that the son appeared in a film entitled *Conspiracy Theory*, in which he spoke the line, "Somebody has to lift the scab ... the festering scab that is the Vatican."

Of course, Gibson's film has an appeal beyond these most paranoid elements—in the first place, to wider layers of fundamentalist Christians. But what does the growth of evangelical Christianity (and its specific Catholic variant) represent, if not primarily a concentrated ideological expression of the increased confusion and disorientation of considerable numbers of people in the US?

And such a phenomenon is not so difficult to understand. We only have to consider the massive changes that have occurred in American society over the past several decades. In the first place, the economic transformations: the wholesale destruction or decline of entire industries and regions, the changes associated with globalization and computerization, the virtual disappearance of traditional rural and even small-town America. Along with these, the demographic changes in family structure, religious affiliation, in union membership—in general, every old allegiance has been loosened or broken.

Momentous decisions are taken—to go to war or prepare for new ones, to eliminate the social-welfare state, to deregulate or scrap essential services—entirely behind the backs of the population. All the while, official society discards its liberal consensus, lurches to the right and promotes every form of backwardness, including religious superstition and bigotry.

And all this goes undiscussed, undebated! American political life seems entirely barren to masses of people, something distant, alien and hostile.

The two-party system, a corpse from the point of view of history, crushes the living with its enormous, apparently immovable weight.

Is it any wonder that wide layers of the population feel powerless, marginalized, even beaten and scourged? There are millions of tortured, anguished souls in America, who feel abandoned, betrayed, at the mercy of persecutors. Unable to associate itself with any broad-based progressive social movement, this mass in desperation finds expression at present in a variety of forms, many of them unattractive and even antisocial. To misdiagnose or turn a blind eye to this reality is to underestimate the depth of the crisis of American society.

I feel safe in predicting that *The Passion* will not encounter precisely the same response in Western Europe, and not because Americans are inherently vulnerable to religious mania, although there are ideological difficulties deriving from US history. Nowhere else in the advanced industrial world have the ruling elites been so successful as in the US, with the indispensable assistance of the trade union bureaucracy, at destroying social programs, reducing living standards in the interests of profit, and paralyzing opposition and resistance.

Gibson is not oppressed. He is a multimillionaire. The "sigh of the oppressed," as Marx termed the religious impulse, is not present in his film.[80] But something of the "sigh of the oppressed" is present *in the response* to the film. *The Passion of the Christ* is a reactionary film, but one ought not draw the conclusion that the majority of those attending it, probably overwhelmingly drawn from the lower middle class and working class, are reactionary. This is not a film with an overt social message. If Gibson, or those he now associates with, in and around the Bush administration, put forward their misanthropic, right-wing political agenda in a film, masses of people would not turn out.

Trotsky once pointed out that a political leader "is always a relation between people, the individual supply to meet the collective demand."[81] Gibson is not a political leader, but one might say that every major cultural phenomenon, even the most retrograde, is also "a relation between people," the response to a social demand. Here the demand, however, is very diffuse, confused, composed of disparate elements.

---

80   Karl Marx, "A Contribution to the Critique of Hegel's Philosophy of Right: Introduction" *The Marx-Engels Reader*, ed. Robert Tucker (New York: WW Norton & Co, 1978), 54.

81   Leon Trotsky, "What Is National Socialism? [1933]," *The Struggle Against Fascism in Germany* (New York: Pathfinder Press, 2004), 461.

Those seeing *The Passion* are reading all sorts of things into it. Its appeal, under the present confused ideological conditions, extends into different and even opposed social layers. As noted above, there are distinctly ultra-right, if not fascistic elements, who respond to its fascination with violence, its paranoia and bitterness, who see America as whipped and persecuted, by Arab and other "terrorists," by the ungrateful, vengeful, Pharisee-like French and Germans! Reactionary forces who also want Americans to get used to making their own "sacrifices."

But the film also attracts the genuinely oppressed, who are valiantly, often futilely trying to "embrace their cross" of everyday life at this point. They take consolation in Jesus' suffering as a means of coming to grips with their own. This is by no means an ignoble effort. This same response, however, has another, debilitating meaning, as an expression of the doctrine of passivity and resignation to one's fate. These are people who largely have no insight yet into their own problems and circumstances.

The Passion of the Christ is a reprehensible work. Those who praise the film, or downplay its reactionary character, or remain silent for fear of drawing fire from the fundamentalist right, serve political reaction themselves.

However, the film, artistically and intellectually negligible, has provoked a response that points far beyond itself and its director. Whatever the immediate fate of Gibson's work, its reception underscores, above all, the increasingly unstable social and moral state of American capitalist society, inexorably coming face to face with its own peculiar Passion.

Kill Bill, Vol. 2:
A Culture at the End of Its Rope

World Socialist Web Site; June 25, 2004

Written and directed by Quentin Tarantino

Every social act has social consequences. Cinema is perhaps the most social of all the arts, by virtue of both the collective, cooperative nature of making films and the mass character of their distribution and exhibition. A film is an aggressive intrusion into the lives and thoughts of those who see it and therefore a factor in social life.

Every work in the cinema is "political" and "polemical"; i.e., it proposes a certain view of humanity—of its aspirations, its possibilities, its current social organization—and at the same time argues against others. An individual film may uncover or conceal important truths; it may demystify social reality or obscure it; it may encourage or help paralyze the viewer, enlighten or help disorient him or her.

Kill Bill, Vol. 2, written and directed by Quentin Tarantino, is a repugnant film, symptomatic of a culture at the end of its rope. The second half of a two-part work, it continues the story of Beatrix, or The Bride (Uma Thurman), a former professional killer, who was shot and left for dead, while pregnant, along with her entire wedding party. Upon waking from a coma four years later, she sets about exacting revenge on the individuals responsible, including, above all, the "Bill" (David Carradine) of the title, her former lover, father of the child she delivered while in a coma and a murderous crime boss.

There is nothing new or interesting in the story and nothing new or interesting in its telling. *Vol. 1*, released last year, was memorable primarily for its extraordinary number of severed limbs (by samurai swords) and geysers of fake blood. The violence was gratuitous and appalling, but the film could be dismissed as essentially cartoonish. One simply forgot about it quickly.

Vol. 2 is a different case. Here, events are slowed down and we have a far more loving attention paid to cruel and sadistic detail. Although Thurman's character ultimately triumphs, the most memorable sequences by far involve her humiliation, subjection and abuse at the hands of three tormentors. She is trapped and bound in each instance—first, physically, by Bill's brother Budd (Michael Madsen); next, "morally," by her allegiance to her Chinese master in the martial arts, Pai Mei (Chia Hui Liu); and, finally, under the influence of a "truth serum," by Bill himself.

Beatrix is essentially tortured in each instance. The Madsen sequence is the most horrific. Beatrix is shot in the chest with a shotgun blast of rock salt, left to writhe in pain, tied up with belts and ropes, dragged across the desert floor, threatened with having her eyeballs burnt out with Mace and finally buried alive in a pine coffin. Budd leers and gloats over her the while, deriving great pleasure from her agony. What is one to make of this?

This is a film whose subject matter is torturing and murdering and bloody revenge. It has the word "Kill," as an imperative, in its title. Remove the pointless dialogue, the self-conscious references to countless other films, the various camera and editing gimmicks, the heaps of self-satisfaction and self-aggrandizement, and what remains? A work about a group of psychopaths eliminating one another. The first speech of the film contains the word "sadism." When asked, under the influence of the truth serum, whether she regrets no longer murdering people, our heroine replies, "Yes." The characters are, with the possible exception of Beatrix, uniformly foul, violent, brutal, cold. Why should we find any of this appealing?

We will be told that Tarantino doesn't mean any of this seriously, that this is simply a great cinematic romp. The director himself tells us, "But also everything I'm doing, there's just a level of playfulness. How can you take it seriously? How can you get hung up on it?" The film critics agree. One, for example, labels the director a "sadistic freak," before expressing the opinion that *Kill Bill, Vols. 1* and *2* are "great fun."[82] Another critic writes that *Vol. 2* is "one wacky magnificent assemblage."[83] A third tells us that the new film is "the most voluptuous comic-book movie ever made" and a "deliciously perverse picture."[84]

And no doubt there are audiences that find this entertaining and amusing. But one must say that this is not a healthy phenomenon, that a great deal of social alienation has gone into making such a response possible. The critical, or rather, *uncritical* reaction reflects the same process, a cultural and moral regression.

The fact that Tarantino "doesn't mean anything by it," that he is posturing, is no argument in favor of the film. In any case, he most certainly does mean *something* by the sadism. Does he think that human beings are this vile? If not, then why does he make films that argue for that proposition?

After all, the sequences mentioned above are the ones on which the director has obviously lavished the most attention. They are the only ones that get under the viewer's skin. Whenever the characters sit and talk to one another, the results are simply tedious (one reason for the violent

---

[82] David Edelstein, "Revenge Stories: The Bride brings the pain in Kill Bill, Vol. 2. The audience receives it in The Punisher," *Slate,* April 15, 2004. Available: http://www.slate.com/articles/arts/movies/2004/04/revenge_stories.html

[83] J. Hoberman, "Vengeance Is Hers," *The Village Voice,* April 6, 2004. Available: http://www.villagevoice.com/2004-04-06/film/vengeance-is-hers/

[84] Elvis Mitchell, "Vengeance Still Mine, Saith the Lethal Bride," *The New York Times,* April 16, 2004. Available: http://movies2.nytimes.com/2004/04/16/movies/16KILL.html

histrionics: to divert attention from the fact that the filmmaker has nothing to say and cannot construct a serious drama). The climactic speech in
which Carradine's Bill goes on about comic book superheroes is simply
inane, an embarrassment. Carradine, never more than an adequate actor,
is very poor here. Thurman, an appealing if limited performer generally, is
not the slightest bit convincing as a cold-blooded killer (fortunately, for her
sake and ours). The entire effort is frankly amateurish, puerile.

We will be told by some that Tarantino is merely reflecting the violence in the society around him, or even that he is holding it up to criticism. Nonsense. *Kill Bill* is not a critique of sadistic bullying; it revels in it.
A calculated, manipulative (and orgasmic) heaping up of violent acts cannot possibly constitute a rejection or a critique. Tarantino's work lacks
entirely that "pathos of distance" characteristic of a reflective critique.
The film itself is oppressive and bullying, as well as unpleasantly pleased
with itself.

Sadism in film is not the same as sadism in life outside the cinema.
But there is a connection between the two phenomena. A representation,
a reflection bears *some* relationship to the thing represented or reflected.
To be "entertained" even by imitations of torture, or to seek to entertain by
such imitations, suggests a disturbing degree of indifference to the pain of
others. It is already the result of a general process of brutalization in the
culture and it helps further inure the population to suffering.

The "porno-sadism" of *Kill Bill* obviously speaks to a wider phenomenon in American society. Ironically, the film opened in North America on
April 16, less than two weeks before the torture and abuse of Iraqi detain-
ees at Abu Ghraib prison was exposed. Tarantino termed *Kill Bill, Vol. 1*,
a "black comedy." He suggested that the violence was so outlandish and
bloody that it was obviously set in "fantasy land. ... This is definitely not
taking place on planet Earth."[85] But there is violence and sadism on planet
Earth—plenty of it. Is it not a fact that the images of American soldiers—
men and women—smiling, leering or giving thumbs-up signs beside naked
Iraqi prisoners would not be out of place in Tarantino's cinema?

This is not to say that Tarantino is in any way morally culpable for
the current situation, which he is obviously not, or that he even supports

---

[85] Mark Bayross, "Kill Bill Volume 1: Q&A with Quentin Tarantino, Uma Thurman,
Daryl Hannah and Julie Dreyfus," *Phase 9*, October 2003. Available: http://www.
phase9.tv/moviefeatures/killbillvolume1feature1.shtml

Bush and the Iraq war, which he probably does not. But the filmmaker is responding to certain social impulses.

Tarantino's personal history and fixations interest us not in the least. By whatever process, however, the director has made himself into a sensitive antenna almost entirely unconcerned as to the signals he picks up. Indeed, he makes a virtue of his indifference to the sources of his material, his addiction to kitsch and the B film, and his anti-intellectualism.

In this manner, Tarantino becomes an ideal transmitter for all manner of pent-up frustration, rage and paranoia that dominate certain social layers in America. He cynically chronicles and at the same time exploits these feelings. He both encourages and mocks them. So we arrive at this "turning on the dime," in Tarantino's words. "Getting you to laugh, laugh, laugh—stop laughing. Stop laughing. Stop laughing. Laugh again."

And we arrive at the filmmaker as sadist: "I think the role of a filmmaker can very well be as a sadistic relationship to the audience's masochist. I've always really believed that the audience needs to be tortured, all right, and the torture is not so bad. It's a lot better than being glazed over. It's a lot better than being bored and have images just glaze over you."

Revenge as a central motif; the loose use of words like "kill"; approving references to sadism and torture—where could we be but in post-September 11 America, where bloody-mindedness has apparently become the stuff of polite dinner parties in Washington, New York and elsewhere? Tarantino thinks he's behind the steering wheel, but every aspect of his work suggests that he's being driven by powerful social forces.

The decayed state of American society is not the filmmaker's fault. One senses that the disintegration of old institutions, the loosening of traditional affiliations, the economic dislocations, the violence and chaos of American life ... that all this sends Tarantino (and not only him) into a tizzy. The task of the artist, however, is to do something other than merely register these facts, much less "be playful" with them.

In accordance with the special means of his or her field, the artist must turn these sometimes abrupt and even terrifying realities into art. It has been done before, even in America, and even in the film industry. How else could we have a *Vertigo*, for example, which transformed a 'dizzying' reality into a moving, haunting drama?

Tarantino, however, is entirely dominated by the social processes. He is thoroughly at their mercy. *Kill Bill* is little more than congealed disorientation, resentment and confusion. It contains no spirit of anger, protest or opposition. The film appeals to the worst in its audience ...

One must say what is: Tarantino is a bad filmmaker. And—artificial, removed from life, self-referential, unmoving, unconvincing—*Kill Bill, Vol. 2*, is very bad art.

Michael Moore's Contribution: *Fahrenheit 9/11*

World Socialist Web Site; June 30, 2004

Written and directed by Michael Moore

The release of Michael Moore's *Fahrenheit 9/11* has provided great numbers of people in the US the opportunity to demonstrate their opposition to the war in Iraq and the policies of the Bush administration, and their general disgust with the political and media establishment. More than 3 million people viewed the film in its first weekend in the theaters, by all accounts overwhelmingly approving its message.

The opening of Moore's film in North America has been a genuine political event, not a stage-managed one. This in itself is rare in a country where official political life has been for decades thoroughly scripted, running in the narrowest of channels.

For many people, buying a movie ticket has suddenly become a means of making a public statement of dissent. It turns out, contrary to the official mythology, that millions in the US passionately oppose the criminal policies of their government.

That is not a small matter. The response to *Fahrenheit 9/11* is a shattering exposure of the American media and its leading personalities. The massive turnout at the box office—unprecedented for a nonfiction film— gives the lie to the claims about the popularity of the "war president" and his regime. Abraham Lincoln was right—you can't fool all of the people all of the time.

How did the media "miss" the fact that there was mass opposition to the war? Why was it denied and concealed, even after the huge demonstrations of February 2003, until the record-breaking turnout to Moore's film has now made it an obvious fact of national life? How did the media, including the "liberal" media, "miss" the fact that Bush was a reactionary cipher, a moral eunuch, whose every word and deed served the interests of the corporate elite?

The popular outpouring confirms that a radicalization is under way in the US, with far-reaching implications.

And the millions who have flocked to the movie theaters have not gone for nothing, they have not been duped. *Fahrenheit 9/11* is an admirable film, remarkable in certain parts, done with considerable and heartfelt sincerity. Moore is a gifted filmmaker who displays intuition, energy and courage.

Even in considering the weaknesses of the film, which are also real and significant, one has to place them in a certain context. If *Fahrenheit 9/11*, for example, attempts to cover too much ground, if it touches on too many issues and not any one of them in sufficient depth, can one blame Moore entirely? After all, if the US media, with all its vast resources and technology, were treating events with a modicum of honesty, would there be such a gaping hole that Moore clearly feels he has to fill up single-handedly? Would he feel the need to cover *everything*, if the official news media had been investigating and exposing *anything*?

Right-wing critics attack Moore for his supposed "egoism" and propensity for "self-aggrandizement." These reactionaries are simply infuriated that the filmmaker has the audacity to take on the powers that be when so many others have been intimidated or bribed. His stance has helped reveal that a vast social constituency has been suppressed and unable to express itself.

The journalistic wing of the American intelligentsia in particular is largely a cesspool of venality and corruption. The principal task the US media has set itself in recent years has been concealment, its inventiveness largely devoted to finding means of preventing the population from discovering the truth about its government and society.

That a war of outright aggression could be launched, which has resulted in the deaths of tens of thousands and with as-yet-unknown and potentially catastrophic repercussions, based on a series of transparent lies, without *a single major voice* in the American media raised against it—this is a crime for which the media moguls and their million-dollar anchormen and anchorwomen and columnists deserve to be answerable.

And even some of Moore's political difficulties—the refusal to break with the Democratic Party, the populist pandering, the obsession with

Bush as an individual—ought to be seen in context. Large sections of the liberal-left milieu in the US in recent years have simply thrown in the towel, enriching themselves, turning to the right, exhibiting an increasing indifference about the fate of broad layers of the population. In this sense, Moore is something of an isolated figure. He retains a feeling and a genuine sympathy for the plight of the oppressed.

Moore (*Roger & Me*, *Bowling for Columbine*) opens his film with a precredit sequence dedicated to the hijacking of the 2000 elections by the Bush camp and the refusal of Democratic candidate Al Gore and his party to resist the theft. Bush takes office, despite protests, and promptly goes on vacation.

After a few shots of the new administration's officials putting their public faces on, the screen goes black and we hear the sounds of the September 11, 2001, terrorist attacks, then see the horrified faces of those watching from the streets below. Extraordinary footage of George W. Bush follows. After being informed of the second aerial suicide attack on the World Trade Center, the president of the United States continues sitting in a classroom and reads a children's book for another seven minutes, looking like a man who does not know what to do.

Moore explains correctly that the Bush administration in the wake of September 11 deliberately set out to create the impression in the popular mind that the Saddam Hussein regime was implicated in the terrorist assault, although no such connection existed and Iraq had never attacked the US.

An extended sequence of the film then treats the wide-ranging links between the Bush family and the Saudi ruling elite. These connections are real and significant, and the general argument that US foreign policy is driven by material interests—oil, profits and greed—is certainly a healthy antidote to the drivel about "liberating" Iraq and bringing "democracy" to the Middle East, but Moore strikes his most truly false note in this section.

Fahrenheit 9/11 essentially portrays the Saudis as the master manipulators and even controllers of the Bush administration. This is simply wrongheaded. The suggestion that "rich Arabs" are taking over the country or have undue influence will not help raise the political-cultural consciousness of the US population. American imperialism is ruthless, criminal and predatory. The Saudi monarchy is a caretaker and puppet of US interests, not an independent actor, no matter how vast its wealth.

The director here has taken the line of least resistance, succumbing to the lure of the easy explanation, rather than providing a more profound analysis. This is not the only such short cut taken in *Fahrenheit 9/11.*

After providing his version of the background to the September 11 attacks, including revealing shots of Taliban officials visiting the US as part of an attempt to work out a pipeline deal, Moore proceeds quite forthrightly to expose the Bush administration's efforts to use the tragic deaths in New York and Washington for its own sinister political purposes.

The USA Patriot Act, passed by Congress, introduced many repressive measures long sought by the ultra-right and law enforcement agencies. Democratic congressman Jim McDermott (Washington) notes that September 11 was "the chance to do something" and the Bush administration took full advantage, unleashing an unprecedented attack on democratic rights, with the full participation of the Democrats in Congress. Moore details some of the more preposterous actions taken by the FBI against entirely law-abiding citizens.

Fahrenheit 9/11 graphically depicts the consequences of the launching of a war of aggression against Iraq in March 2003: the corpses of young Iraqi children (juxtaposed with the insufferable Donald Rumsfeld boasting about "the care, the humanity, that goes into our conduct of this war"), devastated families, terrified women and children in a house invaded by US troops in the dead of night. The film succinctly exposes the litany of Bush administration lies about weapons of mass destruction and alleged Iraqi–Al Qaeda links. It furthermore indicts the Democratic Party leadership for endorsing the war and the American mass media for transmitting the government's lies without criticism or questioning.

The strongest sections of the film are unquestionably those shot in Moore's hometown of Flint, Michigan. The director returns to what he knows best. Here the film takes on a different character and rises above the level of much of "left" middle class commentary. Here the critical social and class questions emerge in a sharp and persuasive fashion.

We learn that Flint, once home to thousands of jobs at auto giant General Motors, now has a real unemployment rate of 50 percent. One young man explains that televised images of a bombed Iraqi city remind him of his neighborhood. The shots of boarded-up homes and devastated, poverty-stricken neighborhoods bear him out.

Fahrenheit 9/11 makes the case that those who join the "volunteer" US military are, in fact, economic conscripts, forced by desperate circumstances to put their lives at risk in hope of receiving education or job training. Moore asks a group of black youth how many have relatives in the military. Nearly everyone raises his hand.

In one of the most revealing sequences, two Marine recruiters cynically trawl a shopping center in an impoverished part of town for likely recruits or even anyone who can be duped into leaving his name and address.

Moore pays attention as well to the moral and mental state of the troops sent to Iraq. His picture is complex enough: we see US soldiers terrorizing Iraqi civilians, abusing and humiliating prisoners and demonstrating psychotic behavior ("It's the ultimate rush," says one US soldier, when you listen to a heavy metal tune during a raid), all this the inevitable consequence of brutal and brutalizing colonial warfare. We also see those who are reflecting on their situation and their own actions, who feel guilt and shame. One young soldier tells the camera, "Part of your soul is destroyed in taking another life." Another says, "If Rumsfeld were here, I'd ask for his resignation."

Horrific scenes from Walter Reed medical center in Washington of American Iraqi war veterans, mostly kids, without legs or hands or arms, are intercut with images of a beaming Bush addressing a fund-raiser full of fat cats, declaring to thunderous laughter and applause, "This is a gathering of the haves and the have-mores. Some call you the elite, but I call you my base."

A conference on the profits to be amassed from the conflict in Iraq brings together corporate jackals, large and small. "There are billions and billions of dollars to be made," they are reminded from the podium. The war, observes one participant, is "good for business, bad for the people."

Fahrenheit 9/11 captures a heartbreaking reality. As part of his research into economic conditions in Flint, Moore interviews Lila Lipscomb of Career Alliance, a job-training and workforce development agency. A self-described "conservative Democrat" and a flag-waving patriot, Lipscomb has a son in the military in Iraq. When we first meet her, she fully supports the war.

By the time we encounter Lipscomb again, tragedy has struck. Her son has been killed in action in Iraq. In an unflinching and honest manner, Lipscomb begins to examine her previously unthinking patriotism and faith in the administration, increasingly aware of the government's dishonesty in taking the country into war. Outside the White House, she confronts a war supporter who accuses Moore of staging Lipscomb's encounter with an Iraqi woman protester.

In a final scene, Lipscomb reads from her son's last letter, denouncing the war, "What in the world's wrong with Bush, trying to be like his dad? ... I really hope they do not re-elect that guy." Her husband asks rhetorically, "[He died] for what? For what?" The scene is deeply moving.

In the final voice-over, Moore returns powerfully to the social questions, reiterating the point about the sons and daughters of the working class having to conduct a war that benefits only the wealthy. He concludes with a citation from British left-wing author George Orwell, which contains these passages: "The war is not meant to be won, but it is meant to be continuous. ... The hierarchy of society is only possible on the basis of poverty and ignorance. In principle, the war effort is always planned to keep society on the brink of starvation. The war is waged by the ruling group against its own subjects, and its object is not victory ... but to keep the very structure of society intact."

Fahrenheit 9/11, in short, ends with a fierce condemnation of the capitalist system—although the words are not used—and the manner in which it regulates social tensions in part through imperialist war. This is extraordinary material for a film that has a mass audience—indeed, for any contemporary film. A domestic box office of $100 million, a figure now being bandied about, would translate into some 15 million viewers in the US, or approximately one in fifteen people over the age of 14. No wonder that certain maddened right-wingers are urging that cinemas showing the film be boycotted.

At its best, Moore's film articulates and can only deepen the social anger building up in America and which must find political expression, although perhaps not in the manner that the filmmaker himself might advocate.

In interviews, Michael Moore repeatedly emphasizes that he is an artist and a filmmaker first and foremost. This is generally interpreted as a disingenuous or evasive remark. Perhaps it is an attempt in part to avoid being accused of taking a partisan position on the current election campaign and thus compromising attempts to reach a wide audience with his film, but the documentarian, inadvertently or not, has hit upon an important issue.

As a politician and commentator, Moore has been woefully inconsistent. He vacillates, for example, between strident denunciations of the Democrats for their lack of backbone and appeals to its traditional supporters to "retake" the party. His support earlier this year for the candidacy of former army general Wesley Clark, the commander of NATO forces in its brutal assault on Serbia, for the Democratic presidential nomination was entirely deplorable—this was Moore at his weakest, his most pragmatic, his most unthinking.

As an honest artist, however, Moore is compelled to go beyond the limitations of his conscious political outlook. Image-making has that quality. This is not a film that provides aid and comfort to the leadership of the Democratic Party. In searchingly examining the history of the past four years, Moore reveals the Democrats as largely complicit in a bipartisan strategy, indeed a ruling elite consensus, aimed at establishing US global hegemony.

Looking honestly at Flint and such communities, Moore is compelled to acknowledge or imply that for American working class youth there is no future within the present economic and social order. Beyond that, he argues convincingly that imperialist war takes advantage of poverty to find its cannon fodder and, at the same time, serves as a safety valve to suppress the class struggle at home. The implications of these insights are revolutionary.

Of course, in creating a work that directly treats political and historical matters, the artist, even the honest artist, cannot entirely overcome his limitations. Unresolved questions will inevitably find their way into the artistic product. And this is the case with Moore's film.

A tension exists in *Fahrenheit 9/11* between the sober and thoughtful tone of the Flint sequences and some of the more superficial, irritatingly jocular, almost sophomoric moments. A tension exists between a deep sympathy for the working population in America and an opportunist orientation to the miserably compromised "liberal" wing of the Democrats, one of the two big-business parties in America. A tension exists between socialist convictions, hostile to all forms of national and ethnic chauvinism, and American populist demagogy, tinged with nativist prejudice.

One of the difficulties with *Fahrenheit 9/11* is that, from the methodological and aesthetic point of view, it ends where it should have begun. It's not the exaggerated focus on Saudi Arabia and the Bush family fortunes that is most telling, but the scenes in America, in Michigan. The horrors in Iraq are not principally the product of Bush's personal greed and stupidity, as real as those are; they express the social contradictions of American society as a whole.

Lacking in Moore's film ultimately is a more seriously considered and consistent analysis of *the type of society* out of which something as monstrous as the Iraq war could possibly have emerged. The political personnel in charge of lying and finding rationales for imperialist invasion at any given instant are a secondary matter. Bush, Gore or John Kerry—the drive for US world domination will continue. The personal demonization of Bush can become a means of evading the critical question: the historic and systemic bankruptcy of American capitalism, at which Moore's film is forthright enough to hint.

The filmmaker's dilemma is not merely his own. Moore passed through the bitter experiences of the working class population in Flint, repeated throughout the US, in the 1970s and 1980s: the vast downsizing, the abandonment of workers to their fate by the trade unions, the devastating economic, social and moral consequences. The limitations of that experience and his own limitations are bound up with unresolved political problems facing the American working class, including the character of the unions, the nature of the Democratic Party, the historic role of liberalism.

Where does Moore go from here? In our view, his further evolution as an artist will largely depend on his intellectual and political development. In the first place, this will mean an open admission of his underlying socialist convictions. A frank and thoroughgoing critique of American capitalism is unavoidable if the filmmaker is not to repeat himself, or worse, fall backward and find his work used for purposes antithetical to his most deeply held convictions.

Moore has obviously done a considerable amount of reading and thinking, and on that basis made a crucial advance with this film. He has come very far. One hopes he can resolve the tensions in his thought and his art.

Ghost Town: *Melinda and Melinda*

World Socialist Web Site; April 6, 2005

Written and directed by Woody Allen

Melinda and Melinda is the latest in a recent series of very poor films written and directed by Woody Allen. Indeed, it has been 13 years since Allen produced a work, *Husbands and Wives*, that was worth something as a whole. The presence of certain performances or personalities—John Cusack and Jennifer Tilly in *Bullets Over Broadway*, Mira Sorvino in *Mighty Aphrodite*, Leonardo DiCaprio and Charlize Theron in *Celebrity*, Sean Penn and Samantha Morton in *Sweet and Lowdown*—partially obscured the fact

that the director-writer had run out of things to say, but the fact has become too obvious to conceal by this point.

The new film's premise is that life is either tragic or comic, depending
on the way one looks at it, or both. A group of four New Yorkers is sitting
around a restaurant table. One writes comedies, another tragedies. They
argue about the respective merits of their efforts. A third man at the table
tells a story about a woman barging in on a dinner party. Two intercut versions of the ensuing story then unfold, one ostensibly "tragic," one "comic."

In the tragic version, Melinda (Radha Mitchell)—it is she who comes
uninvited to the dinner party hosted by Laurel (Chloë Sevigny) and Lee
(Jonny Lee Miller)—is fleeing a desperate situation. Finding herself in a
staid and unsatisfying marriage, she entered into a love affair. She has lost
custody of her children and attempted suicide. "Tragic" Melinda gets involved in another doomed relationship in her new life, too.

"Comic" Melinda (also played by Mitchell) lives downstairs from Hobie
(Will Ferrell) and his wife Susan (Amanda Peet), the hosts of the interrupted dinner party. Hobie falls for her, complicating and disrupting his marriage. She, meanwhile, has started a relationship with a new boyfriend. He
longs for her. One thing leads to another. This version has a happy ending.

The tragic strand is not particularly tragic, the comic not especially
comic. At times, one has a difficult time remembering which is which, and
not because some insightful comment about the "tragi-comic" character
of the human condition is being offered, but because both segments lack
sharpness and purposefulness.

Nothing is worked through to the end. There are countless uninten-
tional red herrings. Characters appear, seem to carry a certain dramatic
weight, and disappear, without anything having been established about
their presence. Nearly everything in the film simply happens, blandly, rather pointlessly. The actors, some of them quite talented, stand there in front
of the camera, with lines and arguments that hardly go anywhere, floun-
dering. *Melinda and Melinda* simply sits there on screen, inert, flat, unmoving (in both senses of the word).

Mitchell is pleasant enough, but, like many contemporary performers,
lacks depth and texture. She is not the remotest bit convincing as a potential suicide and, we learn, worse. Ferrell is the most appealing presence in
the film, but he's given little to work with. Sevigny, a remarkable performer,
as the hostess of the "tragic" dinner party, is almost entirely wasted. The
discussion of the "tragic" and "comic" never rises above the banal.

Allen, a genuine comic talent, never had a great deal to say about the world. In his films from 1977 to 1992, *Annie Hall* to *Husbands and Wives* (*Crimes and Misdemeanors* [1989] was one of the better Reagan-era films), he stood out against the general decline of American filmmaking by defending some principle of old-fashioned, contrarian, self-deprecating, quasi-cultured New York liberalism. A good deal of the comic business stemmed not so much from his embodying anything important, but from what he hadn't succumbed to. He *wasn't* "going Hollywood," *wasn't* making blockbusters, *wasn't* getting fabulously wealthy and indulging himself, *wasn't* abandoning music and literature, *wasn't* giving up on Bergman and Freud and Fellini, etc. He also had the talents of the very gifted Mia Farrow at his disposal for a number of those years.

The Allen persona wore thin a good many pictures ago, but it carried him through until the early 1990s. Various factors, including personal ones, may have caused him to lose his way so dramatically, but no doubt social changes played a decisive role. The milieu that he lovingly, if sardonically, chronicled has disintegrated. At its upper, wealthiest end, it has become a source of support for law-and-order, free-market Republicans. Many of New York City's so-called cultural intelligentsia signaled their shift by supporting Rudolph Giuliani in 1993.

New York City's official web site explains: "His [Giuliani's] message of fiscal responsibility and attention to quality of life concerns [i.e., shunting the homeless off the streets and subways] resonated with New Yorkers, who elected him over incumbent David Dinkins. ... To reduce crime, he implemented a 'zero tolerance' approach, placing an emphasis on enforcing laws against nuisance crimes as well as serious offenses. ... To stimulate the city's stagnated economy, Giuliani reduced the tax burden by eliminating the Commercial Rent Tax in most areas of the city, reducing the Hotel Occupancy Tax, and eliminating the Unincorporated Business Tax. ... [A] national financial magazine named New York City the most improved American city in which to do business ...

"Faced with a $2.2 billion budget gap upon taking office, Giuliani lowered projected spending by $7.8 billion through a series of cost cutting measures and productivity improvements. He reduced the city's payroll by over 20,000 jobs without layoffs. ... In 1993, 1.1 million New Yorkers were receiving welfare. To bring an end to a philosophy that encouraged dependency on public assistance, Giuliani implemented the largest workfare program in the nation. Since his welfare reforms were enacted in March of

1995, 340,000 people have been moved off the rolls, saving $650 million annually in city, state and federal funds."[86]

It would be hard to improve on this as a guide to the general evolution of certain upper middle class layers in Manhattan. One would perhaps only need to add a graph showing the meteoric rise in the stock market in the 1990s. Allen's milieu largely threw its lot in with the barbarians some time ago. And he goes on pretending as if nothing has happened. But these developments have had consequences for his art, hollowing it out, rendering it lifeless.

One scene stands out: the party at which the "tragic" Melinda (at least I think it's the tragic one) meets her new love. First of all, the vast, sumptuously decorated Upper East Side apartment would be out of reach for nearly anyone but a millionaire these days. A leisurely medium shot takes in the guests standing around, in their blazers and ties and tasteful evening dresses, sipping drinks, listening to classical music skillfully played on the piano, presumably discussing love and psychoanalysis and literature and who knows what else, and one suddenly realizes why it all looks so terribly, terribly unreal, almost *touchingly* unreal—this is a gathering of phantoms. One can see why the camera remains at a certain distance; if it were to move in too close, one would surely be able to see right through what *must be* paper-thin, two-dimensional figures.

This is light from a dead star. The party only exists in Allen's brain, as a memory or perhaps a fantasy, a crowd of cultured, moneyed, sophisticated, liberal-minded New Yorkers.

It is impossible to accomplish much of anything, comic, tragic or otherwise, on such a basis. It may be painful at times to look life and reality in the face, but they remain the only basis for art.

---

[86] Available: http://www.nyc.gov/html/nyc100/html/classroom/hist_info/mayors.html#giuliani

Steven Spielberg's *Munich*: Art as Humanization

World Socialist Web Site; December 30, 2005

Directed by Steven Spielberg; written by Tony Kushner and Eric Roth; based on *Vengeance: The True Story of an Israeli Counter-Terrorist Team*, by George Jonas

Munich, Steven Spielberg's latest work, concerns itself with the efforts of a team of Israeli agents to track down and kill Palestinian leaders allegedly responsible for masterminding the hostage-taking episode at the 1972 Olympic Games in Munich that resulted in the deaths of eleven Israeli athletes. As the bloody act of revenge proceeds, the team members grow increasingly skeptical about the morality and efficacy of their operation.

One is entitled to have ambivalent feelings about this film, but, in the end, it strikes me as an honest, relatively complicated and humane effort—in many ways, quite remarkable—and one that provides little comfort for defenders of the status quo, in Israel or elsewhere. *Munich* is a work that took considerable courage to make, as the genuine hostility it has evoked in reactionary quarters demonstrates. This was clearly not a film made with a commercial return in mind. Spielberg is more than a mere celebrity; he has a serious standpoint and, moreover, a definite commitment to craftsmanship. And that latter quality has consequences. To the extent that the filmmaker is artistically honest, this obliges him to make choices that take him beyond the limits of his conscious political and social outlook.

Avner (Eric Bana) is a Mossad agent in *Munich*, the son of a war hero and former bodyguard of the prime minister, Golda Meir, who awaits the birth of his first child. Claiming that the Munich tragedy "changes everything"—an obvious echo of the Bush administration's rhetoric following the September 11 terrorist attacks—Meir (Lynn Cohen) justifies authorizing a plan to assassinate Palestinian leaders around the world on the grounds that "Every civilization finds it necessary to negotiate compromises with its own values." Avner is asked to lead the assassination squad.

The eventual team, of which Avner is the youngest and at first most hesitant member, includes Steve (Daniel Craig), a bloody-minded South African; the Belgian Robert (Mathieu Kassovitz), a toymaker now charged with making bombs; a German Jew, Hans (Hanns Zischler), an antiques dealer and expert forger; and Carl (Ciarán Hinds), a self-described "worrier" and clean-up man.

The team, which has no official link to Mossad and acts autonomously, sets about its work in Europe. Without going into any more detail than necessary, Avner's group carries out a series of operations in Rome, Paris, Cyprus, Beirut and Athens. Initially the most sensitive about the nature of the mission, Avner becomes hardened by the experience. When one of his team remarks how strange it is "to think of yourself as an assassin," Avner cynically rejoins, "Think of yourself as something else, then." But events begin to wear on him.

Avner and others start questioning the proof that their targets indeed had anything to do with the Munich killings. All except Steve, the South African, a fascist type, who declares that "the only blood that matters to me is Jewish blood." Hans, on the other hand, points out that the Palestinians didn't invent bloodshed and terrorism. "How do you think we got the land from them in the first place?"

While in Athens, Avner and his team, claiming to be European leftists, unexpectedly share a room with a group of Palestinian bodyguards. Avner gets into a conversation in a hallway with one of them, Ali (Omar Metwally), who tells him that "European Reds" don't understand the significance of a homeland. Ali goes on: "We can wait forever. You don't know what it is not to have a home. Home is everything." The two groups share a common ideology, based on land and blood.

The Palestinians eventually become aware of the team's operations. The hunters are themselves hunted. Self-doubt increasingly plagues Avner's squad. Members of the group fall victim to attacks, one perhaps to suicide (after arguing, "Jews don't do wrong because our enemies do wrong ... We're supposed to be righteous.").

Back in Israel, Avner's mother (Gila Almagor), who lost her family to the Nazis, justifies his activities, without knowing their precise nature, by unconditionally defending the founding of Israel: "We had to take it because no one would ever give it to us. Whatever it took, whatever it takes, we have a place on earth at last."

But Avner, who has moved his wife and child to Brooklyn, finds no solace. He questions the ethical basis of his operation and comes to the conclusion, "There's no peace at the end of this." In a meeting with his Mossad controller, Ephraim (Geoffrey Rush), in New York, he once again demands evidence that the murdered men had anything to do with the Munich hostage-taking. Provided with only vague assurances, he rejects Ephraim's entreaties.

One can find fault with Spielberg and principal screenwriter Tony Kushner (*Angels in America*) on a number of grounds. Although there are references to the origins of the state of Israel, the film tends to suggest that the history of violence in the region began in Munich in 1972. In fact, the establishment of the Zionist state meant the expulsion of some 800,000 Palestinians. In 1946, Jews owned less than 12 percent of the land in the area that became Israeli territory; that figure rose to 77 percent after the 1948–49 war.

Palestinians fled their land in large measure out of fear of Zionist violence. In the notorious massacre at Deir Yassin in April 1948, Menachem Begin's Irgun group massacred 250 men, women and children. This widely publicized event was part of a deliberate effort to terrorize the Arabs and empty Palestine of its population. Over a two-year period from 1947 to 1949, the Zionists destroyed and depopulated more than 400 Arab villages, systematically replacing them with Jewish communities. By 1972, then, masses of Palestinians had been living miserably in refugee camps distributed throughout the region for more than two decades. They had only recently taken up arms against their condition.

The killing of the Israeli athletes was an atrocity (how many were killed by Palestinians and how many by German police snipers remains unknown), but the ultimate responsibility for the violence lies with the Zionist authorities and their backers in Washington and elsewhere.

Moreover, it is reasonable to assume, and research apparently backs this up, that the decision taken by Meir was only in part a specific response to the Munich events. These rather provided the moral and political pretext for the Israelis to eliminate a portion of the Palestinian leadership, many of whom had nothing whatsoever to do with the Olympic hostage-taking. Avner raises this issue in the film, but, again, the reference is only a fleeting one.

The notion of a timeless Jewish moral superiority to which the assassination team's operation supposedly represents an affront must also be rejected. To the extent that a considerable portion of the Jewish intelligentsia and proletariat had links to progressive social movements (a major impetus for the Nazis' anti-Semitism), this was due to specific historic and social, not "racial," circumstances. In a tragically ironic manner, the evolution of Israeli society and its official racism and oppression of the Palestinians have put paid once and for all to the idea that the Jews are the "chosen people" in any social sense. It turns out there are poor and rich Jews, oppressed and oppressor Jews, revolutionary and fascist-minded Jews, just as there are such categories among every other ethnic group on the face of the earth.

That having been said, *Munich* is considerably more than the sum of its obvious and not unexpected limitations. Spielberg and Kushner have accomplished something important and valuable. The film represents an indictment of the politics of retaliation and revenge. It painstakingly demonstrates that such killing has the most horrifying consequences, for both the victim and the perpetrator. Spielberg is deliberately unsparing in this regard, and it is undoubtedly one of the elements that outrages his right-wing critics: the victims are people too, who die in painful and terrible ways. All the deaths are horrible, including of course the deaths of the Israeli athletes in Munich. Spielberg and Kushner take each one singly and carefully. The murder of a woman assassin is particularly devastating, one of the most chilling such scenes in recent memory. A great deal of thought and sensitivity has gone into this work.

The film asks: How can human beings like Avner and his colleagues proceed on such a killing spree, particularly if they begin to doubt the official claims that justify it? Or, as the film's production notes put it, the team members begin to ask: "Who exactly are we killing? Can it be justified? Will it stop the terror?" Are these not critical themes today, especially in the US? If "left" opponents of the film feel that these are unworthy or insignificant questions, let them explain themselves.

Critics claim that the actual members of Mossad's assassination squads (who, incidentally, murdered an entirely innocent man, a Moroccan immigrant living in Norway, in 1973) never felt the qualms that Avner and his team experience. One can only reply, then they should have, and this is something the artists have contributed, to their credit.

In any event, the existence of the "refusenik" movement in the Israeli military, including more than 1,200 soldiers and reservists who have refused to serve in the Occupied Territories, reveals that this is a burning issue. One of a group of twenty-seven Israeli air force pilots in 2003, which issued a letter declaring its refusal to take part in military operations in the West Bank and Gaza Strip, told a reporter from *Yedioth Ahronoth*, "Something deep broke inside me. I don't sleep well at night.

How many more have to be killed until we realize that we are committing crimes?"[87] Is this not Avner? Spielberg and Kushner are obviously sensitive to this.

Spielberg has gone to considerable lengths, in the face of criticism from pro-Zionist elements, to affirm his love for Israel, his dedication to its existence and so forth. Again, this is entirely to be expected. But the film hardly ennobles the Zionist cause. Are we supposed to celebrate each violent death? Only the most depraved elements in the audience will do so. Whatever the director's intentions, *Munich* traces out a course of official violence and criminality, which only begets more violence.

Clearly, the events of September 11 and their aftermath resonate strongly in the film. A section of the American liberal intelligentsia has concluded that the terrorist attacks in New York City and Washington provide justification for the most deplorable and sinister activities by the US state.

And Spielberg-Kushner also hint at the outlook that for some Israelis and their supporters around the world justifies the violence against the Palestinians, as well as its historical origins. One must look in particular to the words of Avner's mother, when she explains about her arrival in Palestine, in the wake of the Holocaust: "Whatever it took, whatever it takes ..." This hardness, formed in part in the concentration camps, while tragically understandable, is a perverse and ultimately poisonous outlook. A portion of the victims, fresh from the horrors in Europe, concluded: "Enough of that rubbish about the goodness of man! Look at what happened to us! We know what humanity is like, rotten, cruel. Well, we too can be rotten and cruel. Whatever it takes ..." In a terrible twist of fate, some of the victims of the worst crime in history absorbed the outlook of their tormentors. Humanism, the Enlightenment, the traditions of socialism and progressive thought were thrown out the window by these people. A new appeal to blood was launched, only this time to "Jewish blood."

In a painful sense, both the Israelis and Palestinians are victims of history, victims of the twentieth century and its thwarted hopes. Avner is assuredly not driven by personal spite or ambition. Something harsh and terrible was taken out of the Nazi camps. His mother's face is that of someone deeply, irretrievably scarred by the past. And one always has the sense

---

[87] Chris Marsden, "Israel: Air Force pilots reject participation in targeted assassinations," World Socialist Web Site, December 4, 2003. Available: http://www.wsws.org/articles/2003/dec2003/isra-d04.shtml

that these people are trying terribly hard to convince themselves of the righteousness of their cause—in some cases, fortunately, without success. Kushner explains that *Munich* "became more and more the story of a man whose decency just won't let him off the hook."

The Zionist appeal to blood and homeland finds an echo within the Palestinian nationalist movement as well. When Ali rejects the program of the "European Reds," internationalism and socialism, he shares the same debased and reactionary outlook as the Zionists. *Munich*, inadvertently perhaps, points to the bankruptcy of terrorism as a method of struggle of the oppressed. In the murky world portrayed in the film of international terrorism and counterterrorism, one never knows precisely who's who. Avner is never certain whether his information from "Papa" and his group originates ultimately with the CIA, Mossad itself (desiring to remain officially removed from the team's operations), a section of the Palestinian movement attempting to settle accounts, and so forth.

Terrorism is almost inevitably associated today with the politics of tribalism and communalism, in the final analysis with the effort to pressure the great powers on behalf of the special privileges of this or that national bourgeois or petty-bourgeois layer. The working class struggle for socialism, on the other hand, requires the greatest degree of openness, clarity and mass participation and consciousness.

Munich has come under venomous attack by right-wing forces in the US and Israel, particularly the former. As Michelle Goldberg explains in her "The War on 'Munich'" (*Spiegel Online*), the campaign began well before the film appeared in the cinema. Leon Wieseltier, literary critic of the *New Republic*, the fiercely pro-Zionist liberal publication, vented his spleen against Spielberg in early December.

The film's "tedium," Wieseltier declared, "is finally owed to the fact that, for all its vanity about its own courage, the film is afraid of itself. It is soaked in the sweat of its idea of evenhandedness." He continues: "The screenplay is substantially the work of Tony Kushner, whose hand is easily recognizable in the crudely schematic quality of the drama, and also in something more. The film has no place in its heart for Israel ... Zionism, in this film, is just anti-anti-Semitism. The necessity of the Jewish state is acknowledged, but necessity is a very weak form of legitimacy."[88]

---

[88]   Leon Wieseltier, "The case against *Munich*," *Jewish World Review*, December 12, 2005. Available: http://www.jewishworldreview.com/1205/munich.php3

Wieseltier perceives the film's dangerous applicability to the US following September 11, 2001. "The Israeli response to Black September marked the birth of contemporary counterterrorism, and it is difficult not to see *Munich* as a parable of American policy since September 11. 'Every civilization finds it necessary to negotiate compromises with its own values,' Golda Meir grimly concludes early in the film. Yet the film proclaims that terrorists and counterterrorists are alike. 'When we learn to act like them, we will defeat them!' declares one of Avner's men, played by Daniel Craig, already with a license to kill. Worse, *Munich* prefers a discussion of counterterrorism to a discussion of terrorism; or it thinks that they are the same discussion. This is an opinion that only people who are not responsible for the safety of other people can hold."[89] People "responsible for the safety of other people" such as George W. Bush and Ariel Sharon, presumably, two of the world's leading political arsonists.

Wieseltier's defense of American and Israeli "counterterrorism," the policies of aggression and repression in the Middle East, was seconded by David Brooks, right-wing columnist for the *New York Times*. Brooks asserted that Spielberg badly misreads the Middle East because he denies the existence of evil—i.e., Islamic radicalism. Brooks comments, "Because he will not admit the existence of evil, as it really exists, Spielberg gets reality wrong. ... In Spielberg's Middle East the only way to achieve peace is by renouncing violence. But in the real Middle East the only way to achieve peace is through military victory over the fanatics, accompanied by compromise between the reasonable elements on each side."[90] From the safety of his *Times* column, Brooks consistently advances the most bloody-minded and brutal conceptions.

In fact, hostile critics were made so anxious by Spielberg's film and its implications that they began denouncing it at the time of the release of his last film, *War of the Worlds*. Edward Rothstein, also of the *Times*, complained last July about *Munich*, simply on the basis of hearsay. He wrote: "It is said to begin with the murders of Israeli Olympic athletes by Palestinian terrorists in 1972—an attack Martian-like in its ambitions. But the analogy, Mr. Spielberg's comments suggest, will be undermined: injustices suffered by the attackers will need to be understood and their victims' tactics questioned." The *Times*

---

[89] Ibid.

[90] David Brooks, "What 'Munich' Left Out," *The New York Times*, December 11, 2005. Available: http://query.nytimes.com/gst/fullpage.html?res=F30A13F83A550C728DD DAB0994DD404482

columnist added, "Perhaps that idea of terrorists with a cause and defenders with doubts influenced the discomfort felt in the current film [*War of the Worlds*] as well."[91] Earlier this week, it should be added, Rothstein predictably followed up with his own ignorant attack on *Munich*, in the pages of the *Times*.

This reactionary hectoring is entirely to the credit of Spielberg and Kushner. The latter has described himself as "both a God-believing Jew and a historical materialist socialist humanist agnostic. I want the State of Israel to exist (since it does anyway) ... and at the same time ... I think the founding of the State of Israel was for the Jewish people a historical, moral, political calamity." These are ambiguities that cry out for resolution, but nonetheless they contain the possibility of insight, in opposition to the ideological "death squad" represented by Wieseltier, Brooks and Rothstein.

Left and Arab critics have also come out against *Munich*. Again, many correct political points can be made against the film's liberal outlook and its serious omissions in regard to the history of Israel and the plight of the Palestinians. But to suggest that Spielberg and Kushner have produced nothing but a "Celebration of the Israeli Killing Machine," and other such comments, is absurd and unworthy. This is not to view the film's images, but simply to watch one's preconceptions flash in front of one's eyes.

The claim is made that nothing goes on in *Munich* other than the "humanization of Israeli killers." Again, this is patently untrue, but, in any event, art, alas, confronts the unavoidable task of humanizing. Serious art cannot function in any other manner. To portray a human being honestly and deeply requires a high degree of artistic objectivity. What do we ask of the artist? Precisely that he or she sensitizes us to the human personality and condition in all its complexities. If not that, then what? People who want the opposite of humanization want propaganda films, which have a very limited value.

We will be told: ah, so you want to humanize Bush or Sharon! To "humanize" is not to "condone." The actions carried out by Avner and his group are horrible and criminal, and that fact emerges from the drama itself to any sensitive viewer. Anyone not disturbed by the events, or who finds them attractive or exciting in any fashion, had better see a specialist. In any case, a Mossad agent is not the same thing as a mastermind of imperialist policy. In his own way, Avner too is a victim of historical circumstances. And he ultimately responds along those lines. We would ask the critics who claim

---

that *Munich* is mere Zionist apologia, based on your conceptions, what kind of film would you make?

Criticism on this score amounts to empty moralizing of the liberal-anarchist variety. Shall we have no films about US soldiers in Iraq because of the crimes carried out there? Those soldiers, even the ones committing terrible acts, are also victims of imperialism. If their stories, and the horrors perpetrated, are not represented, how is mass revulsion and shame to develop in America?

Of course the Palestinian viewpoint must be seen and heard. *Paradise Now*, directed by Palestinian filmmaker Hany Abu-Assad, about the making of suicide bombers in the Occupied Territories, deserves a far wider audience than it will currently obtain in North America. A film about the victims of Deir Yassin, or the fate of Qibya, the Jordanian village whose residents were massacred by Sharon's unit 101 in October 1953, is entirely in order.

However, if the Jews *as a people* in Israel are guilty of such sins, like the American population presumably in the case of Iraq, that they cannot even be represented in artistic works, then this leads to the most pessimistic and bleak conclusions. We would prefer a hundred *Munichs*, with its faults, to such dire and blockheaded "left" thinking.

Spielberg has an instinctive feeling for history. His next project is about Abraham Lincoln. A radicalization is under way in America, and it will be difficult to stop. Once people get a taste for ideas, politics and history, it will prove contagious.

Terence Davies's *Of Time and the City*: What the Filmmakers Now See

World Socialist Web Site; September 24, 2008

Directed by Terence Davies

Of Time and the City is an intensely personal, but also socially perceptive film by veteran director Terence Davies (*The Long Day Closes*, *House of Mirth*). Davies has made a documentary of a sort, a tribute to his native city of Liverpool, where he lived from his birth in 1945 until he left in 1973.

He has organized black-and-white photos, newsreel footage and contemporary video, beneath a soundtrack composed of classical and popular music, radio programs, oral history and his own intense narration, into a highly individual response to the culture, history and evolution of a major city.

There are many images that appear on the screen, but more than anything else, *Of Time and the City* evokes the Liverpool of Davies's childhood and early adolescence. He was raised a devout Catholic, and the Church figures prominently in his memories. The narrator speaks of his dream of finding peace in his struggling soul, struggling with his sexuality in particular, a dream thwarted by the Church. About religion, he concludes, "It's all a lie," and notes that he became a "born-again atheist."

Days at the beach ("The world was young and oh how we laughed"), football crowds and football scores on radio, radio programs with bizarre sexual *double entendre* (in the 1950s, when homosexuality was illegal in Britain). Narrow streets, long terraced rows of small houses. Footage from the postwar period of women carrying bundles of laundry on their heads down the street to communal laundries. Women at those wash-houses, chatting and singing, while they scrub out the dirt.

And Davies cites Friedrich Engels somewhere here, a portion of this passage from *The Condition of the Working Class in England* (1845): "Every great city has one or more slums, where the working class is crowded together. True, poverty often dwells in hidden alleys close to the palaces of the rich; but, in general, a separate territory has been assigned to it, where, removed from the sight of the happier classes, it may struggle along as it can."

At an early age, Davies discovers the cinema, which replaces the ritual and splendor of the Church with its own. Gregory Peck arrives at the Ritz Theatre in Birkenhead across the river from Liverpool. "We gorged ourselves on musicals, Westerns, and melodramas," the voice-over tells us.

Rightly so, the soundtrack includes "Dirty Old Town," with its evocation of factory walls, canals and the gas works. (Although the version by The Pogues is superior to the one used in the film.)

The monarchy appears—the future Queen Elizabeth's marriage in 1947 and her coronation in 1953. We fear the worst and even prepare ourselves for a somewhat sentimental, national-popular approach on Davies's part. But he surprises and pleases us when he is quite unsparing on "Betty and Phil and a thousand flunkies." He notes the vast sums "wasted on the monarchy ... privileged to the last," while the rest of the population, Davies drives home with deep feeling, "survived in some of the worst slums in Europe!"

Those slums are cleared in the 1960s and replaced with high-rise housing estates, which soon become new and perhaps more depressing dwellings. "We had hoped for paradise, we got the *anus mundi* [the anus of the world]." Two young girls push a stroller through a wasteland of rubble, broken glass. He refers in passing to "Municipal architecture—dispiriting at the best of times, but, when combined with the British genius for creating the dismal, makes for a cityscape that is anything but Elysian."

Of Time and the City is unabashedly, unashamedly elegiac, so much so that it's almost impossible to be offended. "The golden moments pass and leave no trace," he declares, quoting Chekhov. Davies has no use for many aspects of the modern city, where "cocktails are consumed in Babylon" and well-heeled diners eat in restaurants located in "deconsecrated churches."

The film is valuable not because of its carefully thought-through approach to history and social life. No, not at all. This is a poetic version, but genuinely felt and elegantly expressed. What Davies is largely paying tribute to, although he probably doesn't recognize it, is the socialist working class culture that existed in cities like Liverpool into the 1970s. That "dirty old town" is gone, but so too is much of the parochialism and insularity associated with it.

Waltz With Bashir: "Memory Takes Us Where We Need to Go"

World Socialist Web Site; December 24, 2008

Directed by Ari Folman

The 1982 Israeli invasion of Lebanon killed an estimated 18,000 people. The Israelis also collaborated with the fascist Phalangists in the massacre of some 3,000 Palestinian men, women and children at the Sabra and Shatila refugee camps. The brutal operation was part of a global counteroffensive by the ruling classes, initiated in 1979–80 under the Jimmy Carter administration and broadly extended by Ronald Reagan. The year 1982 also witnessed the Malvinas War, ferociously prosecuted by the government of Margaret Thatcher, elected in May 1979.

Israeli director Ari Folman's *Waltz With Bashir* was one of the most extraordinary and haunting films at the Toronto film festival this year. Folman has made an animated film that ends with the tragic events at Sabra and Shatila. The director says "it's a completely autobiographical film."

The film unfolds like this: a friend tells Folman of a recurring dream in which he is chased by a pack of twenty-six snarling, vicious dogs. The friend, Boaz, is certain it has something to do with his experiences as a soldier during the Lebanon invasion. When the Israelis were entering villages, they first "liquidated" the dogs, so they couldn't give warning. Boaz shot twenty-six dogs during the invasion of Lebanon.

Folman, however, discovers he no longer has any memory of the Lebanon fighting. "That's not stored in my system," he says. Only one image remains, of him and his comrades, naked, calmly swimming in the sea. The absence of memory disturbs him, and he determines to track down those he fought with and fill in the blank space. "Memory takes us where we need to go," he explains.

He first visits an old friend, Carmi, who now lives in Holland and has made a fortune selling falafel. Carmi remembers one of his first experiences in Lebanon, he and his fellow Israeli soldiers "shooting like lunatics" at an old Mercedes, in which they later discover the bodies of a whole family.

Folman explains, "I can't remember anything." He retains this one image. "What image?" asks his friend. "You're in it." This is the image of the soldiers emerging from the sea. Carmi says he doesn't remember anything about the massacre at Sabra and Shatila. "That's not stored in my system," he says, echoing Folman.

In a taxi in the Netherlands, "everything comes back" to Folman. He continues to visit old comrades and they tell him about their experiences in Lebanon, many of them harrowing.

Folman eventually recounts how he and his unit marched into West Beirut, following the assassination of Phalange leader Bashir Gemayel (the "Bashir" in the title), and how they took up positions around the Sabra and Shatila camps. The Phalangist forces arrived and claimed they were entering the refugee camps to "purge" them of Palestinian fighters. However, the vast majority of the latter had been evacuated on ships to Tunisia two weeks earlier.

Folman's film makes clear that the Israeli command post was elevated high enough to see what was going inside the camps. For three days the fascist forces carried out their killings. A well-known Israeli television reporter learned of the massacre and telephoned Defense Minister Ariel Sharon. The future prime minister responded, "Thanks for bringing it to my attention. Happy New Year." Sharon was later found guilty by an official inquiry of indirect responsibility for "ignoring the danger of bloodshed and revenge" and for "not taking appropriate measures to prevent bloodshed."

A friend, a therapist, asks Folman, "What did you do?" He explains that he and his comrades sent up flares, which helped the Phalangists in their murderous work. "You took on the role of a Nazi, unwillingly." The television reporter notes that the sight of Palestinians coming out of the camp with their hands above their heads reminded him of the famous image of Jews surrendering in the Warsaw Ghetto.

Waltz With Bashir is done with considerable artistry and intelligence. The images are deeply disturbing, hallucinatory, including Folman's recurring memory of the unclothed soldiers, armed, emerging from the sea in front of a row of Beirut high-rises, under a frighteningly yellow sky.

An exposure of Zionist crimes, or a film simply this painfully honest, would be almost unthinkable in the American film industry at present. It will be interesting to see what happens to the film when it opens in the US in late December.

In an interview, Folman explained that *Waltz With Bashir* "follows what I went through from the moment I realized that there were some major parts in my life completely missing from my memory. ... I discovered a lot of heavy stuff regarding my past and meanwhile, during those years, my wife and I brought three kids into this world. This makes you wonder, maybe I am doing all this for my sons. When they grow up and watch the film, it might help them make the right decisions, meaning not to take part in any war, whatsoever."[92]

He added, "I believe that there are thousands of Israeli ex-soldiers that kept their war memories deeply repressed. They might live the rest of their lives like that, without anything ever happening. But it could always burst out one day, causing who knows what to happen to them. That's what post-traumatic stress disorder is all about."[93]

For many people, over the past few decades, a variety of realities, social iniquities, crimes haven't apparently been "stored in the system." But they were there, nonetheless. Other processes, moods and illusions helped to exclude them from consciousness. What makes the truth about things come flooding in? A complicated combination of subjective effort

---

[92] Available: http://emanuellevy.com/interviews/
waltz-with-bashir-interview-with-director-ari-folman-3/

[93] Available: http://www.festival-cannes.fr/assets/Image/Direct/025319.pdf

and external stimuli, perhaps in the form of new and shocking events (in Folman's case, perhaps a new war in Lebanon, the occupation of Iraq?). The subjective effort itself is objectively driven, an indication that whatever social facts underpinned and sustained the existing belief system have given way to something else.

Waltz With Bashir is one of the most conscious expressions of this complex process.

Luchino Visconti's *Senso*: Drama and History

World Socialist Web Site; June 3, 2010

Senso, the 1954 film directed by Luchino Visconti about the Italian national unification struggle in the nineteenth century, is a beautiful and important work.

Visconti (1906–76) was one of Italy's leading filmmakers in the postwar period. He gravitated from his early neorealistic work (*Ossessione, La Terra Trema*) toward more elaborate historical and psychological portrayals in a series of remarkable films: especially *Senso, The Leopard* (based on the novel by Giuseppe Tomasi di Lampedusa, [1963]), *Death in Venice* (based on the Thomas Mann novella, [1971]) and *Conversation Piece* (1975).

Visconti, descended from Milanese aristocracy on his father's side and great industrial wealth on his mother's, turned to the left in the 1930s. He began his film career in France working on Jean Renoir's *A Day in the Country* (1937). He also declared himself a Marxist around this time and maintained a long relationship with the Italian Communist Party (in 1944, he was nearly executed by the Fascists for harboring partisans). Visconti never made a secret of his homosexuality.

At the time of its release in the mid-1950s, *Senso* was criticized by some on the Italian left for its abandonment of the tenets of neorealism, which favored the naturalistic treatment (in black and white) of working class or peasant subjects, often using non-professional performers.

In the brilliantly hued and operatic *Senso* (with a cast of movie actors), an Italian countess, whose cousin is a radical Italian nationalist leader, falls head over heels for a handsome young soldier in the occupying Austrian army in Venice in 1866. She betrays the Italian cause out of love and lust, only to discover that the Austrian has been using her for her wealth and prestige. She takes revenge ...

Senso has been painstakingly restored, under the auspices of The Film Foundation. The organization explains: "Visconti and his cinematographers Aldo Graziati (who tragically died during the shoot) and Robert Krasker fashioned a palette that was both delicate and vivid, rich in its historical associations and its evocations of landscape painting of the period. For that reason alone, *Senso* has been extremely difficult to restore, and the shrinkage and overall damage to its original three-strip Technicolor camera negatives have only increased the level of difficulty. Now, with the advent of digital techniques the Cineteca di Bologna and L'Immagine Ritrovata have joined forces to restore this magnificent film to its original grandeur."[94]

The effort has been worthwhile. The color and detail are extraordinary. One does not see scenes and décor like this every day. Although, as French critic André Bazin argued at the time, "Visconti continuously seeks to impose upon this magnificent, beautifully composed, almost picturesque setting the rigor and, most importantly, the unobtrusiveness of a documentary."[95]

Famously, director Visconti persuaded Ingrid Bergman and Marlon Brando to play the leading roles, but the producer preferred Alida Valli and Farley Granger. In fact, both Valli and Granger perform very well. Few films bring out as clearly as this one does the complex relationship between public and private life, between political and personal commitment, as well as various means by which people fool themselves about their lives and desires. It is also an extraordinary historical panorama.

Senso begins, sumptuously, in the opera. The national and social elements are distributed throughout the various levels of the Venetian opera house: the Austrian occupiers in the orchestra seats, the Italian elites in the boxes, the middle classes farther up, and so on. A performance of Verdi's *Il Trovatore* ("To arms! To arms!" cries the chorus) inspires the nationalist elements; they shower the Austrians with leaflets demanding their departure and calling for the liberation of Italy.

---

[94] Kent Jones, "Senso" (San Francisco International Film Festival, 2011). Available: http://history.sffs.org/films/film_details. php?id=4445&search_by=3&searchfield=1957

[95] André Bazin, *Bazin at Work: Major Essays and Reviews From the Forties and Fifties.* Trans. Alain Piette and Bert Cardullo. Ed. Bert Cardullo. (New York: Routledge, 1997), 161.

One of the Austrians in the crowd, Franz Mahler (Granger), casually insults Italian national honor. Marquis Roberto Ussoni (Massimo Girotti), a leader of the Italian volunteer forces, challenges him to a duel. Ussoni's cousin, the married Countess Livia Serpieri (Valli), arranges an encounter with Mahler and implores him not to proceed with the duel. Ussoni is exiled for a year instead. He hands over a large amount of money to Livia, to be used to buy weapons for the volunteer forces.

Livia and Mahler begin an obsessive affair, although, before too long, his ardor seems to cool. Eventually, fighting between the Austrians and Italians breaks out, and Mahler is called away. However, he wants no part of the war. Desperate, he shows up at Livia's country estate, where she has been sent by her husband to keep her out of harm's way. Mahler needs money to bribe a doctor so he can obtain a medical discharge. Livia gives him the nationalists' cash, and he leaves. Ussoni's forces and the rest of the Italians suffer defeat at the hands of the Austrians, although the latter are clearly losing the struggle and the new Italian bourgeois-aristocratic alliance, including Livia's husband, is gaining the upper hand.

From Verona, Mahler writes to Livia, explaining how he managed to get out of the army, telling her that he still loves her and insisting that she not visit him. She disobeys and flies immediately to the Austrian, discovering him—drunk and dissolute—in the arms of a prostitute. He insults and abuses her, accuses himself of "cowardice and vice," and finally kicks her out of the apartment. Livia goes to the Austrian high command with the compromising letter, which proves Mahler is a deserter. Punishment is meted out.

Visconti had many profound concerns when he directed *Senso*. Basing himself on the work of Antonio Gramsci, among others, on Italian history, the filmmaker means to indict the Italian bourgeoisie for the counter-revolutionary deal it came to with the landed gentry during the Risorgimento and the betrayal of the democratic, egalitarian aspirations of the people. The Italian elite, personified by Serpieri and others, carries out national unification in mortal fear of the "lower classes."

Ussoni, on the other hand, seems to represent the impotent, demagogic "radical" elements, never short of phrases, but unable or unwilling to organize the mass of the population. He tells his cousin, "We have no rights now, Livia, only duties. We must forget our own interests," but the words are hollow. He is useful to those on top of Italian society for his ability to stir up the crowd but dispensed with when his services are no longer necessary.

Italian censorship apparently made Visconti remove a scene in which Ussoni attempts to supplement the Italian (Piedmontese) army of King Victor Emmanuel II with his volunteers, and is told that his units are of little use. Ussoni, according to film historian C. Paul Sellors, "responds in disgust, articulating that the war is little more than a royal land grab."[96] Another writer on cinema history, Millicent Marcus, argues that this scene's excision "succeeded in removing the film's true revolutionary sting."[97]

Presumably, in Visconti's conception, in this "failed revolution" of the 1860s, the ultimate triumph of fascism under Mussolini finds a foreshadowing. Moreover, by further extension, Visconti intended the work as a condemnation of the newly restored Italian "democratic" government, propped up and financed by American imperialism. Of course, the fact that the party with which he aligned himself, the Communist Party, was principally responsible for the ability of the discredited and despised Italian bourgeoisie to maintain itself in power at the end of World War II was not something that Visconti proved able to treat.

There is another important side to *Senso*, which is complicated, and perhaps several viewings of the film are required to satisfy oneself as to Visconti's own position.

Livia throws herself headlong into the affair with Mahler (named for one of Visconti's favorite composers, intriguingly enough). As an unhappy wife trapped in a loveless marriage, no longer so young, and involved with a handsome young man, Livia's conduct is understandable up to a point.

Of course, when she hands Mahler the 3,000 florins and deprives the volunteer forces of arms with which to fight the Austrian enemy, Livia crosses a line. (The scene is unforgettable, as Mahler distractedly mouths, "My love, my love!," while he concentrates on scooping up the precious gold coins.)

Visconti paints the early stages of the relationship in a manner that underscores Livia's heedlessness in particular. She says in a voice-over: "Time stood still. Nothing existed but my guilty pleasure at hearing him talk and laugh." Later, Franz and Livia have this conversation:

---

96 Paul C. Sellors, "Senso." In *The Cinema of Italy*, ed. Giorgio Bertellini (London: Wallflower Press, 2004), 68.

97 Millicent Marcus, *Italian Film in the Light of Neorealism* (Princeton: Princeton University Press, 1986), 167.

Franz: For Countess Serpieri the past doesn't exist. There's only now and tomorrow.

Livia: Only now.

Franz: Is there no tomorrow?

Livia: If someone told me "You've only today—there'll be no tomorrow," I would feel as if a doctor has said "You're dying. You've only a few hours left to live." And now I know it's true. There's only now, Franz. We'll have no tomorrow.

In my opinion, when Visconti has his character repeat these melodramatic lines, he has not forgotten their context. Livia has been placed by the film in a definite situation: the cousin of a leader of the "national revolution," charged with a considerable responsibility herself in an increasingly threatening political-military situation. Individuals don't merely act in this way or that in the abstract, they choose *to do one thing instead of doing another*.

Visconti is not moralizing, in my opinion, but arguing and showing that there is a desperate, delusional element to Livia's conduct (the fact that the "decadent," cynical Mahler cannot genuinely reciprocate the feelings only emphasizes this). The director has already hinted at Livia's half-hearted commitment to the cause, her susceptibility to blandishments, her vanity and selfishness. People are not simply "swept away by uncontrollable passion," the film suggests; there may also be a semi-calculated desire to evade challenging problems and responsibilities by giving oneself up to emotional excess. Extreme "sensuality" here is something of a refuge for a certain type of personality from a difficult social situation, and, at any rate, a dead end. At the conclusion, we assume Livia will return to her unappealing, repressive husband.

Rarely has this problem of "the political and the personal" been addressed so forthrightly, and in the context of enormous events. Visconti is a unique figure, in many ways. Critics from the French "New Wave" (Jean-Luc Godard) and elsewhere complained that *Senso* suffered from a lack of spontaneity. The film does stagger and stiffen occasionally, one feels, under the weight of its ambitions, and its ideological debt to Gramsci, Georg Lukacs (on the nature of realism) and others. And one should not forget the pressure of the deeply false theories ("socialist realism," "proletarian culture") that was still being exerted on artists in and around the Stalinist milieu.

On the whole, Visconti's determined attempt to make lifelike, dramatically convincing sense of individual human behavior as the expression of historical and social processes is both illuminating and liberating. This is the way *toward life*, not away from it.

Bazin, a political opponent of Marxism, somewhat grudgingly remarked: "Visconti claims that in *Senso* he wanted to show the 'melodrama' (read: the opera) of life. If this was his intention, his film is a complete success. ... *Senso* has the density and the import of reality."[98]

Indeed, while watching *Senso*, one muses: If only contemporary film writers and directors could be compelled to watch Visconti's work ten, fifteen or twenty times ...

Of course, fantasies aside, the process doesn't work that way. The chief problem with today's filmmakers is not their lack of knowledge of past filmmaking, although this *is* a problem, but their lack of important experiences, deep thoughts and feelings, and, consequently, things to say.

Even those "students of cinema history" among contemporary directors, when they attempt to remake an older work, for example, or emulate it in some manner, generally botch the job.

The principal task is not to reshoot a significant film from another period, or even necessarily pay homage to it, but to adopt a similar seriousness toward contemporary life as the "classical" director did toward his or her own time. This is largely missing.

---

[98] Bazin, 161.

Anonymous: An Ignorant Assault on Shakespeare

World Socialist Web Site; November 23, 2011

Directed by Roland Emmerich; written by John Orloff

Roland Emmerich prepared himself to film a story about the greatest literary figure in the English language by directing *Independence Day*, *Godzilla*, *The Patriot* and *The Day After Tomorrow*. In 2000, I commented that *The Patriot*, with Mel Gibson, was "a ridiculous work, which could only be taken seriously in a period like ours in which ideas and ideals are held in such generally low esteem."

In both his disaster and horror films and his misguided foray into the history of the American Revolution, the German-born Emmerich has shown himself given to bombast, simplification and crudity. In *Anonymous*, he has easily matched his previous unfortunate efforts.

The premise of the new film is that English dramatist and poet William Shakespeare (1564–1616) was not the author of the three dozen or so plays attributed to him, rather they were written by Edward de Vere, the seventeenth Earl of Oxford (1550–1604). This claim has been around for more than a century, and has been thoroughly refuted by both internal (Oxford was not a remarkable poet, while the real Shakespeare was) and external evidence (personal and historical facts too numerous to mention). Whether or not Emmerich and his screenwriter, John Orloff, actually subscribe to the theory is unclear. Orloff may, but one suspects that Emmerich, while he defends the Oxfordian thesis in public, could hardly care less. The film is merely another opportunity to display his questionable inventiveness.

To recount the convoluted plot of *Anonymous* is to discredit it. A work entitled "Anonymous" is playing at a contemporary New York City theater. Derek Jacobi marches onstage and presents a sort of prologue, in which he casts doubt that Shakespeare, the mere son of "a glove maker" and a "grammar school" graduate, could have produced such a magnificent body of work. There is a "darker story" to tell, he somberly informs us.

From there we are taken back to a computer-generated London circa 1600, in the latter days of the reign of the officially childless Elizabeth I (Vanessa Redgrave), a period dominated by political intrigue surrounding the question of her successor. Elizabeth's Secretary of State and chief spymaster, Robert Cecil (Edward Hogg), is conspiring to bring James VI of Scotland (eventually James I of England)—the son of Mary, Queen of Scots—to the English throne.

Opposed to Cecil are a number of important aristocratic figures, centrally the Earl of Essex (Sam Reid) and the Earl of Southampton (Xavier Samuel). A more circumspect ally of theirs against the accession of James is the Earl of Oxford (Rhys Ifans), who was raised by William Cecil (David Thewlis), also a key advisor to Queen Elizabeth, and against whom William's son and replacement, the aforementioned Robert, a villainous hunchback, bears considerable enmity.

As the story unfolds, we learn that Oxford had an affair as a teenager with the younger Elizabeth (Joely Richardson, Redgrave's daughter) and fathered a son by her (who also plays a prominent part in the story), that he was blackmailed into marrying Anne Cecil—and giving up playwriting—in exchange for covering up a crime he committed and, most extraordinarily, that Oxford is himself the illegitimate son of Elizabeth, so that incest tops off the whole lovely business.

Meanwhile, as they say, the playwright Ben Jonson (Sebastian Armesto) is recruited by Oxford in the present (i.e., 1600 or so) to introduce the latter's plays, old and new (according to the film, the earl, a prodigy in every way, wrote *A Midsummer Night's Dream* at the age of eight!), into the London theater, while putting his (Jonson's) name on them. Through his dramas Oxford hopes to elevate Essex (and lower Cecil and James) in the eyes of the population (the "mob") and the queen herself. Jonson agrees to put the works in circulation, but draws back from assigning his name to them. An upstart, semiliterate buffoon of an actor, William Shakespeare (Rafe Spall), is not so modest and begins to take credit for Oxford's works.

Anonymous climaxes with the staging of Shakespeare's (Oxford's) *Richard III*, a tragedy with a deformed evildoer at its center (intended to remind contemporaries of Robert Cecil), and the Earl of Essex's rebellion, in February 1601, which has disastrous consequences for a number of the film's central figures.

Emmerich's "dark" film is, first of all, a deeply mean-spirited work. I will leave to the psychologist the task of determining why a couple of demonstrably mediocre contemporary artists feel obliged to portray the greatest single collection of dramatists in the history of the English language (Shakespeare, Jonson, Christopher Marlowe and a number of lesser lights, including Thomas Nashe and Thomas Dekker) as fakers, thugs, imbeciles, informers and worse. Can one detect hints of jealousy and self-justification?

The depiction of Shakespeare is the most stupid and offensive. Does it really strengthen the case for the Earl of Oxford's or anyone else's authorship of the famous thirty-seven plays to present the generally recognized author as a semiliterate braggart, drunk and ... murderer?

When *Anonymous* is not unpleasant and noisy, it is generally tedious and clichéd. Scenes of Mermaid Tavern regulars carousing, Shakespeare "wenching," the Cecils conspiring, Essex and Southampton proudly, nobly riding and striding (their silly scenes manage to bring to mind the costume drama hilariously parodied by Steve Coogan and Rob Brydon in *The Trip*: "Gentlemen, to bed, we arise at dawn!"), the groundlings oohing and ahhing at the Globe Theatre, etc., are taken from a manual of Elizabethan stereotypes.

A good many talented performers are disgracefully wasted here, including Ifans, Thewlis, Redgrave, Hogg and Jacobi. Redgrave, who generally appears in command even in minor or undistinguished roles, is unconvincing and at times simply distasteful as the increasingly senile monarch. Ifans, a fine comic actor, has an impossible job, of representing the Earl of Oxford as a brilliant, lady-killing aristocratic martyr to Elizabethan police-state oppression, with the time on his hands to pen *Hamlet, King Lear* and the rest of the magisterial works. The whole thing is preposterous.

What does it say about the contemporary Hollywood elite that in its empty-headed fantasies about the Elizabethan era it heaps scorn on the possibility that the son of a lowly glove maker and a grammar school graduate could have created the remarkable works in question, and instead prefers a jaded aristocrat from one of the most distinguished families in England?

Emmerich and Orloff like to present any hostile reaction to their effort as proof that they have upset the academic-Shakespeare industry applecart with a "controversial" and "courageous" work. Confronted with the film's idiocies, they fall back to their second line of defense, the pseudo-postmodernist argument that history and historical movies are all made up anyway, so why should anyone be irritated with them?

In any event, there are inaccuracies in Shakespeare, Orloff is quick to point out. "Now Shakespeare plays with history all over the place. Those plays are not history; they are drama. ... We're just following the master," he told an interviewer. What can one say?

As Holger Syme, Associate Professor, Department of English, University of Toronto, and Chair, Department of English and Drama, University of

Toronto-Mississauga, notes in his blog: "Emmerich and Orloff certainly take the licence their philosophy of history gives them to impressive extremes, ignoring, basically, the entire archive of documented evidence for just about anything that happened in the sixteenth century."

Syme goes on, "The film and its ludicrous script clearly just don't care about history at all. That's a filmmaker's prerogative. But why would Orloff and Emmerich then try to have it both ways? It rankles a bit to have to sit through egregious tripe like this [the film itself] only to be told that both author and director have a better understanding of Tudor England than the entire academic community of literary scholars and historians."[99]

Apart from the plot incongruities and absurdities (How many illegitimate offspring did Elizabeth produce? Why don't any of Shakespeare's associates in the theater world, who know perfectly well he can't be the author of the great plays, do anything serious to expose him? Why is it that the brilliant spymaster, Cecil, and his network of hardworking spies have to be informed that a well-advertised production of *Richard III*, with its hunchback protagonist, is going to be produced under their very noses? Isn't the final conversation between Oxford and Elizabeth about their son, by which time he knows (although she doesn't) that the queen is his mother, just a little bit ... unsettling?), apart from all that, there are facts about Elizabethan literary life that the film simply gets entirely wrong.

Professor Syme points out a few. He observes when we first meet the crowd of playwrights in 1598, "Marlowe makes fun of [Thomas] Dekker for the failure of *Shoemaker's Holiday* and claims preeminence among historical playwrights. Which is funny, since Marlowe hadn't written a history play in five years at that point, largely because he was murdered in 1593. And Dekker's play wasn't written until 1599 (a fact recorded in that famous and fraudulent monument to government conspiracy otherwise known as Henslowe's Diary)."

He continues: "How about a few dates? A 1558 *Midsummer Night's Dream* [the year when the Earl of Oxford would have been eight] has a certain charm, to be sure, but a *Richard III*, 'winter of our discontent' and all, advertised as excitingly new in 1601 might have upset the handful of theatregoers who had already bought the *printed text* in 1597. Or the second edition of 1598. There is, of course, the additional slight problem that multiple witnesses spoke of a performance of *Richard II*, sadly lacking a hunchback, on the eve of Essex's

---

[99] Available: http://www.dispositio.net/archives/449

uprising, and the fact that this performance was used as evidence against the Earl and his conspirators at multiple trials in 1601." And so on.

The anti-Shakespeare, pro-Oxford arguments hold no water, from any standpoint. In his valuable *The Genius of Shakespeare* (1998), Jonathan Bate, now at the University of Oxford, introduces his chapter on "The Authorship Controversy" in this fashion: "There is a mystery about the identity of William Shakespeare. The mystery is this: why should anyone doubt that he was William Shakespeare, the actor from Stratford-upon-Avon?"[100]

Bate points to the overwhelming evidence that Oxford could not have been the author, including the references to or hints about events that took place after the illustrious earl's death in 1604 in Shakespeare's later plays.

Anti-Stratfordians claim that none of Shakespeare's letters survive, a claim repeated by Orloff. Bate points out that letters addressed to the Earl of Southampton "may be read at the beginning of the texts of *Venus and Adonis* and *The Rape of Lucrece* [poems by Shakespeare] in any complete edition of his works." He notes the servile tone of the epistles, and adds, "Pride of place was so important to Elizabethan society that the idea of the mighty Earl of Oxford in the forty-third year of his life writing such words to one of [Lord] Burghley's [William Cecil's official position] whip-per-snapper wards is even more fantastic than the thought of him writing plays after his own death."[101]

The Genius of Shakespeare gets to the nub of the matter when it discusses the anti-Stratfordian argument as it emerged in late-Victorian England, when, "for the first time, English culture became resolutely middle class. The middle classes were highly sensitive to intruders from 'below' and firmly committed to the ideals of 'above'. ... Anti-Stratfordianism makes William of Stratford into the peasant, shuts him away, and attributes his work to any lord it can find."[102]

Bate cites the comments of one Christmas Humphreys, Barrister at Law, in his introduction to a mid-twentieth-century work entitled *Who Was Shakespeare?* (1955), which championed the Earl of Oxford's cause: "It is offensive to scholarship, to our national dignity, and to our sense of fair play to worship the memory of a petty-minded tradesman while leaving the actual author of the Shakespeare plays and poems unhonoured and ignored. Moreover,

---

[100] Jonathan Bate, *The Genius of Shakespeare* (London: Picador, 1998), 65.

[101] Ibid, 73.

[102] Ibid, 92.

I have found the plays of far more interest when seen as the work of a great nobleman and one very close to the fountainhead of Elizabethan England."

Aptly, Bate adds, "'Our national dignity', 'a petty-minded tradesman', 'a great nobleman': those three phrases tell the whole story. Like so many English questions, it all boils down to class."

Anonymous is a lazy, careless, irresponsible, latter-day, third-rate, Hollywood-tawdry, postmodernist-charlatan rendering of the Shakespeare "authorship controversy." The imposture and forgery here are entirely the work of Orloff and Emmerich.

The Award-Winning *A Separation* and the Humanity of the Iranian People

World Socialist Web Site – posted as a Perspective *(editorial comment), March 30, 2012*

It is not often we devote a Perspective to a film, or any art work. However, the combination of the context in which it appears and its own merits makes *A Separation*, by Iranian filmmaker Asghar Farhadi, worth acknowledging in this manner. It is a film with a good deal to say, and the present situation gives the work a special poignancy and relevance.

The United States government and military-intelligence apparatus, in complicity with the Israeli regime and allies in Europe, is relentlessly driving toward military action against Iran. The pretext is the Iranian nuclear program.

Such a war would mean unspeakable suffering for the Iranian population and the people of the region. It would have potentially calamitous global consequences as well, including for Israelis, Americans and Europeans.

With machinelike regularity, President Barack Obama, Secretary of State Hillary Clinton and Defense Secretary Leon Panetta make unsubstantiated claims about Iranian nuclear ambitions as though we had not experienced countless US government and mass media lies about Iraqi "weapons of mass destruction" in the run-up to the invasion of March 2003.

Will the world repeat this horrific experience in Iran, on an even more devastating scale?

Americans are bombarded almost daily with reports of Iran's evildoing: its "threats" against the US and Israel, its support for terrorism, its aggressive geopolitical ambitions. The Iranian people themselves, except when it serves propaganda purposes, i.e., in relation to the upper-middle-class Green opposition movement, are presented as alien, hostile, virtually subhuman creatures, driven by religious fanaticism and irrational hatred of Americans.

A Separation provides one of the few glimpses that Americans and others in the West will have into the reality of Iranian life. The film is direct and honest, unlike most products of the US movie industry. The critic for the *New Republic* was obliged to admit that American films on the same general subject matter "are airy, pretty and affluent" compared with Farhadi's work.

The central problems in *A Separation* are deeply human, and thoroughly believable. A middle-class couple in Tehran is on the verge of breaking up. The wife, Simin, wants to leave Iran and take her daughter with her. Her husband, Nader, feels obliged to stay and continue caring for his Alzheimer's-stricken father. When Simin tells Nader that his father doesn't even know him any more, he replies, "But I know he is my father."

When his wife leaves to stay with her mother, Nader hires a devoutly religious, working class woman, Razieh, to look after his father. Razieh is pregnant. Her hot-headed husband, Hodjat, is out of work and creditors are hounding him. Forced by her condition to leave Nader's apartment during the course of the day and visit a doctor, she ties the demented elderly man to his bed. On coming home, Nader is enraged by his father's condition. An altercation occurs when Razieh returns, and Nader throws her out of the house. The next thing we know, she is in the hospital, having miscarried. She and her husband accuse him of causing the death of the baby, by pushing her down a flight of stairs.

As the story unfolds, the almost unbearable pressures bearing down on every character, including the children, make themselves felt. Changing what must be changed, the drama could be set in countless other locations, including many US cities and towns.

A Separation is a realistic, hardly flattering portrait of Iran, a society beset by intense contradictions. The film is frank about all sections of the population. At the same time, each of the central figures is fairly and sympathetically treated, even the judge who has to rule on the conflicting claims. The individual degrees of guilt or innocence fade into the background, as the ultimate responsibility for the tragedy clearly lies with the profound social and economic tensions. In the end, as elsewhere, the more affluent couple retain the upper hand.

The performances are superb in *A Separation*, a film virtually without a false note. Farhadi's film stands in the best, intensely humane tradition of Iranian cinema in recent decades, along with Abbas Kiarostami's *Where Is the Friend's Home?*, *Close-Up* and *Through the Olive Trees*, and Jafar Panahi's *The White Balloon* and *The Mirror*, and numerous others.

A Separation reveals to the viewer a complex and highly cultured society, where daily life, to be blunt, often proceeds along more civilized lines than in the US at present.

This is a country with a long, terrible history of foreign oppression. In 1953, the US and Britain organized a coup against a democratically elected government and installed the torture regime of the Shah, which brutalized the Iranian people and defended the interests of Western oil companies until its overthrow in 1979.

And will a war, in the name of "the American people," based on one transparent falsehood or another, soon be launched against Iran? Will deadly US bombs and missiles shortly be raining down on the streets, buildings and human beings we see in *A Separation*? Will the criminal cabal made up of Obama, Cameron, Sarkozy and Netanyahu have its way? It is almost impossible to conceive of. But it is the harsh reality. Even without a full-scale war, life in Iran is being strangled by economic sanctions and other measures, which no doubt help account for the pressures depicted in *A Separation*.

And why? So the US, and the jackals who follow in its wake, can have greater access to the energy supplies of the Middle East and shove out of their way a regime they consider an obstacle.

The American media is busy misrepresenting the situation and indoctrinating the population. On March 28, for example, the *New York Times*, whose editors already have the blood of innumerable Iraqis on their hands, ran another piece behind whose writing and publication one feels the thuggish presence of intelligence agencies. It is hard to tell in a given instance because the *Times* operates as a propaganda arm of the Pentagon and CIA more or less on "automatic pilot."

The March 28 article chronicles the close relationship between Israeli Prime Minister Benjamin Netanyahu and Defense Minister Ehud Barak as they plot war against Iran. "For Mr. Netanyahu," we learn, "an Iranian nuclear weapon would be the twenty-first-century equivalent of the Nazi war machine and the Spanish Inquisition." Historical ignorance and moral depravity here ally themselves with neocolonial arrogance.

That Israel is the only power in the region already armed with nuclear weapons and has pursued aggressive and murderous policies against the Palestinians and other Arab peoples for decades are not facts troubling the *Times* reporter.

Will an attack on Iran produce a "catastrophe"? Through its presentation of the views of Netanyahu and Barak, the *Times* dismisses the notion. The warmongering Israeli leaders contend "that given a choice between an Iran with nuclear weapons ... and the consequences of an attack on Iran before it can go nuclear, the latter is far preferable. There will be a counterattack, they say; people will lose their lives and property will be destroyed. But they say it is the lesser of two evils." If Iran counterattacks, the US, of course, will invoke its obligation to come to the "defense" of Israel and launch its own military assault.

What cold-blooded criminals all these people are, in the Obama administration and Congress, the Israeli state and the US media!

A relatively small number of people in the US have seen *A Separation*, some hundreds of thousands. Another one million or so have seen the film in France, far fewer in the UK. The governments of these countries are planning to destroy Iran as a regional power, a task requiring the punishment of its population with the most lethal weaponry ever developed.

Americans and Europeans should be seeing this film. Accepting the Academy Award, Farhadi offered the award to the Iranian people, a people, he said, who "respect all cultures and civilizations and despise hostility and resentment." Mass opposition must build to the threat of war with Iran. Everything must be done to stop this crime being prepared before people's eyes.

Film Festivals

Filmmaking Needs a New Perspective

Buenos Aires Third International Festival of Independent Cinema

World Socialist Web Site; May 16, 2001

Buenos Aires is a remarkable city, but the recent film festival in the Argentine capital revealed the same general problems one encounters in Toronto, Berlin, San Francisco, London, Singapore and everywhere else. The very seriousness of the selection of films in Buenos Aires served to underscore the reality that cinema on an international scale has reached something of an impasse. This does not mean that no film artist is doing serious and honest work (for example, Jia Zhangke's *Platform* (see page 57), from China; Lee Chang-Dong's *Peppermint Candy,* from South Korea; Fruit Chan's *Durian Durian,* from Hong Kong; and Jafar Panahi's *The Circle,* from Iran), but it must be said that even the latter suffer from definite limitations that are perhaps *most* revealing about the current difficulties.

One can only arrive at the source of the present impasse, and perhaps indicate a way out, by considering a number of related social and historical issues.

There are those who suggest, somewhat superficially, that the current stagnation in cinema is principally the product of the domination of commercial filmmaking by large conglomerates with their specific social and ideological agendas. No doubt the age of the $150 million budget is not conducive to genuine experimentation and iconoclasm. It is too easy, however, to make Hollywood into a straw man.

If the American "independent" and European and Japanese art cinemas were producing a stream of challenging and oppositional works, if one truly felt that these cinemas were at war with the dead hand of commercial filmmaking, that would be one thing. But that is by no means the case. If anything, the products of the so-called independent cinema in the US, for instance, are weaker than those turned out by the major studios. At least the latter demonstrate some technical and (occasionally) storytelling abilities. In fact, a great many individuals have had the resources and means in recent years to make films independent of the studios; however, they have had precious little to say.

There is nothing more painful than watching the amateurish effort of a 30-year-old middle class North American who has never had a serious thought or participated in a serious struggle. The situation is not much more promising in Europe. A number of French directors have taken self-absorption to new heights (Assayas, Ozon, Carax, Jacquot, Kahn, etc.). Others, having nothing whatsoever to say, film sex scenes (*Romance*, *Baise-moi*, *Intimacy*, and so forth). The latter work is apparently known as the "cinema of the body." The Italian and German cinemas are largely silent, and the Spanish and Scandinavian (*Dogma* group, Icelandic, Finnish) are overpraised.

The former Soviet and eastern European filmmakers continue to be disoriented and confused (or merely gloomy) at best. The Japanese, in the face of a worsening economy and growing political instability, go on making mannered and self-conscious or merely trivial films in a number of genres, which, in my view, will not endure. Argentine cinema, which was naturally on display in Buenos Aires, demonstrates the same general tendencies as its international counterparts.

It does not even appear before the consciousness of most of those involved in the film industry that there is a large and growing gap between the subject matter of their works—principally the not very intriguing dilemmas of middle-class and upper-middle-class layers—and the extraordinary events of the last decade or the convulsive reality facing much of the world's population.

Filmmakers have largely ignored many of the critical events of our time—for example, the collapse of the Soviet Union, war in the Persian Gulf, the historical roots of the Balkan conflict (and not simply impressionistic accounts of the barbarism), the social catastrophe in Africa, Latin America and much of Asia, the decline of the traditional labor movements, the explosive growth of social inequality, the consequences of a globally integrated economy—and shown remarkably little interest in the human problems associated with them.

No artist escapes his or her era in any meaningful sense. The "spirit" of an epoch, as Trotsky suggested, manifests itself in everyone, in those who consciously seek to grasp and embody its realities and those who struggle against or seek to evade them. That the dominant trend in filmmaking makes no effort in the direction of a probing examination of social life tells us a good deal about our day and about sections of the population that have benefited, for example, from the boom in the entertainment industry and the stock market in recent years.

A considerable portion of the intelligentsia has swung to the right. There are increasing numbers of intellectuals and artists "thinking the unthinkable," accommodating or preparing to accommodate themselves to the present system. The dampening of the spirit of opposition within certain layers has been a protracted process, extended over several decades. It is now bearing malignant fruit.

A truly reprehensible example is Werner Schroeter's *The Queen*. Schroeter, a veteran of the German counterculture, although never a political radical, has made a documentary on the life and work of German actress Marianne Hoppe. Hoppe stayed in Germany under the Nazis and carried on with her career, apparently making nationalist and pro-war films, among others. She barely apologizes for her behavior. "One was not brave ... I reproach myself," is the limit of her explanation. She says: "I stayed, but at least I wasn't nice to them [the Nazis]."

Throughout the film, Hoppe and others keep referring to "dear Gustaf," and a shot of an old theater program reveals this to be none other than Gustaf Gründgens, the inspiration for Klaus Mann's 1936 novel *Mephisto* (and István Szabó's 1981 film). Gründgens, once a member of the Communist Party, had a triumphant career in Nazi Germany under the auspices of Field Marshal Hermann Göring. He has come to epitomize the artist or intellectual who, to further his career, collaborated with fascism. Hoppe "wasn't nice" to the Nazis; she was only nice to those *who were* nice to the Nazis. I doubt that Schroeter's thoroughly disgraceful work will provoke much outrage. Outrage and protest are out of fashion. "Live and let live, and let's get on with our careers," seems to be the motto of the day.

This must have a special significance in Argentina, where the military dictatorship murdered some 30,000 people between 1976 and 1983. Would a film that whitewashed an actor who selfishly pursued his or her career in Buenos Aires while thousands were being abducted and tortured arouse hostility? One would like to think so.

Anne-Marie Miéville's *Après la réconciliation* (*After the Reconciliation*), while not reprehensible like Schroeter's work, is significant in its own right. Miéville has been working with French filmmaker Jean-Luc Godard, to whom she is married, since the mid-1970s. The film is a long-winded and pretentious four-handed conversation, at the center of which is a married couple, played by Miéville and Godard.

It is a film filled with epigrammatic gems like these: "Don't trust the storyteller; trust the story," "Speaking about talking can only be an interview," "It's best to stop when you know what will happen next," and so on. It's a miserable effort, pompous and boring. The film may have personal reconciliation as its subject matter, but the title is too suggestive to ignore. At one point, somebody says, "We anticipated something ..." Indeed.

Much of this generation has reconciled itself to the status quo, and not only recently. As I understand it, Godard—who made some extraordinary films in the 1960s, but has done little of consistent value since—(and many others) signed a contract with God or the Devil on the following terms: they would be "extreme leftists" for five years or so, and then, if things did not work out, they would be allowed to pout and feel sorry for themselves for the rest of their lives and explain how everyone and everything (history, the working class) had let them down. Not much can be done with such people!

Veteran Japanese filmmaker Nagisa Oshima (*In the Realm of the Senses*, 1976) has made a dubious work as well. *Taboo*, a story of homoeroticism and repression, treats the *samurai* universe with great attentiveness. I will be told, no doubt, that the film represents a criticism. When an artist displays such an obsessive and reverent attitude toward a fascistic-militaristic milieu, I think one has the right to be skeptical.

Because it sets itself the most ambitious goals and extends itself the most, however, this serious work most graphically illustrates some of the current problems.

I by no means wish to leave the impression that there are no socially critical or oppositional tendencies among film writers and directors. I referred above to a number of valuable works, and there were others (*La fe del volcán*, from Argentina, perhaps *The State I'm In*, from Germany, surprisingly *Il Prezzo*, from Italy).

The best filmmakers are capable of recreating with astonishing accuracy particular environments, historical moments and social ills. One encounters individual moments of breathtaking beauty and extraordinary truth. When it comes to the larger historical picture, however, and this is the level at which the most critical work needs to be done, even the finest contemporary filmmakers are at sea. And this markedly impairs their efforts.

Durian Durian, from Fruit Chan, follows up on the director's *Little Cheung*. The latter takes place in Hong Kong, most of the former on the mainland. *Durian Durian* (the name of a bitter-tasting fruit) principally chronicles the activities of a young woman, a graduate of a classical dance school in provincial China, who is obliged to prostitute herself in Hong Kong for three months to make some money. With this "primitively accumulated" capital she may open a small business, or if it is not enough, return to Hong Kong. The film is remarkable in many ways, but one gets the sense that Chan is repeating himself to a certain extent.

The sincerity of the filmmakers is not in question. But we must ask: do these filmmakers consider themselves to be "left-wing" and, if so, what would they mean by it? What is their view of the Chinese regime? Do they consider it "communist"? If so, from what point of view do they oppose it? If not, do they see any genuinely socialist alternative?

In the most immediate and concrete sense, how can the Chinese, Taiwanese or Hong Kong film directors who consider themselves opponents in one way or another of the status quo proceed much farther without a concrete understanding of the social nature of the Chinese state, without an examination of Maoist Stalinism and its pretensions, without an evaluation of the Chinese Revolution and its contradictions going back at least to 1925–27?

One could direct the same general type of questions toward the Iranian filmmakers, Kiarostami, Makhmalbaf and others, whose "humanist" approach has also reached a certain limit. Can they proceed without grasping how the great mass upsurge of 1979 brought to power a thoroughly reactionary regime? Why was there such a vacuum of progressive political forces at that time? What is the history of the Tudeh party and Stalinism in Iran? What was the impact of the Russian Revolution on Iranian intellectuals and artists?

And this does not apply simply to films that deal explicitly with historical or social themes. How can one draw an accurate psychological profile of anyone without confronting the past? Suppose an Argentine filmmaker, for example, sets out to make a work about a 55-year-old banker or lawyer. Was he or she a leftist twenty-five years ago, subsequently disillusioned or cowed by reaction? Or was he or she a collaborator of the military dictatorship or someone who kept silent?

History cannot be left out of account. Insofar as it is, we witness the result: superficial and insubstantial films. *Peppermint Candy*, from South Korea's Lee Chang-Dong, although it perhaps carries out its work too neatly, is one of the few films that attempts to analyze personality from the point of view of history.

The crisis in perspective, the general historical disorientation, has various elements. The factor of material corruption enters into it in some cases. There are those who willfully remain blind to the plight of suffering humanity. These we will leave to their fate. It is the intellectual condition of the honest and compassionate artists that concerns us, although the pressures generated by class interest and caste narrowness can never be entirely discounted.

In the final analysis, even the most serious of contemporary artists lack a politically and scientifically informed confidence in the prospect of a struggle to change things for the better. This results chiefly from having failed to work through the great experiences of the twentieth century, above all, the Russian Revolution of 1917, the rise of Stalinism and its crimes against the international working class, the socialist and internationalist opposition to Stalinism whose chief partisan and theoretician was Leon Trotsky.

Insofar as those critical experiences are not grasped *consciously*, the official version of events, based on the great falsehood that Stalinism was the genuine expression of Marxism—in fact, it was its opposite—holds sway, leading to the most pessimistic conclusions, i.e., that social revolution is at best a hopeless utopia and at worst a recipe for social disaster. It then becomes impossible to view the present social circumstances in the most critical and truthful manner, that is, from the point of view of their transitory character, as a set of conditions that must give way to higher social principles.

A genuine renaissance in cinema will not occur, in my view, until a strong revolutionary and pro-socialist tendency begins to manifest itself.

Speaking generally, the "union of art and the bourgeoisie" in the nineteenth century, which, as Trotsky observed, was "stable, even if not happy," was possible as long as the ruling classes maintained regimes "both politically and morally 'democratic.'"[103] In the first third or so of the convulsive twentieth century, art found much of its sustenance in opposition to the bourgeois order and its artistic institutions.

The weakness of art in the past several decades stems, in the broadest sense, from the fact that Stalinism undermined the socialist workers movement and the culture of principled opposition that it fostered, while

---

[103] Leon Trotsky, "Art and Politics in Our Epoch," *Leon Trotsky on Literature and Art*, ed. Paul N. Siegel (New York: Pathfinder, 1970), 105.

the decline of capitalist society made a serious rebirth of art and intellectual life dependent on a world view informed by anticapitalist opposition and struggle. Out of these peculiar circumstances arose the unnatural notion of an "avant-garde" without advanced social views, a vanguard simply in "visual style," as though the substance of the phenomena to be treated "visually" and the artist's attitude toward those phenomena were no longer of significance. This hollowed-out notion of an avant-garde has helped produce an insular, cynical and socially indifferent atmosphere in many artistic circles.

The development of art, which, in turn, has such a bearing on the development of society, demands a conscious turn to questions of history and social life by an entire layer of artists and intellectuals. This is not an imposed or arbitrary demand; it is a most elemental and pressing fact of contemporary life.

Art is one of the means at our disposal for cognizing reality. There is no absolute barrier between art and science. Without an infusion of objective understanding as to how human society has reached its present state, and therefore a conception of what might be done to fundamentally change things for the better, art will not advance. Art is about essential human problems, including centrally the problem of freedom from oppression and exploitation, although art has its own means of approaching these questions. How absurd and self-defeating it would be to argue that artists should or can continue to grope blindly, trusting to accident or mere intuition.

The Success and Failure of the International "Style of Quality" in Cinema

2001 Toronto International Film Festival

World Socialist Web Site; September 21, 2001

The devastating attacks in New York City and Washington occurred midway through the Toronto film festival. After a one-day interruption the festival's activities proceeded, somewhat curtailed and obviously on a far more somber note. Inevitably, the attacks did more than simply alter the mood of those on hand. While the course of political developments, even the most traumatic, cannot by itself determine the evaluation of works of art, it is impossible to regard the films screened in Toronto entirely outside the context created by the tragic events and the threat of more to come, as well as the larger set of historical and political circumstances from which they sprang.

The idea has been cultivated in recent years, in both the commercial and art cinemas, that filmmaking forms a universe apart, a magic kingdom of image and sound with its own history and rules, that film, in fact, transcends or even replaces life. This is a tedious notion, a stupid one, and a sign of intellectual disorientation. Much nonsense has been said and done in its name. In reality, filmmaking, like all art, has no other material at its disposal other than that which is given it by the world of three dimensions and the narrower world of class society, as Trotsky observed, and its efforts have no significance apart from its ability to illuminate and make sense of those spheres. Cinema, in short, is bound up with the lives of those who create it and those who watch it.

There were, as always, good, bad and indifferent works among the feature films (250 in all) presented at the festival, including numerous commercial productions. The latter films will no doubt appear in movie theaters over the coming months (*Hearts in Atlantis, Training Day, Novocaine, Life as a House, Last Orders, From Hell, Serendipity, Hotel, Buffalo Soldiers, Prozac Nation, Focus* and *Enigma*, among others). There will be remarkable individual moments in some of the larger-budget productions, as well as performances of value, but on the whole these will not be challenging or complex works. Some will be hazardous to one's mental health. Other categories of contemporary cinema—American and Canadian "independent" films, European social realism of a type presently found in Germany, Austria and the Netherlands in particular, Scandinavian family drama, etc.—were also represented in Toronto.

More promisingly, a number of films attempted, with varying degrees of success, to combine artistic and social seriousness. At least two facts about this group are noteworthy. In the first place, there were more of them than in recent years, perhaps fifteen to twenty worthwhile films from a number of countries. Second, virtually none of the better films broke any genuinely new ground; if anything, they exhibited a tendency toward the formulaic, toward stagnation.

Included in this loosely defined group are works by veterans like Paul Cox (*The Diaries of Vaslav Nijinksy*), Shohei Imamura (*Warm Water Under a*

Red Bridge), Mohsen Makhmalbaf (*The Sun Behind the Moon*), Ken Loach (*The Navigators*), Stanley Kwan (*Lan Yu*), István Szabó (*Taking Sides*), Ermanno Olmi (*The Profession of Arms*) and Jean-Luc Godard (*Éloge de l'amour*).

Aside from these relatively idiosyncratic works, another grouping of art films is identifiable. It seems possible to argue, speaking very broadly, that since the early 1990s certain tendencies in international filmmaking have come to be thought of as the most advanced and have been emulated. These tendencies have been most generally associated with films from Asia: Taiwan, Iran, China and elsewhere. The films in question are characterized by seriousness about their human subjects, who are often disadvantaged economically or socially marginalized. In deliberate contrast to the bombast of the commercial cinema, such works unfold slowly, without fanfare, often with considerable understatement. They are reserved and dialogue is sparse. Elaborate camera movement is avoided—in some cases, all camera movement. Climactic, dramatic confrontations are largely dispensed with. Life is never painted as it should be. Relations between people are generally harsh, sometimes brutal. A relatively bleak picture is drawn of alienated and sometimes destroyed human beings.

The artists' original motives in producing work of this type were, generally speaking, healthy ones: the rejection of Hollywood emptiness, as well as of didactic and simplistic political filmmaking; the desire for an honest, intimate and intense picturing of human relationships; a reawakened interest in the poetic and aesthetically pleasing in cinema.

The success of the new trend is undeniable. On the whole, there has been a rise in the sophistication and intelligence of art filmmaking; a global equalization, quite roughly speaking, has taken place. However, like all other social phenomena, trends in cinema do not float freely in the ether. A decade of unprecedented political confusion and ideological backsliding could not leave anyone untouched. A certain plateau has been reached, and the trend associated with Taiwanese, Iranian and Chinese filmmaking now threatens to deteriorate into merely an international "Style of Quality."

A number of films at the recent festival seem to fit, with varying degrees of appropriateness, into this general category. They include *The Road* (from Kazakhstan), *The Orphan of Anyang* (from China), *What Time Is It There?* (from Taiwan), *Beijing Bicycle* (from China), *Delbaran* (from Iran) and *Millennium Mambo* (from Taiwan). Some of these works are more successful than others, some are even quite admirable, but as a group they seem limited to me, stuck at a certain point, passive, socially amorphous, resigned, unsatisfying.

It is correct for filmmakers to reject moralizing and lecturing, to abstain from concocting works out of even the most politically unassailable recipe books. This is not the same thing, however, as deliberately refusing to analyze and draw conclusions about social life and the great problems of one's time. On the basis of such a refusal, reticence will turn into evasion and accommodation, and even the most attractive aesthetic qualities will tend to become, over time, mere mannerisms. This is most strikingly apparent, in my view, in the work of Taiwanese filmmaker Hou Hsiao-hsien, director of some of the finest films of the 1990s. His newest work, *Millennium Mambo* (about young people in Taipei), is a poor film, weak and uninvolving. His most ardent admirers may convince themselves that it is a masterpiece, but this tedious film and the sharp decline it reveals are among the clearest indications that some process has exhausted itself. It is difficult to proceed when one has a limited grasp of what is up or down, Left or Right, in one's own society and history.

The lack of historical consciousness breeds skepticism and fatalism. Hardly any of the current filmmakers can imagine a world different from the present one, or a mass social movement, or much of any movement at all. Human beings are imprisoned by circumstances, continually reinforced on all sides. Progress appears possible only on the basis of individual moral decisions, a viewpoint not so terribly different from the one promoted on television talk shows.

There is a danger that the art-film world will become increasingly inbred. Few, if any, of the films just listed will make their way to North American movie theaters, or to any movie theaters in great numbers. And one must ask, with as little cynicism as possible, to what extent certain works are even intended to reach and affect a large audience. Of course, the domination of the world's movie screens by Hollywood products is not the fault of the independent filmmaker. The question, however, arises: is there a type of cinema emerging that adapts itself to that domination and principally addresses itself to—in fact, principally seeks to impress—critics, festival directors and programmers and others in the global film festival circuit and its periphery, which constitute, after all, not an insignificant economic arena?

This is not to suggest that the process is the result of a conscious plan. Not at all. It results rather from a limited social outlook, on the one hand— a vague, although deeply felt humanism—encountering, on the other, a variety of financial and logistical obstacles. "There is no way to reach masses of people? Well, brutish and inarticulate as they are, they're probably not interested anyway. We'll speak to those refined enough to listen." ...

The Two Paths

Buenos Aires Fifth International Festival of Independent Cinema

World Socialist Web Site; May 7, 2003

The most recent Buenos Aires independent film festival opened as US forces continued their brutal assault on Iraq, shooting down protesters in Mosul and calmly presiding over the destruction of the country's cultural heritage. Not since the 1940s had the world seen such an act of naked aggression. For its part, Buenos Aires bears witness to the depth of the Argentine and world economic crisis, with more than a quarter of the nation's population now out of work and well over half living below the poverty line. The city is measurably dirtier, poorer and gloomier than one year ago.

The director of the Buenos Aires film festival, in his introduction to the event's catalog, confessed to an impression, given the circumstances, that the endeavor might be "frivolous" and "irrelevant," and indeed wondered "why we are holding this festival" at all. On the other hand, he went on to note that last year's event had been hailed by some as "a pocket of cultural resistance and a small source of hope."

These not unworthy but somewhat confused considerations hint at certain peculiarities of the present situation in cinema. Should a festival organizer, filmmaker or critic be stricken with a guilty conscience about staging or attending such an event? The question would surely not even arise—simple intuition would reject it!—if the level of seriousness in filmmaking corresponded in some manner to the level of seriousness of the political and social crisis. By "level of seriousness" is not meant simply the appearance of works responding directly to current events (although that is necessary), but a more general commitment to expressing the "intimate life" of a people and time "to its innermost depths and pulsation," in the words of the nineteenth century Russian critic V.G. Belinsky.

Every serious and truthful work of art contains an element of protest and, therefore, "justifies" itself, however desperate the social or economic state of affairs, in fact contributes to altering that situation for the better. The bringing into the light of essential aspects of people's lives, no matter how intimate the subject or lyrical the approach, inevitably calls into question the current social organization, which opposes and oppresses elemental human strivings. The deeper and more profound the examination, the greater the element of protest.

The principal task of the artist in our view, therefore, is not to provide immediate solutions to social problems, much less to spin out blueprints for a future society, but to portray in the most indelible manner the complex realities of the existing world, which are so little or poorly understood by great numbers of people. Nothing could be more pressing than this. If the artist bends his or her will, at whatever cost, to the illumination of difficult moral, social and psychological problems, this must sooner or later find a deep response in the population. The life-and-death attitude the artist takes toward fundamental human issues will prove to be "contagious," so to speak. The viewer then has responsibilities of his or her own.

In the event, the Buenos Aires festival, as all such affairs, included both "frivolity" and "resistance," both self-absorbed trivia and genuinely illuminating work. If there was not enough of the latter, that was not primarily owing to lapses on the organizers' part, but an expression of ongoing difficulties.

The festival presented a varied program, including segments devoted to new Argentine cinema, to Palestinian films, to the "secret history" of Australian film, to the new "queer cinema" from China, to a number of individual filmmakers (Harun Farocki, Otar Iosselani, Nobuhiro Suwa, Stan Brakhage and others), to the club of "Lost Films" and more. There are no arguments to be made against this somewhat adventurous approach. One ought to be grateful for the opportunity to see, for example, works by the French director Jean Epstein (1897–1953), including *The Fall of the House of Usher* (1928), and Roberto Rossellini's *India* (1958).

Nonetheless, the programming variety could not conceal an essential truth: that contemporary cinema remains largely impoverished and lags far behind an increasingly explosive social reality. Moreover, the "commitment to obsession" that film festival organizers espouse almost guarantees the presence of a certain number of charlatans and fakers. At some point it will have to dawn on film festival organizers worldwide that extremism in form is not a virtue in itself. Nearly any film school graduate, with a certain degree of effort, can make an incomprehensible or supremely cold and violent or sexually graphic work. Nor is it beyond the reach of many, unhappily, to produce five-, six- or seven-hour films in which no one and no thing moves.

It is more difficult, however, to take the measure of the epoch and the society in which one lives in a dramatically compelling and truthful manner.

For that, one first of all has to have a decided interest in humanity and an objective means by which to make sense of society and history, through grasping the social conditions of existence as rooted in class affiliation.

By and large, the people making films and those criticizing them seem unaware of the contradictions of the present situation in cinema. Things are going rather well as far as they are concerned. They believe that their ideas and lives are terribly important. For the most part, however, they are not. A general middle class self-absorption and evasiveness combines with more-narrow vested interests—the success of this or that film project or festival, the continued prestige of a director whose career one has endorsed, a publishing venture, an academic position— to ensure a degree of blindness as to the inadequacies of contemporary filmmaking.

We are still in need of a richer, more suggestive, humane, sensual, passionate, historically concrete and subversive fiction. Who will create it?

Belinsky, writing in 1834, asserted that there were "two inescapable paths" for the artist. One involved forswearing oneself, suppressing one's egoism and breathing "for the happiness of others," sacrificing all for the good of mankind, loving truth not for the sake of reward, but for its own sake. The other, he observed, was a "wider, less disturbing, easier" path: "love thyself more than anything on earth; shed tears, perform kindness only for the sake of profit; fear not evil when it bringeth thee advantage. Remember this rule: it will assure you comfort everywhere!" These two paths remain.[104]

A number of films stood out in Buenos Aires: two documentaries and one fiction film in particular. *The Flowers of September* (*Flores de septiembre*) treats the tragic abduction and murder of high school students under the Argentine military dictatorship of 1976–83.

Forget Baghdad: Jews and Arabs—The Iraqi Connection, directed by Samir (born 1955), is a fascinating and eye-opening account of the experiences of former members of the Iraqi Communist Party, now living in Israel. In the film's opening, Samir, the child of Iraqi parents who emigrated to Switzerland, explains in a voice-over that he is going to Israel, to "enemy" territory, to search for former Jewish comrades of his father, a onetime member of the Iraqi CP.

---

104   V.G. Belinsky, *Selected Philosophical Works*, "Literary Reveries" (Moscow: Foreign Language Publishing House, 1948), 14–15.

The director does not, in fact, encounter anyone who remembers his father, but he does interview four former members of the party: Sami Michael, a well-known Israeli writer; Moshe Houri, a former kiosk owner and building contractor and still a supporter of the Israeli Communist Party; Shimon Ballas, a writer and professor of Arab literature at Tel Aviv and Haifa universities; and Samir Naqqash, a novelist, short-story writer and playwright still working in Arabic, whose efforts are largely ignored in Israel.

The film addresses itself to a number of problems: the experience of Jews in the Iraqi Communist Party; the trauma of the Iraqi Jews' emigration to Israel and the discrimination they encountered; the treatment of the "Jew" and the "Arab" in cinema, including Israeli cinema (film historian Ella Shohat, herself an Iraqi Jew now living in New York, speaks on this). The questions are all legitimate, but the one with which most spectators will be least familiar is the history of the Iraqi Communist Party.

The accounts of political activity in the late 1940s are anecdotal, but manage to shatter a number of myths. One of the interviewed men notes that he grew up in a Baghdad neighborhood without mosques, churches or synagogues anywhere in sight; "Iraqis are anti-religious" by nature, he suggests.

Shimon Ballas recalls his first party meeting in 1946 at the age of 15. Necessarily secret, because the organization was illegal at the time, the gathering was held in a Shiite quarter in a coffeehouse "for Muslims only." Asked to explain the difference between idealism and materialism, Ballas gave the common garden-variety answer, that idealists pursued noble aims, while materialists concerned themselves with the base things of this world. A shoemaker then proceeded to offer the meeting the Marxist interpretation of the question, referring to Hegel, Marx and others. Ballas admits to his shame. Clearly, a new world opened up to him.

The Iraqi Communist Party, which had Muslim, Christian and Jewish members (with a considerable number of the latter in leading positions), was the "strongest in the Middle East," according to the interviewees, with 100,000 members. One of the former members recalls the depths of popular support, as he was protected against the police at one demonstration by women in traditional dress, on a later occasion by prostitutes in a brothel. "Help me, I'm a communist!," he shouted another time to a farmer, who hid him in his cart. Sami Michael had to make his way to Iran, where he worked with the Tudeh Party.

The politics of the Iraqi Stalinist party are another matter, which largely avoid scrutiny in the film. A mention of the party's "patriotism" is the only reference to the Stalinists' subordination of their efforts to the Iraqi national bourgeoisie, according to the notorious "two-stage" theory of social revolution in the colonial countries.

The four are ambivalent, to say the least, about their emigration to Israel. In the early 1950s, the overwhelming majority of the Iraqi Jewish population felt obliged to leave. Each man seems convinced that the Iraqi government collaborated with the Israeli regime in forcing them out and that Zionist forces carried out the bombings of Baghdad synagogues and libraries in 1950–51, which hastened the departure of the city's Jewish population. They speak of the deep sadness they felt on leaving Baghdad.

The four report on the humiliations they endured as Iraqi Jews on arriving in Israel. One recounts being dosed with DDT as a form of disinfectant on disembarking from an airplane. "They [the Israelis] bought us and we became their slaves," another asserts. The Iraqi Jews carried out strikes in some of the refugee camps in protest against their conditions. Samir Naqqash observes, "Israel changed people, from better to worse. It released diabolical instincts." Sami Michael, a popular writer in Israel, remarks that "everything is narrow, artificial, organized to ideology."

The film traces the process by which the four, despite their misgivings, reconciled themselves to Israeli society. "What had become of the communism of my youth?" one asks. The Arab Jews were silenced, told that they were splitting the Jewish nation by their complaints of discrimination, their suffering overshadowed by the Holocaust. However, Ballas, who left the Stalinist movement in 1960, comments, "My thought remains rooted in socialism. I didn't change." *Forget Baghdad* is one of those rare works that manages to be simultaneously tragic and inspiring.

Mang jing (*Blind Shaft*) is the remarkable first feature film directed by Li Yang (born 1959). It concerns the fate of two coal miners who earn their living by staging accidents that kill fellow workers they have passed off as relatives and collecting the compensation due family members. *Blind Shaft* opens and closes with violent deaths, but the film devotes itself primarily to a depiction of the everyday brutality of life under the Chinese Stalinists' "free-market" policies. The murders or attempted murders flow logically from an economic paradigm in which "only money matters."

In the opening sequences, the two are sitting with a third miner down a shaft. "All the men in my village have left to look for work," he says. They kill him and open negotiations with the boss, a self-important yuppie, who wants to cover up the death. The latter's henchman suggests, "Why bother? Why not just kill the two of them?" In the end, the mine owner agrees to pay 30,000 yuan ($3,600) in compensation to the dead man's "brother," one of the two murderers. "Pack your bags and burn the corpse! Get the f*** out of here!" the boss screams.

The two go visit a brothel. In an extraordinary scene, they propose to sing an old favorite, "Long live socialism!" The prostitutes tell them "the words changed years ago." They sing the revised version, "The re-actionaries were never overcome. They came back with their US dollars, liberating China."

The pair next pick up a 16-year-old, desperate for a job, and explain they can find him work in a coal mine, but only if he pretends to be a neph-ew of one of them. He's a youngster, straight from the country, who has never had a drink or slept with a girl. One of the two older men begins to soften, "It's not right; he's too young." The other responds, "You feel sorry for him. Who feels sorry for you?" They try a new mine, with a crude thug for a boss. "What's a few deaths?" he asks rhetorically at one point.

The softhearted one tells his colleague, "If we kill him [the youth], we'll end his family line." The pair take him to a brothel. Afterward, the boy feels remorse: "I've shamed myself. My life's over. I've turned into a bad man." Violence prevails in the end. The final scene is a cremation, the final shot the chimney of the crematorium. A holocaust of sorts. Unofficial estimates put the total dead in Chinese coal mine accidents last year at 7,000 or more.

Mang jing is not the end-all and be-all of filmmaking, but it is a sharp-eyed, truthful work done with compassion. Where is the European, North American, Japanese or Australian equivalent?

World Cinema and the World's Problems

2005 Toronto International Film Festival

World Socialist Web Site; September 23, 2005

In recent years, how could one have countered the argument that the state of international cinema refuted the materialist conception that the evo-lution of the world determines the evolution of art? After all, the products of the film industry grew increasingly trivial even as economic conditions worsened for masses of people and political life grew ever more ominous.

Of course, to argue that social life ultimately determines the course of art is not to suggest that the one is ever identical to the other, that art under any conditions reflects social truth in some automatic or seamless fashion. Events, traumas can and do intervene and divert art from its truth-telling course. The film industry as a profit-making industry in particular is susceptible to social pressures. At its best, Hollywood hardly offered a "close reading" of American or any other society.

In any event, the retrograde character of American studio works in particular *has been itself* an expression of social trends: the vast social gap opening up between the wealthy elite (including the Hollywood upper crust) and everyone else, a related intellectual and cultural decline and a growing evasiveness on the part of a prosperous middle-class layer in the face of troubling events.

The American circumstance was the most pronounced, but similar processes were at work elsewhere: increasingly privileged and socially indifferent layers came to prominence in France, Japan, Scandinavia and beyond (add profound political disorientation to the mix in those countries formerly run by Stalinist regimes).

In the mid-1990s, certain Asian filmmakers (in Iran and Taiwan, in particular) swam against the stream, upholding the principle of a democratic interest in the lives of ordinary people and the details of everyday life against the culture of celebrity and money. Unsurprisingly, they were not so impressed by the American example, Iran and Taiwan both having suffered under vicious US-backed dictatorships for decades.

However, the abstract humanism many of these filmmakers adhered to, which was largely unmixed with an understanding of the great events of the twentieth century, proved an unreliable guide to the complexities of the late 1990s and the early years of the new century. Taiwanese cinema has almost completely lost its way, and while the Iranians continue to produce serious, humanistic works, they do not reach the heights of those made a decade earlier. We have entered perilous and demanding times.

Objective reality provides a powerful impulse. The truth about things cannot be eternally swept under the rug. New tendencies are emerging. Notwithstanding the immense obstacles, cinema has begun to register the way things are for masses of people, albeit in a confused, preliminary and not always thoroughly artistic fashion. This latter weakness is perhaps inevitable. Significantly new artistic form is a response to stimuli originating outside art. For years, art and cinema have appeared dead to this kind of stimulation. Various formal twistings and turnings have taken place, with the artists pretending that nothing mattered except themselves and their art objects. "Innovation" of a generally hollow kind has been the order of the day. Events have now taken the film artists unaware. All the things that art had supposedly "said good-bye" to—political life, the conditions of masses of people, history—are once again making themselves felt. The artists are unprepared, by and large, and begin clumsily. But, nonetheless, a cultural process that is on the whole a healthy one has begun.

Naturally, evasiveness continues to flourish along a broad front. The recent Toronto festival had more than its share of self-involved, tedious and trivial works ... and personalities, especially the ones who are photographed and gossiped about the most. Even while Hurricane Katrina devastated a portion of the southeastern US and, at the cost of a great many lives, exposed much of what is rotten and depraved about official America, the culture of celebrity and money was alive and well in early September. Insignificant people only grow more insignificant.

The film festival, however, also gave voice to those concerned about humanity and its future.

The results were quite disturbing and even exhausting. First of all, under any circumstances, the viewing of several dozen films in a concentrated manner, if they have any substance to them, has a peculiar effect on one's sense of space and time. The viewer is dislocated, removed from his or her immediate environment and enters a quasi-dreamlike state. The cinema's dark space, with brilliant, moving images projected on one wall, becomes the "real world" and the intervals between films something of an intrusion. Moreover, if a film is dramatically convincing, the viewer leaves his or her "own" time frame to a certain extent and enters into that of the work. One experiences at some unconscious level the duration of the events portrayed. At the conclusion of the entire event, the viewer feels that he or she has been away an indefinable but extended length of time, not a mere week or ten days.

At this festival, *quantity* tended to dominate at the expense of *quality*. While the various films did not attain the greatest aesthetic heights, they did give some expression to the weight of the world's problems and, to a certain extent, its pain.

Over the course of little more than a week, one witnessed the murder of Ukrainian Jews by German forces in World War II (in Liev Schreiber's very inadequate *Everything Is Illuminated*); the massacre of Algerians by French police during the Algerian war of independence (*October 17, 1961*); the savage operations of French colonialism during that same conflict (*La trahison*); the anti-Sikh riots in India in 1984 that claimed the lives of thousands (*Amu*); the tragic consequences of the Iran-Iraq war (*1*) and the Lebanese civil war (*A Perfect Day*); the making of suicide bombers (*Paradise Now* and *The War Within*); the enduring tragedy of the Palestinian people (*Attente*); the wretched conditions in Cameroon (*Les Saignantes*); the plight of African refugees in South Africa (*Conversations on a Sunday Afternoon*); the brutal exploitation of Chinese textile workers (*China Blue*); the present dismal state of affairs in the Czech Republic (*Something Like Happiness*); repression and religious fanaticism in Iran (*Iron Island* and *Border Café*); religious fanaticism in India (*Water*); the barbarism of the death penalty in modern-day Iran (*Day Break*) and postwar Britain (*The Last Hangman*); the brutality of the Argentine military dictatorship (*Sisters*); the disastrous impact of civil war in Sri Lanka (*The Forsaken Land*); a bloody coup and repression in South Korea (*The President's Last Bang*); and the history of US militarism (*Why We Fight*)!

Perhaps none of these works were indispensable, indeed some were quite unsatisfactory, but the cumulative picture of human distress was disturbing, as it should have been. Jean-Pierre Bekolo concludes his film *Les Saignantes*, about corruption and power in Cameroon, with the intertitle: "How can you watch a film like this and do nothing after?" Presumably a good many of the filmmakers would have adopted such a question as their own.

A degree of seriousness prevailed in these works, and probably in others we were not able to see. This seriousness is reflected in the directors' various remarks about their lives, works and methods.

Shonali Bose, the director of *Amu*, begins her director's note in this fashion: "I was a 19-year-old student in Delhi when Prime Minister Indira Gandhi was assassinated at the end of October 1984. In the days and nights that followed, thousands of Sikhs were massacred. The city burned. Like many other people, I worked in the relief camps, transcribing postcards from widows to their relatives, writing down their stories of the horrors that had taken place. It was unforgettable."

The director of *October 17, 1961*, Alain Tasma, writes about his art: "In my view of my profession as a director, erasure is a major quality; making sure that the [artistic] work goes unseen … making people forget the fiction, the fabrication, and the tricks …"

Hany Abu-Assad, director of *Paradise Now*, the story of a pair of would-be suicide bombers from the West Bank, says: "The full weight and complexity of the situation is impossible to show on film. No one side can claim a moral stance, because taking any life is not a moral action. The entire situation is outside of what we can call morality. If we didn't believe that we were making something meaningful that could be part of a larger dialogue, we wouldn't have gambled our lives in Nablus."

In an interview, Vimukthi Jayasundara, director of *The Forsaken Land*, about Sri Lanka suspended between war and peace, comments: "For me, filmmaking is an ideal vehicle for expressing the mental stress people experience as a result of the emptiness and indecisiveness they feel in their lives. With *The Forsaken Land*, I wanted to examine emotional isolation in a world where war, peace and God have become abstract notions. I wanted to address, but also question, the tension, misunderstanding, tenderness and human interaction inherent in every human relationship. Anywhere on earth."

Mohammad Rasoulof, director of *Iron Island*, about a group of homeless people in Iran who live aboard a rusting hulk of a ship under the benevolent dictatorship of a tribal chief, told an interviewer: "The story that happens on this ship may occur anywhere in the world. Betrayal by leaders of a society is not limited to a specific geography. It has been an issue for humans in every part of the world since long ago."

About the consequences of the Iran-Iraq war, *Gilaneh*'s co-director Rakhshan Bani-Etemad argues, "War has caused disaster all over the world in all times. Although it is the men who fight the wars, the catastrophe of it is devastating for women for years to come."

One is not likely to forget the conditions of the teenage girls documented in *China Blue*, obliged to work in a southern Chinese jeans factory from 8 a.m. until 2 or 3 in the morning, who resort to clipping clothespins on their eyelids to keep themselves awake.

In *The Last Hangman*, Albert Pierrepoint (Timothy Spall), Britain's final executioner, reaches the breaking point when he is obliged to place a noose around the neck of a former friend. Later, drunk, he cries out to his wife, "I murdered the bloody lot of them. I can't bear it anymore!"

And Indian-Canadian director Deepa Mehta can be forgiven a great deal, including the rather stereotyped romance at the center of her *Water*, the film about the terrible fate of widows (forced to live in seclusion, never able to remarry) that Hindu fundamentalists prevented from being made in India in 2000, for a moment in which certain facts of life are spelled out clearly. Why are we forced to live like this? one of the wretched women asks. Someone answers that "disguised as religion, it's just about money—one less mouth to feed, four less saris, and a free corner in the family home."

All in all, serious efforts. To a certain extent, their cumulative effect was all the more stark because of a certain lack of perspective on the part of the filmmakers themselves. They tend to portray one tragic historical episode or social moment apart from a consideration of the long-term processes that produced it and the social forces that could set things right. In most cases, these artists see no way out of the dilemmas or tragedies they depict. Their pessimism or despondency may weigh on the viewer.

Few of the works in their entirety impressed me with their sincere, obligatory truth (*October 17, 1961* is one of the exceptions). I did not often think, "Yes, from beginning to end, it could not have been any other way!" There was a tendency toward an overly rational approach in some cases, a certain pragmatic narrowness, "art as a tool." These artists lack full confidence in their intuition. And indeed, the filmmakers' collective intuition is far from adequate, starved by decades of a reactionary cultural climate.

Social and historical films are called for, no question. Are the present efforts sufficiently rich and complicated? Clearly not. But there are signs of life, of struggle.

To see the world as it is, what does this mean? To look at the world wisely, directly, honestly, to pursue artistic truth without compromise. This needs to be encouraged with all our strength.

The "New Seriousness" in Cinema ...
2007 Vancouver International Film Festival

World Socialist Web Site; October 27, 2007

The Vancouver film festival presented some 240 feature films this year, among them numerous interesting and provocative works. Some of the strongest of those came from China and other parts of East Asia.

A film like *Little Moth* (directed by Peng Tao) is a sharp-eyed picture of Chinese society and the cruelty inevitably inflicted on its weakest members.

Bing Ai (Feng Yan), a documentary, gives some indication of the extent of social antagonisms in China and the outrage felt (and openly expressed) by wide layers of the population.

Global politics intruded into festival organizers' efforts to showcase Chinese independent filmmaking. In an unprecedented action, Canadian authorities denied visas to five of six Chinese directors invited to participate at the festival's "Dragon and Tigers" Asian film series. Two of the directors reapplied successfully to the Canadian embassy in Beijing, according to the *Vancouver Sun*, while "three decided not to bother."

One of the filmmakers who reapplied and was accepted, Zhang Yuedong (*Mid-Afternoon Bark*), showed a *Sun* reporter the humiliating and insulting letter he received from an immigration officer, rejecting his visa based on Section A11 (1) of the Immigration and Refugee Protection Act.

"I am not satisfied that you are sufficiently well-established and/or have sufficient ties in your country of residence to motivate your departure from Canada at the end of your authorized period of stay," the officer wrote, adding: "Should you wish to [re]apply, I would suggest that you do so only if your situation has changed substantively or you have significant new information to submit."

In an e-mail to a film festival official, Zhu Rikun, producer of *Timber Gang* (a documentary about a work crew cutting trees in harsh wintertime conditions), quite legitimately asked, "As a person who received an invitation from you, I'd like to ask, do only rich people have the right to attend film festivals?" *Timber Gang*'s director, Yu Guangyi, wrote, "I am very grateful for the invitation. But knowing the conditions required for the visa, I doubt that anyone will pass."

Bing Ai director Feng Yan commented in an e-mail, "If people with no property want to attend a film festival, do they always have to be forced to submit a non-existing 'bank statement,' forced to lie and lose credit?"

One can only interpret the rejection of the Chinese filmmakers' visas as an effort by the Conservative government in Ottawa to align itself ever more closely with the belligerent and reckless foreign policy of the Bush administration.

The responses of the Chinese filmmakers to the Canadian government action indicate a sensitivity to social issues that is rare in global cinema. The directors live and work in a country undergoing a massive social transformation. Millions have rapidly fallen victim to capitalist predators. A new class of vulgar and thuggish entrepreneurs, often making use of the slogans of the Chinese

"Communist" Party, has arisen. For the mass of people, reality is harsh almost beyond measure. The harshness of everyday life tends to fill these works.

"Two children lost"

"Money, money. You only think about money," Guihua tells her husband, Luo, at one point in Peng Tao's *Little Moth*. It's too late by then, and the comment makes no impression, in any event.

In the film's opening sequence, Luo pays a visit to his uncle, in some rural backwater. Over noodles, they get down to business. Luo's uncle tells him, "I found a girl for you. She's 11 years old. She can't walk. Her father's too poor to take her to a hospital."

Luo buys the girl, Xiao Ezi ("Little Moth"), for 1,000 yuan ($135) from her father, unemployed and a drunkard. The little girl has a blood disease; Luo plans to use her, an object of pity, to beg on the street.

Guihua develops feelings for the little girl. When she attempts to boil Chinese herbs prescribed by a doctor, Luo prevents her, saying, "I bought her to make money, not to cure a patient."

The begging effort begins. Luo stands around and watches while Guihua and the little girl sit silently by a sheet stretched out on the sidewalk that reads "Help my child" and explains her condition. Although initially lucrative, the begging operation runs into difficulties. Luo has invaded the "territory" of a gang of local lowlifes. They want a share of the profits in return for protection.

The three move to another locale. Again, someone sets Luo straight on the "rules" in this new territory. Yang, as he calls himself, claims to be a friend of Luo's uncle. His own meal ticket, a one-armed boy, is out begging. The boy, 13, proposes to Xiao Ezi that they run away: he'll carry her on his back and he will beg to support them, while they look for his "birth father." Distraught, Guihua goes in search of the girl: "I pity her. How can she make a living?"

There are more unhappy twists and turns. "Yang" turns out to be a truly sinister figure, a vendor of body organs, with designs on Guihua. A wealthy woman interests herself in Xiao Ezi, until a doctor offers a chilling diagnosis and proposes an expensive operation. In the end, Guihua puts up posters around the city, "Two children lost."

The director, Peng Tao, explains, "I wanted to show the unique status of people living at the bottom of the Chinese social ladder." His film goes a long way toward doing that, intelligently and sensitively.

There are various possible approaches to this sort of painful material. In Europe and North America at present, on the rare occasion that filmmakers treat society's "lower depths," more often than not they sensationalize, become hysterical. The poor are as familiar to those filmmakers as creatures from another planet.

The approach taken in *Little Moth* has definite limitations, about which we will speak later, but Peng proceeds cautiously and seriously. Dialogue is at a minimum here, even at the most critical junctures. Indeed, this is *life* at a minimum, from exhaustion, lack of resources, lack of culture. Small gestures, indirect comments say a great deal.

Everything is grey and shabby and grim, the buildings, the muddy or paved streets, the clothes, the unfortunate people themselves. Is there a single joyful or relaxed moment in the film? Whether such an approach captures life in all its aspects may be a problem, but the sincerity of the film can't be called into question.

Terrible poverty and terrible social backwardness, not the individuals' wickedness, drive the events. In fact, Guihua, an accomplice in the begging scheme, proves to be warmhearted, and even Luo, capable of the most callous comments ("She'll lose us 1,000 yuan if she dies," he says, in front of the little girl), becomes quite inconsolable when he learns that his wife may be in danger. On the other hand, Xiao Ezi's wealthy would-be benefactress plays the cruelest trick of all. The director has his head screwed on the right way.

"If I was a government official ..."

Bing Ai is a remarkable and illuminating portrait of a Chinese peasant woman. Zhang Bing Ai, her sickly husband and two children grow oranges by the Yangtze River. The family lives in an area that will be flooded as part of the gigantic Three Gorges Dam Project. They are ordered to relocate, but Bing Ai rejects the compensation offered by the government and digs her heels in.

There are many fascinating aspects to this film, made over the course of nearly a decade by independent filmmaker Feng Yan. There are elements we expect to see: the peasant's unending, backbreaking labor, his or her thrift, the primitivism of rural Chinese life. But the unanticipated moments are what make the film genuinely interesting.

Obviously, the filmmaker has dedicated herself to the subject. Not everyone spends eight or ten years on such a project. Presumably, a bond developed between the director and her subject. Bing Ai speaks quite articulately about a range of subjects, including quite intimate ones.

She didn't know her husband when they married and had no feelings for him. "His mother didn't like me." The night before her wedding, she slaved away in the kitchen until 2 a.m. "Our affection grew over the years." Still, in an early scene, Bing Ai complains bitterly about his ill health and their resulting difficulties. "The only reason I didn't kill myself was because of the children."

She speaks about her numerous abortions. I would have had the children, even if I'd had to go hungry," Bing Ai explains, but the law prevented it. She also had miscarriages "because I worked too hard." Nowadays in the cities, she says, women have people attending them when they have children, "like servants waiting on their master," but adds, "Nobody cared when we had our kids."

Bing Ai tells the camera that city folk, including the new "self-made men," are more clever than she, but "most of them make money by illegal means." She wouldn't want her daughter to make "dirty money."

The most revealing moments concern Bing Ai's struggle with the authorities. Certain species of filmmaker, including the hysterical and socially demoralized, self-servingly imagine that the population is largely submissive, practically inviting the blows that rain down upon it.

Nothing could be further from the truth. The absence as of yet of a mass movement against capitalism speaks above all to the rottenness of all the traditional organizations through which social protest once found expression and the population's sense that the authorities are impervious to their concerns. But submission, resignation?—that is a serious misreading of the present situation.

The film reveals the anger of the residents of Bing Ai's village against the miserable compensation offered them. At a June 2002 meeting with government officials, the villagers protest against the unfairness of the evacuation process. One says: "We aren't getting anything out of the migration policy. The policy of access to water, roads and electricity and land. We haven't got any of it. We have to carry the water in a container from right over the mountain. In the past, we never had to do that." They're confused, they don't know how or whom to fight, but the crowd seethes with resentment.

Bing Ai is a thorn in the side of the officials, because she refuses the compensation and refuses to move. "I am stubborn," she says with pride. In one of the most revealing scenes, she tells a visiting group of bureaucrats,

"Party officials got compensation. The land you gave me permission to build on has no electricity, no water." She wants a permit to build at a site closer to her farmland. "If I was a village official, you would have given me a permit long ago. If I was the village head, the village party secretary or an official, you'd definitely give me permission. If I had money, you'd give in." One replies: "Now you're accusing us of being corrupt." If the shoe fits ...

On another occasion, another group of officials accompanies Bing Ai and her husband to the proposed location of her new home. The couple is not satisfied at all—the land is on a slope and far from the river. An official tells the crew to stop filming (which they do momentarily, but then continue surreptitiously). He threatens: "You better decide what you want. ... I've told you before, when the time comes, you'll relocate, like it or not. We'll arrange for some men to move you here. ... You'll build here, that's it. ... I've been polite long enough." The party secretary tells Bing Ai, "The government won't abandon you."

She sees through the whole pack of thieves. "I'll survive, just wait and see. They won't come to a good end. ... Just think how much money they make. Their pockets are full of other people's money. It's not fair. ... They don't have a conscience." She tells the filmmaker, "I'll die with a good reputation, that's good enough for me." A final title notes that her house was eventually submerged under the flooding waters, and that with her 4,800 yuan in compensation ($640) "she bought a shed by the road where she still lives." This is a detailed and unusual portrait of a complex human being and a complex social situation.

Our Difficulties and Obstacles

It is necessary to praise the better films being made and encourage their makers but at the same time criticize their limitations, which are palpable. The critic Aleksandr Voronsky noted that "Every epoch, every period of social development, every class, group or layer has its own difficulties and obstacles on the way to artistic truth and, it goes without saying, its own favorable circumstances."[105]

What are some of our difficulties and obstacles? Film depends on life and on the state of life. It has been and remains as a total process (production,

---

[105]   Aleksandr Voronsky, "On Artistic Truth," *Art as the Cognition of Life* (Oak Park: Mehring Books, 1998), 335.

distribution, exhibition) one of the least "portable" of art forms. It relies on the cooperation and interaction of human beings on a large scale, in essence, on a global scale. A period of reaction and stagnation such as we've lived through over the past three decades, in which the best human types are discouraged and draw back and the worst come forward aggressively, is not favorable for art and culture in general. But perhaps for a musician or a singer, even a painter, the change in social mood is not so decisive, as he or she tends to be less directly dependent on the current state of social relations.

The wretched trajectory of filmmaker Jean-Luc Godard might help illustrate the point. In 1965, he observed, "The cinema is optimistic because everything is always possible, nothing is ever prohibited; all you need is to be in touch with life."[106] Forty years later, he sighed to an interviewer, "It's over. There was a time maybe when cinema could have improved society, but that time was missed."[107] It's difficult to imagine anyone working in another art form drawing such drastic (and, of course, utterly wrongheaded) conclusions about his or her medium as a whole. Would a composer or an architect be quite as likely to make the same sort of remark?

Godard notwithstanding, filmmaking as a whole is pulling out of the alternately cynical and socially indifferent or "playful" (postmodernist) moods of the 1990s and early 2000s. There is a new seriousness that continues to make itself felt. This was evident at both the Toronto and Vancouver film festivals. Changes in global economic and political conditions, the outbreak of neocolonial wars and the emergence of staggering levels of social inequality have had an impact, as they must.

The "new seriousness," however, is not without its problems and limitations. A considerable gap exists between the generation now beginning to grapple with the world in images and that which produced remarkable works in the postwar period.

Ingmar Bergman and Michelangelo Antonioni died this year, but they were essentially inactive for years. Robert Altman died last year, Robert Bresson in 1999, Akira Kurosawa in 1998, Federico Fellini in 1993, Satyajit Ray in 1992, John Huston and Douglas Sirk in 1987, Orson Welles in 1985, François Truffaut in 1984, Luis Buñuel and Robert Aldrich in 1983, Rainer Werner Fassbinder in 1982, Alfred Hitchcock and Raoul Walsh in 1980,

---

[106] Jean-Luc Godard, *Godard on Godard* (New York: Viking Press, 1972), 233.

[107] Geoffrey Macnab, "'Cinema is over. Its time was missed.'" *Guardian Weekly*. Available: http://www.guardian.co.uk/guardianweekly/story/0,,1476076,00.html

Nicholas Ray in 1979, Roberto Rossellini and Howard Hawks in 1977, Luchino Visconti in 1976, Pier Paolo Pasolini in 1975 and John Ford in 1973. Anthony Mann died in 1967, Yasujiro Ozu in 1963 and Kenji Mizoguchi in 1956. Godard is alive, but artistically more or less a corpse.

Polarization and Protest

2009 Toronto International Film Festival

World Socialist Web Site; September 30, 2009

To make useful sense of an event as large and contradictory as the Toronto film festival, which screened 273 feature films from sixty-four countries this year, is no easy matter. A given commentator sees only a fraction of the films, and he or she is bound to wonder as a consequence whether something terribly important might have been missed, and whether, as a result, any generalizations might be inadequately grounded.

Moreover, film festivals like this have tended, in recent decades, simply to take place year after year without significantly noticeable development or extraordinary purpose, aside from relatively narrow ones. Those with a personal or financial stake in the matter—directors, performers, producers, distributors—might have reasons to sharply distinguish in their memories the 2002 Toronto festival from the 2005 edition, but is anyone else likely to?

However, events inevitably take place that provide some perspective on every aspect of social life, including global filmmaking. The economic crisis that began with the collapse of Lehman Brothers in September 2008, and which has meant a steady worsening of the conditions of millions over the past year, is one such event. The deepening crisis has been accompanied by a growth of political tensions, militarism and neocolonial violence.

The new Obama administration, which so many in the North American film industry greeted with euphoria, has intensified the war against the Afghan people and spread the brutal conflict into Pakistan, and is currently staging new provocations against the Iranian regime centered on allegations about Tehran's nuclear program, a campaign that menacingly resembles the one organized by the Bush-Cheney government to justify its criminal invasion of Iraq in 2003.

Nor have global-economic and industry trends left the Toronto film festival untouched. It has become a major focus for certain sections of the film industry, a launching pad for numerous commercially and critically successful movies. Such an operation must set in motion large amounts of money and create the conditions in which "important" careers and reputations are created (or perhaps destroyed). The swelling presence of movie stars, red carpets, and other trappings of the celebrity culture testifies to the Toronto festival's thoroughgoing inclusion in the international entertainment trade.

This process has to have an impact on those who organize the event, who no doubt take its growing commercial stature as a sign of their cultural prescience and insight. A process of social differentiation occurs here, too, within the festival itself, as the various components of the film world (studio, "independent," art-house, etc.) compete—one-sidedly of course—for publicity and funds.

Honest artistic elements, at a certain point, must come into conflict with the tendency of the festival to become more and more of an establishment event, socially indifferent and oblivious, under the conditions of economic disarray and imperialist barbarism.

As it happened, Israel's murderous assault on Gaza and the provocative decision of the Toronto film festival, in the face of this atrocity, to single out Tel Aviv eight months later ("a young, dynamic city that ... celebrates its diversity"), as part of a new festival program, provided the spark for a protest from a number of radical-minded filmmakers.

Whatever the intention of festival organizers, there can be no doubt that the Israeli regime and its representatives saw the Toronto festival spotlight as a propaganda coup, part of the effort to improve the country's image around the world.

When a number of Toronto filmmakers made the case in a face-to-face meeting, not against the screening of Israeli films, but against the decision to celebrate Tel Aviv and falsify its history, festival officials were obdurate, refusing to listen to entirely reasonable arguments. In that refusal, one sees reflected in part the impact of the processes referred to above.

The decision to organize the spotlight in the first place and to go through with it despite serious objections by longtime film festival participants, as well as the polarized response that decision generated, brought a number of processes into focus.

The protest against the Toronto festival's collusion with the Israeli "rebranding" campaign was eventually signed by 1,500 filmmakers, writers and intellectuals. Right-wing, pro-Israeli elements in the film industry (a list that included virtually no one of artistic significance), who sprang to the defense of festival organizers, resorted to McCarthyite smears, accusing the protesters of attempting to "blacklist" Israeli filmmakers. This is rich coming from forces who have worked might and main for years to suppress all criticism of Zionist policy and remain entirely immune to the suffering of the Palestinian people.

Of course, insularity and political blindness are certainly not uniquely the property of the Toronto festival hierarchy.

From our standpoint, a discernible connection exists between the positions taken by the festival organizers and their defenders, on the one hand, and the self-centered, bland, superficial quality of much of contemporary filmmaking, on the other.

For instance, Canadian filmmaker Atom Egoyan, in a letter to the *Globe and Mail* posted September 17, noted that he had "watched with dismay as many of my colleagues" signed the open letter of protest. He further argued that "a tone of partisanship has been cast on a cherished oasis of civility and artistic free expression."

"What I resent about the Toronto declaration," Egoyan commented, "is that for the first time in the history of this magnificent event, an agenda was imposed before the festival even began."

Unhappily, the letter speaks to the political naïveté and general obtuseness of our present-day "intellectual classes." According to such an outlook, the dominant national ideology and politics are more or less the natural state of things. Thus, for example, Egoyan would not consider the decision to open the 2008 Toronto festival with the wretched, pro-military *Passchendaele*, a film intended by its creator to ignite "interest and justifiable pride in the grit and valour of all the Canadians who fought for their country," and backed by the Chief of the Defence Staff and the ultra-right government in Alberta, as the expression of an "imposed agenda."

That a respected contemporary film director should consider "partisanship" a quality to be deplored and avoided, and the antipode of "artistic freedom," speaks volumes about our current difficulties. How else has artistic freedom, tenuous at the best of times, ever been defended except through the most resolute, and "partisan," struggle against the powers that be and the forces of reaction? What is one to say of an artist who evidently regards the directors of the Toronto film festival, and the Canadian establishment that stands fully behind them, as the guarantors of intellectual and creative freedom?

The task of the artist is to speak the truth, not offer "a treacherous impartiality." The artist who cannot choose between those who suffer and those who cause that suffering proves him or herself thereby a poor and untrustworthy observer of life, generally incapable of profound insight into the human condition. Why should we value his or her opinion about any important matter? A conscientious study of the facts, and their real interconnections, which inevitably leads to taking sides, is what's first of all called for, in the historian, the scientist, and the artist.

It is necessary to point out that while the protest against the Tel Aviv spotlight was legitimate, it never went beyond definite political bounds. Even by opponents of the festival's stance, certain things can be said, and others cannot. These limitations, too, find their reflection, or equivalent, in contemporary artistic life, in works that intend to be critical of existing social relations. So much passivity and timidity remains.

To be more concrete: as we noted on the WSWS, the actions of the Israeli state do not represent some remarkable violation of imperialist moral standards. Canada's "humanitarian mission" in Afghanistan, for example, dovetailing neatly with US aims and plans, is nothing more nor less than a predatory colonial enterprise, which increasingly demands the bloody suppression of the Afghan population. The recent massacre of more than 100 civilians in Kunduz, ordered by the German army and executed with American bombs, is in no way morally superior to Israeli action in Gaza.

Sincere, concerned people registered their protests, and even stuck their necks out, over the Tel Aviv question. Inevitably, however, professional "left" opportunists were also active—and they are not entirely unknown in Toronto—who seek to isolate protests against the Israeli elite's crimes from an opposition to imperialism as a global system. According to these people, capitalism has an "ugly face" that needs to and can be cleared up. For them, globalization, "neo-liberalism," and even imperialist belligerence are merely policy choices that can be reversed if sufficient pressure is exerted on the powers that be.

In our view, on the contrary, the savage assault on the Gazan population showed the world what this social order dominated by convulsive crisis and decay has in store for it. For the artists, increasingly, a true accounting of reality will require defining their work by its relation to socialism and revolution. It is next to impossible for those making a conscious effort to portray social reality, in particular, to make measurable progress without examining and criticizing the foundations of the existing economic and political setup. There are no limits to the artistic means and conclusions that flow from such an intellectual effort ...

The World at Large and Closer to Home

2011 Toronto International Film Festival

World Socialist Web Site; September 30, 2011

The recent thirty-sixth Toronto International Film Festival (TIFF) screened some 335 features and shorts from sixty-five countries. The event is often described (and likes to describe itself) as "the most successful public [film] festival in the world," although the meaning of that phrase is a bit obscure.

In any case, the festival apparently grows more and more significant to the film industry each year, and the "talent" on hand becomes more and more tabloid-newsworthy. Each morning during this year's festival, the one thousand or so journalists received e-mailed instructions on that day's "Red Carpet" events—i.e., major screenings. For example: "Red carpets **lock 15 minutes prior to talent arrival**—this means media cannot access the carpet after that time. Media check in starts **one hour** prior to carpet lock. Please note: media cannot leave until talent has cleared the carpet." One could only feel mild repugnance.

(During one press conference this year, it was reported to me, journalists were so irritated by the behavior of a particular film's producers, who prevented anyone from exiting the room until the "talent" had first all left, that they momentarily refused to allow the producers themselves to depart. That sort of mutiny, unhappily, is a rare event.)

The festival organizers attempt to navigate a course between the imperatives of large financial interests and the objective impulse of global filmmaking, which tends toward criticism of a society dominated by those same financial interests. In that contradiction, which is an untenable one in the long run, lies the peculiar character of the annual event.

On the one hand, the picture that emerges of contemporary global society from the most substantial works presented at the Toronto festival is not a flattering one. The artistic approaches and themes in the various examples of more socially minded filmmaking are varied (and *by no means* uniformly successful or convincing), but over the course of dozens of screenings, one is brought face to face with poverty past and present in North America; political repression in Turkey and Iran; corruption and social misery in Uzbekistan, Slovakia, Britain, South Africa, China, Tunisia, India, Portugal, Morocco and the Gaza Strip; official violence in Australia and Spain; the plight of African refugees in Europe; political conspiracy in the UK; the brutality of French imperialism in its overseas territories; and other realities.

Some of the films that seemed most interesting to us, from the dramatic and social points of view, included *Omar Killed Me* from France, about the frame-up of an innocent Moroccan immigrant for murder in the 1990s; *Think of Me*, about a single mother trying to stay afloat in contemporary Las Vegas; *Rebellion*, about the suppression by the French authorities of a revolt in New Caledonia in 1988; *Future Lasts Forever*, a moving film about the legacy of political repression in Turkey; *Habibi*, about the plight of a Palestinian couple, confronting many obstacles to their love, in Gaza; *The Tall Man*, an Australian documentary about the police killing of an Aborigine in custody in 2004; *11 Flowers*, about life in small-town China during the mid-1970s; *Beauty*, the portrait of a brutally repressed and repressively brutal middle-aged Afrikaner in South Africa; *Free Men*, about Algerian Muslims in Paris during World War II rescuing Jews from the Gestapo; Wim Wenders's documentary study of the late dancer Pina Bausch and her company, *Pina*; *The Deep Blue Sea*, another consideration of doomed love from Britain's Terence Davies; and *Edwin Boyd*, about a small-time bank robber in Toronto during the postwar years (more about this below).

On the other hand, the noxious presence of major corporate sponsors at the Toronto festival has become ubiquitous, from the name of the new downtown festival headquarters itself—TIFF Bell Lightbox—to every public screening of a film at the festival, where those sponsors are endlessly thanked. The *Globe and Mail* noted in September 2010: "The Lightbox demanded a significant investment on the part of corporate sponsors (which include Bell Canada, Royal Bank of Canada and Research In Motion, whose brand is stamped on the building's BlackBerry lounge), private donors, the federal and provincial governments, and the developers themselves. Mr. [Noah] Cowan [artistic director of programming] said the single biggest donor was the King John Festival Corp. The Lightbox sits on Reitman Square, land owned by Hollywood producer Ivan Reitman and his family, which also partly runs KJFC."

With the development of social struggles in North America and else-where, how long will it be before the presentation of a given work, one that strongly challenges the status quo, proves unpalatable to the establish-ment figures who currently facilitate and even fund the festival's smooth running? What sort of crisis will that precipitate?

We had a foretaste of this two years ago when festival organizers re-sponded with considerable hostility to a protest against their official cel-ebration of Tel Aviv, only months after the horrific massacre perpetrated by the Israeli military in the Gaza Strip. When events come closer to home, the degree of hostility is likely to grow. Although, the entertainment industry being the singular beast that it is, political opposition may also emerge in surprising quarters.

Currently, the festival organizers seem dizzy with a success that, frankly, more or less fell into their laps as the result of changes in global economics and the structure of the film industry over the past two decades and the vari-ous benefits of holding such an event in Toronto.

In early 2010, officials trumpeted the results of a study which estimat-ed that the film festival generated an annual economic impact of C$170 million. With the opening of its new headquarters, the TIFF Bell Lightbox, the festival was expected to generate C$200 million by 2012.

According to the *Commerce Times* website, Peter Finestone, film com-missioner for the city of Toronto, asserted that the festival helped the city be more competitive in terms of tourism, business visitors and conven-tions. "[The Festival] makes a huge contribution in terms of raising the profile of the city," declared Finestone. "As a film festival it drives film studio executives to Toronto and has them get a bit more familiar with the city. In that sense it assists in selling the jurisdiction to major studios [and] independent film companies, as a place to come and make their movies."

The economic impact study indicated that tourists drawn to the film festival spent C$27 million in Ontario in 2008 and that C$60 million of tax revenue was generated through year-round film festival activities and con-struction associated with the Lightbox.

It is permissible to take some of the more grandiose claims about the economic benefits of the film festival with a grain of salt. The festival commissioned the year-long study in 2008–09, which was funded by the

Ontario Ministry of Tourism and Culture, the Ontario Media Development Corporation and the City of Toronto, all interested parties. "In addition, the Ontario Ministry of Tourism and Culture engaged an independent study by TNS Canadian Facts to determine the tourism impact of the 2008 Toronto International Film Festival."

Nevertheless, there is no question that companies and individuals spend millions of dollars during the festival's ten days or so. What sort of economic or cultural benefit this produces for the average working class resident of Toronto, many of whom would likely find the cost of a single ticket (about C$21) an obstacle to attending, is another question.

This is an issue that bears thinking about for a number of reasons. To most of those who come on business to the festival, social conditions in the host city are of little interest. (That 57 percent of the industry "delegates" who attend enjoy household incomes of more than C$100,000, and 23 percent more than C$150,000, according to the same 2010 economic impact report, is not immaterial in this regard.) To many attendees, "Toronto" is merely an adjective that goes first in the festival's title, an event more readily identified with a handful of upscale hotels, bars and restaurants.

In fact, general conditions of life in Toronto are changing for the worse, in line with decades-long trends and, more immediately and dramatically, attacks on the working population everywhere since the financial crisis of 2008. One sees it on downtown streets. The number of people picking through the garbage or sleeping on sidewalks, including only a block from the festival's Lightbox, has increased.

Statistics bear out one's personal observations. More than 600,000 people in Toronto now live at or below the official poverty line. The city's welfare caseload grew by 15 percent between December 2008 and December 2009. Food bank use increased by 14 percent from 2009 to 2010.

As the WSWS noted a year ago, "On any given night, an estimated 5,000 people sleep in shelters or on [Toronto] city streets. In 2009, 33,000 people were homeless sometime over the course of the year. For those who do have jobs, the average hourly wage has been virtually flat for two years, coming in at $22.86 per hour in one of the most expensive cities in the world. Rental rates are so high that a quarter of a million households spend at least 30 percent of their monthly income just to keep a roof over their heads. And of those households, fifty thousand are forced to devote half of their monthly income to housing. Meanwhile, Toronto rents continue to rise at more than twice the national average."[108]

According to a poverty fact sheet, the annual income needed to afford a one-bedroom apartment in Toronto is C$38,000. Fifty-five percent of single parents in the city earn less than that, 31 percent of couples and 69 percent of people living alone. In other words, the struggle to make ends meet is an increasingly painful reality for hundreds of thousands in the city.

A study released by the United Way in January 2011 pointed to the increasing concentration of poverty in decaying high-rise rental housing. By 2006, nearly 40 percent of all the families in high-rise buildings in the City of Toronto were poor, up from 25 percent in 1981. The authors point to various reasons for the concentration of low-income tenants in high-rise buildings, including the targeting of new private-sector housing "almost exclusively at better-off families."

"Housing market forces are only part of the story however," the report points out. "It is the broad forces of income inequality that have been gaining momentum since the 1980s which have created the conditions for concentrated poverty. This has resulted in a significant decline in the incomes of families, in real terms, over the past twenty-five years, and an increase in the number of families living in poverty.

"In the City of Toronto, the median income of all households, in adjusted 2006 dollars, declined by $3,580 over the twenty-five year period, from 1981 to 2006. But the decline among renter households was nearly double this amount, at $6,396. In the inner suburbs, renters suffered even bigger losses in their annual incomes over this period." Taking inflation into account, household incomes in Toronto have declined by 10 percent over the past fifteen years.

Toronto's right-wing millionaire mayor, Rob Ford, is now spearheading an attack on municipal services and jobs that will result in a further deterioration in the quality of life for the vast majority of the city's population. The violent suppression of the G20 protests in Toronto in June 2010 by police, 7,000 of whom were deployed in the downtown area, with 1,000 arrests and the use of snatch squads, tear gas and rubber and

---

[108] Carl Bronski, "Toronto Star investigation highlights police brutality, rigged disciplinary system," World Socialist Web Site, November 12, 2010.
Available: http://www.wsws.org/articles/2010/nov2010/toro-n12.shtml

plastic bullets, revealed the real state of social relations in the city and the country as a whole.

One would think that conditions of life in the nation's largest city and metropolitan area might intrigue Canadian filmmakers (southern Ontario as a whole contains some 25 percent of the country's population). Yet, alas, in the nearly two decades I have been attending the festival, I can count on the fingers of one hand the number of works dealing dramatically with that general subject.

However, films made in Canada treating matters generally lumped into the category of "identity politics," gender, sexuality, race, etc., have never been in short supply. No, never in short supply, but not very interesting or illuminating either, for the most part.

For that reason, it seemed of some objective significance that the 2011 festival presented a work that depicted social relations in Canada in a relatively harsh light, that did not take as its premise the "kinder, gentler" nature of capitalism there, that scraped away the surface and discovered the brutality of the social order.

This was *Edwin Boyd*, directed by Nathan Morlando. The film offers a fictionalized account of a real-life bank robber in Toronto in the late 1940s and early 1950s.

In Morlando's film, Boyd (Scott Speedman) returns from World War II, with a British wife (Kelly Reilly) and two children, and finds few opportunities for veterans. The family lives in poverty. "I didn't bring you over from England to live like this," he says.

Boyd turns to robbing banks, successfully knocking off several before his wife discovers the truth. "I'm not crazy," he explains in the face of her shock and fright. "The world is crazy. I'm its mirror." The film captures something important about the realities of postwar life in Toronto, with virtually all its scenes seemingly (and fittingly) shot in raw, cold, grey weather. This was an economically grim time, but also socially volatile. After six years of war and sacrifice, following on the harsh Depression years, Canada experienced a powerful strike wave. In 1949 in Toronto, the year Boyd began robbing banks, a socialist (Trotskyist) candidate won 23 percent of the vote in the city's mayoral election.

Again, whatever the filmmaker's conscious intentions, he manages to capture some of this social volatility in an initial scene in Toronto's notorious Don Jail, where Boyd eventually ends up and from which he breaks out twice. Kevin Durand gives a remarkable performance as the explosive

Lenny Jackson, another bitter veteran and one of Boyd's eventual partners in crime, who lost a foot back in Canada working for the railway.

Although a period piece, *Edwin Boyd*'s potshots at the banks (during one robbery, Boyd asks customers and tellers, "What good have they [the banks] ever done you?"), its concern with the fate of war veterans, its unsympathetic attitude toward authority, all this speaks to the present-day and present realities in Canada. The inclusion of a scene of a double hanging (Jackson and another gang member were executed in 1952, for shooting a policeman) is grisly and disturbing.

Someone is paying attention, not everyone is fooled.

Interviews

"Human Beings and Their Problems Are the Most Important Raw Material for Any Film"

An Interview with Abbas Kiarostami

International Workers Bulletin; October 10, 1994

Abbas Kiarostami (born 1940) is one of the most important Iranian filmmakers of his generation. Born in Tehran, Kiarostami studied painting in university and worked in advertising and the film industry before beginning his directing career in 1970, with *Bread and Alley*. One of his first significant films, *The Traveler* (1974), a short feature, centers on a boy who goes to great and somewhat unscrupulous lengths to attend a football match. Kiarostami's first feature-length film, *The Report*, about a man accused of corruption, was released in 1977, on the eve of the popular eruption that drove the US-backed Shah of Iran from power.

Following the Iranian revolution, Kiarostami made a number of other short works before he wrote and directed the film that would bring him an international reputation, *Where Is the Friend's House?* (1986), a deeply compassionate drama in which a young boy searches for his friend to return a school notebook. In *Homework* (1988), a documentary feature, the director asks a number of children and a few parents about school and the treatment the former undergo.

In my view, Kiarostami made his most enduring films in the early 1990s—*Close-Up* (1990), a documentary about a man who impersonates fellow filmmaker Mohsen Makhmalbaf because his own life is empty; *Life, and Nothing More ...*, in which a fictional director and his son, following an earthquake, set out to find the lead actors in *Where Is the Friend's House?*, filmed in the devastated region; and *Through the Olive Trees* (1994), the subject of the following interview. (See review on page 22).

I saw *Through the Olive Trees* at the Toronto film festival in 1994, at a low point for global filmmaking. The film's strong concern with poor people and their emotional lives struck me forcefully. As I told Kiarostami when we spoke, the work was startling because it was not about supermodels, sports stars or other celebrities.

The work of other Iranian filmmakers was also important in the 1990s and into the new century, including Makhmalbaf, Jafar Panahi, Bahman Ghobadi, Rakhshan Bani-Etemad and Samira Makhmalbaf, many of whom we interviewed. Along with Kiarostami, however, these Iranian filmmakers came up against the limits of their "humanism" under the complex global and domestic conditions of the past decade. Kiarostami's most recent films have not been compelling or substantial.

The reactionary clerical regime in Iran has now cracked down harshly on artistic freedom, jailing certain filmmakers and threatening others, but the artists have had no answer by and large except to turn to the pro-Western Green Movement and seek allies within the "democratic" imperialist camp.

David Walsh: What was the interest in making a film about a film?

Abbas Kiarostami: It wasn't my intention to make a film about a film; I just wanted to tell a story. Because I knew that it was very dangerous to make a film about a film. This is very familiar to people, and many, many filmmakers have done it before. But I couldn't find any other means for telling this story. And afterwards I wasn't at all dissatisfied with the way it worked out.

DW: How does the presence of the film crew change the lives of the people in this village, or does it?

AK: I've made three films over a period of five years in this village. All in all, these are very intelligent people, and they soon realized that cinema is just this created world, it's not real. Initially, it was hard for them to believe that local people like themselves could be in a big film. It was very hard to come to terms with that. They always thought that actors had to be from the big city. Two days before I came here, I showed the film to the actors. Initially, they would laugh at themselves on the screen. But once the film was over, they behaved just like all other actors or viewers. And they were saddened by what they had seen.

DW: How can film or art in general contribute to the lives of ordinary people?

AK: First of all, the people in the village are very distant from the cinema or the artistic world. When they only see a couple of films a year, it cannot have an impact on their lives as such. The biggest impact of cinema on the viewer is that it allows his imagination to take flight. There are two possible results of this. Perhaps it will make his ordinary day-to-day life more bearable. On the other hand, it may result in his day-to-day life seeming so bad that as a result he may decide to change his life. We become more aware of the day-to-day hardships. As Shakespeare says, we're more like our dreams than our real lives.

DW: You are choosing to make films about ordinary people, poor people. That itself is quite rare today.

AK: I get my material from around me. When I leave my house in the morning, those are the people I come into contact with. In my entire life I've never met a star, somebody I've seen on the screen. And I believe that any artist finds his material from what's around him. Human beings and their problems are the most important raw material for any film. So as a result, when I'd made the film before this, I couldn't put out of my mind the problems of the lead actor. Which is why I returned to make the third film.

I had many interviews in Cannes and people asking me why I had made a trilogy. I have many answers every day. But I found the most important answer on the final day; my link to these people was never cut off. And every time I finish a film in the village and I leave, I realize that there are dozens of other subjects I haven't covered. It's difficult for me to forget these people. So that initially when I had finished this film, I thought that it was a trilogy and that was that, but in the past few months, I've thought about it and I've decided to make the next film there.

DW: Is there any ambiguity in the final sequence?

AK: Yes, it is both ambiguous and it is not. Because if you follow the story, you see that the situation in the film is so complex, it's not possible for the couple to get together. Because the social norms and customs are very powerful and ingrained, they cause a problem. But I didn't want to have a very bleak ending to the film. So I added my own dreamlike ending. And in a way I was wishing for something brighter. I'm reminded of this sentence from [screenwriter] Jean-Claude Carrière: We should continue dreaming until we change real life to conform to our dreams. So the ending of the film is more dreamlike rather than something that is possible in reality. Because those two people have become very close to nature. And they've metamorphosed into small white flowers. And they grow softly closer together and they almost become one.

An Interview with Film Critic Andrew Sarris

World Socialist Web Site; July 1, 1998

[Authors Note: Andrew Sarris died on June 20, 2012, at the age of 83.]

I have been reading film critic Andrew Sarris on and off for the past thirty years. I consider him the most interesting and perceptive writer on American films over that period.

Sarris wrote for *Film Culture* in the 1950s and 1960s and now writes for the *New York Observer*. He is best known, however, and deservedly so, for his work as film critic on the *Village Voice*, the liberal-radical New York City weekly newspaper, in the 1960s and 1970s. His two major books from that period—the groundbreaking *The American Cinema: Directors and Directions, 1929–1968* and *Confessions of a Cultist: On the Cinema 1955–1969*, a collection of more than 100 reviews and essays—remain my favorites among his works.

We spoke in his Manhattan apartment.

David Walsh: Could you briefly discuss your early life and how you came to be interested in film?

Andrew Sarris: A lot of people say that they loved movies from an early age. That wasn't really my situation so much. I liked movies. The family story is that when I was three years old I ran into a movie theater, and was just completely entranced by what was on the screen. When my mother came in to get me, I raised such a ruckus that the manager let her stay if she would keep me quiet.

But we didn't go to that many movies when I was a kid. I can remember the posters for *Show Boat* in 1936 at the Loews theater, an expensive theater. We used to go to the Rialto in Brooklyn, in Flatbush. When I was 11 in 1939 I saw eleven double-bills, twenty-two movies.

In 1946 I was one of fifty civilian students admitted to Columbia. The first year and a half I did fairly well—not great, but fairly well. For the first time my father started to make some money, probably off the books. He was running a boat rental business, row boats. We were right on the beach, in Howard Beach. That was about all my father salvaged. He'd had a lot of real estate. We were rich until about 1931, then he lost everything.

So I had money at that time. I fell in love with movies. I was hit by a truck in 1948 or 1949 after seeing *That Hamilton Woman* for the thirty-seventh time or something. I was crossing the street. After that I was on crutches for about a year, I started going to the movies all the time. My studies completely suffered.

In 1952 I went into the army. I didn't leave the States; this was right after the Korean War. They used to show three movies a week on the army post for free, and so I kept up with American movies in the early fifties. I had a huge backlog of movie memories that I had no idea what to do with. When I got out of the army in 1954 I wasn't getting anywhere; I had writer's block. I thought about teacher's college, just to make a living. I wasn't really doing anything. I was living off my mother. I had no appreciable income.

A couple of things happened. They were giving a film course at the Center of Mass Communications that dealt mostly with sociological subjects and television, which was just starting up. It was one of the first in the US. Very solid, instructive course. For the first time I started to think systematically about movies.

I met two people in that course. One was Eugene Archer. He'd just come out of the Air Force. He was from somewhere in southern Texas. He was a very strange guy. I've always known nerd types, who had odd qualities but were wonderful conversationalists. I love to talk. Very serious, he'd only smile occasionally. Very authoritative, but there was humor in it, irony. He was a real film nut; he made me look dilettantish.

The second thing that happened, Jonas Mekas came into the class. He was starting a magazine called *Film Culture*. The first issue had already come out. There were a lot of big names, sponsors, people like Agee, documentarians, the usual fringe people in New York. He had manuscripts, from Europe and elsewhere. They were in different stages of erudition. But their English, their syntax was not too good. He wanted to turn them into reasonable English. I said, I'll do it, if you let me review movies.

There matters stood. That was 1955. In the next five years various things happened. I kept a half-assed job at Fox as a reader. And I'd do occasional articles for *Film Culture*. I did a career article on Carol Reed. I got a fan letter from Australia.

With very little money I took off in 1961 to the Cannes film festival. I had three letters from the *Saturday Review*, the *Atlantic Monthly* and the *Village Voice*. I didn't write a word about the festival; I got writer's block. I spent six or seven months in Paris—you know, went to the Cinémathèque. When I came back from Paris I just walked into the *Village Voice.* I hadn't given them anything. I right away resumed doing my column. I was lazy, disorganized and very casual about the whole thing. When Pauline Kael attacked me I was amazed that I was considered so important. I didn't react very quickly. I didn't realize what had happened. I had just been plodding along.

DW: You treated films that were either dismissed as trash or worshipped somewhat uncritically in a serious manner. How did you arrive at the intellectual point of being able to do that?

AS: I think it's a combination of things in my makeup. My father was very grandiose; he was very Victor Hugo. I always took great subjects. So I have a grandiosity and a kind of seriousness. I also had an awareness of neglected writers, critics. James Agee, Otis Ferguson. I had read these people and they were more socially conscious. So was I for a while. I used to put the Stanley Kramer films on my ten-best list and leave the Hitchcocks off. André Bazin and the French critics, and the New Wave way of looking at American movies—that was one of the big influences, specific influences. So gradually my whole orientation changed. But my manner of speaking ... Everyone asked, who is he? I wrote with a kind of seriousness, as if I were writing the final word. I was learning to write as I was writing.

Also, I was a contrarian. I always felt there was something underneath everything. I was an original conspiracy theorist, you know. My favorite genre was the spy genre. I was always thinking of things under the surface, that nothing was what it seemed, there was some other explanation. So all of these things created this tone, which infuriated a lot of people.

DW: What is unique about film as a medium, in your view?

AS: Film has everything. I think it's an emotional medium, above all. Anyone who depends on movies to educate himself, I think, is on the wrong track. What you derive from a film depends very much on what you bring to it. It allows you to focus emotionally on things you already know. It brings things to a point. Like music. Film is the art to which all other arts aspire. It produces the most sublime emotions.

I'm something of a Christian. What concerns me are issues like guilt and redemption. The dramatic progress to self-knowledge.

DW: I found one of your comments in the new book on Ernst Lubitsch revealing. You write about a screening of Lubitsch's *Heaven Can Wait* (1943): " ... the timing of every shot, every gesture, every movement was so impeccably precise and economically expressive that an entire classical tradition unfolded before a stunned audience. Contemporary sloppiness of construction brought on by the blind worship of 'energy' makes it almost too easy to appreciate Lubitsch's uncanny sense of the stylized limits of a civilized taste. Almost any old movie looks classical today."

AS: There was always a technical floor under movies, you know, and there was a kind of restraint; there were things you didn't try, you didn't do. A nondisruptive quality that, at its best, amounted to a kind of serenity. I didn't mean to give a blank check to old movies. I look at some of them on Turner Classic Movies and they're stupefyingly boring and tedious, and they shut out so many things.

One of the hooks that people have picked up on is that I'm a nostalgia freak, "Oh, the good old days." I deal with the best of the movies, but I'm not implying that today is not interesting. I'm fascinated by what's happening right now. The fascination comes in the explosion of content, the type of things you can deal with. But form, not so much.

DW: How do you feel about the reception to your own writing?

AS: I've gotten to the age now where I think I'm being given a free ride to a certain extent, so I think I'm overrated. I was underrated at one time. I'm satisfied with the reaction to this book. I'm aware of things that are certainly not beyond criticism. I use the aphorism that I'm too much a journalist for the academics, and that I'm too academic for the journalists. I'm a mixed bag, like movies. I'm not pure; I'm not this or that. I'm a lot of things. Sometimes rather flat, banal, lazy perhaps.

DW: We don't see eye to eye on political issues, but the growing social polarization is an issue that disturbs many people. Do you think the situation is tenable?

AS: I think things are awful in that sense. I don't see how any fair-minded person with any eyesight can say that the situation is ideal. We've reached in political debate a stage of bourgeois complacency such as even a bourgeois like me finds unthinkable. Years ago I used to read *The New Republic* every week. It was never a radical publication ... I stopped reading it because it depressed me. I got depressed because every week there was a variation of the same thing, people consenting to their own exploitation.

I'm a doomsday person. I keep waiting for the stock market to go down 3,000 points or something. It will. The big beneficiaries, however, would be the worst sort of Christian fundamentalist Republicans.

I can see all the ways that you're right, but I don't think it makes any difference. If you're right, I'll shake your hand, "Yes, people have come to their senses. They now realize the system cannot continue, this exploitation of human beings, this selfishness, this greed, this horrible ... whatever." Things are pretty awful for most people. I feel like I'm sitting in the Winter Palace and the crowds are gathering outside. I'm fairly comfortable. I don't have to worry about where my next meal is coming from. But I'm old, too. I'm secure. But I can understand the pain out there.

A Conversation
with Film Critic Robin Wood

World Socialist Web Site; October 16, 2000

Robin Wood, who died in December 2009, was one of the most perceptive film critics of the past forty years. Born in Britain in 1931 and educated at Cambridge, Wood first came to my attention with his book on American filmmaker Howard Hawks, published in 1968.

The book was noteworthy for the seriousness (still rare in those days) with which it approached a Hollywood director, its moral rigor and emotional honesty, and its enthusiasm.

I think these were the hallmarks of Wood's work throughout his career. Even when one disagreed with his views, and I quite often did, one never doubted the sincerity of the opinion. Wood was the opposite of a poseur.

He published extensively in film magazines and was the author of numerous works, including studies of Arthur Penn, Ingmar Bergman, Claude Chabrol, Michelangelo Antonioni and, perhaps most famously, Alfred Hitchcock. His forthright and critical examination of Antonioni, for example, stood out in a sea of overblown praise. Wood was not afraid to fight against prevailing opinion.

Wood's initial study of Hitchcock came out in the 1960s; he published a critical reevaluation in 1989, *Hitchcock's Films Revisited*. He was also the author of *Hollywood from Vietnam to Reagan and Beyond* and *Sexual Politics and Narrative Film: Hollywood and Beyond*.

Wood moved to Canada in the 1970s and was long associated with film studies at Toronto's York University.

Wood came to left-wing ideas in middle age, and not under the most favorable conditions. His comment in the interview that "World revolution is the only thing" is admirable, but for many in the decades in which Wood was most active, "leftism" increasingly meant the politics of personal lifestyle, not the effort to organize the working class as a consciously socialist, revolutionary force. Wood was not unaffected by this development, and his immersion in identity politics damaged much of his later work, in my view.

As the interview in 2000 indicated, the political difficulties of the recent decades weighed heavily on him. He expressed the desire for a revival of socialist principles, but immediately added that he felt such a perspective was "hopeless." In an amicable fashion Joanne Laurier and I expressed our disagreement.

We spoke at his Toronto apartment.

David Walsh: I was curious about your feelings about this [2000 Toronto] film festival and about film festivals in general.

Robin Wood: If I was running it I would be much more selective. I've seen a number of films which I don't think merit being in a festival.

DW: Off the record, which ones?

RW: On the record. Well, the first one I saw—*Maelström* [Denis Villeneuve]. I thought it was facile and cheap. I don't know how many films should be in a festival.

Two that I was rather impressed by were the rather obvious ones, *Code Inconnu* [Michael Haneke] and *Yi Yi* [Edward Yang]. Two opposite poles of cinema. One extreme, sort of formalist, structural experimentation; the other, old-fashioned, about characters and what they do and how they relate, how they develop, what they find out about. I'm a great admirer of Michael Haneke.

DW: Do you feel that the festival has changed in character?

RW: I think it has become more and more what it always was. I came here two years after the festival had already begun (23 years ago), so I don't know how it actually started. But it has certainly grown enormously, it's become much more embedded in corporate capitalism, with all these sponsors. Everybody, all these firms, putting money into it. I hate all that. Again, you can see why they've done it, because it gets them more money and all that. I would have preferred a more modest festival and not have to stick to that kind of thing.

DW: Do you think this has had any aesthetic or artistic consequences?

RW: I haven't thought about it. Not just off the top of my head. Do you?

DW: I've only been there seven years; it just gets bigger and bigger. I just wonder how long these various worlds will coexist. Maybe they can! It's hard to believe that there isn't going to be a price to pay at some point.

RW: I'm sorry they no longer do anything like the horror film retrospective, like Richard Lippe and I did in '78, called "The American Nightmare." ...

I retired from York ages ago. I'm a "professor emeritus," and such. I'm actually giving a course in January, a graduate course in Canadian film.

DW: What is your general feeling about Canadian films?

RW: It's unfortunate, but there are so few Canadian films that I really feel a strong commitment to. I would rather like some time to see all the Canadian films I can, to see whether there is more there than I thought. Or to answer the question: why aren't there better Canadian films? One reason perhaps is the way funding operates in Canada. Because I know the situation of my favorite Canadian film director, William McGillivray—I continue to think that *Life Classes* is by far the best Canadian film I've ever seen—it's a wonderful film, it's a masterpiece. He's gone on to make one other film; I understand it's not quite at the same level, but very strong, very innovative. He's spent at least four years trying to raise money to make another film, for which he has a screenplay, which he let me read, which I think is excellent. He can't get any money for it. None of the funding agencies will provide the financing. I would love to see the films they do finance, to see what sort of films they're backing and why...

DW: What is your attitude toward the contemporary commercial film industry?

RW: Only the most obvious things, I'm afraid. I've got nothing original to say. I find it enormously depressing. I hate a cinema that's been taken over by special effects. I've given up going to almost all of the contemporary action movies. I still enjoy action movies, I like exciting films, but I don't find the contemporary ones exciting. They're just boring. Often the first half-hour is interesting when the characters are being introduced, after that it's just explosions, explosions, more explosions, bodies being shattered, people falling off roofs. I find it noisy and boring.

There was a great deal of excitement at the end of last year about a wonderful new rebirth of Hollywood, supposedly all of these highly intelligent films—*Magnolia*, *American Beauty*, which I'm afraid I never went along with in the first place. Insofar as there was a revival, in any case, it's gone. I dislike *American Beauty* quite strongly, and I thought *Magnolia* was watchable, interesting. My favorite Paul Thomas Anderson film is his first, *Hard Eight* [1996]. I thought it was a really terrific small movie, really tight, beautifully made, beautifully acted, beautifully directed, very well written. I thought, how wonderful, there's somebody here, then *Boogie Nights*, *Magnolia*…

DW: What about so-called American independent films?

RW: A lot of the excitement seems to have gone here too. I remember the early days of the Sundance festival. It all seemed so exciting back then. I was really excited by the work of people like [Gregg] Araki and Richard Linklater. Araki seems to have gone downhill. I didn't like *Splendor* [1999] very much. Linklater continues to be interesting, but I wish he'd stop trying to make big Hollywood movies. He belongs in the independent arena. I loved *Before Sunrise* [1995]. *Newton Boys* was a very decent film, not a great film.

I enjoyed the *Hamlet* with Ethan Hawke very much. I thought he was terrific. He was the best screen Hamlet. Much better than Olivier and certainly than Kenneth Branagh. He was without the Olivier affectation and all of Branagh's self-consciousness. Branagh always seems to be saying, "Now to help you get this line, I'm going to put on an expression. This is important. Watch this."

I thought the women were marvelous in Branagh's *Hamlet*, Julie Christie and Kate Winslet. … I had very mixed feelings about the film.

DW: I had mixed feelings too, but I do believe that Branagh sincerely believes that Shakespeare can be popular and desires to present his work to a mass audience.

RW: I don't know. I'm less and less sure. I used to think so …

DW: Who are some of the contemporary filmmakers you admire?

RW: I'm afraid my answer is going to be very mainstream. The obvious names—Hou Hsiao-hsien, Edward Yang, Tsai Ming-liang from Taiwan.

And Ang Lee, ex from Taiwan. But not for his most recent film, *Crouching Tiger, Hidden Dragon*, which was a great disappointment. And then [Abbas] Kiarostami from Iran. I've seen two other very fine Iranian films at the festival, *Smell of Camphor, Fragrance of Jasmine* [directed by Bahman Farmanara]. A director who was persecuted all these years making a film about himself and what a terrible life he's had. It could have been maudlin and self-pitying and none of that was there. I liked *The Circle* very much, by Jafar Panahi. And another Iranian film, *The Day I Became a Woman* [Marziyeh Meshkini]. A lovely film. So unexpected, the little girl, quite unpredictable and charming. And conscious, not charming in an innocuous sense.

I like a number of Icelandic film directors. I liked Fridrik Thor Fridriksson's film, *Angels of the Universe*. I liked the Hans Petter Moland film, *Aberdeen*, from Norway. *Zero Kelvin* [1996], by Moland, is a very fine film. On one level it's a kind of intelligent version of *Straw Dogs*. There are other things going on as well.

The director I'm longing to see some more of is Thomas Vinterberg, from Denmark. I thought *Celebration* [1998] was tremendous. I loved it. I saw it several times. A very unusual film. I interviewed him; I was very impressed with him as well. It's been two years and he hasn't made another film. Lars von Trier I haven't made out yet. I still don't know what I think of *Breaking the Waves* [1996]. It's very impressive on a certain level, but I don't think I care for the theme of the sacrificial woman. And all that extraordinary religious stuff at the end, with the miracles, I didn't know what to make of that.

DW: How do you feel about Terence Davies?

RW: I liked his early films. I didn't see *The House of Mirth*.

DW: I liked it very much. I thought it was far better than Scorsese's *The Age of Innocence* [1993].

RW: Oh, I loved that film.

DW: What about Europeans?

RW: Michael Haneke. I have a lot of catching up to do. An awful lot I haven't seen.

Joanne Laurier: How do you feel about the films of Bertrand Tavernier?

RW: I like them very much. I think it's shameful that his films are not shown here. I don't know why. They do come out on video. *Capitaine Conan* [1996], *L'Appât* [1995], *Daddy Nostalgie* [1990], *L.627* [1992]. Deeply human. We interviewed him for *CineAction*. I don't think a film of his has been released generally since *A Sunday in the Country* [1984]. It's very odd. I still like Claude Chabrol. *Ceremony* [1995] was a terrific movie. Eric Rohmer I sort of dropped out on a long time ago, and I've only just started getting back to him. I liked *Autumn Tale* [1999] very much. Now I want to see all of his recent films. You can't see everything. I dropped out on [Jean-Luc] Godard a long time ago.

DW: Godard dropped out on Godard a long time ago. Most of the French films I saw at this festival I didn't like very much. I thought they were cold and impersonal and pretentious—produced from recipe books. They had all the right ingredients, all the right influences, but no real feeling or serious thought.

RW: I've only seen one Olivier Assayas film. I've forgotten what it was called. I thought it was pretty good.

DW: In terms of some of the filmmakers you wrote about in the past, have you maintained the same views, or reevaluated them, or changed them in any way?

RW: Hitchcock, of course. I've written a good deal about him. Hawks, no, I feel more or less the same about Hawks. Although *Rio Bravo* is possibly becoming my personal favorite film of all time; ever since I came to the conclusion that the whole world situation was hopeless, and that nothing would arrest the horrors, and the only thing left was to maintain one's self-respect, if one can. I don't see what's going to arrest the onslaught of global capitalism. I hope that I'm wrong.

DW: I think you are.

RW: World revolution is the only thing, and I can't see how that could possibly happen.

DW: That's our perspective. I don't share your pessimism, but perhaps we could set that question aside for the moment.

JL: Your view of Hitchcock ...

RW: I wrote my first book on Hitchcock in the 1960s, when I was just a 30-year-old kid. I did a kind of update, *Hitchcock Revisited* in the 1980s.

DW: Could you possibly summarize some of your reconsiderations?

RW: I think what's been crucial to any work on Hitchcock has been the work of radical feminists in the late 1960s, early 1970s. First, they launched an attack on Hitchcock because of all the persecution of women in his films, and then to amend that ... although women are constantly tormented, terrorized and murdered in his films, the women emerge as the most sympathetic characters and the ones with whom Hitchcock seems to most deeply identify. The whole thing is turned on its head, and the films become about male oppression, rather than about the terrorization of women. I think the best of Hitchcock films continue to fascinate me because he's obviously right inside them, he understands so well the male drive to dominate, harass, control and at the same time he identifies strongly with the woman's position. The struggle against that—his films are a kind of battleground between these two positions.

DW: Hawks, you said ...

RW: I don't think my view of Hawks has changed fundamentally. I love his films as much as I ever did. I would reevaluate some of them. I think I like *Red River* [1948] less than I did. I think I like *Gentlemen Prefer Blondes* [1953] more than I did. It's terrific.

Hawks never receives credit, but *The Big Sky* [1952] is just about the first film in which a white man and an Indian woman end up together, and alive. And nobody noticed. Because Hawks treats it in a completely unshocking, unproblematic way. He never says he is making a great statement, or a protest against racial discrimination. Nothing like that at all. It's the most natural thing in the world.

DW: How do you find teaching?

RW: It varies. Some of the students see themselves as much too sophisticated and knowing for the films of the past. They know better now. I show them a film like *Letter From an Unknown Woman* [Max Ophuls, 1948], and they say, "Well, this is a terrible film because we wouldn't behave like that nowadays. It just shows a woman who's making herself into a victim. It's terrible to make a film like that." No sense of the social analysis in that film. The position of women, the position of men, what options are available; nothing of that at all. They think that all problems are solved. "Of course, we're not feminists. We don't have to be, we're liberated."

First of all, many of them are so damned satisfied with the way the world is at present, I can't understand it. The films they see are Hollywood action films. Not all students, obviously, but I get it a lot. You get people coming up to you at the end of the class who say, "Are we going to see a lot of films in black and white? I don't watch black and white films."

JL: We wrote about *Titanic*, and the mail was astonishing. We tried to understand why so many people were attracted to that film.

RW: It's such an old-fashioned film. Take away all the spectacle and everything and what you've got is a simple little 30s Hollywood story.

JL: Too simple. A mediocre film.

...

DW: There are difficulties [in the present situation]. The idea of an alternative has been weakened. History causes us difficulties, but not arbitrarily. There are processes at work that will make something quite different possible.

RW: I'd love to live to see it. A great deal has got to be done, I think, to revive socialism and socialist principles. And to make it clear that this is not synonymous with Stalinism. In the popular mind at present socialism and communism are identified with Stalinism. They're synonyms. At best, you'll get the view that "Socialism had great ideals, but look what it leads to, it must lead to that." I don't know how you turn that around. Socialism is a dirty word.

DW: Some of the complex lessons of the twentieth century have to be assimilated by a significant layer of the population.

RW: I think it's crucial as well to find ways to break through to young people. There's so much dissatisfaction, rebellion. It takes a totally incoherent form at present. Raves and drugs, anything shocking, against what they take to be the establishment. The possibility is there; so much potential.

DW: The cultural questions are so important. The rejuvenation of a socialist-political culture, which was so damaged by Stalinism, physically and morally, is absolutely critical. I have confidence that it can be done.

RW: Again, I hope you're right. I think it's a positive sign that people are communicating on the Internet. I try to be a radical in political and social ways, but I'm a terrible conservative when it comes to technology. I'm terrified of computers. I do my writing on a computer, but that's as far as I've gotten. But I'm getting hooked up to the Internet soon.

An Interview with Jia Zhangke, Director of *The World*

World Socialist Web Site; September 29, 2004

Jia Zhangke (born 1970) is a prominent Chinese filmmaker, a member of the so-called "Sixth Generation" movement (referring to the "generations" of Chinese filmmakers since the origins of cinema in that country).

Jia graduated from the Beijing Film Academy in 1997, the same year he directed his first feature film, *Xiao Wu*, or *The Pickpocket*, a remarkable work about a small-time crook operating in a dirty, poor provincial Chinese town.

Platform (2000), one of Jia's strongest works, in the words of our comment, "considers the economic changes that occurred in China in the 1980s, the promotion of capitalist relations, and their social and personal consequences." (See review on page 57).

At the 2004 Toronto film festival, Jia presented *The World*, his fourth feature. The film, which forms the basis of the following conversation, concerns the lives of various employees at World Park, located on the outskirts of Beijing and displaying kitsch replicas of internationally renowned buildings and sites, including the Eiffel Tower, the Taj Mahal, the Leaning Tower of Pisa, London Bridge, etc.

As our review commented: "Of course it's an imitation world. None of the characters has ever really been anywhere. Not only has Tao [a central character] never been on an airplane personally, she explains somewhat resentfully, 'I don't *know* anyone who's ever been on a plane.' The façade of cosmopolitanism and Chinese 'modernization' is entirely false."

We noted further: "One cannot help sensing that the difficulty in arriving at general conclusions about Chinese history and society has a bearing on the narrative approach of many of the Chinese and Taiwanese filmmakers. No doubt specific cultural traditions come into play, but the elliptical style, the deliberate fracturing of so many works into many small and apparently discrete dramatic units—cinematic *non sequiturs*, so to speak—may reflect in part this absence of an overall perspective. The filmmakers see individual fragments and moments of life in the region with astonishing clarity and even brilliance, but developing a comprehensive picture is more challenging."

Jia's subsequent films have shown that this concern about overall perspective was warranted. His most recent work has centered on more privileged and self-centered layers in Chinese society and lacks the energy and sense of protest of his earlier films.

David Walsh spoke to Chinese filmmaker Jia Zhangke in Toronto through an interpreter.

David Walsh: I understand this film was made through official channels, with government approval. Why did you decide to take this route?

Jia Zhangke: With the political changes taking place, there is more freedom of speech. For more than a decade, filmmakers in China have talked about this, argued for this in the media and tried to negotiate with the censors, and this is the result.

DW: Is it possible to be just as critical as before while taking this route?

JZ: Things went well, because we had permission. The concern is there, the worry is there, but we did not get anything cut out of the film after the censors viewed it. But there's also the concern as to whether I will change as an individual, so ...

DW: Do you feel a pressure?

JZ: A lot of pressure.

DW: From the government, or the world film industry? Or both?

JZ: Mostly the pressure from the government. There are two things that we need to keep in mind. First, to create a good film, that people enjoy, and, second, to try and transform the general situation, to create more freedom of speech for filmmakers and the population.

DW: You're something of a celebrity in the film world. I meant that pressure as well.

JZ: There's not too much pressure in that. Filmmaking is a relaxing activity; I don't care what other people think about the films.

DW: Will this film be shown in China, and what do you think the reaction will be?

JZ: It will be released in November, and this will be my first film shown in seven years. It will be shown in Beijing, Shanghai and Canton. I'm quite nervous about it, also quite excited.

DW: Do films like this get a big audience?

JZ: I don't know, we'll see. There's not a very good system in terms of promotion and distribution. Young directors have limited resources with which to promote their films.

DW: Your films are composed of small dramatic units. What is the relationship between these small units and the overall effect you want to create?

JZ: I feel like I learn the world in small episodes, bits and pieces of life. This is a new narrative method for me to connect everyone together in this film, similar to the way you use a computer—you click here, you click there, each time leading you to another location. This is how the world and its experiences are connected to one another. These small episodes create the big picture, or that's the intention.

Also, in China now, society has so many different levels, new levels, and people fit into these different levels, that's why we tried to create stories about these different strata that would connect with each other, to create a single, whole image. It's a complicated country.

DW: In this film and others, you treat workers who die in accidents or face very bad conditions—the construction worker in this film, a coal miner in another. Are these bad conditions and deaths an issue that particularly concerns you?

JZ: Very much so. The modernization in China brings a great many people from the provinces to work in the big cities. They sacrifice their lives in the service of this "modernization" in the great cities, which benefits other people. This is why this concerns me.

DW: Your work is very austere, very understated, but in the films there are often musical numbers, theatrical numbers. Are you aware of a tension in your film between this austerity and a desire for something more spectacular, more theatrical?

JZ: The musical part of this film, and the theatrical, is a symbol of people escaping from their real lives. Also, a lot of young people in China don't know how to express their emotions, so by creating this artistic-theatrical environment, this mask, they can express themselves more openly. Even though every day they do the same routines at this park, the same dances, it's an escape for them.

DW: The "world" in the film, a theme park, is a false world, an imitation world. Do you mean to suggest that Chinese people are fooled or fool themselves into living in a false world?

JZ: Yes, it's a fabricated world with which I'm trying to say something about China. "Modernization" and globalization have arrived in China, but the country seems modern only from the outside. There are many problems in China right now, including how the Chinese deal with themselves. There are many problems concerning freedom of speech. It may look very cosmopolitan, but it's not.

DW: China is a major source of cheap labor for many companies all over the world. What is your attitude toward globalized capitalism?

JZ: Major companies, especially from the US and other big countries, are benefiting from these low-paid workers, and also Chinese companies too. So these workers are the victims of this globalization. So before the country becomes wealthy again, there's a stage in which a lot of people are going to sacrifice, but the business people don't care about this. They don't care at all.

So the government should intervene and defend people. Because these workers work the longest hours, the most dangerous jobs and get the lowest wages. Some of these workers work eighteen hours a day. Like the conditions of another century.

DW: Are there protests, strikes, opposition?

JZ: No, everybody is silent about this. That's why we make films about it. It's one of the ways we can express ourselves about this problem.

DW: What is your opinion of the US war against Iraq?

JZ: I don't like war at all.

DW: How can Chinese filmmakers continue to make progress?

JZ: Freedom of speech is the most important thing today, not to be scared by the rules and regulations of the government, and not to be too concerned by what audiences will think, but to do your own work. To be more independent.

DW: Are you optimistic about Chinese cinema?

JZ: Right now, I'm optimistic about the situation. But there are so many ups and downs in China, so that one never knows how it will turn out.

DW: Are there others of your generation whose work you admire?

JZ: Yes, more and more young directors, doing independent work, on digital video, documentary films. Inexpensive films.

DW: Are these films seen by people?

JZ: Yes, people watch these films in many ways. Universities show them. Cinema clubs show them, fan clubs watch them. But still it's a very small portion of the potential audience.

An Interview with British Filmmaker Mike Leigh

World Socialist Web Site; December 5, 2008

Mike Leigh is perhaps the most interesting British filmmaker of the past two decades. Nominated for five Academy Awards and the winner of accolades and prizes at every major international film festival, including Cannes, Berlin and Venice, Leigh has established himself as a significant figure in global cinema.

After more than a decade writing and directing for British television (*Nuts in May*, *Abigail's Party*, *Four Days in July* and other works), he became known to a wide international audience with his *Life Is Sweet* (1991), an account of a deeply dysfunctional but strangely endearing working class family, and *Naked* (1993), a lacerating picture of alienation and frustrated idealism.

Leigh's greatest box office success to date has been *Secrets & Lies* (1996), the story of a white woman who comes face to face with the half-black daughter she gave up for adoption years earlier. In *Topsy-Turvy* (1999), the filmmaker examined the artistic-theatrical process in a work about the Victorian lyricist-composer team of Gilbert and Sullivan. He treated the problem of illegal abortions in the 1950s in *Vera Drake* (2004).

Leigh (born 1943 in Salford, Greater Manchester), the director of eighteen feature films in all, has been at work during a difficult political and cultural time—"impossible," as he described it to me. In a generally bleak artistic landscape, he has stood out importantly as someone who has attempted to make complicated and sensitive—and socially engaged—films, also accessible to broad audiences. His method of building up characters and plots out of intense discussion and improvisation lasting months often yields remarkable results.

As Leigh notes, he is anything but a naturalist. He refers to his love of circus, vaudeville and theater. His films do not imitate everyday human activity, nor do his characters repeat ordinary conversation. The events and dialogue are deliberately heightened, as part of an effort to get behind the reality of day-to-day life. The exaggerated, sometimes grotesquely exaggerated, goings-on take their place in a certain British tradition. André Breton once commented something to the effect that there was no need for a surrealist movement in England because life and art there were already surreal enough.

One of Leigh's most interesting features as a film writer and director has been his willingness to bite into reality at a somewhat different angle than both the British "neorealists" of the early 1960s and director Ken Loach in his working class portrayals, along with the general school of "docu-" and "kitchen sink" drama. He has seemed considerably less parochial and "national" in this regard.

That his film career has had its share of ups and downs, veering occasionally toward sentimentality and occasionally toward condescension, owes much to the unfavorable climate. The Thatcherite counteroffensive against the working class and the protracted rightward lurch of the Labour Party and the trade unions, which entirely abandoned the population to its fate, have framed the past several decades. The systematic dismantling of the welfare state, the destruction of entire industries and communities, the attempt to eradicate social solidarity in favor of ruthless individualism and related socio-cultural processes have made their impact felt. In a traditional society such as Britain, the traumatizing consequences have been particularly severe.

More than he perhaps suspects or has intended, Leigh has registered and often critiqued these trends. He considers himself a socialist and a proponent of social equality. In person, he is intelligent, sometimes combative, always articulate. He hopes his next project will be a film about the great British painter J.M.W. Turner (1775–1851), for which, disgracefully, the financing has been difficult to organize.

I began our discussion at his offices in London with a question about his most recent movie, *Happy-Go-Lucky*. I wondered how he responded to the comment that the film, about an irrepressible north London teacher, was "lightweight" in comparison to the best of his previous work.

Unsurprisingly, Leigh rejected the notion, arguing that the film was an examination of the real world, which had its "dark underside." He referred to its "Chekhovian" sensibility and pointed out that *Vera Drake*, a pretty grim work, had had its tragicomic aspects.

Happy-Go-Lucky, the filmmaker continued, "confronts easy assumptions" about our present condition, by which I took him to mean easily gloomy or cynical assumptions. "Because we're screwing up the planet and ourselves, and there's a great deal to lament at present," we should not forget that there are caring people teaching children, he pointed out.

He couldn't understand the view of those who simply find the film's central character, Poppy (Sally Hawkins), "irritating. I've heard people say, 'I want to kill her,' and I can't understand that. You should love her by the end of the film."

As for "dark" and "light," Leigh asserted that Poppy and Johnny (David Thewlis), the angry lead figure in *Naked*, were "flip sides" of one another. "They complement each other. Johnny and Poppy are both idealists. They believe in certain values. Johnny, of course, is bitter, frustrated; he's grown in on himself."

Happy-Go-Lucky is about "what you don't often see, teaching and learning." There are teachers of various kinds in the film, including a flamenco teacher who brings her problems in love into the class. Leigh remarked that the moral there was "you leave your personal rubbish outside the classroom."

When I mentioned that a teacher from north London had praised his movie for its verisimilitude, but noted that whereas in the film a social worker had arrived on the scene in two days to deal with a troubled child, she had been waiting for eight months for help, Leigh remarked, "That's a valid criticism." He acknowledged that *Happy-Go-Lucky* had not been first and foremost an exposé of the conditions in the British education system. You begin a film by intending to discuss "everything," he said, and then you narrow it down to what you consider the most essential problems.

The conversation then carried on as follows:

David Walsh: One of the admirable features of your work is that it's both artistically serious and popularly accessible. That's unusual these days.

Mike Leigh: I don't even think about that, consciously or self-consciously. That's a given with me. My natural instinct is to communicate and entertain.

I don't regard my early and natural gravitation toward film, the theater, writing, etc., as being anything other than some natural and instinctive and compulsive gravitation toward show business, entertainment, making people laugh, a fundamental need to capture life and share it with people. In other words, I'm not one of those people who needs to say, "Well, we ought to strive to do something that's kind of popular."

On the other hand, I'm equally unafraid of confronting the audience with difficult and not always easily explicit notions. I think people, in the strict sense of the word, are entertained, and thereby stimulated, not only by being asked to care, and to enjoy, but also to think and have their emotions confronted by stuff.

DW: There are theories that to demonstrate artistic integrity is to be inaccessible, impossible for wide audiences to follow.

ML: Nonsense. It's exactly those notions that lead me to say what I just have. I think it's crap. It would be patronizing to both of us to recite the infinitely long list of artists of all kinds who simply remind us that the two things—artistry and popularity—are naturally and thoroughly compatible.

DW: Absolutely. At the same time, you have been making films in a difficult time, and often flowing against the stream ...

ML: Oh, an impossible context. You know, Ken Loach and I, and everybody else, from the late 1960s till the early 1980s, we couldn't make feature films; we did it all in television, as you know very well. Incidentally, apart from everything else, in the context of the BBC Play for Today [anthology drama series, 1970–84] and all that, I know from experience that one can reach wide audiences in a popular way.

You're absolutely right, and you've already said this, the problem is not the work, one's intentions, one's work or anything else; it's the bloody system that stands between the work and the audience. And also the indoctrination of the audience, as intelligent as they may be, to the assumption that a movie is a Hollywood movie. That is hardwired in by the very nature of the Hollywood machine and culture.

DW: And of course the "Hollywood movie" is something quite different from the "Hollywood movie" of half a century or more ago.

ML: That is absolutely correct. We were raised on those films.

DW: When you were beginning to make films, or before, what was your feeling about French and German filmmaking, for example?

ML: The truth of it is, historically, biographically, I was 17 in 1960, and it was that year that I left Manchester and came to London. Prior to that moment, I had virtually never seen a film that wasn't in English. You didn't see world cinema, you saw Hollywood movies and British movies. About the only film I recall having seen was *Le Ballon rouge* [1956], the sentimental French film.

However, when I hit London as a student in 1960, that is exactly the time of [Jean-Luc Godard's] *À bout de souffle* [1960], John Cassavetes's *Shadows* [1959], and the French New Wave, plus I discovered the rest of world cinema. What were my feelings about all that? I was completely blown away by everything. The most interesting answer to all that is to take note of the fact that this was also the time of the parallel British "New Wave."

DW: Which I was going to ask about next ...

ML: The films of Tony Richardson, Karel Reisz, Lindsay Anderson, and so on. Now, I personally felt that the purest, most important and most organic of those films wasn't actually made till the late 1960s, and that was *If ...* [1968]. And that was not a film about working class life, that was Lindsay digging into his own upper-middle-class, public school experience.

About the so-called British New Wave films ... good as many of them were and inspirational as they were in some respects, because they were looking at working class life, the fact is that none of them, without exception, was an original movie; every one of them was an adaptation of a play or a book.

And although it's historically true that [François Truffaut's] *Jules et Jim* [1962] was an adaptation of a novel, nevertheless, the inspiration for me was that *À bout de souffle*, [Godard's] *Vivre sa vie* [1962] and Truffaut's *Les Quatre cents coups* [1959] were films that actually used film, like painting uses painting, to investigate something in a direct and original way.

DW: There's no question that there is something to those British films of the early 1960s, but there are also problems.

ML: They're script-bound. The truth of it is there was great integrity. You know, [Karel Reisz's] *Saturday Night and Sunday Morning* [1960], [Tony Richardson's] *A Taste of Honey* [1961], [Lindsay Anderson's] *This Sporting Life* [1963]—there was considerable seriousness and integrity; that's not in question.

Curiously, and historically, and importantly, the first film that did what those films did was really outside the fold. It was *Room at the Top* [1959], directed by Jack Clayton. The real revolution, in a way—which I didn't pick up at the time, because I didn't watch television—was what [producer] Tony Garnett and Ken Loach did, which was to say, "Why don't we get away from this terrible studio-bound convention of doing plays? Let's get out on the streets with lightweight cameras, newsreel equipment," like the French were doing, and that was the revolution. It was that that I joined in on a few years after it started. With Tony Garnett —he got me into the BBC.

DW: My concern at the time was a feeling that there was a certain occupational hazard in Britain, so to speak. To write and work in a country with such an immense literary tradition, Shakespeare, Dickens ... it's like having a very, very powerful father, and I felt there was a certain parochialism and insularity that went along with that. The kitchen sink drama seemed to me to be somewhat provincial.

ML: Yes, I agree. This goes back to something I said earlier. For me, the natural influences, really early influences, were not only movies, but theater, vaudeville, circus, pantomime, and the Marx Brothers, Chaplin, [Buster] Keaton, Laurel and Hardy, the Three Stooges, Mickey Mouse and cartoons, and all the rest of it. Those things were as important ... and this is where I would differ from Ken Loach, Tony Garnett. Yes, *The Ragged-Trousered Philanthropists* [a classic of British working class literature, published in 1914] is important; yes, Dickens is important; and, yes, there's no question that a major influence is the time I spent as a youth in a socialist—a socialist-Zionist, but a socialist—youth movement, and that's all important too.

But the fact of the matter is that the heightened, theatrical, vaudeville aspect of what goes on in my films is as important as the hard, social way of looking at the real world. Those two elements are absolutely and mutually inseparable.

DW: To be blunt, I think that's one of the elements that gives the films their particular quality. I think that is what distinguishes them.

ML: In *Topsy-Turvy*, it does the same thing, but in a topsy-turvy way. That is an apparently chocolate box subject, but what we're actually looking at, in a hard and real way, is real people, doing real jobs, doing the very thing we've been talking about, taking seriously and rigorously the job of entertaining and amusing and otherwise stimulating other people.

DW: The films seem to begin less from a theme as a lump, but rather as an attitude toward a particular aspect of life, something you want to investigate ...

ML: I guess so, although I don't know that I'd say "an attitude" toward an aspect of life, because what I'm trying to do is precisely, if possible, look at the world from a multi-perspective.

My natural instinct is to see people, to see society as society, but really as a society that works because of the nature of the individuality of individuals. I can't look at a crowd without seeing a thousand individuals. What's fascinating to me is that each of us is different. So in each of my films, each of the characters, large or small, is properly and organically and thoroughly, in a three-dimensional way, at the center of his or her universe.

So that, therefore, by implication, even though there may be a clear objective or thing that I'm exploring, nevertheless, you get multi-perspective, because the characters, even though they might be subordinate, don't become ciphers. They're not non-people; the detail of everybody is the nature of what it's about.

DW: Again, this is important. As opposed to much of what is unhappily called "political filmmaking," these are genuinely spontaneously created human beings. And that's not an easy thing to do.

ML: No, although, in my view, the films are entirely political and entirely concerned with investigating and reflecting on how we lead our lives. But I would challenge anybody to say that they've walked out of a film of mine with one single clear notion as to what I'm telling them to think, because that's not what happens basically. I want you to walk away with things to argue about and ponder about and reflect on and procrastinate about and, you know, supply for yourselves.

DW: Presumably that's connected to your own process, through which you are not simply passing on something pat or entirely solved.

ML: That's true, although it's important to draw distinctions.

DW: The artist makes judgments and makes decisions.

ML: And, not only do I consider it as my job, but as the stimulating experience of making art, that one does distill everything and arrives at a point where it's clear what it is. It's not simply a random collection of lazy stuff.

DW: Absolutely. And I suppose that's what's complicated and that's what's art. So the viewer leaves having felt or thought something he or she hadn't felt or thought before.

ML: Yes, and the important thing is that the spectator walks away and the film carries on, that you take something with you.

DW: Yes, I wanted to ask about "realism," not with a capital R, but an interest in reality and life.

ML: I certainly would—for what it's worth, and it's not worth much— endorse the probably academic distinction between naturalism and realism. What I do is not naturalism; it's not the replication of surface naturalism. I want to get to the essence of things, in a heightened and distilled way, so I certainly think it is realism.

DW: About your methods …

ML: What we shoot is very precise, but really I make up the film as we go along. That's preceded, however, by a long period—half a year these days—of working with the actors and everybody else to prepare them. I don't have an idea and then talk to the actors. I never tell the actors anything, and they never know anything other than what their character would know. I collaborate with each actor individually first to create a character, and I put the characters together, and gradually we build up a whole world through discussion and research and improvisation, and we arrive at a three-dimensional world, implicit in which are the dynamics for the potential film.

Then I do a kind of structure. But the precise way in which the dialogue comes into existence scene by scene is to go to each location and improvise and, through rehearsal, to break it down and build it up and distill it and structure it into a very precisely scripted thing. But I don't go away into a separate room and write a script; I do it through rehearsal. It does become very precise, down to the very last semicolon.

DW: That kind of process is very rare. To take months like that. The time and freedom ...

ML: These are low-budget films. The strict principle has always been to organize the budget so that that time is there, at whatever cost. So, for example, when I used to go and make films at the BBC, where the budget already existed, and the filming dates already existed before they knew what the film was, I would go in and the first thing I would do was sit down with whomever it was and say, "What do we pull out of the budget and put into extended rehearsals?" So, for example, no overseas locations, no helicopter shots, very limited crowds, no elaborate action vehicles, nothing is going to be blown up.

The most remarkable thing about *Topsy-Turvy* is that it was made for ten million pounds, which, considering what you see on the screen, is extraordinary. But we had a six-month rehearsal, we did research; it's about an imaginative use of money, and nobody's ever done it and not got paid for it.

The point is, I can't make films any other way. It's not the matter of a choice. We have to do that. If we don't do that, we can't make the film.

DW: I think of Chaplin and how he stopped working on *City Lights* [1931] for several months ...

ML: But we should remember that his roots, his metabolism as a filmmaker, like Keaton, like [D.W.] Griffith, [Louis] Feuillade, like everybody who made films before the talkies came in, were precisely in the philosophy that you could get out there and explore things, that you could get out of bed each day and you didn't necessarily know what you were going to do next. It was all about using film to be thoroughly and properly creative.

DW: We have been living through difficult times for the past several decades, the cult of wealth and greed, with Reagan and Thatcher and all those who have come after them. The present economic crisis is going to put an end to that, one way or another, because you're dealing with the destruction of myths about capitalism.

Can you imagine a different political situation, one of discontent, of upheavals ...? How would that—or would that?—affect your own work?

ML: I suppose the answer to that, at a fundamental level—it's a dodgy thing to discuss, because nothing is ever black and white—would have to be no. I think what I make films about is how we are, although it's pompous to say, in a universal way. Although the milieu is always specific, the actual things that are on the go, at a fundamental level, are endemic to what human life is about.

Now, people talk about three of my films—*Meantime* [1984], *Four Days in July* [1985] and *High Hopes* [1988]—as a kind of anti-Thatcher trilogy. *Four Days in July* is a film about Northern Ireland.

Meantime was quite consciously directed toward what was happening, four years into Thatcher, but *High Hopes*—although the characters talk about Thatcher, they have a cat called Thatcher—was really about putting your money where your mouth is. Not to sit on the fence, and if you're going to call yourself a socialist, what does that actually mean? Not just paying lip service to it. On one level, anyway, like a lot of my films it was also about having children and not having children, and all the rest of it. It's also about class and materialism, and stuff.

People have said to me, "Ah!, *Naked* was a post-Thatcher film." This is all nonsense. The correlation between the passing of Thatcher and *Naked* is virtually nonexistent, if we're going to be honest.

Now, you could say quite legitimately, and a faction on the hard left has said it ... I've been to screenings in London and Sydney where people stood up and harangued me, particularly when we did *Meantime*, basically for having the tools to make a film and not making a film about the manning of the barricades, not dealing with those issues. I accept the criticism because that is not what I'm concerned to do; I'm concerned to do other things.

Comes the turmoil, the revolution, whatever, for me, the job, in fundamental terms, would be—sure, to be taking the temperature, as I always do; sure, to be dealing in surface terms with the world that we'd be looking at—to look at people in terms of human needs, human behavior, and feelings and emotions, how men and women function, what it is to be a parent and child, how to survive.

Having said that, nothing makes sense to me except a world in which there is real equality. I can't believe, for example, I live in a country where, after more than a decade of a so-called "socialist" government, we still have a railway system, an education system, a health care system, a steel industry which are riddled with the curse and disease of privatization. This is the only country in Europe where the railways are a complete mess.

DW: A final point. We know that no individual book or film changes the world, yet books and films do change the world. Do you have any thoughts about the relationship between art and social change, an indirect, complex, often subterranean, long-term relationship?

ML: Look, this goes back to something that we've been saying during this conversation. If I make films where people walk away with stuff on the go, if you tell me about the response of a teacher to *Happy-Go-Lucky*, I feel like I'm justified in thinking that, in some minuscule way, I'm making a contribution to that person's life, or to individual people's ideas.

I call my films subversive. I think it's subversive to tell the truth about things, not the obvious political truths, and how people are. That's what I do.

Essays & Film History

On What Should the New Cinema Be Based?

International Workers Bulletin; June 17, 1996

In previous articles we have attempted to give some indication of what was best in the San Francisco film festival. A number of valuable films, with truthful, passionate and even lyrical moments, were screened. Many of the filmmakers present, from a variety of countries, demonstrated their intelligence and sincerity. Individual films from Korea, Iran, the former Soviet Asian republics, India and the US in particular stood out.

No one who takes a serious look at the current cinema as a whole, however, would be fooled by the assertion that all is well in filmmaking. On the contrary, the sentiment that serious filmmakers, performers, students of film and audience members probably share more than any other is profound dissatisfaction. This is a healthy indicator that a new mood is already gaining ground. But first, we must ask, what has film been like in the past decade or two?

Everywhere one hears complaints about the sterility and mediocrity of the commercial cinema. Very little is to be expected from the large American studios, firmly in the grasp of giant conglomerates. When executives from these outfits speak of "artistic decisions" it is only a slip of the tongue. The gap between the technology at the large studios' disposal, capable of producing breathtaking illusions, and the intellectual and moral poverty of their productions has grown to alarming proportions. Hollywood filmmakers, by and large, have everything at their disposal except something to say. Whatever their conscious aim, the immediate effect of their impersonal, bombastic productions is to stultify and numb the viewer and render him or her temporarily incapable of critical thought.

Western European and Japanese filmmaking are not in much better shape: farces without real laughs, melodramas lacking drama, "erotic thrillers" which don't even scratch the surface of the psyche. Everywhere—pretty, blank and interchangeable faces. The absence of Hollywood's pyrotechnics only throws into greater relief the paucity of ideas. South American filmmaking, with a few exceptions, merely leaves the impression of moral and political retreat. The great majority of directors from Australia and New Zealand appear to have only one ambition—to head for Los Angeles and lose their personalities and integrity as rapidly as possible.

Has the collapse of Stalinism, proclaimed with fanfare as the rebirth of intellectual freedom, produced an artistic renaissance in eastern Europe and the former Soviet Union? This question answers itself. It is now clear that the former artist-"dissidents," even those who courageously opposed the old dictatorial regimes, nourished themselves on very thin ideological gruel indeed. The most honest have produced nothing of substance, the worst simply sold themselves not necessarily to the highest, but the first, bidder.

When it comes to so-called alternative film, the picture, in general, is no brighter. American "independent" filmmaking has been in recent years an exercise in trivia. The not very dramatic or picturesque exploits of confused, middle-class 25-year-olds will remain in no one's memory for long. The entire international milieu of self-pitying "radical" feminists and gays has produced next to nothing of enduring value. Any serious critical treatment of the smirking fellowship of "hip, urban" cynics (Jim Jarmusch, the Kaurismaki brothers, etc.) can only be considered another symptom of intellectual decline.

There have been, of course, honorable exceptions to all this: Asian film directors such as Hou Hsiao-hsien and some of his colleagues in Taiwan; Iranians Abbas Kiarostami and Mohsen Makhmalbaf; certain members of China's "Fifth" and "Sixth" generations; Korean Park Kwang-su and others. And there are of course others, but the number is strictly limited.

Conformity and Glorification of Wealth

One could make the same severe accusations against so many of our contemporary films: that they lack intensity, depth and purpose and exhibit the most wretched conformism in glorifying wealth, law and order, and the existing state of things. What has become of the spirit of revolt that animated the most serious artists in the first half of the twentieth century? It wasn't only the French Surrealists who would have subscribed to the notion, advanced in 1930, that "Everything remains to be done, every means must be worth trying, in order to lay waste to the ideas of family, country, religion." What can be said in defense of a film industry whose most consistent hero, in various guises, is the policeman?

The arguments, made by studio representatives and their apologists, that the public gets what it wants and deserves what it gets are simply self-serving. Particularly when the decisions about what the public gets (and, therefore, by this logic, what it "wants") are made by the ignorant, wealthy executives of huge corporations that monopolize greater and greater control over a multibillion-dollar entertainment industry. In reality, whenever an intelligent piece of work dealing with social or historical problems has been made accessible to masses of people, they have responded. And if more artistically and emotionally demanding works do not capture a large audience, whose fault is it? The individual fed on nothing but pablum for years on end is surely not to blame if he or she has digestive problems when suddenly presented with boeuf bourguignon.

The economics and social relations of filmmaking explain some of the problems. One-hundred-million-dollar budgets do not permit experimentation or encourage examinations of social problems. A greater share of moviemaking than at any previous time is firmly in the hands of large enterprises, with a vested interest in the status quo. Filmmakers and performers tend to come, as perhaps never before, from the more privileged layers of the upper middle class. When successful, they receive fantastic amounts of money and live behind high, well-guarded walls, far removed from the social reality of the overwhelming majority of the population. Such people, motivated only by greed and careerism, have never produced anything of value. But the obvious fact that the film industry is precisely a privately owned industry does not explain, for example, the emptiness of the independent cinema or, in general, the lack of protest and resistance, the lack of intellectual and artistic ferment and ferocity. It's not simply that things have been awful, but that so few have been disturbed by it!

At long last, as we suggested above, a new mood appears to be gaining ground. Dissatisfaction, disgust and even shame are potentially revolutionary sentiments. Many people recognize that the current cinema reflects modern life very poorly. The question becomes: on what should the genuinely new art and cinema be based?

The problems in the arts do not result from the light of human genius having suddenly dimmed or gone out. One has only to look at the extraordinary advances that have been made in various theoretical and applied sciences, medicine, computer technology, media technique, and so on. Or in athletic achievement. Or even in certain areas, involving a high degree of craftsmanship and formal discipline, of musical performance.

The greatest stagnation and even decline have occurred in the spheres of politics and art (particularly the literary and dramatic arts). This is not accidental. It is in the areas of humanity's understanding of its own social organization and history—including the struggle to alter them—and of those arts most associated with the development of that understanding, where the most severe blows have been sustained.

The current situation in filmmaking and art can only be understood as a historical product. Cinema is 100 years old. Its history, more than that of any other artistic form, is intimately bound up with the great issues of the twentieth century.

It is beyond the scope of this article to examine those issues in depth, but this much can be said: the great artistic ferment of the post–World War I era is inexplicable outside an analysis of the expectations (and fears and disputes) aroused by the Russian Revolution, itself a product of half a century of socialist culture. This is not the same thing as saying that the artists, as a whole or even in large part, who participated in the artistic movements of the day were conscious revolutionaries. Far from it. But they lived and breathed in an atmosphere in which a revolutionary socialist tendency possessed great moral and intellectual weight. The critical-minded culture built up from the last third of the nineteenth century—interpreted in the broadest sense to include, for example, the development of psychoanalysis—was the crucible in which were formed the artistic geniuses of the first decades of this century.

The artists may not have agreed with the Marxists about the contradictions of capitalism, but there was a general, instinctive acknowledgment by the most insightful intellectuals in Paris, Berlin, London, Vienna, Budapest and, of course, Moscow, that the existing society was on its way out and thought had to be given to the cultural problems of the future human organization. Anyone who doubts that this has relevance to the American film industry need only consider the following list of filmmakers—all of whom worked in Hollywood—who were born or raised in Germany, Austria and Hungary between 1885 and 1907: Erich von Stroheim, Michael Curtiz, Fritz

Lang, Ernst Lubitsch, William Dieterle, Josef von Sternberg, Douglas Sirk, Robert Siodmak, Edgar Ulmer, Max Ophuls, Billy Wilder, Otto Preminger and Fred Zinnemann.

Stalinism and the Attack on Socialist Culture

One might say that the atmosphere in the great cultural centers in the 1920s was an intellectual preparation for a revolution that, tragically, did not take place. The primary responsibility for this lies with Stalinism, which delivered the greatest blows, physically and spiritually, to that accumulated critical-socialist culture. The nationalist, counterrevolutionary bureaucracy in the USSR did not merely exterminate by the hundreds of thousands the socialist intellectuals and workers in the Soviet Union in the late 1930s; it shattered the confidence of the best minds and spirits around the world in the possibility of creating a society freed of exploitation and oppression. It corrupted or demoralized generations of intellectuals. Put another way: in 1925 or 1935, the thinking of a serious artist dissatisfied with capitalism would have naturally gravitated in the direction of socialism. Is that the case today? It is not, and Stalinism, which has dragged the words "communism" and "socialism" through the mud, is principally to blame.

The first condition of a genuine artistic renaissance then is some degree of clarity—or at least a break with the most obvious falsifications—as to how humanity got itself into its present predicament. The false identification of Stalinism and Marxism, for example, must be rejected by anyone serious about addressing the crisis of culture. Film, theater and fiction in particular are too close to social life for anyone involved in their creation to be able to afford avoiding this task. Hegel maintained that art and social life were not accidentally related: "... rather we shall discover that only through the one we shall fully comprehend the other." Their "overlap," as he termed it, has an objective character that the greatest Marxists have never ignored. Art is thinking and feeling in images. If social science requires artistry, so too does the filmmaker or novelist require a degree of science. The artist of today, to put it bluntly, has the task, in addition to the training in his or her own specialty, of studying history, especially the history of the 1917 October Revolution and the struggle against its degeneration. These remarks of André Breton in 1935 take on the character of an inescapable imperative in our day: "Not only can literature not be studied outside the history of society and the history of literature; it also cannot be written, in each era, unless the writer reconciles two very different concrete facts: the history of society up to his time, and the history of literature up to his time."[109]

Art and Social Understanding

This is not primarily a call for works of a historical or social character, although such works are undoubtedly needed. It is a broader and, at the same time, more practical issue. We simply maintain that the art of the next period—whether epic in dimension or at the level of the most intimate—if it is to be enduring, must be animated by a far greater degree of social and historical understanding. It will be called upon to be so by circumstances beyond the artists' control.

This is not a call for work of an explicitly political character, although such work too has its place. The conflict between man's conscious thought and his lyrical expression, as Breton phrased it, cannot be resolved so easily. The artist must above all be true to his or her inner self, as long as this is not shallowly interpreted as taking the line of least resistance. There should be no taboos. Every aspect of human life, social relations and psychology must be freshly explored—"the dizzying descent into ourselves" undertaken, as well as the examination of more objective social processes. The aim is the creation of works that, in Breton's words again, "bring about a perfect balance between the inner and the outer; it is this balance that objectively confers authenticity upon them."[110]

The struggle today for more authentic art and cinema, from the point of view of either substance or form, does not begin from zero. In the first instance, there is the great body of past achievements to build upon. And no doubt much of the recent formal innovation that has so often struck one as empty and cold will prove to be of use, when joined to a purposiveness. A world of materials, forms, techniques will open up to the artist gripped by the understanding that the activity of interpreting the world imaginatively is linked with the activity of changing it.

---

[109] André Breton, "Speech to the Congress of Writers (1935)," *Manifestoes of Surrealism* (Ann Arbor: University of Michigan Press, 1972), 239.

[110] Ibid.

Creative authenticity has only been attained through devotion to artistic and historical truth. This seems to us to be the general orientation that filmmakers and artists need to adopt.

Hollywood Honors Elia Kazan: Filmmaker and Informer

World Socialist Web Site; February 20, 1999
(Originally published in three parts on February 20, 23 and 24, 1999)

The Decision to Give Elia Kazan an Award

"I do not hate you at all. You are simply not of my kind. You had the choice, my dear fellow, between nobility and a career. You made your choice. Be happy with it, but leave me in peace."
—Mephisto, *Klaus Mann*

The decision by the board of the Academy of Motion Picture Arts and Sciences to bestow an honorary award on filmmaker Elia Kazan at its annual Oscar ceremony March 21 is an act with definite political implications. Kazan, the director of nineteen feature films between 1945 and 1976, was one of the most prominent figures to turn informer during the anticommunist witch-hunts of the early 1950s. After a first appearance before the House Committee on Un-American Activities (HUAC) on January 14, 1952, at which he refused to "name names," Kazan reappeared on April ten and identified eight people who had been members of the Communist Party with him in the mid-1930s, along with certain party functionaries. His testimony damaged the careers and lives of a number of individuals and helped consolidate the Hollywood blacklist. Kazan's decision to collaborate with the HUAC inquisitors epitomized the devil's bargain into which a significant section of the filmmaking community and the American liberal intelligentsia as a whole entered during this period.

The Academy board's January 7 decision, by a unanimous vote, to give Kazan an award has been for the most part warmly received in the media. David Freeman in the *Los Angeles Times* January 19, in a piece entitled "Kazan's Works May Now Outweigh His Transgressions," writes: "This award would have been unlikely without the end of the Cold War.

Communism as an international force is spent. HUAC itself seems out of a black-and-white past. Though there are divisive issues today, the economy is good; Hollywood's dominion in popular entertainment has never been stronger. It's a good time to set the house in order."

The headline of Bernard Weinraub's January 24 article in the *New York Times* says a good deal: "Time Frees the Hollywood One." Weinraub argues that the award "will not only crown Kazan's career, but, in many ways, spell the end of the tormented legacy of the Hollywood blacklist." In a particularly foul piece ("A Salute to Elia Kazan") in the *Washington Post*, Richard Cohen writes: "Why, then, has it taken so long to honor this 89-year-old genius? The answer is clear: He was blacklisted." He goes on: "I would say that Kazan is finally being honored not because his anti-communism no longer matters but because it does—and it is triumphant. No longer does anyone of note believe either that the Soviet Union or communism represented an essentially—if flawed—progressive cause or, for that matter, that Moscow and Washington were equally at fault for the Cold War. That debate has ended. ... His cause (anti-communism) was good, his method (informing) was bad, but now it is only the cause that seems to matter." This is simply a case of defending yesterday's swinishness to justify tomorrow's.

The extreme right-wing press is naturally jubilant. In a piece published in William Kristol's *Weekly Standard* ("The Rehabilitation of Elia Kazan"), Stephen Schwartz writes that on March 21 "a long-standing and bitter injustice will be rectified." He continues: "Now, what amounts to Kazan's rehabilitation after decades of blackballing and smears marks a notable breach of the Iron Curtain that has long surrounded Hollywood's collective memory."

Schwartz is an ideologist, not a film critic. His knowledge of cinema history can be gauged by an ignorant reference to blacklisted filmmaker Abraham Polonsky as "a Hollywood writer who would never have been heard of had he not received a House subcommittee subpoena long ago." Before his career was cut short by the witch-hunt, Polonsky was involved in the production of two critical works of the late 1940s, *Body and Soul* (as screenwriter and perhaps more) and *Force of Evil* (as director), both starring John Garfield. Critic Andrew Sarris, no friend of the Stalinists, called Polonsky "one of the great casualties of the anti-communist hysteria of the fifties." (Ironically, thirty years ago, Sarris noted that the Garfield–Beatrice Pearson taxicab scene in *Force of Evil* "takes away some of the luster from Kazan's Brando-Steiger tour de force in *On the Waterfront*.")

Perhaps to make themselves feel better, some liberal commentators suggest that Kazan's filmmaking is being honored by the Academy, not his politics. Ellen Schrecker, author of *Many Are the Crimes: McCarthyism in America*, told the *Times*'s Weinraub: "Although I certainly don't approve of what Kazan did during the McCarthy period ... one can maybe learn a lesson from Bill Clinton and compartmentalize, and separate Kazan, the informer, and Kazan, the artist." Victor Navasky, author of *Naming Names*, commented: "First of all, it's a human thing. ... He's not physically well and he made this great cinematic contribution. Second is, with the passage of time, some of the passions have cooled and things are being put in a different perspective."

This line of reasoning fails to take into account that the Academy is planning to celebrate Kazan's *lifetime* achievement. No one with any sense would deny the filmmaker's talent or suggest boycotting or ignoring his films, but his role as an informer cannot be walled off so neatly from his artistry. Kazan's renegacy was essential to what and who he was, and subsequently became.

Not satisfied with caving in to reactionary forces, Kazan attempted to transform ratting on one's former comrades to the state into a matter of principle. His belated opposition to Stalinism, about whose crimes he remained entirely silent during the 1930s, was of a right-wing and opportunist character. It coincided with a shift in the needs and policies of American capitalism. One needs to cut through the self-serving arguments and excuses and say what is: Kazan behaved like a scoundrel, becoming an informer in 1952 to save his career in Hollywood and all that went with it.

After the officially manipulated patriotic zeal of the early and mid-1950s had subsided somewhat, and Americans were permitted the luxury of reflecting on what had happened, Kazan and other informers became the objects of a natural and instinctive revulsion. Even many political opponents of those who had been blacklisted found it difficult to stomach such contemptible conduct. Kazan deservedly became something of a pariah. Time and a general rightward shift of various social layers have done a good deal over the last several decades to change the mood within Hollywood's upper echelons.

Whatever the board members' conscious motives, their collective decision to honor Kazan is a means of absolving those who collaborated with and assisted HUAC and the McCarthyites. It is likewise an announcement by the film industry establishment that it would do nothing to oppose and resist a new witch-hunt, should it emerge. This is not an academic question. One can see the right-wing political elements who would spearhead such an operation engaged in countless attempts across the country to ban films and books and, of course, the recent effort to keep a sex scandal going in Washington.

A brief review of Kazan's career and the circumstances of the Hollywood blacklist might help place the Academy's decision in its proper artistic and historical context.

Kazan as a Film Director

"Hendrik was incapable of imagining emotions beyond the compass of his own heart. The passions to which he yielded generally had consequences that were beneficial to his career; on no account were they allowed to endanger or disturb it."
—Mephisto, *Klaus Mann*

The director was born Elia Kazanjoglou in Constantinople (now Istanbul) in 1909. In 1913, his family, Anatolian Greeks, emigrated to the US and settled in New York City, where Kazan's father became a rug merchant. The future filmmaker graduated from Williams College and went on to study drama at Yale. He joined the left-leaning Group Theatre as an actor and assistant stage manager. The Group, led for much of the 1930s by Harold Clurman, Cheryl Crawford and Lee Strasberg, was one of the focal points of artistic life, and, inevitably, radical thought and activity, in New York City during the Depression years. It attracted actors and directors, as well as a variety of writers, including Clifford Odets.

Kazan became a member of the Communist Party in the summer of 1934, and quit in the spring of 1936 in protest, he asserts, over the party leadership's heavy-handed and undemocratic attempt to wrest control of the theater company. He maintained close relations with many in and around the Stalinist movement until his HUAC appearance in 1952.

As an actor, he performed in a number of notable works, including Odets's *Waiting for Lefty* and *Golden Boy*. Kazan directed his first play in 1935 and over the next decade established himself as one of Broadway's leading figures, directing the debuts of Thornton Wilder's *The Skin of Our Teeth* (1942), Tennessee Williams's *A Streetcar Named Desire* (1947), Arthur Miller's *Death of a Salesman* (1949) and Williams's *Cat on a Hot Tin Roof* (1955). Much courted by the Hollywood studios, Kazan began his filmmaking career in 1945 with *A Tree Grows in Brooklyn*. In 1947, he and Strasberg founded the Actors Studio; its leading pupil, Marlon Brando, became the American cinema's most dynamic performer in the early 1950s.

A viewing of a dozen or so of Kazan's films produces contradictory responses. Two connected impressions stand out: there is hardly a single one of his films without a remarkable scene or performance; and there is hardly a film that stands up as an integrated, fully realized work. As a discoverer and director of (certain) actors, Kazan obviously stood out. After all, what other film director can claim the distinction of having guided performances by so many of Hollywood's "sensitive" or "tough-sensitive" leading men: Garfield, Brando, James Dean, Montgomery Clift, Warren Beatty, Robert De Niro and Jack Nicholson? Or of a remarkable, if generally lesser known, group of female performers: Barbara Bel Geddes, Dorothy McGuire, Kim Hunter, Eva Marie Saint, Julie Harris, Carroll Baker, Patricia Neal, Lee Remick and Natalie Wood?

One has a more difficult time, however, in establishing consistent themes that run through Kazan's work. There is a general hostility to bigotry and philistinism, to official abuse of power and a mistrust of dogmatism and rigidity. A demanding or oppressive father and a troubled son make appearances in several of his films (*Sea of Grass, East of Eden, Splendor in the Grass*). But these are rather diffuse notions or relationships and rather diffusely represented. One might say that Kazan is less attracted to any particular idea or ideas than to representing a certain type of heightened romantic or sexual moment. Instead, however, of probing the source of attraction of these moments and, moreover, cultivating their inner qualities in conscious opposition to the norms of everyday life, Kazan is content to stay on or near the surface. He lets the more disturbing and subversive implications slip through his fingers.

After all, an incandescent moment in film involves more than simply an accidental coming together of talented performers and technicians. Somehow, the artists must have pierced the countless layers of conventional thought and behavior that daily existence heaps upon living men and women. To undertake such a task, one must have powerful motivation and resources, which, in the final analysis, find their source in dissatisfaction with the existing psychological and social conditions. Lyricism is the beginning of a protest, as the surrealists understood.

In my view, Kazan's filmmaking, which seems to take the form of a steady decline after a somewhat interesting beginning, cannot have been helped by his strenuous and public efforts to put his radical past behind him. After all, how much did the director owe to the fact that he had developed within a socialist cultural milieu, albeit one distorted by Stalinism? In rejecting that milieu, or, rather, in *turning with hostility on* that milieu, how much of what was daring and original in himself did he also repudiate or excise?

In any event, *A Tree Grows in Brooklyn* has a certain charm, despite its sentimentality, in its evocative recreation of turn-of-the-century working class life in Brooklyn. *Sea of Grass* (1947) and *Gentleman's Agreement* (1947) are fairly tedious studio-commissioned works. The first is in the *Effi Briest* mold—a story of a woman's apparent adultery and her separation from her children enforced by an unforgiving husband; the second a liberal critique of anti-Semitism in postwar America. *Panic in the Streets* (1950) is a jittery effort about a manhunt for gangsters in New Orleans, one of whom is carrying pneumonic plague. Regarding Kazan's first half-dozen films, Jean-Luc Godard, then a youthful critic, noted their "impersonality" and an "absence of style which reveals an affectionate contempt for art on the part of the author."

Kazan made three of his next four films with Brando—*A Streetcar Named Desire* (1951), *Viva Zapata!* (1952) and *On the Waterfront* (1954). I have to admit a prejudice here: relatively little sympathy for the Williams–Arthur Miller–Strasberg–Kazan school of drama and acting. I've always thought there was something provincial and stunted about the conceptions of its leading lights. Most of their work, it seems to me, suffered from a false "depth," a kind of cluttered psychologizing that covered up at least as much as it revealed. This is obviously a subject that deserves a special study.

In any case, I've always found *A Streetcar Named Desire* particularly problematic. A recent viewing tempered my hostility somewhat. There are some telling moments and genuine feelings in the piece. I still find it hard to take, however. Brando and Kim Hunter make it watchable, particularly the former. I do not know how much credit Kazan deserves for Brando's performance, but its restraint, in the midst of a great deal of noisy thrashing about, is remarkable. Brando's Kowalski is wonderfully relaxed and amused, at least in the early scenes. After that, everything goes to pieces in this story about "a neurotic Southern girl on the last lap to the mental ward," in critic Manny Farber's words.

Viva Zapata! has its excesses and its silly moments, but this is one of Kazan's most creditable works, in my view. Brando is excellent as the Mexican revolutionary and the film as a whole, from a screenplay by John Steinbeck, is done with a certain degree of tact and intelligence. The film's vision of a revolutionary so appalled by the occupational hazards of holding power that he walks away from it remains a compelling, if not entirely satisfying one. From the sociopolitical point of view, this is the one film of Kazan's, if one can make such narrow distinctions, that might be characterized as anti-Stalinist, not anticommunist.

On the Waterfront tells the story of Terry Malloy (Brando), a longshoreman and former boxer, who ends up telling a crime commission everything he knows about the operations of the corrupt and murderous local union leadership. Kazan and screenwriter Budd Schulberg, also a HUAC informer, made the film in large measure to justify their own actions. In his autobiography, Brando makes two remarkable claims: first, that "I did not realize then ... that *On the Waterfront* was really a metaphorical argument" by Kazan and Schulberg "to justify finking on their friends"; second, that when shown the completed film, "I was so depressed by my performance I got up and left the screen room. I thought I was a huge failure." The film stands up, despite its reactionary and self-serving theme, primarily because of the performances of Brando and Eva Marie Saint and its overall grittiness. It also has an extraordinary score by Leonard Bernstein.

The notion, however, that *On the Waterfront* captures metaphorically the truth of Kazan's relationship to the Communist Party, on the one hand, and HUAC, on the other, is fanciful, as is the idea that the film somehow brings out the "dilemma" facing the potential informer. Where is the "moral ambiguity" in Malloy's position that Kazan has referred to on various occasions? If Brando's character does not speak to the authorities and seek their protection, he is likely to be rubbed out. He is fighting for his life and has no choice, within the framework established by the film's creators, but to turn on his former associates. Kazan and Schulberg have stacked the deck entirely in their favor.

How do the fictional circumstances in *On the Waterfront* resemble the reality of the early 1950s in the US? In turning informer, it was Kazan who joined a political lynch mob. The Communist Party was not simply synonymous with its Stalinist leadership and program. It contained devoted and self-sacrificing individuals who believed they were fighting for progressive social change. Terry Malloy's traumatic experiences have more in common with those endured by the actors, directors and writers *who faced the blacklist* than with those who accepted and profited from it.

If Kazan had made *"On the Set"* instead, about a well-paid and successful director who cravenly surrendered to right-wing political forces, would it have had the same resonance? (Brando's failure to see any connection between Kazan's informing and his own character's behavior is comprehensible precisely because the situation set up in the film is so at odds with the director's actual circumstances. Indeed, the strength of the film is that one would not regard it as a defense of cowardice and opportunism without a knowledge of the historical and personal facts.)

James Dean aspired to be another Brando. He never came close to being that, but he is occasionally affecting (and sometimes irritating) in Steinbeck's *East of Eden*, a modern retelling of the Cain and Abel story. The film drags on, however, and the various relationships, which are not all that startling or revealing to begin with, take an interminable amount of time to establish. It takes Kazan forty-five minutes to lay out relations that a Douglas Sirk or a Michael Curtiz could have made clear in three or four shots. (In his memoir, blacklisted screenwriter Walter Bernstein recalls that in the aftermath of Kazan's HUAC appearance, Dean expressed contempt for the director and vowed never to work with him. After *East of Eden* came out, Bernstein and director Martin Ritt ran into Dean on the street. "He came up to us," Bernstein writes, "and spoke without slackening his stride. 'He made me a star,' he said, and walked on.")

Tennessee Williams did not much like his own script for Kazan's next film, *Baby Doll* (1956), and one can hardly blame him. Carroll Baker, as a still-virginal wife, and Eli Wallach, as an interloper trying to do business in hopelessly backward rural Mississippi, stand out.

Abe Polonsky once asserted that Kazan suffered from a "bad conscience" in the films he made after giving his HUAC testimony. *A Face in the Crowd* (1957), also written by Schulberg, could be seen in this light. The Capraesque story of a malevolent country singer and huckster who becomes a huge television star and the agent of a fascistic US senator is semi-hysterical in its efforts to demonstrate its makers' progressive social views. Andy Griffith, apparently at the director's urging, plays at top volume from beginning to end and simply grows wearisome. Much in this film is over-inflated, unconvincing. Patricia Neal is affecting, however.

Wild River (1960), the story of a Tennessee Valley Authority official in the 1930s trying to convince an old woman to vacate her property to make way for a hydroelectric project, has its genuine pleasures, above all in certain moments between Montgomery Clift and Lee Remick. Natalie Wood is a girl in late 1920s Kansas suffering a breakdown after experiencing disappointment in love at the hands of Warren Beatty and his family in *Splendor in the Grass* (1961). Andrew Sarris complained at the time that "Kazan's violence has always been more excessive than expressive, more mannered than meaningful. There is an edge of hysteria even to his pauses and silences, and the thin line between passion and neurosis has been crossed time and again."

In *America, America* (1963), Kazan told the story of his uncle's emigration from Turkey to the US at the turn of the century. For all its pain and pathos, this treatment of the immigrant's dream of passage to the new world is markedly uncritical. That the story stops and starts a dozen times, gets sidetracked, loses its way, befits a film that cannot make up its mind what it wants to say about its hero or his new country.

The Last Tycoon (1976) is based on F. Scott Fitzgerald's final, uncompleted novel; playwright Harold Pinter wrote the screenplay. Robert De Niro intelligently portrays a film studio head, patterned by Fitzgerald on MGM executive Irving Thalberg. The film was not successful, but its subdued and slightly depressed tone seems appropriate to Kazan's final film effort.

On the whole, in my view, there are more minuses than pluses in Kazan's work. Stylistically, he borrowed from a number of sources—Eisenstein, Ford, Welles, neorealism, the *Nouvelle Vague* et al.—without ever seeming to establish a definite artistic viewpoint. One feels that, alongside the legitimate desire to communicate what he knows and thinks about the world, the director is always seeking to impress the viewer, to establish his, Kazan's, credentials, above all.

I do not think there's any question about Kazan's "touch" with actors, but there is some question as to what precisely that touch involved. Brando has some interesting things to say on this subject. He writes in his autobiography: "I've never seen a director who became as deeply and emotionally involved in a scene as Gadg [Kazan's nickname]. ... On *Streetcar* ... I discovered he was the rarest of directors, one with the wisdom to know when to leave actors alone. He understood intuitively what they could bring to a performance and he gave them freedom."

I do not question Brando's judgment, or the results Kazan achieved with him and others of or near his caliber, but I feel obliged to point out a number of things. First, Brando is as humble about his own abilities as Kazan is ordinarily overconfident about his. But even so, what is the actor fundamentally saying? That Kazan was one of the few who gave him room to apply his artistry.

In his autobiography, *A Life*, Kazan has the grace to credit Brando with finding the "tone of reproach that is so loving and so melancholy" in the taxicab scene in *On the Waterfront*. He writes: "I didn't direct that; Marlon showed me, as he often did, how the scene should be performed. ... Marlon was always presenting me with these small miracles; he was more often than not better than I, and I could only be grateful for him."[111] I suspect that points to an elementary truth, which is nothing for Kazan to be ashamed about: that Brando was a more significant figure in relation to film acting than Kazan was to film directing.

This is not to deny or denigrate the latter's role. He was there, he presided over some extraordinary moments, he encouraged them. He possessed in full measure that critical ingredient of the film director's art. But there are other ingredients. One is the ability, while allowing each actor and technician to make the richest contribution he or she can, to stamp one's personality and conceptions on every performance and image. Kazan was an extraordinary director of the extraordinary actor, Brando, but why are there are so many poor performances in his films, even by remarkable performers? Why were Zero Mostel and Jack Palance permitted to chew up the scenery in *Panic in the Streets*? Or Vivien Leigh in *Streetcar*? What was Kazan thinking when he directed Griffith in *A Face in the Crowd* and Pat Hingle in *Splendor in the Grass* to bellow at the tops of their voices to no useful effect?

One might easily be accused of interpreting Kazan's art in the light of his performance in the political and moral realm, but I think there is a certain shortsightedness and "opportunism" to his direction. Everything is thrown into the effort to achieve a particular effect without adequate thought to the whole, not simply to the whole film, but to the *body of work* as a whole.

To be considered an "actor's director" is a double-edged sword. Actors are the human material of drama. The best give of themselves wholeheartedly and produce results that far exceed the mere sum of a human brain and body and preexisting lines of dialog. But the actor's viewpoint, bound up with the obligation to concentrate on the truth of self, is almost always a partial and even *necessarily* distorted one. (The relative strength of the acting and relative weakness of the writing in the American theater of the 1930s and 1940s hints at an underlying problem: the shallowness and provincialism of

---

[111]   Elia Kazan, *A Life* (New York: Da Capo Press, 1997), 526.

a good deal of the artistic Leftism of the day in the US, the degree to which it became trapped either within "socialist realist" conventions, or, after that had run its course, a somewhat tepid, self-absorbed expressionism.)

Moreover, there is cause to mistrust directors who are legendary, as Kazan was, for manipulating performers to get a desired reaction—i.e., angering or exciting or causing them anxiety by artificial means. (For example, during the filming of *Viva Zapata*, Kazan apparently told Anthony Quinn that Brando was saying things about him behind his back to sharpen the conflict between their two characters on screen. Brando calls the director, approvingly, an "arch-manipulator of actors' feelings.") Such maneuvers may be necessary occasionally, but as a pattern they suggest cynicism and a lack of confidence in one's ability to convince actors of the emotional truth of a scene and provide the means to arrive at it.

A Hawks or a Welles or a Visconti or a Fassbinder is not primarily known as an "actor's director," but as a film artist who integrates the work of his actors into a larger and all-sided aesthetic effort. One of their films is instantly recognizable in a fashion that a Kazan film never is. His films, in style and subject, go all over the map in search of something the director never found. In a January 1964 review of *America, America*, Sarris observed that "Kazan is generally better with individual scenes than with a whole scenario, and ... his players are remembered long after the import of their playing has been forgotten." I would subscribe to that view. A genuine talent, yes; a "genius," by no means. His career considered as a whole, Kazan belongs in the second or third rank of Hollywood directors of his era.

Is there, speaking generally, a link between Kazan's artistic weaknesses and his role in the 1950s? This, it seems to me, is on somewhat shaky ground. There were, after all, far less complete artists who acted with principle and courage. It might be said that in Kazan one finds a particularly unfavorable constellation of personal and intellectual flaws: a relatively superficial political radicalism; a genuine artistic talent sufficient to gain him recognition, but inadequate to the task of fully working problems through; and an extremely powerful desire to maintain his position and reputation.

In *America, America*, Kazan portrays a man prepared to go to any length to reach the shores of the Promised Land. He slaves, steals, betrays to make his way to the US. When he reaches New York City, he kneels and kisses the ground. Kazan, the ambitious immigrant's son, learned some bitter lessons about America in the early 1930s and was radicalized by the experience. The country, above all, had disappointed him. But why, he must have felt a decade later, should he maintain that resentment when America had, at long last, fulfilled its promise—at least to him? And, moreover, under conditions in which to continue opposing the status quo threatened his continued prominence and celebrity. From the point of succeeding in America, who would dispute Kazan's claim that he had his "own good reasons," as he called them, for turning informer?

Anticommunism and the Film Industry

"Now I have contaminated myself, thought Hendrik. Now there is a stain on my hand that I can never wash off. ... Now I have sold myself. ... Now I am marked for life ...
—Mephisto, *Klaus Mann*

At least from the onset of the great economic crisis of the early 1930s, the authorities in the US have been alert to the potential danger represented by motion pictures. They consistently acted to weaken or, if necessary, suppress any radical or socially critical tendencies in filmmaking. One historian has asserted that the Production Code imposed in 1934 was intended both to exclude sexual conduct and violence from the screens and to "use popular entertainment films to reinforce conservative moral and political values." Adherence to the Code, for example, required such changes that MGM dropped plans to film Sinclair Lewis's *It Can't Happen Here*, the author's vision of the rise of American fascism. The Production Code Administration insisted that Fritz Lang's anti-lynching film, *Fury* (1936), not include a black victim or any criticism of the Jim Crow South.

The House Committee on Un-American Activities (HUAC) was formed in May 1938. Under the chairmanship of Rep. Martin Dies (D-Tex.), the committee pioneered many of the techniques later used by Sen. Joseph R. McCarthy: indiscriminate accusations, pressure on witnesses to name former associates, hearings in which being questioned or mentioned became an indication of guilt, guilt by association. The committee was permanently established by the House of Representatives in 1945; two years later, a federal appeals court upheld its power to cite uncooperative witnesses for contempt of Congress.

In the late 1930s and early 1940s, HUAC and State Senator Jack Tenney's California Joint Fact-Finding Committee on Un-American Activities launched attacks on left-wingers in the film industry. Dies spearheaded an attack on the Federal Theatre Project, which succeeded in getting its funds cut off in June 1939. When leading liberal and radical figures in Hollywood attacked his committee's operations, the Texas congressman told the press that the movie industry was a "hotbed of communism." On February 27, 1940, 2,500 people gathered at the Philharmonic Auditorium in Los Angeles to protest this outburst.

The following year, Tenney—Dies's California counterpart—announced that he was going to launch an investigation of "Reds in movies." The inquiry was in part a union-busting operation. Walt Disney, whose operations had recently been struck by cartoonists and animators, was particularly anxious to root out radicals. Tenney's hearings proved something of a fiasco.

In the campaign to suppress *Citizen Kane* in 1941, William Randolph Hearst and the gossip columnists who did his dirty work set an important precedent by smearing Orson Welles as a radical and a "red."

The US-USSR alliance during the Second World War led to a temporary suspension of such activities. Interestingly, on the eve of US intervention, an attempt by right-wing, isolationist senators to probe individuals and groups in Hollywood who were urging American entry into the war, including "anti-fascist" and Stalinist elements, was rebuffed by the film studios and unfavorably treated by the press. The film producers retained Wendell Wilkie to represent them before the Senate Subcommittee. In the war years, Hollywood even produced a few vaguely or not so vaguely pro-Soviet films, such as *Mission to Moscow* (1943), *The North Star* (1943) and *Song of Russia* (1944).

The witch-hunt began in earnest in the film industry in October 1947, when HUAC held a series of hearings on the subject of "subversives" in the film industry. After several days of testimony from "friendly" witnesses—anticommunist producers, directors, actors—HUAC began its questioning of "unfriendly" witnesses, the group that became known as the Hollywood Ten. These leftist screenwriters and directors—CP members or supporters—refused to cooperate and were cited a few weeks later for contempt of Congress. (Many of them later served one-year prison terms.) In the face of HUAC's determination, backed up by the media, liberal support for the Ten in Hollywood rapidly evaporated.

Film producers meeting November 24–25 at the Waldorf-Astoria Hotel in New York adopted a resolution, declaring, "We will not knowingly employ a Communist." The blacklist was officially on, or, rather, unofficially on, since there was no authoritative list of unemployables. As historian Ellen Schrecker puts it, "writers stopped getting calls for work, actors were told they were 'too good for the part.'"[112] A variety of reactionary organizations, including the American Legion, and Hollywood's own network of anticommunists and informers worked closely with the studios to enforce the blacklist. From this point onward, the combined efforts of the government, industry, and right-wing and church groups did not let up until a systematic purging of left-wing and radical elements from the filmmaking ranks had been effected.

This was only part of a much larger effort by the American ruling class, after decades of political instability, to settle accounts with radical-ism and socialism. Anticommunism became virtually a state religion in the United States in this period. In 1947, President Harry Truman established a loyalty program for federal employees and asked the attorney general to draw up a list of "subversive" organizations. Between March 1947 and December 1952, some 6.6 million government employees were investi-gated. During that same period, 1947–52, congressional committees held eighty-four hearings into "Communist subversion." HUAC provided data on 60,000 people to employers. At least 15,000 federal employees were fired or forced to resign by government loyalty boards. By one estimate, 13.5 million Americans came within the scope of federal, state and private loy-alty programs. Approximately 20 percent of the working population had to take an oath or receive clearance as a condition of employment.

There was a general ideological assault on the American population—in-tended to stigmatize concepts such as Socialism, Marxism and Revolution—to encourage their identification in the popular consciousness with infinite wickedness and social catastrophe and, more generally, to cultivate an atmo-sphere of stifling conformity. A Communist, according to the official version, was un-American, non-Christian, an alien, a creature from hell.

The assault took a variety of forms. HUAC distributed millions of copies of a pamphlet, "One Hundred Things You Should Know About Communism" ("Where can Communists be found? Everywhere.") A dramatic series, based on the career of FBI informer Herbert Philbrick, *I Led Three Lives*, ran for three years on television. Hollywood churned out a series of "anti-Red" films: for example, *The Red Menace* (1949), *I Married a Communist* (1950), *I Was a Communist for the FBI* (1951), *Walk East on Beacon* (1952), *My Son John* (1952), *Big Jim McClain* (1952) and *Trial* (1952).

---

[112] Ellen Schrecker, *The Age of McCarthyism: A Brief History with Documents* (Boston: St. Martin's Press, 1994), 89.

The last of the Hollywood Ten went to prison in September 1950. The HUAC inquisitors returned to Hollywood in the spring of 1951. As Ceplair and Englund write in their history of political life in the film industry from 1930 to 1960, the new hearings followed a series of events that strengthened the committee's position: "the conviction of Alger Hiss, the fall of China to the Communists, the first successful atomic explosion by the Soviet Union, the arrest of atomic spy Klaus Fuchs in England, the dawning of Joseph McCarthy's special brand of anti-communism, the passage of the McCarran Internal Security Act, ... the outbreak of the Korean War, the Supreme Court's approval of the Smith Act [under which the Trotskyists had been persecuted in 1941] ... and the arrest of the Rosenbergs."[113]

One hundred and ten men and women were subpoenaed during the second set of HUAC hearings from 1951 to 1953; fifty-eight turned informer. The more prominent ones—thirty-one individuals with at least four film credits—gave an average of twenty-nine names to the committee. Most gave way abjectly. The first witness, actor Larry Parks, "reduced himself nearly to groveling and pleading" in face of the committee's demand for names. In the end, after a certain amount of public soul-searching, he identified ten individuals. The price of hesitation was high. A headline in the *Los Angeles Examiner* two days later read: LARRY PARKS LOSES $75,000 SCREEN ROLE. Parks's career was more or less finished. The lesson was not lost on most of the others who testified.

Four prominent directors became informers: Frank Tuttle, a dependable journeyman, perhaps best known for *This Gun for Hire* (1942) with Alan Ladd and Veronica Lake; Edward Dmytryk, the "Judas" of the Hollywood Ten, director of *Murder My Sweet* (1944) and *Cornered* (1945); Robert Rossen (*Body and Soul* [1947] and *The Hustler* [1961]), who refused to name names in 1951, capitulated in 1953, and was apparently tortured by the decision the rest of his life; and Kazan.

Of the four and perhaps the entire group of informers, Kazan certainly possessed the greatest stature as an artist and intellectual. His decision to collaborate with the witch-hunters had far-reaching consequences. One "director-victim" told Victor Navasky, for his book *Naming Names*, "If Kazan had refused to cooperate ... he couldn't have derailed

---

[113] Larry Ceplair and Steven Englund, *The Inquisition in Hollywood: Politics in the Film Community 1930–60* (Berkeley and Los Angeles: University of California Press, 1979), 362.

the Committee, but he might well have broken the blacklist. He was too important to be ignored."[114] Navasky comments: "Probably no single individual could have broken the blacklist in April 1952, and yet no person was in a better strategic position to try than Kazan, by virtue of his prestige and economic invulnerability, to mount a symbolic campaign against it, and by this example inspire hundreds of fence sitters to come over to the opposition."[115]

As it turned out, Kazan did not have it in him to do that. In the various attempts at self-justification he has made over the years, he asserts that matters of principle—opposition to the conspiratorial methods of the Communist Party and the crimes of Stalin—impelled him to name names. In his autobiography, Kazan denied doing it "for the money." He writes: "It [saving his career in Hollywood] was not the reason. In the end, when I did what I did, it was for my own good reasons and after much thought about my own experiences."

Testimony from his contemporaries suggests otherwise. Lillian Hellman, not the most reliable of witnesses it must be admitted, claimed that Kazan told her, "I earned over $400,000 last year from theater. But [Twentieth Century-Fox president Spyros] Skouras says I'll never make another movie [if I don't cooperate]." Theater producer Kermit Bloomgarden informed Navasky that Kazan "told me he'd been to Washington and met with J. Edgar Hoover and Spyros Skouras and they wanted him to give names. ... He said 'I've got to think of my kids.' And I said, 'This too shall pass, and then you'll be an informer in the eyes of your kids, think of that.'"[116] Kazan refers in his autobiography to Skouras's proposing a meeting with Hoover, but never specifies whether or not it took place.

In that same work, the director makes fairly plain his own frame of mind, citing a diary entry from 1952 that described a conversation with Arthur Miller: "I mentioned that Skouras had implied I couldn't work in pictures anymore if I didn't name the other lefties in the Group, then told Art I'd prepared myself for a period of no movie work or money. ... But that I didn't feel altogether good about such a decision. That I'd say (to myself) what the hell am I giving all this up for? To defend a secrecy I didn't think right and to defend people who'd already been named or soon would be by

---

[114]   Victor Navasky, *Naming Names* (New York, Viking Press, 1980), 201.

[115]   Ibid, 200.

[116]   Ibid, 201.

someone else? I said I'd hated the Communists for many years and didn't feel right about giving up my career to defend them."[117]

Some gave names to the Committee with obvious reluctance; a few later repudiated their conduct (actor Sterling Hayden, for example); others were deeply troubled by the decision. Kazan obviously had to see himself acting not out of self-interest, but in defense of principle. Two days after his HUAC appearance, Kazan took out an ad—written, he says in his autobiography, by his late first wife—in the *New York Times* justifying his behavior. It is a fairly filthy document.

Kazan's essential claim is that "Communist activities" represent "a dangerous and alien conspiracy" that needs to be exposed. The American people "can solve this problem wisely only if they have the facts about Communism." He asserts that "any American who is in possession of such facts has the obligation to make them known, either to the public or to the appropriate Government agency." This is apparently what Kazan has done by placing the facts about his own life "before the House Committee on Un-American Activities without reserve."

He explains, in his ad, that up until this point he has refrained from telling his story sooner because he has been held back by "a piece of specious reasoning which has silenced many liberals. It goes like this: 'You may hate the Communists, but you must not attack them or expose them, because if you do you are attacking the right to hold unpopular opinions and you are joining the people who attack civil liberties.'"

This argument, he has come to realize, is "a lie. Secrecy serves the Communists. At the other pole, it serves those who are interested in silencing liberal voices. The employment of a lot of good liberals is threatened because they have allowed themselves to become associated with or silenced by the Communists. Liberals must speak out."

Kazan's membership in the Communist Party has given him "Firsthand experience of dictatorship and thought control. ... It left me with an abiding hatred of Communist philosophy and methods and the conviction that these must be resisted always."

The contention that the Communist Party was nothing more than a GPU conspiracy is gutter political reaction of the McCarthy type. Budd Schulberg, Kazan's co-informer and screenwriter, tried to put a more exalted twist on his own testimony in conversations with Victor Navasky. He

---

[117] Kazan, 460.

claimed that the tragic fate of Soviet artists motivated him and that he acted to block the growth of a totalitarian movement in the US. The informers,
he said, were "premature anti-Stalinists."

The genuine anti-Stalinists, as anyone who has studied the history of
this century knows, were the Trotskyists, and they did not discover the cause
in 1952. Trotsky and his co-thinkers fought for the regeneration of the Soviet
regime and the Communist International from 1923 until 1933, when the
latter organization's worthlessness from the point of view of social revolution became manifest, and thereafter for political revolution in the USSR and
the building of a new socialist international. Their opposition to Stalinism
was of a Marxist character, an opposition from the left. They explained that
the regime in the Soviet Union had betrayed the October Revolution and that
its crimes did not result from the growth of socialism in the USSR, but from
its opposite, the growth of tendencies that would lead to the restoration of
capitalism. Subsequent events have vindicated that view.

Marxists in the USSR by the tens of thousands paid for their opposition to the bureaucratic dictatorship with their lives. On the other hand,
many of the social types who had denounced the Bolshevik-led revolution
in 1917, with its perspective of world revolution, flocked to support the
Stalin regime in the 1930s, precisely because it had abandoned the path
of social revolution. One has only to remember the support given by such
respected liberal organs as the *New York Times* and the *Nation* to the infa-
mous Moscow purge trials of the late 1930s.

Kazan, Schulberg and others aligned themselves with the Soviet bureaucracy and the American party during the era of the Popular Front,
when the Stalinists were supporters of Roosevelt and held significant
positions in the CIO unions. Stalinists or fellow travelers controlled theater companies, publishing houses and a variety of publications. Kazan
and many others like him were never by any stretch of the imagination
Marxists, but left reformists. Whether the political evolution of these individuals was predetermined, whether some other prospect might have
opened up for them if the Communist parties had not been thoroughly
Stalinized, is now a moot point.

Schulberg's notion that oppressed Soviet artists would be served by
the strengthening of the American state rested on a fundamental political
lie: that American "democracy" and Stalinist "totalitarianism" were deadly
enemies. This vulgar, false and self-serving notion served to justify a whole
host of perfidious deeds during the Cold War. Schulberg never bothered to

explain how ceding the struggle against totalitarianism to Joseph McCarthy, John Foster Dulles, Dwight Eisenhower and Richard Nixon, the CIA, the FBI and the US military would advance the cause of human liberation.

What were the consequences of McCarthyism within the US? In his *Times* ad, Kazan claimed he valued "free speech, a free press." Under the cover of pursuing the Communist menace, right-wing and corporate interests consolidated their hold over the media, helping establish a conformist, pro-capitalist climate unlike anything that exists in any European country. The paralyzing narrowness of American political life, with its minuscule differences between two big business parties, can be traced back to this period.

However, for all the rubbish that was produced in Hollywood in the 1950s it would not be correct to argue that the immediate impact of the witch-hunt was the artistic collapse of the American film industry. Classical studio directors, whose careers predated the McCarthy era and who had largely remained aloof from the political controversies of the early 1950s, continued to produce serious works for at least another decade. The generations that have come after them, however, have had progressively less to say and have possessed, in general, neither political nor artistic principles.

In any event, I suspect the powers that be had already grasped that another medium had supplanted film as the most powerful and direct influence on the populace: television. Although some blacklisted writers got jobs in the new industry under assumed names, as a whole, television programs of the 1950s promoted some of the most repressive conceptions ever advanced about the human condition.

Kazan also pledged his commitment to the "rights of labor" in his declaration. However, eliminating radicals from the labor movement and thereby weakening workers resistance was a top priority of the McCarthyites. While the ruling class was in no position to drive workers back to the economic conditions of the 1930s, it was determined to render the unions politically harmless. The bourgeoisie was prepared to make sizable concessions in the form of wages and improved living conditions if it could ensure the dominance of a pro-capitalist bureaucracy in the labor movement.

Employers worked closely with various state investigative bodies to identify "troublemakers." Unions that refused to purge CP leaders were expelled; in some industries, mass dismissals took place. In the auto industry, UAW leader Walter Reuther took advantage of the Stalinists' unpopularity due to their role as policemen of the no-strike pledge during the war to whip up a pogrom-like atmosphere against left-wingers.

The overall result of this process was the political neutering of the labor movement and, ultimately, the establishment within the unions and factories of a virtual dictatorship presided over by right-wing thugs. This had immense and disastrous consequences for American society. Working people are continuing to pay, in the form of steadily worsening living standards and a variety of other ways, for their failure to organize themselves as an independent political force and their general acceptance of the framework of capitalism. And there have been consequences for humanity as a whole. After all, would it not have been far more difficult for the American state to implement its foreign policy—from its support for bloody dictatorships in Asia, Africa and Latin America, to its decade-long war in Southeast Asia, to its direct role in mass murder in Indonesia, Chile and elsewhere—without the existence of an entirely docile, pro-imperialist AFL-CIO, an organization, in fact, intimately tied to the intelligence and military apparatuses?

Conclusion: Some Behavior Is Inexcusable

"Each knew what the other was thinking. Höfgen thought of Ihrig and Ihrig of Höfgen: Yes, yes, my friend, you're just as great a bastard as I am."
—Mephisto, *Klaus Mann*

The citations at the beginning of each section of this piece come from *Mephisto*, the remarkable novel written in 1936 by Klaus Mann, German novelist Thomas Mann's son. The book's central character is Hendrik Höfgen, in whose figure, a recent English-language edition explains, the author painted a "thinly veiled portrait of his former brother-in-law, the actor Gustaf Gründgens. Gründgens, who had been married to [Klaus] Mann's favorite sister, Erika, and had once been a flamboyant champion of Communism, had a magnificent career in Nazi Germany under the auspices of Field Marshal Hermann Göring."[118] Höfgen found himself unable to resist careerism, self-delusion and opportunism. Nor was he the only artist or intellectual to heed the siren song of National Socialism. The choice Kazan faced in the early 1950s—opposition or acquiescence to reaction—was posed in the sharpest fashion in the artists' experience with German fascism.

---

[118]   Publisher's Note to Klaus Mann, *Mephisto* (New York: Penguin Books, 1977), front matter, no page number.

Reviewing Kazan's fate, a number of questions pose themselves, none of which can be answered exhaustively here: From the point of view of the ruling class, why was McCarthyism necessary? Why did this very reactionary trend meet so relatively little resistance? And, more generally, why is it so difficult to take a principled stand in America?

Contrary to the superficial notions of bourgeois historians of the liberal or conservative persuasion, the American population is not by nature hostile to radical change or even social revolution. The US came far closer to social revolution in the 1930s than the experts would care to admit. Significant layers of the population came into contact with left-wing ideas for the first time and found them appealing. The entire experience was frightening and chastening for the bourgeoisie. The argument that McCarthyism was simply an eruption of paranoia that bore no relation to the actual strength of the radical movement is not substantiated by the facts. The Communist Party, the Trotskyist movement, the social democratic parties may have been relatively small numerically, but the commitment of the population, emerging from a war with fascism, to what it perceived to be progressive and democratic social change was genuine.

After all, the history of the United States has left a peculiar ideological patrimony. For the purposes of bamboozling the population, the political establishment finds it helpful to refer to past struggles for "freedom," "equality" and "democracy," and falsely claim their heritage. The difficulty, of course, is that struggles over those principles did take place, great sacrifices were made, and there is always the danger that people will take them seriously and, moreover, want to continue and deepen them.

In no country in the world is there a greater discrepancy between the promise, on the one hand, and the social and political reality, on the other. Given an opportunity to examine the problem, masses of people would have no difficulty working out that the overthrow of capitalism follows logically upon the great eighteenth- and nineteenth-century battles against monarchy, colonialism and slavery. Indeed, one could argue that the powers that be make unrelenting war on socialism, given the highly proletarianized population and advanced economic conditions of the US, precisely because, all things being equal, it is such a rational and attractive proposition.

Social development, of course, does not take place in this manner, through formally logical sequences, but through living struggles in which the consciousness, preparedness and self-confidence of the various contending parties play crucial roles. To explain why the McCarthyites had such a relatively easy time of it, despite the strong democratic traditions of the American population and its potential sympathy for socialism, certain social and cultural questions have to be considered.

It should be kept in mind that while the witch-hunt was a sustained and zealously pursued campaign, it was not for the most part accompanied by physical repression. There was, of course, the horrifying example of the Rosenbergs. Some Communist Party members went to jail; many left-wingers lost their livelihoods. But large numbers of people, like Kazan, capitulated without fear of any particular reprisals. Many commentators note that Kazan could have pursued a career in the theater or in Europe. This makes his behavior all the more revealing.

Why did so few, particularly in the liberal and artistic intelligentsia, play honorable roles?

One cannot simply cite personal weakness, singly or collectively, by way of answer.

An irony is surely at work here. The US is famously the land of individualism, yet perhaps nowhere else is there such an intense, unrelenting pressure to conform. Kazan is probably telling the truth when he says he did not inform "for the money." It is more likely that he testified from fear of social ostracism and the loss of recognition.

In the final analysis, the immense rewards for conforming and the high price of resisting have been bound up with the condition of US capitalism. The American bourgeoisie launched its ideological scorched-earth policy in the late 1940s in part because it *could*. It emerged from the war the most powerful ruling class in the world, with nearly unchallenged economic hegemony and enormous financial resources. Its state had the credibility of having played a major role in defeating Nazi Germany, a credibility reinforced by the US Communist Party with its dreadful super-patriotic line ("Communism is twentieth-century Americanism"). The ruling class in the US was in a unique position to combine bribery, flattery and intimidation to neutralize real or potential opposition.

The ideological weaknesses of the population came into play as well. Their lack of strong socialist traditions, relatively low level of class consciousness and difficulty in drawing generalized political conclusions from experiences rendered large numbers of people vulnerable to anticommunist propaganda, particularly under conditions of generally rising living standards and economic prosperity. Within the intelligentsia specifically, the absence of traditions of opposition along clearly defined social and class lines played a damaging role. Stalinism had contributed significantly to this problem, with its cynical promotion among intellectuals and artists in the late 1930s of "friendship for the Soviet Union" (i.e., "friendship" for the bureaucracy and silence about Stalin's crimes) instead of socialist politics.

Figures like Kazan went along with an anticapitalist social wave at the height of the Depression. Everything these individuals lacked, however, everything that was unthought-out and uncritical, proved their undoing when the current dramatically shifted. Now (by the late 1940s) prosperous or on the road to being prosperous, recognized, even feted by the entertainment industry, Kazan and others were not inclined to remember responsibilities to the working class or the social cause in which they had once believed. Having tasted of celebrity, they found the thought of isolation terrifying. In America, after all, if you are not an immense success, a star, you are nothing, a human zero. To take a stand against official society means, above all, leading a life out of the limelight.

In asking, why is it so hard to take a principled stand in the US, one is also hinting at a related question: why is it so hard to be a great artist in the US? Because great art requires extraordinary mental independence and rigor, immense powers of resistance to external pressures and unyielding commitment to the truth of one's inner self. Where these qualities are in short supply, artistic work will not rise to the highest levels.

Kazan, Budd Schulberg and the rest of the informers acted like scoundrels and cowards to save their careers. Sterling Hayden in his autobiography had the elementary honesty to acknowledge this. "I think of Larry Parks," he wrote, "[who] consigned himself to oblivion. Well, I hadn't made that mistake. Not by a goddamned sight. I was a real daddy longlegs of a worm when it came to crawling. ... I [then] swung like a goon from role to role. ... They were all made back to back in an effort to cash in fast on my new status as a sanitary culture hero." Kazan saved his skin and made another eleven films after his informing. But what was left of him?

I may be accused of concerning myself excessively about the fate of someone who acted in such a disgraceful manner, but a concern for art and the artist obliges me to make some kind of accounting. Acts committed against one's better self, like Kazan's, set off a process, lengthy or otherwise depending upon the moral state of the individual, of inner annihilation. Marlon Brando, perhaps the greatest performer with whom he worked, underestimates the damage the filmmaker did, but there is something at least profoundly humane in his observation that Kazan "has done great injury to others, but mostly to himself."

"Kazan" and "informer" became forever inseparably linked. From the point of view of Kazan's own intellectual and artistic development, the most terrible thing about his deed was that it ineluctably condemned him to a life that would be largely devoted from then on to self-justification. He would never again have the luxury of being able to devote himself single-mindedly to any other problem. He effectively destroyed his own freedom of artistic movement.

No doubt Kazan simply wished to rid himself of a past toward which he no longer felt any attachment or sympathy and which threatened to disrupt his promising career. No one is obliged to hang on to ideas he or she rejects. Going over to the side of the most deadly enemies of social progress is another matter. Kazan thought he could play games with history and escape unscathed. But if there is one lesson that might be drawn from the debacle of his life and career, it is that such actions have consequences.

A perusal of Kazan's autobiography leaves a peculiarly unpleasant taste in one's mouth. It contains a number of relatively acute observations about this or that individual, this or that artistic effort, as well as a good deal of name-dropping and a good many stories about women he's slept with. At its heart, however, the book is an exercise in self-pity, self-absorption and self-justification. "Everyone has his reasons," he writes. This phrase, popularized by Jean Renoir, in Kazan's hands has sinister implications. What he means is: Everyone has his reasons to be a swine.

A Life is written along somewhat provocative lines. It's a style of artistic confessional that has become fashionable in the past few decades. The author recounts all the vile things he's done, and, more or less, taunts the reader: Yes, I'm a bastard, what are you going to make of it? The implication always being that swinishness is intrinsic to the artistic personality, and indeed that the greater the artistic genius, the greater the swinishness. Kazan would have us believe, and perhaps he believes it himself, that informing on his former comrades was no more dishonorable than manipulating an actor on a film set or cheating on his wife.

In any event, talent or even genius does not excuse everything. Marxists emphasize the need to make an objective assessment of artistic achievement. This inevitably requires making a certain distinction between the artist and his or her art. We do not go searching through garbage cans for all the ways in which the writer, painter or composer falls short. But the distinction is a relative, not an absolute one. Humanity has the right to expect that the artists have its concerns, in the most general sense, at heart. Here we are not speaking of official society with its empty and philistine moralizing, but suffering and for the most part inarticulate humanity. Compassion, a democratic spirit, even a kind of nobility—these do not seem too much to ask.

Naturally, imperfect human beings produce art, along with everything else. They inevitably sin against others and against themselves. But why make a virtue out of those inevitable errors and misdeeds, much less a program? History teaches us that class society occasionally mutilates very gifted people beyond recognition, so that artistic genius and personal vileness coexist within a single human being. Why not simply recognize this as an unfortunate fact of that society, another sign of its incompatibility with the demands of human happiness, and not as a proof that genius feeds on vileness?

Art counts for a good deal, but not everything. We listen to Richard Wagner's music (or some of it) with enjoyment, but that does not dissipate the stench of his anti-Semitism and generally filthy ideas. He is remembered, frankly, for both his music and his ideas. Doesn't it mean something that humanity is more likely to cherish in its collective memory a Mozart and not a Wagner, a Van Gogh and not a Degas, a Döblin and not a Céline, a Breton and not an Eliot?

As for Kazan, somewhere around page 600 in his autobiography he sums things up fairly well: "For years I declared myself an ardent liberal in politics, made all the popular declarations of faith, but the truth was—and is—that I am, like most of you, a bourgeois. I go along disarming people, but when it gets to a crunch, I am revealed to be a person interested only in what most artists are interested in, himself."

A remarkable comment. Kazan thinks he is being very clever here, that he is revealing an essential, if unpalatable, universal truth. In reality, he only displays his extraordinary philistinism. What is the logic of his comment? Life is, first and foremost, about taking care of oneself; art presumably serves a function insofar as it enables one to do that. The individual who considers art as a means, as something extraneous to the purpose of his or her existence, is not a serious figure. The great artist, one might say the *truly ambitious* artist, is one who understands that the fate of his art is of far greater consequence than his personal destiny.

Marx, writing in 1842, understood this: "In no sense does the writer regard his works as a means. They are ends in themselves; so little are they means for him and others that, when necessary, he sacrifices his existence to theirs, and like the preacher of religion, though in another way, he takes as his principle: 'God is to be obeyed before men.'"[119]

Kazan's comment is a libel against art and an attempt to minimize his own sins by suggesting that anyone might be capable of committing them. Not anyone, *a certain type*. To the extent that the current cultural landscape is overpopulated with artists who think only of themselves, it is in part due to the example and legacy of Elia Kazan and those like him. The media praise Kazan because he fits their idea of the artist: a man or woman capable of sophisticated work—but nothing overly disturbing; prepared to stand on political principle—as long as it does not create problems with the authorities; dedicated to art—unless it demands too much.

The honoring of Kazan is part of a trend, the general rehabilitation of anticommunism and McCarthyism. It was fashionable for a time in some circles to be on the "left." Now, one senses a deep hunger, an irrepressible impulse on the part of some erstwhile liberals and radicals to ingratiate themselves, after the fact, with the witch-hunters, to be, at last, on the "winning side." This is a prelude to and a justification in advance for a new and serious assault on democratic rights.

In applauding Kazan, the members of the Academy are applauding themselves. What are they saying? "In similar circumstances, we would behave in precisely the same way." The film industry establishment is setting up the artist-informer as a model for the present and the future. Nothing good can come from such a celebration. We condemn the decision of the Academy. Beware of those who reward cowardice and lack of principle! As James P. Cannon, a genuine anti-Stalinist, observed two months after Kazan's HUAC testimony, in regard to another specimen of the McCarthy days, Whittaker Chambers: "American capitalism, turning rotten before it got fully ripe, acclaims the stool pigeons and informers, who squeal and enrich themselves, as the embodiments of the highest good they know. By their heroes ye shall know them."

---

[119] Karl Marx and Frederick Engels, "Capitalist Alienation and the Damaging of Aesthetic Values," *Marx and Engels On Literature and Art*, ed. Lee Baxandall and Stefan Morawski (St. Louis, Telos Press, 1973), 61.

An Interview with Blacklist Victim Abraham Polonsky

World Socialist Web Site; February 24, 1999

[*Author's Note: Abraham Polonsky died on October 26, 1999, at the age of 88, eight months after the following interview was conducted.*]

Abraham Polonsky was born in New York City in 1910. He attended the City College of New York and Columbia Law School. He practiced law, taught at CCNY, wrote radio scripts and several novels, and signed a contract with Paramount before leaving for the Second World War, during which he worked with the OSS. After the war, his first screenwriting job was on Mitchell Leisen's *Golden Earrings* (1947); none of his material survived to the final script. His next job was on Robert Rossen's *Body and Soul* (1947), a boxing drama with John Garfield. He was encouraged by Garfield to direct the actor's next picture, *Force of Evil* (1948).

In April 1951, Polonsky was subpoenaed to appear before HUAC, and after refusing to cooperate, was blacklisted by the industry. He could not use his own name in credits until *Madigan*, for which he wrote the script, in 1968. He directed two more films, *Tell Them Willie Boy Is Here* (1970) and *Romance of a Horsethief* (1971).

In 1999, the board of the Academy of Motion Picture Arts and Sciences voted unanimously to give Elia Kazan, a willing participant in the Hollywood blacklist, an honorary award. I spoke to Abe Polonsky about the issue.

David Walsh: What is your response to the Elia Kazan award?

Abraham Polonsky: He's a member of the Benedict Arnold Society, and he got the memorial award for "kiss and tell." What more do you have to know?

DW: Did he play a role in legitimizing the witch-hunt?

AP: All he did was play a legitimate role in his own advancement. And in betraying his personal friends, which was kind of sweet. At least it shows that he's not against the United States, he's only against friendship.

DW: Wasn't he one of the more prestigious people who talked?

AP: Oh, yeah. But a lot of prestigious people talked, as well as a lot of people who weren't so prestigious. But what's the difference? Who cares about him? I don't really care about him. I'm really surprised at the Academy.

DW: Why are they doing this?

AP: Someone talked them into it. They're boobs anyhow, what do you think? We ought to give everybody an Academy Award. That's what I say. The Academy has now become the legitimizing organization for double-crossers.

DW: Did he do it to save his career?

AP: No, I think he did it because he's a creep. He didn't have to save his career; his career was made, and he could have directed on Broadway all he liked.

DW: So why did he do it?

AP: Did you read his autobiography?

DW: Yes.

AP: So how could you ask?

DW: But he gives about six different reasons.

AP: He rejoices in the fact that he betrayed his family, his wife, his friends, what more do you need?

DW: He says in the book that artists are only interested in themselves. Is that true of the best artists?

AP: Au contraire. The opposite is true. Art is not about nothing. It's about an interpretation of the world around you, right? And your understanding of it. People say that, after all, he's a great artist, all he did was betray his friends, what's the big deal? They say all artists are bad characters. Yeah, but their bad character consists of doing what the president did, not keeping his pants buttoned—not betraying their friends.

DW: There's a big difference.

AP: If they can't see the difference ...

DW: Do you think it's possible to look at his films without thinking about what he did?

AP: Well, most people don't know what he did. This is a whole generation in America which has been brought up without studying history. They're as ignorant as hell.

DW: What do you think about his films?

AP: Everybody says they're wonderful, right?

DW: No, not everybody.

AP: Who criticizes them?

DW: Andrew Sarris, Manny Farber, I do, other people.

AP: Good. That means that maybe we can get rid of him without creating a crisis in the world of art.

DW: I think it's possible.

AP: Well, good, let's do it. It's a good opportunity. If we could get rid of the Academy too, it would be marvelous.

DW: The Academy is setting up the artist as informer as a model. That can't be very healthy.

AP: It is very healthy. Because in that way everybody can be a founding member of the Benedict Arnold Society.

DW: No, thanks, not me.

AP: Not you?

DW: Not you, either.

AP: I'm the one who created the organization. I didn't join though. In the world I came from, in the streets I came from, if he did that on the East Side where I come from, he'd be floating on his way to Samarkand by now.

DW: Samarkand, specifically? Do you know if there's going to be a protest?

AP: Well, I got a letter from someone saying there was. But, you know, with the disappearance of the radical movement in the United States, as it has, and the disappearance of strong unionism and stuff like that. ... In the old ways, if something like this was going on, you'd make a few telephone calls, you'd have a thousand people there. No more. Nobody believes in anything, except in the finance capitalist. It's terrible. Listen, I'll just say one thing more to you, and release you from bondage. Remember Swann in Marcel Proust?

DW: Yes.

AP: Toward the end of his life he went to a hairdresser, and suddenly he looked in the mirror, and he said, "To think I've spent the best years of my life making love to a woman who wasn't my style." I make the same remark about the film industry. I've spent the best years of my life in an occupation that's not my style. Where I come from, we don't do things like that.

I've lived a long life, I'm 88, but I've been annoyed by CBS, NBC; ABC is doing it today; CNN was over here. I've been photographed, they've wasted a lot of camera stuff and everything, and they all ask the same questions. I even had the honor of talking to Charlton Heston. Good old Chuck called. I was talking to some people on the air, I guess, and he called in. Chuck, I said to him, you're in charge of the guns in the United States, aren't you? I said, why don't you give this guy a gun, he commits suicide on the stage, and he goes down in history. So when he goes to hell he'll have plenty of company. But he didn't understand it. He may have played Moses, but he didn't listen to what he said. It's awful. But I don't mind, after all, I'm 88. Even if I'm enjoying good health, I can't live too much longer. So to hell with that. But I won't go to the Academy, of course. Why do they think he's such a great director?

DW: I just rented thirteen videos of his films, and I was not particularly impressed.

AP: What's impressive about it? You know what he has? He gets energy out of it. Actors find it very difficult to play around with energy, and a director who can get that out of them is good. Even if he doesn't know what the hell he's talking about, and even if he's on the wrong side. And also there's a theory going around about all artists, that their art is important, but their personal characters are not. Who creates the art, if not the personal character? That's what I want to know.

DW: And also, as you say, there's a difference between cheating on your wife and turning your friends in to the state.

AP: That's right, and turning your friends over to death, to starvation. Because when they got jobs even outside the industry, the FBI came around and said, so-and-so working for you? They'd say, yeah. And they'd say, we're the FBI. The employer would say, is he a criminal? The FBI would say, no, no, we just want you to let us know when he leaves the job and where's he's going. Well, you know what happens to this fellow the next morning. He lost the job. Who needs anyone like that around? So the blacklist functioned economically, too. Of course, J. Edgar Hoover was very busy at this stage; he used to change from his dressing gown into the dress he was wearing that day at the office. You remember him? What a world! Listen, don't lose hope.

Film, History and Socialism

World Socialist Web Site; January 22, 2007

This is a talk given by David Walsh to a meeting organized by graduate film students January 17 at York University in Toronto, Ontario.

My purpose this evening is to address certain problems in cinema from the point of view of Marxism, that is to say, an outlook that considers art as an element of human social development. The contradictions and difficulties in filmmaking are necessarily bound up, in such a view, with the broad social and historical process.

Film is little more than a century old. It is an art form whose entire history is contained, for all intents and purposes, in the twentieth century, a century of convulsive and often tragic events, of global civil war, of gigantic and as yet unresolved social struggles.

If art in general is "the most complex … the most sensitive and at the same time the least protected" part of culture, as Trotsky suggested, then how could it have avoided receiving some very serious, even devastating blows in the course of the past hundred years?

And when one considers cinema in particular, which from the technological point of view is associated with the growth of modern industry, which mobilizes vast physical and human resources for its accomplishment, which created and depends upon a mass audience and which has been regarded as the most powerful medium of communication by regimes of every political stripe—I think one is safe in saying that the vicissitudes of cinema are inseparable from the political and social vicissitudes of the twentieth century. On that basis, I would argue that to have a theory of film history in its most general outlines, first of all, one must have a theory of the twentieth century.

We will return to that. In fact, it's a central theme of this talk.

The state of art in general and the state of the cinema in particular are of great concern to us. The socialist movement has great and noble goals: the elimination of exploitation and poverty, the establishment of genuine democracy and social equality, the creation of a classless culture and society, truly human for the first time.

How are such goals realized? In the first place, out of the objective contradictions of capitalism. We are not voluntarists. We base ourselves firmly on the logic of world economic development. The preconditions for a new society exist within the old, in this globalized, complex, highly developed system of production, which today is colliding so explosively against the boundaries of the nation-state system and the private ownership of humanity's vast industrial and technical resources. This is the source of the ever more tense and volatile international political situation, in which the American ruling elite has undertaken the mad and doomed project of bringing the entire world under its sway. As I say, for a Marxist, these objective facts and processes are decisive.

Nor, however, are we fatalists. A social revolution in the modern era depends upon the conscious democratic choice and activity of the overwhelming majority. No profound social transformation will occur accidentally or spontaneously.

A higher cultural and moral level of the population, a greater degree of self-awareness, solidarity, self-sacrifice—all of this is vital to the future progressive development of human society. We understand that the man and woman of the future will be created by transformed material conditions. We are not utopians, but the willingness to undertake such a transformation itself requires an expansion of consciousness.

We are very much concerned with the cultural development of the working population, that overwhelming proportion of humanity that earns a wage, including wide layers of what used to be considered the middle classes. A progressive social change on the order called for by the contradictions of contemporary society demands that a far greater proportion of the population be able to think clearly and independently about a variety of issues, to reject the lies and manipulations and pressure of the media and manufactured "public opinion," to exercise political and moral judgment in difficult circumstances—all of which involves a deepening of the understanding of the human condition in its manifold dimensions.

One of art's roles is to hold a mirror up so that the population can see itself without illusions, particularly so that it can see its weaknesses, its backwardness, even its crimes and inhumanity. What is a theme common to all significant literary and cinema works in the modern era? That indifference to human suffering is one of the greatest failings. A culture worth its name, first of all, strives to create a climate in which such indifference is considered odious and ignoble, reserved for the people at the top of society, government leaders and cabinet ministers, corporate directors, bankers, generals and police officials.

Art ought to tell even the most painful truths about people, about their social and personal relationships. The Russian revolutionary thinkers and writers, before 1917, often referred to Russia's awful poverty, "our backwardness," they would say. In North America, we have our own vexing problems to expose and overcome.

Culture is vital to the revolutionary process. The transformation of society is not the result simply of a political program or slogan, much less clever tactics; it comes about as the result of a massive cultural and moral awakening as well, which has its objective roots in the irreconcilable internal conflicts of the old society.

It is difficult to conceive of the October Revolution of 1917 without taking into account the role of Russian literature and democratic sentiment in the nineteenth century. The more advanced layers of the society were saturated with humane conceptions.

Consider Tolstoy. Not a socialist revolutionary, a pacifist, a believer that all would be right if society lived according to the principles of Christ's Sermon on the Mount. But an enemy of cruelty and oppression. In his late, powerful novel *Resurrection*, his protagonist has bitter experiences with the judicial system. Considering the various prisoners he has come across, Tolstoy writes, he "clearly saw that all these people were arrested, locked up, exiled, not really because they transgressed against justice or behaved unlawfully, but only because they were an obstacle hindering the officials and the rich from enjoying the property they had taken away from the people. ... This explanation seemed very simple and clear ... but its very simplicity and clearness made him hesitate to accept it. Was it possible that so complicated a phenomenon could have so simple and terrible an explanation? Was it possible that all these words about justice, law, religion, and God, and so on, were mere words, hiding the coarsest cupidity and cruelty?"

Do we have at present a culture, including a film culture, that champions such sentiments? Everyone here knows the answer to that. Our film and popular culture generally tends, on the contrary, to revel in violence, to boast of its callousness and indifference to others. To paint human beings in the blackest colors, and to wallow in the process, is considered the "radical" viewpoint. This is getting to the "dark heart of things." Brutality and four-letter words represent the unadorned truth. The overall message is: this is what people are like, we're not going to kid ourselves any more. The violence in Tarantino, Scorsese, Gibson has reached the level of the pathological. Something is terribly wrong with this social layer.

Our attitude toward contemporary film work is very critical. We write about this a great deal on the World Socialist Web Site. I don't intend to go into detail here. Much of today's filmmaking is very poor—bombastic, trivial or narcissistic, sometimes all three at once. For the most part, it neither enlightens, moves nor delights. And not only commercial filmmaking. American (and Canadian) "independent" cinema is very weak, by and large, amorphous, self-indulgent. European art cinema is in the doldrums. There are honest and well-meaning individuals in Europe whose work I think is overvalued and undercriticized at present, precisely because they work in such a vacuum. Italian and Japanese cinema, two of the pillars of postwar culture, are in very sad shape. There are indications of a global change, but they remain fitful.

The case could be made that the decade of the 1990s as a whole was the weakest in cinema history, taking the 1910s as the first decade in which feature production took hold. In the US, that was the era of the first film stars, Hollywood's replacement of the East Coast as the center of the film industry, D.W. Griffith's remarkable works, Chaplin's first efforts, Mack Sennett's Keystone Cops and the establishment of studios. One of the first epics, Italy's *Cabiria*, a three-hour film, was made in 1914.

In the 1920s, of course, the silent film reached its high point, in American, Soviet, German and other films—we think of Eisenstein, Chaplin, Murnau, Lang, Buster Keaton, Dreyer, Erich von Stroheim and countless others. *The Cabinet of Dr. Caligari, Nanook of the North, Nosferatu, Greed, Battleship Potemkin, Napoleon, Metropolis, The General, The Passion of Joan of Arc, The Man With a Movie Camera* are a few of the notable works.

The 1930s brought the full-scale arrival of the sound film, the flowering of classic Hollywood cinema, the arrival of the German and Jewish refugees en masse in the US, the strong work of the French poetic realists, including Jean Vigo. A remarkable cast of characters inhabited Hollywood, from the Marx Brothers, to James Cagney, Greta Garbo and Jean Harlow. *M, Scarface* and *Dracula* were released in the same year. Frank Capra's populist efforts arrived, Alfred Hitchcock became an internationally known name. Chaplin's *Modern Times*, Jean Renoir's *The Rules of the Game* came out.

The next decade we identify with *Citizen Kane*, Chaplin's *The Great Dictator* and the best of the wartime films; *The Maltese Falcon* and, later, *film noir*, as in *Double Indemnity*, Ulmer's *Detour*, Tourneur's *Out of the Past*; the first Technicolor films. In Italy, Luchino Visconti's *Ossessione* and then the full blast of neorealism: Roberto Rossellini's *Open City*, Vittorio De Sica's *The Bicycle Thief* and many others. *The Best Years of Our Lives* and *They Were Expendable* indicated a critical attitude toward the official patriotic versions of things. Also from John Ford, his great Westerns.

In the 1950s, despite McCarthyism, Hollywood is not exhausted—Hawks, Ford and Hitchcock had some of their best films still in them; also *Sunset Boulevard*, Brando in *On the Waterfront* and "adult Westerns" such as *Shane* and *High Noon*. Japanese cinema makes its mark, with a number of giants: Kurosawa's *Rashomon* is released in 1950. In India, the films of Satyajit Ray; in Sweden, Ingmar Bergman; in France, the birth of the New Wave. Toward the end of the 1950s, a series of darker American films, Hitchcock's *Vertigo*, Douglas Sirk's *Written on the Wind* (1957) and *Imitation of Life* (1959), Orson Welles's *Touch of Evil* (1958), Vincente Minnelli's *Some Came Running* (1959) and Otto Preminger's *Bonjour Tristesse* (1958).

The 1960s brings Fellini's *La Dolce Vita* and Antonioni's *L'Avventura*. The best films of Godard and Pasolini. Kurosawa and Bergman continue to be prominent. There is certainly a definite decline in Hollywood, despite the occasional bright spots. John Cassavetes' first films. Sergio Leone's spaghetti Westerns, *Bonnie and Clyde* and *Easy Rider, 2001: A Space Odyssey*. The end of the restrictive codes in Hollywood. The British neorealist films; Joseph Losey and Dirk Bogarde combine for some interesting efforts; Lindsay Anderson's *If...* Also, the Brazilian new cinema and Luis Buñuel's sophisticated surrealist efforts.

In the 1970s, in the US: Coppola's *The Godfather* and *Apocalypse Now*; *Chinatown* and *Five Easy Pieces*, a series of remarkable films by Robert Altman, *The Deer Hunter*, Woody Allen's *Annie Hall* and *Manhattan*, Scorsese's *Mean Streets.* The Australian New Wave emerges. Above all, in the 1970s, the new German cinema, including Herzog, Wenders, Schlöndorff—and within that, above all, Fassbinder's films from 1971 to 1975, from *Beware of a Holy Whore* to *Mother Küsters Goes to Heaven*.

The disaster surrounding *Heaven's Gate* in 1980–81 helped sound the death-knell for the American independent cinema of the time. Kubrick makes interesting films in the 1980s, but this is a bleak period overall for US filmmaking. In France, there is Tavernier, Pialat and Rohmer; Godard is barely alive artistically, and Fassbinder lives only a part of the decade. Bresson and Tarkovsky make their last films. In Taiwan in the 1980s, there is an eruption in cinema, after decades of anticommunist dictatorial rule; in Iran as well, after the fall of the Shah. China comes on to the scene also. These last three developments prove to be virtually the only ones that extend into the 1990s.

Of course, I'm speaking very generally, and there is an obvious element of subjective opinion in this, but I think a case could be made that the years 1995–2005 were the weakest in cinema history.

Let me make a few points about this. First, there is not a hint of nostalgia in this. Both the Hollywood and European art cinemas had serious limitations. I don't wish to idealize, either. Briefly, in my opinion, filmmaking's greatest days lie ahead. In any case, as long as cinema remains a business under capitalism, it will never reach its potential.

Here it is necessary, as elsewhere, to disagree with so much of film theory. This is not the fault of the individuals involved; rather, it's the result of historical traumas that knocked the confidence in an alternative to capitalism out of so much of the intelligentsia in the latter portions of the twentieth century. For example, Jean Mitry, in his interesting and monumental work, *The Aesthetics and Psychology of the Cinema*, in the first section entitled "Preliminaries," writes: "The production of films entails such resources that no fortune would suffice were only the consideration of art to be taken into account. It is only the commercial aspect which can ensure the continuation of production and, as a consequence, any possible progress, whether it be technical or artistic ..." And later, driving home the point, "To repeat: one does not make a film to make a film, one does it to *make money*."

He is not criticizing these facts—these are his starting point. Such comments should not arouse indignation perhaps so much as a sorrowful shake of the head. As I say, behind them lie a great many political difficulties—in particular, the emergence of Stalinism in the Soviet Union, its historic crimes, which did so much to discredit socialism in the eyes of millions, the subsequent betrayals and defeats of the working class and the resulting decline in the influence of socialism and Marxism. Mitry's common-sense language represents an example of what Trotsky called "the worship of the accomplished fact." For cinema to be only conceivable as *profit-making* cinema, at the mercy today of hedge fund managers and global speculators, would be for me a profoundly dispiriting notion.

In any event, we should have no nostalgia for any type of "golden age"! That doesn't help anyone and it would be mistaken.

Moreover, I don't suggest that the 1990s or perhaps the 1995–2005 period represented a low point to discourage anyone or to paint a universally bleak picture. Not at all. Those who simply find modern life nightmarish and unbearable will never do anything but hide under the covers. If the present is uniformly detestable, where are we to find the possibilities for a future, alternative culture? As we've argued before, the light of human genius, including human artistic genius, has not suddenly dimmed. One only has to consider the strides that have been made in so many fields, particularly scientific, medical and technical.

Over the last half-century, humanity has been thrown back, in our view, in the areas of politics and art, especially film, drama and literature, where the issue of an understanding of historical laws and social organization plays so large a part. All serious art in the modern era, in our view, contains an element of protest against the conditions of life, whether that protest is lyrical or epic. All criticism of social life gravitates toward Marxism, the current that offers the most comprehensive and unrelenting critique of the existing social order. A decline in the influence of Marxism, as the result primarily of Stalinism and the endless official barrage of anticommunism, produces a decline in critical thought and art work.

The present problems are a historical product. It is not accidental that the 1990s also witnessed, in the US at least and probably worldwide, the lowest level of social protest and strike activity in a century or more. The collapse of the USSR in 1991 provided the ruling elites with a certain breathing space, exploited to the full, within which to roll back social programs and attack living standards; launch neocolonial wars; and stultify the population with propaganda about the "end of history," the ultimate triumph of free enterprise, the miracle of the market, and so forth.

Cultural life, too, paid a price for this ignorant chatter. We were promised an era of peace and prosperity. Instead, we see unending war, which threatens to engulf the globe, international instability and a chasm of immense proportions that has opened up between the handful of super-wealthy and the rest of the earth's inhabitants. This reality is sinking into the consciousness of great numbers of people. Reaction has its limits, and the present reaction is rapidly reaching its limit. A worldwide radicalization is in the offing.

So, our present cultural and cinema malaise is a product of definite historical and social circumstances. With the end of those circumstances, a new cultural atmosphere will emerge. But we are far from suggesting that anyone should wait around with folded arms. No, it's our responsibility to do whatever we can to prepare the groundwork for a different state of artistic affairs.

I would like to discuss somewhat more concretely that historical process, in particular as it relates to American filmmaking, to Hollywood, in short. I think this is reasonable, because the American film industry has had at its disposal the greatest technical and financial resources, and represented, from its earliest days, essentially an international undertaking. Without flattering anyone's national sensibilities, it is worth noting that the first legitimate film star, the first performer to be identified on screen and in film advertising was Florence Lawrence, the "Biograph Girl," around 1910, born in Hamilton, Ontario; the first superstar, "America's Sweetheart," Mary Pickford, was born on University Avenue near Gerrard Street in downtown Toronto; and one of the first organizers of comic mayhem, Mack Sennett, was born in Quebec's Eastern Townships.

"Hollywood" is less a spot on the map than an ideological, cultural and commercial nexus. Thomas Jefferson, in the wake of the French Revolution, with its universal significance, declared that every man had two countries, "his own and France." One might say that filmgoers in every country have two film industries, for better or worse, their own and "Hollywood."

Another objection arises. Hasn't "Hollywood" been a swear word, an epithet for leftists since at least the 1930s, the epitome of manipulative, conformist kitsch, a relentless fount of middle class ideology, and so forth? Brecht wrote his famous poem, entitled "Hollywood," during his exile there: "Every day, to earn my daily bread / I go to the market where lies are bought / Hopefully / I take my place among the sellers."

Hollywood is, to say the least, a contradictory phenomenon. As Marxists, we have least of all any reason to idealize it. However, a little perspective is required. Large-scale narrative filmmaking emerged in the form of privately owned, competing enterprises. How could it have been otherwise? Filmmaking, which is itself dependent on a series of scientific and technical innovations, was born with modern industry. The stamp of capitalism, private property and bourgeois ideology is obviously there in cinema from the beginning, with all the falseness, dishonesty, sentimentality and cheap appeals that the defense of this system inevitably entails.

However, is the film industry now or has it ever been *merely* a giant black hole that sucks in and retains every ray of light? Has it been nothing but a machine for the propagation of falsehoods? I would say that that would be a very foolish, blockheaded conclusion. After all, filmmaking depends on an audience, not made up of fools. In a certain sense, to sell their product, to make a deep impression on an audience, the studios were obliged to call upon the integrity and conscientiousness and skill of a considerable number of talented human beings—in some cases probably, great artists.

Marxists argue that the evolution of art is determined by the evolution of the world. Did Hollywood cinema in its heyday tell us something about life in the US? Is there an objectively truthful element—disregarding for the moment the inevitably limited character of the representation—in *Little Caesar* or *Bringing Up Baby* or *High Sierra*? Do we learn something about human beings, about how they live together, about their psychology and behavior? Or is it mere propaganda? I think the answer is clear. The films endure because of their truthful elements, not their historically determined limitations.

Every cultural phenomenon has a dual character. It represents both an objective advance, a deepening of humanity's understanding of the external world and its own activities. A serious art work is not simply one individual's opinion or subjective "narrative"; it allows something essential about life to emerge. It has objective validity.

On the other hand, art is not created by free-floating atoms but by social creatures, the product of specific environments and historical conditions, which, in the end, are the conditions of class society. The artists themselves belong to certain social layers and inherit the prejudices and limitations of those social layers.

Hollywood, from this point of view, is an extreme example of the double character of culture. Its artistic life took shape within this hothouse atmosphere of capitalist competition and the drive for profit. To become indignant about that fact misses the point, in my opinion.

Hollywood filmmaking needs to be treated objectively. It generated extraordinary advances in storytelling addressed to a mass audience, within very definite objective limitations, sometimes crippling limitations. We would argue that, in the end, the radical implications of filmmaking, its truth-telling abilities, proved to be incompatible with the profit system. American capitalism in the 1930s, despite its terrible economic condition, still had great reserves. In that sense, the New Deal and the flowering of Hollywood cinema exist on the same historic plane.

In the postwar period, America became the dominant capitalist power, taking into itself all the contradictions of the world system, and proved unable to coexist with an honest and critical cinema. Thus, the McCarthyite witch-hunts, the blacklist, the illegalization of anticapitalist views or serious criticism in the cinema. Criticism to the bone, criticism of private property and American global ambitions, and the criminality of the ruling elite, became impermissible. But even then, in the late 1940s and early to mid-1950s, films that obviously opposed McCarthyism appeared—*High Noon*, *Kiss Me Deadly*, *Johnny Guitar*, perhaps Allan Dwan's *Silver Lode* and others. It's an intensely complex process.

Why has there been such a terrible falling off in American cinema? I've suggested some elements of the explanation, but I would like to make that more specific, if only briefly. Again, the present cinema is not simply a nightmare, nor is television or popular music. We're not beginning from zero; the events of the past century have not occurred for nothing.

I don't believe, however, that any objective comparison of films from the period 1930 to 1955, let's say, and the past fifteen years or so would work to the advantage of the latter, in terms of texture, depth, seriousness, even social insight.

This is clearly not a technical problem. Cinema has made great strides. No doubt the freshness of the medium made a difference in those earlier years, but color film, video, digital technologies, the Internet, are relatively recent innovations. Why has the content of films, that living complex of moods and ideas, deteriorated and become so unenlightening, so uninspiring, so generally trivial?

Goethe writes that "Literature deteriorates only to the extent that people deteriorate." How do we explain the deterioration in those making American cinema?

Jean Mitry says, "It is indisputable that the photographic image is always the consequence of a certain interpretation." If this is so, and undoubtedly it is, then the question becomes: why have the interpretations weakened? What has become of those doing the interpretations? Why are they seeing the world less deeply, less richly, less evocatively?

Another approach might be: under what historical and intellectual conditions do images become more dense, more complicated, more textured, more highly charged with meaning? Is this something that can happen by accident? Does the filmmaker simply stumble on important images and truths? Does the result of his or her efforts have something to do with the general social situation?

To examine this fully in the context of Hollywood would require a lengthy investigation of what gave rise to the film industry, which is far beyond this discussion.

I will argue for this: that what was best in the American film industry emerged in large measure out of world culture and politics in the late nineteenth and early twentieth century, culture and politics in which the socialist labor movement was a prominent element.

This is by no means simply a question of left-wing filmmakers or writers, but since that history has been so buried in the official version of Hollywood's history, it's probably best to make some reference to their existence. Paul Buhle and Dave Wagner in *Radical Hollywood* and Brian Neve in *Film and Politics in America*, among others, have documented some of this usefully.

The Wall Street Crash and the Great Depression had a shattering impact on the American population, as elsewhere, including artists and intellectuals. All the myths and claims about the free enterprise system were called into question virtually overnight. The mass suffering made "business" and "banking" and "Capitalism" itself into dirty words for millions. Under those conditions, the American Communist Party, founded in 1919 in the wake of the Russian Revolution, gained a great following, including within the film industry.

Tragically, by the mid-1930s this had become a thoroughly Stalinized outfit, run by scoundrels. The American CP, one of the most slavish in the world toward the Kremlin bureaucracy, had swung around to supporting Franklin Roosevelt and the Democratic Party, a betrayal with long-lasting consequences. The crimes of the American Stalinist leadership, including participation in the attempts to assassinate Trotsky, are legion. However, thousands of honest people joined the CP, mistakenly believing that it stood in the tradition of the Russian Revolution and fought for a socialist transformation of the US.

Its influence was widespread. Much of this history has been hushed up, in many cases by the repentant individuals themselves. How many Americans would be shocked to learn that many of their favorite film or television stars supported or belonged to a "communist" party, and that many of their favorite films were written or directed by "communists" or socialists?

For example, Buhle and Wagner write that, according to FBI reports, which probably exaggerated but did not make things up entirely, "Lucille Ball, Katharine Hepburn, Olivia de Havilland, Rita Hayworth, Humphrey Bogart, Danny Kaye, Fredric March, Bette Davis, Lloyd Bridges, John Garfield, Anne Revere, Larry Parks, some of Hollywood's highest-paid writers, and for that matter the wives of March and Gene Kelly along with Gregory Peck's fiancée [were] all in or close to the party."[120] Buhle and Wagner later include Franchot Tone, then married to Joan Crawford, Jose Ferrer and apparently Ronald Reagan, as among those in or around the CP periphery. One could add Sterling Hayden, who turned informer later on, then regretted it, Sylvia Sidney, Shelley Winters, Lauren Bacall, and

---

[120]   Paul Buhle and Dave Wagner, *Radical Hollywood: The Untold Story Behind America's Favorite Movies* (New York: The New Press, 2002), 81.

many, many others. Melvyn Douglas and Frank Sinatra were also named by an FBI informant, along with Paul Muni, born in Ukraine and a veteran of Yiddish theater in New York, whose career was wrecked by the blacklist.

Among the screenwriters, the names are too numerous to mention. They include the writers or co-writers of *Holiday*, *The Awful Truth*, *Mr. Smith Goes to Washington*, *The Naked City*, *A Guy Named Joe*, *Casablanca*, *High Noon*, *A Place in the Sun*, *It's a Wonderful Life*, *The Public Enemy*, *She Done Him Wrong*, *The Philadelphia Story* and so on, along with literary figures and occasional screenwriters such as Dorothy Parker, Lillian Hellman, Dashiell Hammett, Clifford Odets.

Directors in and around the Communist Party included Abraham Polonsky, Nicholas Ray, Joseph Losey, Elia Kazan, Robert Rossen, Jules Dassin, John Berry, Martin Ritt, Edward Dmytryk. As I say, the list is extensive. One should not forget Chaplin himself, a prominent "friend of the Soviet Union," who traveled in left circles.

There were independent figures of the left, socialists like Romanian-born Edward G. Robinson, who was a friend of Diego Rivera, the revolutionary Mexican artist, and held a private conversation with Trotsky in Mexico in 1938; James Cagney, who was redbaited as early as 1934; directors John Huston and Orson Welles; two of the greatest cinematographers of all time, Gregg Toland and James Wong Howe, and many others. No serious treatment of the classic American cinema can avoid the fact that opposition to capitalism animated a considerable portion of those writing, directing, performing and filming some of its most interesting films.

Little Caesar and *The Public Enemy*, for example, were two of the definitive gangster films of the 1930s. The screenplay for *Little Caesar* was written by Communist Party member Francis Faragoh and starred Edward G. Robinson; James Cagney starred in *The Public Enemy*, which was co-written by John Bright, another party member. Robert Rossen, also in the CP, wrote *The Roaring Twenties*, with Cagney and Bogart, and *The Sea Wolf*, which featured Robinson and John Garfield.

Black Fury, released in 1935, is a film worth noting. Directed by Michael Curtiz and featuring Paul Muni, it recounts the story of an immigrant coal miner caught in the crossfire between crooked union leaders, Machiavellian coal operators and brutal strikebreakers. Its ultimate message is confused to say the least, but the film's sympathy for the miners and hostility to the forces of law and order are clear.

A review from the *New York Times* in 1935 makes interesting reading. It begins: "Hollywood, with all its taboos and commercial inhibitions, makes a trenchant contribution to the sociological drama in 'Black Fury,' which arrived at the Strand Theatre yesterday. Magnificently performed by Paul Muni, it comes up taut against the censorial safety belts and tells a stirring tale of industrial war in the coal fields. ... [W]hen we realize that 'Black Fury' was regarded by the State Censor Board as an inflammatory social document and that it has been banned in several sectors, we ought to understand that Warner Brothers exhibited almost a reckless air of courage in producing the picture at all."

Black Fury was proscribed in several states due to its depiction of the beating death of a miner by company thugs. The fictional murder was based on an actual incident in Imperial, Pennsylvania, in 1929, when a miner was beaten to death by the coal and iron police.

With all its peculiarities, the film, like many of those turned out at Warner Brothers, is forcefully done. And these things don't come out of the blue. The personalities, histories and thinking of those involved collectively generate the intensity of the work. Pick a favorite film from the 1930s or 1940s, check into the background of the director, writer, lead actors, cinematographer, composer, art director—in many cases, you will be astonished. A world of culture and often politics lies behind their efforts.

Take another film by Curtiz, *Casablanca*—not his finest, in my opinion, but certainly memorable. First of all, there is the director himself, about whom I will say a few words in a moment. Then there's Bogart, a man of the left; Ingrid Bergman from Sweden, with her refinement and artistry; Paul Henreid, born in Trieste, then part of Austria-Hungary, and later blacklisted in the 1950s; Claude Rains, one of the greatest figures of the British stage in the 1920s, taught by Sir Herbert Beerbohm Tree, the founder of the Royal Academy of Dramatic Arts, and who went on to teach John Gielgud and Laurence Olivier; Peter Lorre, a Hungarian Jew and refugee from Germany, a former member of Brecht's acting troupe, who played Gayly Gay in Brecht's *A Man's a Man* in Berlin; co-writer, Howard Koch, who was in the Communist Party; and composer Max Steiner, who had studied with Gustav Mahler, written for the theater and emigrated to the US along with Erich Wolfgang Korngold and numerous other composers.

A few years ago I conducted this experiment on *A Canterbury Tale*—as I observed at the time, "an odd and vaguely unsettling film directed by Michael Powell and Emeric Pressburger, released in 1944. The film, whose title echoes Chaucer, is an exploration of 'Englishness,' made under war-time conditions and for patriotic purposes."

I discovered this about the filmmakers, aside from Powell: "The co-director of *A Canterbury Tale,* Emeric Pressburger, was born Imre József Pressburger in 1902 in Miskolc, Hungary (then Austria-Hungary). According to a biographer, 'Educated at the Universities of Prague and Stuttgart, he worked as a journalist in Hungary and Germany and an author and scriptwriter in Berlin and Paris. He was a Hungarian Jew, chased around Europe (he worked on films for UFA in Berlin and in Paris) before World War II, who finally found sanctuary in London.'

"Cinematographer Erwin Hillier, born in 1911 to a German-English family, studied art in Berlin in the late 1920s. The famous director F.W. Murnau was so impressed by Hillier's paintings that he asked him to work on *Tabu.* Instead Hillier ended up working for Fritz Lang on *M.*

"Born in 1886 in Germany, production designer Alfred Junge began working in silent films in 1923. By the time of *A Canterbury Tale* he had worked with Alexander Korda, Marcel Pagnol, King Vidor, Carol Reed and Alfred Hitchcock as production and art designer.

"The composer of the film's score, Allan Gray, was born Josef Zmigrod in Tarnów, Poland (then Austria-Hungary) in 1902. He studied under the pioneering modernist Arnold Schönberg. A biographer notes, 'To pay for his tuition he composed popular, jazz-influenced tunes for cabaret acts in Berlin. Josef took his pseudonym from Oscar Wilde's narcissistic hero, Dorian Gray.'

"The individual in charge of visual effects, W. Percy Day, had worked on Abel Gance's celebrated *Napoleon* (1927)."

And I asked: "Is it any wonder that today's films often appear pale and weak by comparison?"

Curtiz, director of *Black Fury* and *Casablanca,* offers an instructive example. Born Mihály Kertesz, "in a well-to-do Jewish family in Budapest," according to a biographical account in the *New York Times,* "he ran away from home at age 17 to join a circus, then trained for an acting career at the Royal Academy for Theater and Art. He worked as a leading man at the Hungarian Theatre before directing stage plays and then films." In 1919, a socialist republic was declared in Hungary, which was drowned in blood by the forces of counterrevolution only a few months later. The *Times* account goes on, "When the Hungarian film industry was nationalized by the new communist government in 1919, Curtiz packed his bags and headed for Sweden, France, Germany, and Austria." Various other accounts make the same point.

This is fine, and would warm the heart of any red-blooded anticommunist, except it doesn't happen to be true. Far from packing his bags, Curtiz was a member of the revolutionary arts council that supervised the newly nationalized film industry in the Hungarian Soviet republic. Other leading participants included Alexander Korda, later prominent as a director and producer in the British film industry, and Bela Lugosi. Georg Lukacs, of course, was also a participant in the short-lived Hungarian socialist government, along with film theoretician Bela Balázs.

Thirty-one films were made during the four months of revolutionary rule in Hungary, only two of which have survived. One is a twelve-minute film by Curtiz, entitled *My Brother Is Coming*. The work is based on a revolutionary poem by Antal Farkas whose words appear on the screen intercut with the images of the hero returning from political exile and imprisonment, seen at first as an individual waving a huge red flag and finally being joined by an ever-growing crowd as he nears home and is reunited with his family. This is the man who "packed his bags" at the approach of the revolution, according to the *Times* and others.

I'm not suggesting Curtiz was a Bolshevik in Hollywood. The evolution of his political views is unknown to me, but one can tell that he brought a certain Central European vivacity, energy and tension to every film he undertook, shaped by the cultural environment and his participation in a revolutionary social experiment. Fassbinder called Curtiz an "Anarchist in Hollywood" and paid tribute to his work. I strongly recommend many of his films, including *Captain Blood, Kid Galahad, The Adventures of Robin Hood, Four Daughters, Angels with Dirty Faces, The Private Lives of Elizabeth and Essex, The Sea Hawk*, and in particular, *Mildred Pierce* and *Flamingo Road*.

Of course, the eventual and for the most part ignominious collapse of the leftists in Hollywood was far from admirable. To account for the relative ease with which a purge of many socialist artists and the intimidation of the rest were carried out would take us beyond our subject. The rotten politics of the Communist Party had something to do with it. The artists, lulled to sleep by the notion that postwar America would see some continuation or extension of the New Deal, or even an American "Popular Front," were utterly unprepared for the monstrous imperialist predator that emerged in the late 1940s during the Cold War.

There is also the problem of celebrity in America. The horrifying execution of the Rosenbergs and the imprisonment of the Hollywood Ten—those CP members who were cited for contempt of Congress—notwithstanding, leftists in America did not face the prospect for the most part of outright repression in the postwar years. But the left-wing directors and writers faced the possibility of exclusion, of being out of the limelight. In America, conventionally, you are everything or nothing. An Elia Kazan could not bear the thought of losing his celebrity status. To withstand public opinion in America especially requires not only courage but a long-term historical perspective.

No fascist counterrevolution took place in America, but a period of profound political and cultural stagnation set in, dominated by opportunism, the strangulation of the labor movement and the emergence of anticommunism as virtually a state religion. Anticapitalist criticism was outlawed and remains outlawed. For the film industry, the ultimate consequence, with the disappearance of the last great figures, by the 1960s, was a severe deterioration and dissolution of what was finest and most insightful in Hollywood cinema.

The artist needs to be inspired by great purposes. American Cold War liberalism proved far too narrow and uninspiring a base upon which to construct a great and lasting cinema. A new cinema will have to arise on a new, far more critical foundation. In our view, the emergence of a consciously socialist current in North American filmmaking, which sets itself up in irreconcilable opposition to the entire economic and political structure and its psychology and morality, is crucial to that development.

This is an important part of the explanation for the decline, I believe. But certain things need to be added. Sometimes we're told that the problem today is "money," the domination of giant conglomerates. The problem of money and art didn't begin with Louis B. Mayer. The Dutch painters of the seventeenth century were at the mercy of the market, and suffered for it. That didn't prevent them from doing some extraordinary work. Mitry is correct in this regard: as long as capitalism exists, filmmaking will involve commerce. No, there are plenty of people around with sufficient financing and artistic independence, and very few of them are saying anything important. The problem is one of perspective, artistic and social.

The politics and the experience of recent decades represent one element of the problem. What have people experienced, what have they seen? You would have to be 30–35 years old for the Soviet Union to be more than a fleeting memory. You would have to be older than that to remember when American liberalism had some substance. The last great successful strike in the US took place in the late 1970s. We speak of the filmmaker with the unfurrowed brow, with relatively few important life experiences, no experience of a socialist or communist movement or of great struggles. It's not his or her fault, of course. Some of this will only be overcome with a great mass movement, which will break up much that's stagnant, skeptical, uncommitted in the present-day artist.

There is, however, a specifically aesthetic question, which is bound up with the broader problems. Something has largely been lost in recent decades. What do all great films, from any source, have in common? What Trotsky called a definite and important feeling for the world. They make a genuine engagement with reality, with the way people are, the ways in which they behave. I'm not speaking of realism as a style or a literary school. One can treat life seriously in a cartoon or a science fiction film, or a reenactment of Greek myth or a musical set on the moon.

Trotsky speaks beautifully of this quality, which, he says, "consists in a feeling for life as it is, in an artistic acceptance of reality, and not in a shrinking from it, in an active interest in the concrete stability and mobility of life. It is a striving either to picture life as it is or to idealize it, either to justify or to condemn it, either to photograph it or generalize and symbolize it. But it is always *a preoccupation with our life of three dimensions as a sufficient and invaluable theme for art.*"[121] (Emphasis added).

It's difficult to add much to that. We need to revive an interest in the artistic concentration on character and human personality, on the plausibility and authenticity of the human situations that are dramatized, on psychological and social realism (not Stalinist "Socialist Realism," which had nothing realistic, or socialistic, about it). It's a matter of a certain approach to life. Nothing will come of a desire to show off or impress, to be the most coldhearted or frenzied or bloodiest or cynical among your contemporaries—this is a race to the bottom.

The individual starting out in cinema today can't immediately surmount all the objective difficulties; one can't invent what one hasn't experienced. But this approach to life, this deep concern "with our life of three dimensions as a sufficient and invaluable theme for art," *that* it's possible for *anyone* to assimilate and adopt.

A few points in conclusion. When we speak of our Marxist approach, we mean by that, if you like, a "classical Marxist" approach. We reject most of what passes for Marxism in academic circles. I would like to make a few comments in that regard.

---

[121]   Leon Trotsky, *Literature and Revolution* (London: RedWords, 1991), 264.

First, a small example of what I mean, which may be instructive. In J. Dudley Andrew's *The Major Film Theories*, published in the mid-1970s, the author is describing the views of certain "militant" French leftists at the time. Speaking for them, he says, in bourgeois art "a lie ... destroys every possibility of meaning except for the neurotic repetition of the dominant ideology. This lie is the product of our culture's insistence on the representation of the real. It insists first that reality is visible; second that the scientific instrument of the camera can capture it. The Marxist-Leninist critics"—please, note, "Marxist-Leninist critics"—"launch their attack even here, claiming that the supposedly scientific instrument of the camera is far from neutral, that, like all science, it serves the ruling class. It does this by propagating the visual codes of Renaissance humanism (perspective) which put the individual at the center of a kind of theater spectacle unrolling before him," etc., etc.

Of course, everyone has the right to clown around at one time or another, but it's bad form to do so in false colors. This is not "Marxism-Leninism," but the leftism of clever French schoolboys and girls, some of which we still hear today. Genuine Marxism has always had the deepest commitment to the achievements of culture, which are humanity's property, not the property of the ruling elite. In 1920, precisely to counter the efforts of the Russian counterparts of these "militant critics," Lenin proposed a resolution explaining that "Marxism ... far from rejecting the most valuable achievements of the bourgeois epoch ... has, on the contrary, assimilated and refashioned everything of value in the more than two thousand years of the development of human thought and culture."[122]

The notion that reality is invisible and the camera can't capture it is another bit of foolishness. First of all, any serious film work strives precisely to uncover what is not immediately visible. This is true for Howard Hawks as well as for Eisenstein. If what's meant by this is that the filmmaker is always so imprisoned by his or her class position that no general truth can emerge from the work, this is simply false for the reasons we've already discussed. The honest artist is not merely a congealed expression of his social standing; he or she transcends that in penetrating reality, as the scientist does. Otherwise, every previous art work created within class society would have to be thrown on the scrap heap.

---

122   V.I. Lenin, "On Proletarian Culture," *Collected Works, Vol. 31* (Moscow: Progress Publishers, 1965), 316–17.

Of course, the artist never goes beyond his or her social limitations *absolutely*, but then he or she never goes beyond other sorts of limitations absolutely *either*—age, sex, nationality, and so forth. The question is: is the artist capable of generating *relatively* truthful pictures? It's on this that the French and other "left" metaphysicians stumble. Because of the impossibility of a *single* work achieving absolute objective truth, they rule out partial, imperfect truths, which contain "grains" of absolute truth. We can't jump out of our skins entirely, but that doesn't prevent the human mind from reflecting and expressing reality truthfully. And those truly thoughtless and stereotyped views are presented as "Marxism."

A more serious trend, the Frankfurt School, is certainly one of those often presented as a Marxist tendency in art and literary criticism. Its leading members were immensely educated, cultured and articulate individuals, but their thinking was greatly influenced by the defeats and tragedies suffered by the working class and socialism, in particular, the triumph of Hitlerism in Germany. Politically, they remained aloof. They also remained silent during Stalin's genocidal war against the Old Bolsheviks and Russian socialism generally in the Soviet Union in the late 1930s, finding that the "most loyal attitude" and not wishing "to publish anything that might damage Russia."

Theodor Adorno, whose comments about Stalinism those were, is one of this tendency's principal representatives. In his postwar writings on the "Culture Industry," he expressed dismay at the condition of art and culture. He abhorred the "industrial" standardization of art works; the narrowing of the gap between empirical reality and culture; the elimination of the distinction between image and reality that "has already advanced to the point of a collective sickness"; the transformation of culture into "baby-food"; the leveling down of art within itself so that there are "no longer any real conflicts to be seen"; the "iron grip of rigidity despite the ostentatious appearance of dynamism" in modern culture; and many other features of mid–twentieth-century culture. Many of these criticisms and descriptions are accurate and just.

However, they are deeply onesided and ultimately superficial. Adorno and his co-thinker Max Horkheimer viewed the growth of the productive forces itself as planting the seeds of destruction. They anticipated various contemporary forms of Green thinking by blaming the Enlightenment (with its emphasis on man's domination of nature), technology and industry for society's supposed regression.

As a German colleague, Peter Schwarz, explained in a recent lecture, "According to Marx and Engels, the productive forces developed by capitalism come into conflict with the capitalist property relations, initiating an era of social revolution and providing the basis for a higher, socialist form of society. Horkheimer and Adorno hold the opposite view. According to them, progress of the productive forces inevitably results in the stultification of the masses, in cultural decline, and finally in a new kind of barbarism."[123]

This conception infuses Adorno's postwar writings on culture. He writes: "The entire practice of the culture industry transfers the profit motive naked onto cultural forms. Ever since these cultural forms first began to earn a living for their creators as commodities in the marketplace they had already possessed something of this quality. But then they sought after profit only indirectly, over and above their autonomous essence. New on the part of the culture industry is the direct and undisguised primacy of a precisely and thoroughly calculated efficacy in its most typical products."

Adorno, to be frank, often writes like the petty bourgeois who is dismayed by the disappearance of the small corner store and the independently owned bookstore, who bemoans the building of a supermarket in a rural area. These are the inevitable cruelties of modern capitalist development. He laments, in one comment, that no homeland "can survive being processed by the films that celebrate it, and thereby turn the unique character on which it thrives into an interchangeable sameness."[124] There is something of the nostalgic philistine in these comments.

No one is more scathing than our movement about present-day culture. The commodification and trivialization of art is a pressing problem. However, we view this problem historically and objectively. Culture is a contradictory phenomenon. The machine enslaves humanity, but it also holds the key to its liberation. Under capitalism, technology is turned against humanity in a destructive fashion. Socialism and opposition to technology have never had anything in common.

As Trotsky noted, "A voyage in a boat propelled by oars demands great personal creativity. A voyage in a steamboat is more 'monotonous' but more comfortable and more certain. Moreover, you can't cross the ocean in a row-boat anyway."[125]

---

[123] Available: http://www.wsws.org/en/articles/2005/10/le91-o11.html

[124] Theodor W. Adorno, *The Culture Industry*, (London and New York: Routledge, 1991), 99.

[125] Leon Trotsky, *Culture and Socialism*, (London: New Park, 1963), 25.

Adorno concluded that modern monopoly capitalism "abolishes art along with conflict." The film industry, he wrote, "strikes the hour of total domination." These morbidly pessimistic conclusions were false. Art and culture have certainly entered a deep crisis. Even today, several decades later, however, it would be wrong to speak of the abolition of conflict or total domination. Art cannot save itself. The crisis of the entire social order will generate opposition from the most farsighted artists. The great technologies created by capitalism will help to undermine its influence.

Adorno, Marcuse, Horkheimer and the others lived through great tragedies. They were deeply disoriented by the events and drew the direst conclusions. One cannot justify their thinking and action, but they lived under very difficult moral and political conditions.

Far less excusable are those postmodernists and left postmodernists who accommodate themselves to or even celebrate the debased culture that Adorno and the others decried. I would like to refer briefly to the work of Fredric Jameson, longtime professor at Duke University and the author of numerous books of criticism, another figure presented to students as a Marxist in the field of art and culture.

As a writer, Jameson is guilty of verbal exhibitionism, working in a dense and obscure manner, which makes portions of his work incomprehensible except to the elect. How someone can even refer to the Marxist tradition, which concerns itself with the political education of wide layers of the population, and hermetically seal himself off through his language remains a mystery. I would suggest that the linguistic obscurantism, consciously or not, serves to conceal the relative poverty of the ideas expressed.

In various essays and books published in the recent decades, Jameson makes clear his own morbid pessimism. The collapse of the Soviet Union and the other Stalinist regimes, the universal triumph of global capitalism, the absence of any alternative to the present order, the absence even of a "new international proletariat," render the possibility of social convulsion, much less "the ultimate senescence, breakdown and death of the system as such,"[126] a virtual impossibility, at least for the foreseeable future.

Present-day society, in his view, is a nightmarish "multinational global corporate network" so complex that it is essentially ungraspable

---

[126]   Fredric Jameson, *Postmodernism, or, The Cultural Logic of Late Capitalism* (Durham: Duke University Press, 1992), xxi.

intellectually and unrepresentable artistically, except through allegory. He writes that the present system is "so vast that it cannot be encompassed by the natural and historically developed categories of perception with which human beings normally orient themselves."[127]

This is a remarkable statement. Why should we take Jameson's word for it? The present state of global capitalism surpasses the "natural and historically developed categories of perception." How can this be so? We don't find this to be the case in our political or intellectual work. It is certainly beyond the capacities of any one individual to grasp the essence and operations of this world system, but that has always been the case. The task of the artist has never been to work out a full-fledged global perspective, but to discover and grapple in concentrated form with the greatest dilemmas of his or her age, to explore and ultimately concretize those dilemmas into imagery.

At any rate, in opposition to that undertaking, Jameson proposes his theory of the "political unconscious." According to this conception, which owes a good deal to Ernst Bloch, as well as Ernest Mandel,[128] the mysteries of the "cultural past" and presumably the present can be solved "only if they are grasped as vital episodes in a single vast unfinished plot," the history of the class struggle as it has unfolded through its various stages. He writes, "It is in detecting the traces of that uninterrupted narrative ... that the doctrine of a political unconscious finds its function and its necessity."[129]

On the one hand, this is a truism. Every work of art, no matter how flimsy, tells us something about the class struggle, that is, social reality. What else could it do? "However fantastic art may be," Trotsky said, "it cannot have at its disposal any other material except that which is given to it by the world of three dimensions and by the narrower world of class

---

[127] Fredric Jameson, *The Geopolitical Aesthetic: Cinema and Space in the World System* (Bloomington: Indiana University Press, 1992), 2.

[128] Ernest Mandel (1923–95): In the post–World War II period, a leader of an opportunist tendency in the Trotskyist movement that adapted to Stalinist, Social Democratic and petty-bourgeois nationalist movements. Pabloism (after another leading figure in this trend, Michel Pablo) sought to transform the Fourth International into a pressure group on those existing tendencies. The Pabloites developed the concept, in relation to Fidel Castro in particular, of the "unconscious Marxist," a contradiction in terms. Jameson appears to borrow his "political unconscious," an adaptation to the existing culture, from such political forces.

[129] Fredric Jameson, *The Political Unconscious: Narrative as a Socially Symbolic Act* (Ithaca: Cornell University Press, 1981), 19–20.

society."[130] The most dimwitted television program provides some insight, for instance, into the mentality of the social layer that created it, its banality and indifference, and so forth.

Jameson suggests that literary works need to be treated as symbolic acts revealing contradictions that a society cannot solve and tries to conceal. The work is then read carefully, by the specialist, to uncover the contradiction.

This literary creation takes place unconsciously. And here, I believe, is the truly pernicious side to this theory, which can only work against the most pressing cultural issue of our day, the development of *conscious historical and social knowledge* by the artist.

Jameson argues that "self-consciousness about the social totality"—i.e., some grasp of the present world situation—is not arrived at by a conscious process. He writes, "My thesis, however, is not merely that we ought to strive for it, but that we do so all the time anyway without being aware of the process." He describes the "conspiratorial text," the work that best sums up our condition apparently, as "an unconscious, collective effort at trying to figure out where we are and what landscapes and forces confront us in a late twentieth century whose abominations are heightened by their concealment and their bureaucratic impersonality." He goes on to speak about the "geopolitical unconscious," and, further, to assert that "it is only at that deeper level of our collective [unconscious] fantasy that we think about the social system all the time."[131]

It's difficult for me to imagine anything more irresponsible at this moment in history, when art and culture suffer so severely, provide such weak and impoverished pictures of life, precisely due to the lack of conscious, rational cognition of reality in art, than this sort of appeal, which amounts to little more than a throwing up of one's hands and an accommodation to the present terribly backward cultural condition. Marxists look at the present culture and propose a struggle; Jameson argues that it will all work out because our unconscious is registering world reality in any event.

Our view runs in the opposite direction. The unconscious comes into play in art in a rich and meaningful manner only to the extent that there is conscious, purposeful intent, that the artist *knows* what he or she is about. Only under those conditions do intuition and the nonrational assist in the

---

[130] Trotsky, *Literature and Revolution*, 204.

[131] Jameson, *The Geopolitical Aesthetic*, 2–3, 9.

artistic creation. At present, we have loads of unconscious fantasy, mostly the self-involved, narcissistic fantasy life of middle class individuals with no experience of life and little to say.

Our conviction is that no one carries out enduring artistic work without knowing important things, without exhaustive study of his or her art form *and* the world. Hegel writes that the serious artist "has to call in aid (i) the watchful circumspection of the intellect, and (ii) the depth of the heart and its animating feelings." It is therefore an absurdity to suppose that poems like Homer's "came to the poet in sleep. Without circumspection, discrimination, and criticism the artist cannot master any subject-matter which he is to configurate, and it is silly to believe that the genuine artist does not know what he is doing."[132]

As a final word, that will suffice. The genuine artist *knows* what he or she is doing. It's our conviction that progress in filmmaking lies along the line of knowledge, study and struggle, both artistic and social. We have great confidence that a new generation of film artists will choose that path.

An Evaluation of Roman Polanski as an Artist

World Socialist Web Site; November 20, 2009

Filmmaker Roman Polanski, as of this writing, remains in a Zurich jail cell while his lawyers fight the efforts by US authorities to extradite him. Polanski pled guilty more than thirty years ago in Los Angeles to unlawful sex with a young teenage girl, then fled the country when the judge in the case reneged on a plea bargain agreement and threatened to sentence the director to a lengthy prison term.

[*On July 12, 2010, Swiss authorities rejected the US government's extradition request and released Polanski from custody.*]

Every aspect of the case against Polanski reeks of dishonesty, hypocrisy and expediency. It has far more to do with current political and economic interests than with an incident that occurred in 1977 and whose two participants have long ago wished to see put to rest.

---

[132]   G.W.F. Hegel, *Aesthetics: Lectures on Fine Art, Vol. 1*, Trans. T.M. Knox (Oxford, Clarendon Press, 1998), 283.

The central concern of the Swiss authorities, by all accounts, is in this instance—as in every instance—the protection of their financial institutions. Embarrassed by a corruption scandal involving UBS and concerned about further investigations into their banks, the Swiss tipped off American officials that Polanski would be in Zurich for a film festival as a means of appeasing Washington.

For Los Angeles authorities, the vindictive Polanski witch-hunt serves the ends of settling a score with an individual who poked them in the eye. The American political establishment generally regards the Polanski affair as a useful means of further stoking up social backwardness and hysteria over alleged sex offenses.

Other factors may have played a role, including the recent efforts of Polanski's lawyers to have the case dismissed, based on the evidence of judicial misconduct, and their charge that Los Angeles officials had shown no seriousness about pursuing the director in recent years. It is at least intriguing to note that Polanski's new film, *The Ghost* (adapted from the novel by Robert Harris), uncompleted and unreleased because of the director's arrest, accuses a fictional former British prime minister (clearly based on Tony Blair) of war crimes and other perfidious acts.

It should be evident to anyone who thinks about it for a moment that the case against Polanski involves a political agenda. His continued prosecution represents an injustice and conforms to reactionary aims.

The fake populist claim that Polanski is a member of the "Hollywood elite" receiving special treatment is false, and even sinister. It echoes (and encourages) the repeated claims of anti-intellectual and often anti-Semitic forces that the entertainment industry is a hotbed of sin and corruption sapping the nation's "moral foundations." To join in the effort to set "Middle America" against "Hollywood," as a series of liberal commentators at the *Nation* and *Salon* have done, is unprincipled and politically reprehensible.

In reality, certain individuals (Michael Jackson and others) are picked out *because* they are wealthy celebrities and served up as human sacrifices to the most backward layers of the population, in an effort to divert their confused but seething anger over deteriorating conditions of life. The punishment of the rich and famous provides a vicarious (and illusory) satisfaction in such cases. It is not accidental that the manipulated outrage against Polanski comes in the midst of the deepest economic crisis since the Great Depression and a continuing flood of layoffs, wage cuts, foreclosures and personal bankruptcies.

Beyond the political and legal questions, there is something more involved here. After all, Polanski has considerable artistic gifts. In discussing the concerted effort to lock him up, we are obliged to consider his artistic contribution.

Polanski himself, through his French lawyer, Hervé Temime, has termed "counterproductive" arguments from defenders citing his artistry as an exculpatory factor. The filmmaker, Temime told reporters, felt that some of the commentary "was perceived as support for the immunity of an artist, and I think that's a false debate. ... He has never demanded special treatment for himself or his career."

Of course, there is no "immunity" for the artist; we would not even consider the question in those terms. However, Polanski's artistry and body of work demonstrate that he is not a sociopath; he is clearly not a pedophile, which would in any case raise the issue of treatment more than punishment.

Does it matter at all then that Polanski is a remarkable artist? We believe it does.

The evidence demonstrates that Polanski is not a sexual predator, but a gifted artist capable of colossally bad judgment.

As a preface, it must be said, the circumstances of his life, dismissed by his self-righteous enemies as irrelevant (the director tends to discount them too, insisting that he doesn't "linger" on unhappy memories), would be taken into account in any humane consideration of his personal difficulties. (That the case should most likely have been thrown out years ago on the grounds of judicial misconduct alone is another matter altogether.)

To be born in 1933, the year of Hitler's ascension to power, was perhaps a tragic omen. Polanski's family returned to Poland from France in 1936, and after the outbreak of the Second World War were forced to move into Krakow's Jewish ghetto. As a boy, Polanski witnessed many horrors. One day, for instance, he saw a German soldier shoot and kill an old woman simply because she couldn't keep up with a group of other women being herded down the street. "There was a loud bang, and blood came welling out of her back," he later recalled. Certain memories and images from this period of Polanski's life were incorporated into the award-winning *The Pianist*, based on the memoirs of Polish Jewish musician Wladyslaw Szpilman.

The following experience inspired the direction of a scene in his film version of Shakespeare's *Macbeth*: "The SS officer had searched our room in the ghetto, swishing his riding crop to and fro, toying with my teddy bear, nonchalantly emptying out the hatbox full of forbidden bread." Polanski's mother was eventually deported to Auschwitz, where she died, and he witnessed his father being marched off to another concentration camp (where he survived). Polanski barely escaped deportation to a camp. He was hidden first in Krakow and later in the countryside, largely fending for himself. More than 90 percent of the 3.5 million prewar Polish Jewish population were dead by 1945.

In the brutal conditions of postwar Poland, Polanski was attacked by a psychopath (already guilty of three murders) who struck him on the head repeatedly with a stone and left him for dead.

In 1969, his wife—actress Sharon Tate, eight and a half months pregnant—and three friends were brutally murdered in Los Angeles by followers of cult leader Charles Manson. Before the real culprits were apprehended, the American media had a field day attempting to link Polanski, or at least his "hedonistic" lifestyle, to the horrible tragedy.

It is difficult to conceive what effect all this must have on his nervous system.

And what about Polanski's artistic efforts themselves? Is he a serious figure? How have his films stood the test of time? Moreover, has he pursued themes that belie his media image as a "monster" and a "pervert"?

There is no possibility here of treating in detail a body of work that spans half a century, but certain points can be made.

Polanski began making short films in Poland in the late 1950s and directed his first feature film, *Knife in the Water*, in 1962. One can raise all sorts of criticisms, artistic and ideological, about his efforts, but it is difficult to think of more than a handful of directors globally who began working in the 1960s, or earlier, and continued to make important films into the first decade of the twenty-first century.

Polanski has expressed a variety of sentiments in his films, but a constant has been a concern for the fate of the vulnerable individual—often a child, an immigrant, a young woman, a victim of persecution (*Tess, The Tenant, Oliver Twist, Death and the Maiden, The Pianist*, as well as *Chinatown,* in its way)—in a generally menacing environment, threatened by different forces, from the insensitivity or social prejudices of others to the outright violence and cruelty of the authorities.

Sometimes, in extreme cases, the external world proves so crushing and destructive in Polanski's films (in *Repulsion* and *The Tenant* most obviously, but there are also elements of this in *Cul-de-Sac, Rosemary's Baby, Bitter Moon, Death and the Maiden,* even *Macbeth* and *The Pianist*) that it invades the individual and brings about an internal collapse.

Could anyone reasonably argue, given the difficulties of the last three quarters of a century, that in representing such a frightening state of affairs Polanski has not offered insight into important aspects of modern existence? In other words, Polanski has applied himself consistently—sometimes successfully, sometimes unsuccessfully, but seriously, at any rate—to one of the central questions of our time: "the conflict between the individual and various social forms which are hostile to him."[133]

His terrifying experiences in Nazi German–occupied Poland surely prepared him for that. Stalinist repression in the so-called "People's Republic of Poland" under the rule of the "Polish United Workers Party" would have added to his skepticism about the powers that be in modern society. His encounters with a spiteful American legal system and media have probably not improved his opinion of media-organized "public opinion" and the forces of law and order.

Polanski began his artistic career as a child actor on radio and with a puppet theater. He also "became a well-known street person" in Krakow, according to biographer Barbara Leaming, "little, loud and aggressive." He landed a part in Andrzej Wajda's *A Generation*, released in 1955, the first part of the renowned trilogy (along with *Kanal* and *Ashes & Diamonds*).

Poland never experienced "socialism," much less "communism," but the formation of the postwar Stalinist regime in Poland brought certain social benefits to the population—rooted in the nationalization of basic industry and related measures—that were, in the end, surviving gains of the Russian Revolution of 1917, extended into the Eastern European–bloc countries.

Polanski was able to attend the National Film School in Lódz in the mid-1950s—at the time one of the finest in the world. He told interviewers Pascal Bonitzer and Nathalie Heinich in 1979 that "Polish technique was developed by filmmakers who were in the Soviet Union during the Second World War. And Soviet cinematography was based entirely on the principles of American production which had been studied and copied in the post-[Russian]revolutionary era, at a time when they had as much enthusiasm as the Americans have today."

He said in a *Playboy* magazine interviewer in 1971 that the school's intense, five-year program was "advantageous." Polanski explained: "Besides all the practical training, like editing, camera operating, etc., you had

[133]   Leon Trotsky, Diego Rivera, André Breton, "Manifesto: Towards a Free Revolutionary Art," *Leon Trotsky on Literature and Art*, ed. Paul N. Siegel (New York: Pathfinder, 1970), 118.

courses in the history of art, literature, history of music, optics, theory of film directing—if such a thing exists—and so forth. The first year was very general and theoretical, and you got to know intimately the techniques of still photography, which is essential, I think, for anyone who later wants to be an expert in cinematography. The second year, the students made two one-minute films of their own. The third year, a documentary of eight to fifteen minutes. The fourth year, a short fictional film of the same length; and then in the fifth year, you made your diploma film, which could go up to twenty minutes."

Polanski explained that "The school was tightly connected with the Polish film archives and we could see anything we wanted." Elsewhere, he notes that the students were divided into artistic factions: "Personally, I was part of the [Orson] Welles group, but there were also groups of neo-realists and students who liked the heroic Soviet cinema."

He left the film school in 1959, he told *Playboy*, "with very firm aesthetic ideals about films. … For me, a film has to have a definite dramatic and visual shape, as opposed to a rather flimsy shape that a lot of films were being given by the [French] *Nouvelle Vague*, for example, which happened in more or less the same period. It has to be something finished, like a sculpture, almost something you can touch, that you can roll on the floor. It has to be rigorous and disciplined—that's *Citizen Kane vs. The Bicycle Thief.*"

It is worth citing these comments at length. They indicate some of Polanski's artistic and intellectual advantages at the outset of his career: a firm grounding in film technique (a commentator notes that his "collaborators on *Rosemary's Baby*, his first American film, were astonished at his exacting camera requirements and precise understanding of the optics and geometry of lenses"[134]; a thorough knowledge of film history and an orientation toward some of its most complex, aesthetically exacting figures (as a member of the self-declared "Welles group"); participation in a seething artistic environment that was a relative oasis of freedom in Stalinist Poland; an aversion to nationalism, which has proved fatal to more than one Polish filmmaker ("These subjects never interested me and from the start I worked outside nationalistic interests," he told an interviewer in 1992); and despite his avowed anticommunism, Polanski had at least enough historical

---

[134] Mark Cousins, "Polanski's Fourth Wall Aesthetic," *The Cinema of Roman Polanski: Dark Spaces of the World*, ed. John Orr, Elzbieta Ostrowska (London: Wallflower Press, 2006), 3.

understanding to know that the Russian Revolution had generated "enthusiasm" among artists until the Stalinist clampdown of the 1930s.

It is perhaps telling about modern history that knives should figure so prominently in the work of one of its major artistic figures. In Polanski's first completed short at the Lódz film school, *Murder*, only two minutes long, a man enters another's room, stabs and kills him. We see the older man's plump, complacent face and demeanor, fleetingly, only as he turns to leave. Knives (or other sharp blades) feature prominently in *Repulsion*, *Rosemary's Baby*, *Macbeth*, *Chinatown* and *Tess*.

And Polanski's first feature, after all, was entitled *Knife in the Water*. In that film, a couple, Andrzej and Krystyna, nouveau riche Poles, reluctantly pick up a young hitchhiker, a poor student. They own a nice auto—like an "embassy" car, says the young man—and a boat. They are going sailing.

The two men, from the start, go at each other. Andrzej invites the younger man to go along with him and his wife for the day, almost as a dare. "So you want to go on with the game?" says the student. The reply: "My boy, you are no match for me."

Tensions mount on board the sailboat, as the older man, a well-heeled, arrogant (and generally unpleasant) sportswriter, pits his nautical skills and savoir-faire against the other's youth and good looks, with the young wife, presumably, as the prize. The hitchhiker's most valued possession is a knife of the switchblade variety. It becomes central to the conflict between the men.

Andrzej needs to control everything and everyone around him. Later, when the student gains a measure of emotional revenge, Krystyna tells him, "You're not one bit better than he is, you understand? He used to be the same as you. ... And you'd really like to be the way he is now. And you are going to be, as long as your ambition holds out."

Numerous commentators agree that the main issue in *Knife in the Water* is a "struggle for power." Andrzej himself says, "If two men are on a boat, one man is skipper." A critic writes, "Power, and the violence used to sustain it, emerged as central elements in Polanski's cinema."[135]

No doubt. But the battle captured beautifully in black and white (with hints of Welles's *The Lady from Shanghai*) by Polanski and his

---

[135] Herbert J. Eagle, "Power and the Visual Semantics of Polanski's Films," *The Cinema of Roman Polanski: Dark Spaces of the World*, ed. John Orr, Elzbieta Ostrowska (London: Wallflower Press, 2006), 38.

co-screenwriter Jerzy Skolimowski (the future filmmaker: *Barrier, Deep End, Moonlighting*) reminds one of siblings quarreling violently. One wants to say: it isn't their fault. Someone else has set them at each other's throats. Something is wrong in the whole situation.

Andrzej and the college student are struggling so fiercely over a knife, over an attractive, but rather passive woman, who doesn't seem terribly interested in the outcome, because, in reality, neither one of them has any real control over his life. The slightly overwrought character of the film, in the end, comes from *everybody's* social powerlessness (including the film-makers'). The ultimate source of unhappiness is a repressive society, rife with inequalities and hypocrisies, that cannot be criticized openly.

Polanski then left Poland for good and made his first feature film in English, *Repulsion*, released in the US in October 1965. Catherine Deneuve plays a repressed young woman who shares an apartment with her sister. Also an outsider, Carol is a Belgian working in a London beauty salon. When her sister leaves on vacation, Carol suffers a nervous breakdown, hallucinates, and ends up slashing two men, an attractive suitor and her lecherous landlord.

Years ago, the film terrified me out of my wits (I recall spending a good deal of the time more or less under my seat), especially the sequences in which arms come out of the walls and reach for the unfortunate girl. On a more recent viewing, it seems somewhat dated and also a little over-wrought. Again, the effort to cram all the fearfulness of postwar life into a purely psychosexual framework overburdens the drama. *Repulsion* sags under the weight and feels contrived as a result.

One might say some of the same things about *Cul-de-Sac* (1966), except that it is a good deal more fun, at least in parts. Two wounded gangsters (Lionel Stander and Jack MacGowran), following a botched holdup, arrive at an isolated castle in northern England inhabited by an ex-businessman and his wife (also markedly different in age), George and Teresa, played by Donald Pleasence and Françoise Dorléac (Deneuve's older sister, who died tragically in an auto accident in June 1967).

One critic (Paul Coates, "*Cul-de-Sac* in Context: Absurd Authorship and Sexuality") comments that the film "can be situated in the Polish and English absurdist tradition, to which it is arguably the most closely related of all Polanski's features, with the possible exception of *The Tenant.*"

An attraction for absurdism and related trends is clearly evident in Polanski's art. The influence of Samuel Beckett, as well as Franz Kafka and blackly comic Central European traditions, is present in his early Polish shorts (*Two Men and A Wardrobe, The Fat and the Lean, Mammals*). The conjoining of sexual aggression and class tension brings Harold Pinter's writing to mind, including his film work with Joseph Losey (*The Servant*).

The somewhat too tempting appeal of absurdism is not difficult to figure out, taking into account Polanski's personal history and the general state of things in postwar Europe: a shattered economy and population, the resulting horror with fascism, the discrediting of "communism" as a result of the crimes of Stalinism—all of this producing an intellectual impasse (reflected in existentialism and other philosophical trends) of an epochal character.

Whether Polanski was conscious of it or not, the ideological atmosphere and physical conditions of life in postwar Eastern Europe, where the regimes set themselves the historically ludicrous goal of building isolated socialist states, were elements too in encouraging his absurdist sensibility. The image of Sisyphean, repetitive, and pointless labor recurs in a number of the early short films, in *Knife in the Water*, and even in *Cul-de-Sac* and *The Fearless Vampire Killers* (1967).

In any event, *Cul-de-Sac* has its pleasures, especially the initial, relatively lighthearted interplay between Stander (a victim of the Hollywood blacklist), Pleasence and Dorléac. Again, sexual and other power struggles ensue, with a rather murky outcome—the gangster dead, the young wife fled, and George curled up in a fetal position on an outcropping as the tide comes in. A "dead end" (*cul-de-sac*) indeed, but from what precisely?

Among other things, it's possible—although it may not have been the meaning of Polanski and longtime collaborator, screenwriter Gérard Brach—to interpret the film loosely as a comment on Britain's declined and decayed state. The presence of an American thug, a dying Irishman, and an irresponsible Frenchwoman, all creating difficulties for the retired, wealthy and nervous Englishman on his secluded, island home is at least suggestive.

Polanski disowned *The Fearless Vampire Killers* (or *Dance of the Vampires*), shot in England and Italy, after its producer Martin Ransohoff severely re-edited the film and made it incomprehensible from the director's point of view. Still, there are the delightful performances of Jack MacGowran as the inept "vampire killer," Professor Abronsius, and Polanski himself as Alfred, Abronsius's equally fumbling assistant. Polanski met his future wife, the ill-fated Sharon Tate, on the film, in which she played one of chief vampire Count von Krolock's (Ferdy Mayne) comely victims.

The film has something of the flavor of a Central European Jewish tale, understated, droll, earthy, taking a sharp-eyed but still sympathetic and amused view of humanity. And there is the lovely moment when "Shagal," the Jewish innkeeper (named no doubt for the modernist painter, who frequently depicted Eastern European Jewish village life), who has himself become one of the "living dead," enters the bed chamber of the blonde servant girl he's been lusting after. ... When she holds up a crucifix—in the time-honored tradition—to ward him off, he scoffingly tells her: "Have you got the wrong vampire!"

Rosemary's Baby, Polanski's first Hollywood film (and major success), for Paramount Studios, shot in the fall and winter of 1967 and released the following June, is a story of the occult. Polanski hastened to assure an interviewer, "You don't have to be superstitious to enjoy a fantasy. ... Myself, I am down to earth in my philosophy of life, very rationally and materialistically oriented, with no interest in the occult."

The story, about a young woman in New York whose ambitious husband makes a pact with a group of devil worshippers and offers her up as a receptacle for Satan's child, is one of the so-called "apartment trilogy" (along with *Repulsion* and *The Tenant*), which treats the behavior of "people under stress" in confined spaces, with some of that behavior stemming from the very fact of being in a confined space, comforting and alarming at the same time.

(The boats in *Knife in the Water* and *Bitter Moon*, and the isolated castles or houses in *Cul-de-Sac*, *Macbeth* and *Death and the Maiden* are all, in their own ways, confined spaces—as is the apartment in which Wladyslaw Szpilman is obliged to remain for a time, at the peril of his life, in *The Pianist*, and Fagin's lair, where Oliver is held against his will in *Oliver Twist*.)

All sorts of psychological issues present themselves in connection to this attraction for and repulsion from enclosed spaces, but at the center of them all probably lies the image of the sealed Krakow ghetto, frightening in itself, but the exit from which is even more frightening.

Rosemary's Baby is a fantasy, and a well-done one at that. The filmmakers assembled an excellent cast, including Mia Farrow (although she was not his first choice), John Cassavetes as her selfish, opportunist actor-husband, and veteran character or stage actors Ruth Gordon, Ralph Bellamy, Sidney Blackmer, Maurice Evans, Elisha Cook Jr., Patsy Kelly, Phil Leeds, and Hope Summer.

The victim of her husband's careerism and her sinister neighbors' plans for her, Rosemary (Farrow) suffers horribly in her pregnancy. She turns pale and at first (unaccountably) grows thin; she's in constant pain. Her elegant, spacious Upper West Side apartment becomes a prison cell, a place of torture. Those she reaches out to, when she realizes the nature of the plot, betray her. The film builds up a disturbing level of paranoia, at the same time as it maintains, until the very end, its peculiar sense of humor.

Roman Polanski attended the Cannes film festival during the May–June 1968 events, the massive general strike that shook French capitalism to its foundations. Contrary to myth (for example, in Vanessa Redgrave's autobiography), he did not support the leftist attempt to shut down the festival that year. As he makes clear in his own autobiography, Polanski found the "revolutionary" filmmakers' efforts rather self-indulgent and even "absurd," which they may well have been, to a degree.

Nonetheless, whatever his ambivalence or even hostility, the experience of a mass movement in the West against capitalism ("By this time the general strike was spreading throughout France. Train and plane services were grinding to a halt, gas stations running dry. Exhibitors began to pack up and go home, and the festival ended in complete disarray," he writes) had to have had an impact on him, as opposed to the experience of a later generation of "dissidents" in the Stalinist countries.

In August 1969, tragedy struck when the so-called "Manson family" members murdered the pregnant Sharon Tate and four friends at the Los Angeles home Polanski and Tate shared. He was in Europe on a film project at the time.

Two years after the tragedy, Polanski told the interviewer from *Playboy*: "Sharon was the first woman in my life who really made me feel happy. I mean literally aware of being happy. That's a very rare state. Strangely enough, about a week or two before her death, I remember an instant when I was thinking of it, and I was actually thinking: 'I am a happy man!' ... I also remember thinking—and here is my middle-European background, probably—I remember thinking: 'This cannot possibly last. It's impossible to last.' And I suddenly got scared. I was thinking that you can't maintain such a status quo. I didn't have anything tragic in mind, but I was afraid, being quite a realist, that such a state cannot last indefinitely."

Polanski's next film was an understandably bleak version of Shakespeare's *Macbeth*, filmed in North Wales and released in 1971. The director explained that after his wife's murder, "everything I was considering seemed futile to me. I couldn't think of a subject that seemed worthwhile or dignified enough to spend a year or more on it. ... As a kid, I loved Shakespeare, and when I was a teenager I saw Laurence Olivier's *Hamlet* twenty times. I always had this great desire to make a Shakespearean movie some day, and when I finally decided I must go back to work, I thought to myself: 'That's something I could do, that's something I could give myself to. That's worth the effort.'"

Polanski adapted the play along with left-wing British theater critic Kenneth Tynan. Their version (perhaps inspired too by well-known comments from the German playwright Bertolt Brecht) emphasizes the shabby, dirty, provincial character of the medieval Scottish nobility's existence. Pigs run through one castle's grounds. The witches, not three, but a crowd, are ugly, ill-clothed, sometimes unclothed. Polanski and Tynan present Macbeth's murder of Duncan, normally done offstage, in all its chaos and painfulness, as the usurper jabs at the reigning king with his dagger.

Macbeth has a perpetually moving frontline of violence and treachery, insecurity and blood. It contains some of the bitterest, grimmest lines in Shakespeare, reaching a high point in the famous soliloquy, "Tomorrow, and tomorrow, and tomorrow," which ends with Macbeth indicting life as "a tale told by an idiot, full of sound and fury, signifying nothing."

Polanski's is an intelligent, creditable version of Macbeth, with many picturesque and striking moments. However, by and large, the film lacks the necessary intensity and fury. Jon Finch and Francesca Annis (as Macbeth and Lady Macbeth) perform with sincerity, but the work as a whole lacks great purpose, except to establish the potential of human beings to do terrible things to one another. Orson Welles, Polanski's "idol," in his 1948 version, makes the play a study in despotism, in the psychology and mechanics, and ultimate irrationality, of a tyranny.

In the Tynan-Polanski modernist (or perhaps already "post-modernist") version, no one is innocent; Macbeth is simply one assassin among many. The difficulty is, if everyone acts horribly, then no one does.

Polanski's next major film was *Chinatown*. Released in June 1974 (at a volatile time, only weeks before the resignation of President Richard Nixon as a result of the Watergate scandal), the film is perhaps his most complete achievement to date. It is a remarkable work, both accessible to a wide audience and artistically and politically complex.

Set in 1937, *Chinatown* is loosely inspired by the so-called "California Water Wars" of the 1910s and 1920s. Los Angeles officials at the time, led by the Department of Water and Power's superintendent, William Mulholland, conspired to divert water to the metropolitan area at the expense of farmers in the Owens Valley. The water was used to irrigate the

San Fernando Valley, large parcels of which had secretly been bought up by a syndicate. The investors reaped a fortune.

Polanski's film centers on private detective J.J. Gittes (Jack Nicholson), who is apparently hired by the wife of the water and power department chief engineer, Hollis Mulwray, to look into her husband's infidelity. Gittes and his associates spy on Mulwray meeting his supposed youthful mistress at their "love nest." In reality, the woman who retained the detective was not Mulwray's wife, and Gittes has become a pawn in an effort to discredit the chief engineer, who has learned of the effort to divert water and other corrupt goings-on, and plans to expose them.

After Mulwray is murdered, his real wife, now a widow, Evelyn (Faye Dunaway), hires Gittes to investigate the crime. Gittes looks deeper into the water issue, getting his nostril sliced open in the process (thanks to a knife-wielding "midget" thug played by Polanski). He presses the fragile and neurotic Evelyn, "I think you're hiding something." She tries to put him off. As to her personal life, she says falteringly, "I don't see anyone for very long. ... It's difficult for me."

Meanwhile, her sinister father, Noah Cross (John Huston), a wealthy businessman and Mulwray's former partner, offers Gittes even more money, $10,000, to find Mulwray's "girlfriend." At their lunchtime meeting, Cross tells Gittes, "You may think you know what you're dealing with, but, believe me, you don't."

In fact, "large-scale capitalist interests [are] arrayed against the people of Los Angeles and the small farmers of the nearby Valley," who are all "coerced and duped" so that Cross can become "even wealthier than he already is."[136]

Events unfold. Gittes's efforts to protect Evelyn and the other young woman only end up leading to a tragic denouement.

Chinatown evokes with great effectiveness the world first depicted in the "hardboiled" novels of Dashiell Hammett, Raymond Chandler, and James M. Cain, among others. Polanski explained to *Interview* magazine that he was "trying to create ... this Philip Marlowe atmosphere [Chandler's private detective], which I had never seen in the movies the way I got it in the books."

At their best, what those novels captured—and Polanski and screenwriter Robert Towne succeed in this as well—was the shocking contrast between the glamorous surface of life in southern California in the 1930s— the lush vegetation, ocean, sunny skies, movie stars, creamy stucco houses,

---

[136] Ibid., 48.

sleek cars—and the rotten, money-grubbing reality at the heart of its cancerous economic growth.

The genial, avuncular Cross is guilty of everything. Toward the end, he tells Gittes, "Most people never have to face the fact that at the right time and the right place, they're capable of anything." The private eye has earlier challenged Cross about his plans to make additional piles of money: "Why are you doing it? How much better can you eat? What could you buy that you can't already afford?"

A critic describes Cross in *Chinatown* as the "very incarnation of the political conspiracy in a single figure of voracious will." What has already happened "can only get worse," because the businessman-developer "indicates that his goal is to buy up the future: the increasing voraciousness of Capital has no limit."[137]

The exile from "communism," Polanski, but an honest artist, with his eyes open, made a meticulously constructed, devastating and deeply felt indictment of American society. One wonders if the political establishment, especially in Los Angeles, ever truly forgave him.

Polanski and Towne created *Chinatown* on the crest of a wave of radicalism that was sweeping the globe. The former considered *Chinatown* an "important and serious" work, he told an interviewer years later. (Although he noted in another published conversation shortly after the movie's release that it was his most formally conventional work.) The director described his approach as being that of "an invisible witness to the events," with the camera following. He went on: "If you have a story to tell, try to tell it in a simple, or maybe, elegant manner, and care about the emotions it can evoke in those kind enough to watch it."

Speaking of *Chinatown*'s tragic ending, he observed, "If you want to feel for Evelyn, if you ... feel in general that there is a lot of injustice in our world, you want to have people leaving the cinema with a feeling that they should do something about it in their lives." Or, as he explained in his autobiography, he wanted audience members to get out of their seats "with a sense of outrage."

The director, of course, had the benefit of the participation of Jack Nicholson at the height of his acting powers (Dunaway, Huston and the entire

---

[137] Dana Polan, "*Chinatown*: Politics as Perspective, Perspective as Politics," *The Cinema of Roman Polanski: Dark Spaces of the World*, ed. John Orr, Elzbieta Ostrowska (London: Wallflower Press, 2006), 113–14.

cast are also excellent). There is little question that Nicholson in the 1970s was one of the finest performers working in films. In, among others, *Easy Rider* (1969), *Five Easy Pieces, The Last Detail, The Passenger, One Flew Over the Cuckoo's Nest, The Shining* and *Reds* (1981), as well as *Chinatown*, he stood out.

His Jake Gittes can be taken as representative: here Nicholson personifies a certain lower-middle-class American type: somewhat vulgar, but honest and quite forceful; skeptical yet not cynical; still naïve and occasionally a little wide-eyed; not too impressed with himself; a bully perhaps in some circumstances but essentially good-hearted; someone you would want on your side; someone capable of an enormous effort to get at the truth.

Polanski directed two more films in the 1970s, *The Tenant* (1976) and *Tess* (1979), both serious, if flawed, efforts.

The former (from a novel published in 1964 by Roland Topor, a French artist of Polish-Jewish descent) is his most "Kafkaesque," if that overworked phrase has much left in it by this time. Polanski plays a mild-mannered clerk, a Polish immigrant living in Paris, who rents an apartment that previously belonged to a woman, an Egyptologist named Simone Choule, who threw herself out of the window. He visits her in the hospital, where, wrapped head to toe in bandages like a mummy, she emits a terrible scream.

Trelkovsky moves into the unappealing flat (everyone tells him "it is difficult to find a good apartment" in Paris), but immediately comes up against the intolerance and repressiveness of the building's owner, its concierge, and the majority of his neighbors. He's not allowed to have female visitors, he mustn't make noise, every move he makes is watched and disapproved of ...

The mental torment generated by his inhospitable surroundings and his loneliness eventually drives him mad. He begins to hallucinate, he starts to dress up in the previous tenant's clothes; in the end, he loses his identity entirely and becomes Simone, even imitating her method of suicide.

As Polanski later admitted, the lead character's transition is rather abrupt and not entirely convincing. *The Tenant* (humanity as a whole perhaps, with its rather tenuous, continually threatened status on this planet) is at its best when it is most concrete about Trelkovsky's difficulties: a nasty landlord, nosy and bigoted neighbors, a police official hostile to foreigners.

Polanski is charming in those portions of the film, as the much-put-upon, endlessly patient "little man," who shrugs at setbacks, lets abuses roll off him like water off a duck's back, while somehow maintaining his dignity. French actress Isabelle Adjani, as a friend of the former tenant who seems ready to help him stay or get back on his feet, is also a delight (Adjani is nearly unrecognizable in the role, which is unlike the enigmatic or self-pitying persona she played in a number of films).

The Tenant collapses under the weight of its own amorphous ambitions, but not before it has demonstrated the "'terrible uncertainty of one's own existence,' as Kafka once put it, that is so often central to the haunting aspect of the director's work."[138] In the film, argues Ewa Mazierska, Polanski "draws attention to the social context of the emergence of schizophrenia."[139]

Tess was Polanski's second adaptation of a classic of English literature (Thomas Hardy's 1891 *Tess of the d'Urbervilles*) and his first film after pleading guilty to unlawful sexual intercourse with a minor and fleeing the US in 1978.

Nastassja Kinski starred as the young farm girl who undergoes a series of tests that eventually drive her over the brink. When her impoverished, broken-down father, John Durbeyfield, learns of his descent from an ancient noble family, Tess is sent to make a connection with a wealthy branch of the d'Urberville family that lives nearby. As a matter of fact, the family has purchased the name and coat of arms.

Alec d'Urberville attempts to seduce his lovely "cousin," and when gifts and sweet words fall short, he rapes her. She leaves, eventually giving birth to a sickly baby that soon dies. She goes to work as a milkmaid and falls in love with the charismatic, reform-minded Angel Clare. They marry, but when she tells him of her past, he finds it difficult to accept, and abandons her. Tess is forced to turn to Alec to help her family avoid starvation. When a remorseful Angel returns for her and finds her living with Alec, tragedy ensues.

Polanski has again done a thorough and convincing job. Hardy's novel is a heartbreaking story of class and sexual oppression. A good deal of that comes through in *Tess*, in its most affecting parts. Peter Firth is especially good as the high-minded but repressed and hypocritical Angel Clare, who destroys his own and Tess's chance for happiness with his "idealism" and stupid male egoism.

---

[138] Tony McKibbin, "Polanski and the Horror from Within," *The Cinema of Roman Polanski: Dark Spaces of the World*, ed. John Orr, Elzbieta Ostrowska (London: Wallflower Press, 2006), 53.

[139] Ewa Mazierska, *Roman Polanski: The Cinema of a Cultural Traveller* (London, I.B. Tauris, 2007), 41.

The director told interviewer Max Tessier in 1979: "Tess's rebellion is of-ten seen as something that occurs only at the end of the novel, but it's actually present all the way through. Everyone has a place within society, and rebelling against it brings grave consequences. When Tess does rebel, it kills her."

Unhappily, this element is not really worked through dramatically in the film. Kinski is fine when called upon to convey a smoldering resent-ment, but lacks the overall depth and dynamism required by the "unspoken rebellion" to which Polanski refers.

The falling off in Polanski's work in the 1980s and 1990s was part of a general falling off. He directed only two films in the former decade, the sporadically amusing *Pirates*, with Walter Matthau, which failed badly at the box office, and the competent thriller *Frantic*, with Harrison Ford and a young French actress, Emmanuelle Seigner, whom Polanski eventually married (they have two children). *Bitter Moon*, released in 1992, an "erotic melodrama," is a poor, unconvincing film.

Polanski's adaptation of Ariel Dorfman's painful *Death and the Maiden* came out in 1994. The playwright was cultural advisor to the Allende "Popular Unity" regime in Chile, overthrown by a CIA-organized military coup in 1973. In his play, a woman in an unnamed South American country believes a man she accidentally encounters to be her chief torturer years before, who repeatedly raped her to the music of Schubert.

Dorfman, who has signed the petition calling for Polanski's release from Swiss prison, explained at the time why he chose the Polish-French film-maker to direct his work: "There were six or seven directors who wanted to make the film, but I felt Roman was the right person. He identified, as you say, with all three characters for his own biographical reasons; he has lived these situations of repression over and over again in his life. And therefore I had nothing to explain to him. I knew that in Polansk I had a director who would understand what the story was about without me having to explain it."

Around that same time, Polanski expressed his dismay about the state of contemporary moviemaking in an interview: "It's already getting more and more difficult to make an ambitious and original film. There are less and less independent producers or independent companies and an increasing number of corporations who are more interested in balance sheets than in artistic achievement. They want to make a killing each time they produce a film."

Unhappily, his own *The Ninth Gate* (1999), with Johnny Depp and Seigner, is something of a confirmation of the very syndrome he describes.

It is a rather bland and anticlimactic, if visually striking, horror film, once again with satanic overtones.

In *The Pianist*, released in 2002, Polanski for the first time addressed himself directly to the terrible fate of the Polish Jews under the Nazis. The director based himself on the memoirs of Wladyslaw Szpilman (in an adaptation by Ronald Harwood)—a pianist and composer who miraculously survived German-occupied Poland and lived another five decades after the war—as well as his own experiences. The result is a difficult-to-watch but restrained and dignified account of a population's descent into hell, and an individual's eventual reemergence.

The first part of the film deals with the step-by-step brutalization of Warsaw's Jews in the first years of the German occupation. Szpilman's family attempts to carry on under the increasingly humiliating and dangerous conditions. After two years, deportation orders come for the family. As they walk to the railway cars that will transport them to their deaths, a Jewish policeman, a collaborator with the Germans, recognizes Wladyslaw and permits him to escape—an episode with marked similarities to Polanski's own getaway in Krakow.

Then comes Szpilman's two-and-a-half-year struggle to survive, both inside and outside the Warsaw Ghetto. From an apartment just beyond it, he watches the heroic Ghetto uprising of April 1943 and later witnesses the general Warsaw uprising in August 1944. In the last period of the war, a German officer discovers him in an abandoned building, hears him play the piano, and helps keep him alive.

In its review in 2002, the WSWS noted a number of weaknesses in the film, observing that "there is something misleadingly passive and empty about Szpilman on screen," and that Polanski, for his own ideological reasons, had softened "some social and political elements in the memoir," including Szpilman's contact with a socialist oppositionist inside the Warsaw Ghetto.

Nonetheless, the WSWS described the film as "a moving evocation of the Nazi Holocaust, depicted through the experience of a single survivor of the Warsaw Ghetto. Polanski does not break new ground, but tackles the subject with intelligence and dignity. He has been largely successful in bringing to the screen the impressive memoir of Wladyslaw Szpilman."

The film was well received and generally viewed as an artistic "return to form," gaining Polanski the Best Director award at the 2003 Academy Award ceremony, accepted for him by Harrison Ford.

On the strength of that success, Polanski turned to another English classic, Charles Dickens's *Oliver Twist* (2005, also from an adaptation by Harwood)—in part, he explained, so that his own children could watch one of his films.

Polanski's version is a straightforward and compelling recounting of the story of the famous orphan boy in early Victorian England. In the Polanski rendering, Oliver (Barney Clark) escapes abuse at the hands of his master coffin-maker's wife and senior assistant by running away on foot to London. There, he falls in with a gang of boy pickpockets, led by the Artful Dodger (Harry Eden) and managed by Fagin (Ben Kingsley).

Falsely accused of stealing a handkerchief, Oliver is brought before a sadistic magistrate, eager to hand down a harsh sentence. Oliver is proven innocent, and his supposed victim, the kindly and affluent Mr. Brownlow (Edward Hardwicke) takes Oliver to his mansion and proposes to raise him.

Fearful that the boy will finger them to the authorities, Fagin and his brutish associate, Bill Sikes (Jamie Foreman), conspire to kidnap Oliver, with the help of Bill's girlfriend, the young prostitute Nancy (Leanne Rowe). With Oliver under lock and key at Fagin's hangout, and following a failed break-in at Mr. Brownlow's house, Nancy takes pity on Oliver and attempts to organize his rescue. Bill finds out about her betrayal and beats her to death. In a climactic scene, at Fagin's, the police close in on Bill, who comes to a pitiful end. Oliver, in the film's epilogue, pays a visit to Fagin awaiting execution in prison.

His version of the Dickens novel brings out themes and motifs close to Polanski's heart: the abandoned child, alone in strange and unforgiving surroundings; the bewildering, apparently arbitrary cruelty of the authorities; the general persecution of the weak and defenseless; and, as well, a confidence, which sometimes flickers very low, in the essential goodness (and immense resilience) of human beings. Kingsley, who on occasion strikes the viewer in all his precision as mannered and lacking in spontaneity, delivers a moving performance as the avaricious, grotesque, but still oddly sympathetic fence.

All in all, this is a film career worthy of serious attention. One might learn something important about our world and our times by watching Polanski's films. He has done honest and artistic work, given characters and events "a definite dramatic and visual shape," in a difficult and often regressive cultural climate.

And now ... Polanski, at the age of 76, has been arrested by Swiss authorities who intend to hand him over to US officials, who would like to lock him up. Given his life history, it seems fairly safe to assume that whatever emotions are washing over the filmmaker, astonishment is not among them. But this travesty of justice, accompanied by all manner of pious and self-righteous bleatings, should also evoke outrage.

Polanski once told an interviewer: "One of the profound experiences of my youth was seeing *Of Mice and Men* [1939]. That has stayed with me. I couldn't stop thinking about this big, lovely man and his friend, and their friendship, and I thought that if I were ever a film maker, I would certainly try to do something along those lines, something against injustice and intolerance and prejudice and superstition. And I have. These elements are weaved through my films."

It's true, and he should be allowed to keep doing "something along those lines," which is no small contribution to his fellow human beings.

Filmography

Oliver Twist (2005)
The Pianist (2002)
The Ninth Gate (1999)
Death and the Maiden (1994)
Bitter Moon (1992)
Frantic (1988)
Pirates (1986)
Tess (1979)
The Tenant (1976)
Chinatown (1974)
Che? [What?] (1972)
Macbeth (1971)
Rosemary's Baby (1968)
Dance of the Vampires (1967) or *The Fearless Vampire Killers* (USA)
Cul-de-Sac (1966)
Repulsion (1965)
Knife in theWater (1962)

Short films

Mammals (1962)
The Fat and the Lean (1961)
When Angels Fall (1959)

The Lamp (1959)
Two Men and a Wardrobe (1958)
Let's Break Up the Dance (1957)
A Toothful Smile (1957)
Murder (1957)

The Crisis of American Filmmaking and Cultural Life

World Socialist Web Site; March 18, 2010

The following is an edited version of a presentation delivered by David Walsh in New York City and the Detroit area.

When one considers the state of filmmaking, and art in general, one's first response is, or ought to be, in my view, a profound sense of dissatisfaction. The spectator, or reader, or viewer, currently experiences a troubling lack of depth, texture, and social and psychological complexity. In short, there is an absence of the world, largely.

Certainly the world that great numbers of people know and experience on a daily basis: the world of work, or lack of work, the vast and complicated series of everyday social relationships, the startling changes in life in recent decades, the enormous inequalities and iniquities, the slipping into the social abyss of so many, the struggle to keep one's head above water that characterizes the lives of tens of millions in this country, billions worldwide ... and the emotional conditions, the drama, tragedy and comedy associated with all that.

Telling the truth is difficult, as George Eliot and Tolstoy both noted, but contemporary art and film, in our view, are failing badly in telling important truths, the truths that are vital to people.

No doubt there is a great deal of ideological and political, and even moral, confusion in this country. We aren't mesmerized by that and struggle to overcome it on a daily basis, but one must say that the failure of film and novels and plays, in the first place, to hold up a mirror to the country adequately in recent decades, to expose American society's crimes and injustices, to show the population its own shortcomings, is a factor in the confusion.

Have contemporary American filmmakers and writers exerted themselves, made enormous sacrifices in the struggle to clarify and demystify reality, the nature of American society itself? Have they helped the population understand its predicament? The answer is obvious, I think.

Representing the world more fully and richly is not a matter of mere surface details, or of passive recording. When we speak about "the presence of the world" in art, we mean its real presence, which includes centrally its social and historical character. As the Austrian novelist Robert Musil (*The Man Without Qualities*) commented, creative effort involves not mere description, but an *interpretation* of life.

At present we lack serious artistic interpretation influenced by the most advanced understanding of reality. The emergence of modern art and culture was inextricably bound up with the growth of Marxism and the socialist workers movement. The decline in the influence of genuine Marxism—not academic leftism, postmodernism, the Frankfurt School, and so forth—has had a serious, harmful impact on art and culture.

A seriousness about showing life in art needs to be revived, for the sake of society and for the sake of art, and that requires the reemergence of a *consciously socialist* current in art and filmmaking. That is one of the central themes of this talk. We argue that only the active presence of a critique that takes society down to its bones and holds out an alternative can encourage artwork prepared to tell the whole truth.

Film remains a powerful medium. Some 1.5 billion movie tickets were sold in North America last year, representing about a third of the global total.

However, changing what needs to be changed, I believe much of this discussion applies to fiction and theater relatively directly, and to the other art forms more indirectly—no medium has truly blossomed, except in the formal or technological sense, in the recent period, in my view.

We are confronted with filmmaking's shortcomings as an artistic and social fact. In terms of mainstream movies, for example, one only has to turn to the mostly dreadful list of Academy Award nominations for Best Picture this year. *Up in the Air* has possibilities, about a man who lives without relationships and accumulates air miles instead, but it is weakly worked out, in the end. There is Quentin Tarantino's exercise in historical falsification and sadism, *Inglourious Basterds*, "fighting fascism with fascism," as we noted on the WSWS. And *Avatar*, directed by James Cameron, which offers fascinating technology and little else.

There are several intelligent performances that received nominations—Colin Firth in *A Single Man*, Anna Kendrick for *Up in the Air* and a number of others—but, in general, the nominations are a miserable showing.

And this in 2010! What have we lived through in the first ten years of the new century?

The US media widely acknowledges that the first decade of the twenty-first century was a disastrous one for American society. *Time* magazine's headline read, "Goodbye (at Last) to the Decade from Hell."

To what extent, directly or indirectly, have the critical developments found expression in movies, which tens of millions of people affected by these events go to see? Is there a film or are there films that sum up the 2000s in a conscious and meaningful fashion? I'm open to suggestion, but I can't think of one.

In fact, what sort of a picture of the world could you assemble from the various images generated by most Hollywood films of the past ten years? Reality as seen through a narrow prism, of people without financial cares, obsessed with trivial concerns; these are dull films by and large, with the great drama of life missing (and the life of the upper middle class has not been seriously depicted either, for that matter).

American filmmaking has been able in the past to think more critically, to grasp the whole, or important portions of it. Consider these films from the mid 1930s to the early 1940s, just a few of the many extraordinary works made at the time:

Charles Chaplin
Modern Times, 1936
The Great Dictator, 1940
John Ford
The Informer, 1935
Grapes of Wrath, 1940
Orson Welles
Citizen Kane, 1941

These are arguably the three greatest figures in the American cinema, Chaplin, Ford and Welles. All, at the time, considered to be figures of the Left.

The FBI viewed John Ford as some sort of a subversive. *The Informer* is a magnificent study of treachery in the political struggle, with an atmosphere worthy of Alfred Döblin's *Berlin Alexanderplatz. Grapes of Wrath,* despite its occasional sentimental streak, conveys tremendous sympathy for the characters' plight. This story of suffering and resistance in the Depression made Henry Fonda himself a deeply beloved figure. Is there any equivalent today?

Or is there anything resembling Chaplin's persona? Or are there personalities as profoundly worked out, as passionately portrayed as Welles's *Kane*?

Where is the writer or director or actor today who has become identified with the plight of wide layers of the population?

We don't feel a trace of nostalgia. There is no golden age we're seeking
to re-create, but there were periods in American filmmaking and individual
works that were seen as offering a deep, universal insight into social life.
Do we have that today? Or anything near it? Again, the question, I think,
answers itself.

Also, it must be said, audiences were more knowledgeable and demanded more. We have to be frank about this: too many mediocre or worse
films receive a free pass. American audiences at this point, sadly, ask for
and expect far too little. It's certainly not the fault of the individual spectators, but it remains a problem. We receive email: you don't like anything,
you're too critical, you shouldn't expect so much ...

We don't agree. Of course, we make mistakes—one might overvalue
a certain work, and undervalue another. However, if we are critical in
our appraisals, it's not our fault there are so many poor and inadequate
works—to speak more plainly, so much rubbish. To tell the truth about the
problems in a sharp fashion is part of the process of changing things. The
population, along with economic and political resistance, needs to build up
its powers of *cultural* resistance.

I would suggest some of the same general difficulties hold true in fiction, drama.

Consider this:

Theodore Dreiser
An American Tragedy, 1925
F. Scott Fitzgerald
The Great Gatsby, 1925
Tender Is the Night, 1934
Ernest Hemingway
The Sun Also Rises, 1926
A Farewell to Arms, 1929

Where are the comparable figures and novels? Where are the strong
and telling images, the unforgettable characters? The authors, especially
Dreiser and Fitzgerald, attempted to make broad, universal statements

about American life. Where is the sense conveyed today of a historical period and of important popular moods, reality caught at a very high level, in
fact, at the highest level?

If we turn for a moment to some of the films of the 1930s and early
1940s ... This is not an exhaustive list, or a scholarly undertaking, but a
sample of memorable works:

Little Caesar, 1931
The Public Enemy, 1931
I Am a Fugitive from a Chain Gang, 1932
Wild Boys of the Road, 1933
Black Fury, 1935
Fury, 1936
You Only Live Once, 1937
Kid Galahad, 1937
The Roaring Twenties, 1939
They Made Me a Criminal 1939
They Drive by Night 1940
High Sierra, 1941
The Maltese Falcon, 1941
Casablanca, 1942

A good number of the movies come from Warner Bros.; several are
directed by Michael Curtiz, later joined by Raoul Walsh. Warners had James
Cagney, Edward G. Robinson, Paul Muni. The films, many of whose very
titles are suggestive, are characterized by lively, fierce and snappy dialogue,
unsentimentality, realism of a sort—they offer a feeling of the decade. One
could *learn something* about the country, the times, the population, by
watching these films.

There are also films on the list by German émigré Fritz Lang and John
Huston. Lang's *You Only Live Once* and *Fury*—the latter about a lynching—
are frightening films about injustice.

High Sierra, with Humphrey Bogart and Ida Lupino, one of the most
expressive performers of the era, is a particular favorite. It conveys a definite sense of the Depression years, their harshness, including their psychic
harshness, but also enormous tenderness and sensitivity that somehow
survive, like flowers growing through cracks in rock.

Casablanca, Maltese Falcon, of course, are well-known films.

In the end, these movies and others can only be accounted for by the fact that Hollywood had a large left wing and also a politically aware European émigré constituency in the 1930s and 1940s. The Depression, the rise of fascism and the example of the Russian Revolution had an enormous impact on the film community. It is a very contradictory phenomenon, with many tragic aspects, because of the role of the Stalinist Communist Party, but it remains a fact that when the anticommunist purges came, in the late 1940s and early 1950s, the authorities had to drive out, discredit or intimidate hundreds and hundreds of writers, directors, and actors ...

Let's consider this somewhat arbitrary list of postwar films:

The Best Years of Our Lives, 1946
The Big Sleep, 1946
Notorious, 1946
The Lady from Shanghai, 1947
Out of the Past, 1947
Body and Soul, 1947
Desperate, 1947
Lured, 1947
Force of Evil, 1948
They Live by Night, 1948
The Treasure of the Sierra Madre, 1948
Key Largo, 1948
The Naked City, 1948
Ruthless, 1948
Pitfall, 1948
D.O.A., 1949
White Heat, 1949
Caught, 1949
Whirlpool, 1949
Dark City, 1950

A film such as William Wyler's *The Best Years of Our Lives,* about returning World War II veterans and their discontents, dealt with experiences through which masses of people passed, the experiences of a generation. The title is ironic. The film takes an "unpatriotic," realistic view of things. It is critical of the treatment of war veterans.

Or one could point to John Ford's wartime film *They Were Expendable* (1945). The title refers in part to the US Navy's attitude toward PT boats and their crews. Would anyone in mainstream Hollywood dare today to make a work critical of the military?

It is worth mentioning as well other wartime films such as Howard Hawks's *To Have and Have Not* and Billy Wilder's *Double Indemnity* (both from 1944), the latter a savage film about American lower-middle-class mores.

Or take some of the leading actors of the period. Simplification, caricature and emotional "rounding off" were very much present, but, at their best, performers embodied something about the American personality, or personalities.

Take Edward G. Robinson and John Garfield—Jewish working class types, or working class intellectuals: Robinson, who met with Trotsky in Mexico; Garfield, a supporter of the Communist Party, essentially hounded to his death. James Cagney, born in the tough Yorkville section of Manhattan, anticlerical and left-wing, at least until the authorities got to him.

Or Bogart, who grew out of the gangster parts in the late 1930s into something interesting in films such as *High Sierra, Maltese Falcon, Casablanca, To Have and Have Not, Key Largo* and others. In *Casablanca* and *To Have and Have Not*, in particular, he plays the pragmatic, efficient individualist, who initially rejects a political or social appeal, but, in the end, responds strongly to the plight of the oppressed, proves capable of solidarity and of democratic sensibilities.

Women's roles expanded, and became more interesting—an important indicator of the relatively democratic, popular character of the films and filmmaking. A Barbara Stanwyck, for example, and numerous other tough working class or lower-middle-class girls, women—Joan Crawford, Jean Harlow, Ginger Rogers (aside from her dancing pictures): prepared to go to nearly any lengths to survive. The pre-Production Code films are even more explicit. Stanwyck, the former Ruby Stevens from Flatbush in Brooklyn, who worked as a wrapper in a department store …

Women who are intelligent, quick-witted, no pushovers, like the population itself: Bette Davis, Carole Lombard, Mary Astor, Greta Garbo, Marlene Dietrich, etc. In the 1940s, Lana Turner, Gene Tierney, Lauren Bacall, Joan Bennett, Veronica Lake, Ann Sheridan and many others.

Compare these personalities to the present state of things. There's a George Clooney, for example, a talented performer. His characters are clever but don't take themselves too seriously. Ready to improvise and roll with the punches, if necessary. Capable of showing a darker, tougher side. But his persona is far less defined so far, in social terms. Among female performers, there are even fewer figures who have been given the opportunity to represent something substantial. There are enormously talented actors; that's not the issue at all.

The opposite today of a Henry Fonda—in *You Only Live Once*, *Young Mr. Lincoln* and *Grapes of Wrath*—might be the unfortunate Tom Hanks. Considerable effort has been made to turn him into an "American Everyman," in *Saving Private Ryan* and elsewhere. In *Forrest Gump*—a terrible film—he was meant to represent that Everyman as an idiot. Hanks has lent himself to efforts intended to strengthen myths about America, about the Second World War, about the "Greatest Generation," and all that. None of that, however, has won him spontaneous public affection.

Numerous titles on that list of postwar films are suggestive of nightmares and delirium, "whirlpool," "caught," "ruthless," evil, nighttime, haunted … Several factors come into play—in the first place, the horrors of the Second World War and the Holocaust; but, as time passes—by 1948, let's say—there is also the pressing matter of the reality of postwar America, which is revealing itself. One thinks of such films as *Lady from Shanghai, Key Largo, Force of Evil*, for example. An important new theme emerges: the powerful presence in postwar society of profiteers and criminals (with a hint of fascism about them), including criminals in business suits.

Contrary to the illusions spread by the Communist Party and its periphery, the postwar years did not mean the expansion of the New Deal, a flowering of democracy. This conception was bound up with an entirely false conception of the war itself, which was not a war for democracy, although millions went to fight fascism, but a war between great power blocs, an imperialist war. The American Stalinists ignored the brutality of the Allied bombings of German cities, applauded the incineration of Hiroshima and Nagasaki. They and those around them were utterly unprepared for the Cold War, the anticommunist witch-hunt and the purges—with disastrous consequences.

Despite McCarthyism, Hollywood was not finished in the 1950s and 1960s. Indeed, in the former decade certain "classical directors" —Alfred Hitchcock, Ford, Hawks and Raoul Walsh, along with Anthony Mann and others—did some of their best work. And there were new voices, such as Douglas Sirk and Robert Aldrich.

The 1960s witnessed the collapse of studio filmmaking and the emergence of the independents, some of whom are or become identified with the radical wave of the latter part of the decade and the early 1970s.

The early part of that decade, connected to the anti-establishment mood among masses of youth in particular, produced some films that "got" certain situations and realities, that still attempted to make wide-ranging comments about American life ...

It seems worth noting, however, that the socially critical films of the 1970s, as valuable as some of them were and *remain*, generally lacked something present in earlier left-wing American filmmaking, with all its contradictions: a substantial interest in and the presence of the working class, or wide layers of the population, and their lives and problems in general. There is also a noticeable lack of interest in the great historical events of the twentieth century. These limitations speak to the nature of the radicalization of the time and all the complex questions it left untouched.

In the 1980s, in the face of the Reagan administration's attacks on the population, carried out with the collaboration of the Democrats, and a sharp turn to the right in the American elite, the films that stand out are those that resisted the generally reactionary tide:

Warren Beatty's *Reds* (1981), about John Reed and the Russian Revolution; Woody Allen's *Crimes and Misdemeanors* (1989) on the ruthless selfishness of New York's upper middle class; Barry Levinson's *Rain Man* (1988), a criticism of the prevailing worship of greed; Michael Cimino's *Heaven's Gate* (1980), a view of bitter class struggle in the 1890s in Wyoming; Oliver Stone's *Wall Street* (1987), about the criminal element rising to the top in American financial circles. Stone, to his credit, also made important films about the Vietnam War, *Platoon* (1986) and *Born on the Fourth of July* (1989); Michael Moore made his first feature, *Roger & Me* (1989), about the decline and fall of Flint, Michigan.

There were numerous serious or well-intentioned efforts, including Edward Zwick's *Glory* (1989) and John Sayles's *Matewan* (1987), but one must say: given the character of the assault on the population begun by Carter and undertaken vigorously by Reagan and the first Bush, the cinematic and artistic response overall was very weak and limited. By and large, the population was not clarified, whereas in Britain, in the work of Mike Leigh, Ken Loach, Stephen Frears and numerous others, there was a more concerted and conscious response to Thatcher, although one would not want to idealize the situation there either.

Things only got worse in American filmmaking over the next two decades, the 1990s and 2000s. Although it was not entirely a wasteland, and there were some lively works: in 1995 (*The Underneath, Palookaville, Welcome to the Dollhouse, To Die For* and *Safe*) and in 1998–99 (*Buffalo 66, Bulworth, The Newton Boys, Pecker, The Truman Show, A Simple Plan, The Thin Red Line, The Insider, Election, Rushmore, Boys Don't Cry*) in particular, for some reason. There are also the last interesting movies by Woody Allen, Richard Linklater's films, Steven Spielberg's *Schindler's List* (1993) and Robert Redford's *Quiz Show* (1994).

The decade produced a number of insightful works, but, interestingly, very few have been followed up on by the various writers and directors.

The World Socialist Web Site was launched in February 1998, and one of the first cultural issues we confronted was the immense success of James Cameron's *Titanic*. We criticized the film very sharply. We received hundreds of letters about *Titanic*, most of them protesting our view, but a discussion was initiated that has never stopped. Cultural criticism, film criticism in particular, is not an exact science. We have made mistakes, but I think the general trend of our analysis has been vindicated.

In the 2000s, there were the last films of Robert Altman, the films of Wes Anderson, the Coen brothers, Michael Moore, Alexander Payne ... I thought Wim Wenders's *Land of Plenty* (2004) was one of the most moving and complicated films about the American social situation and mood. Michelle Williams also appeared in *Wendy & Lucy* (2008), which, along with *Frozen River* (2008), indicated a deeper social interest and concern on the part of filmmakers—still very much a rare occurrence.

We noted a tendency, which I referred to previously: the inability of many filmmakers to follow up, mature, deepen initially interesting, even provocative work. One had to ask: why did the filmmakers find it so difficult to develop? Were they working from too narrow an intellectual, artistic basis?

"If ... disappointment becomes a quite noticeable phenomenon, this may point to a more generalized problem. Why is it at present that the work of so few young filmmakers becomes deeper, riper, more mature as their careers evolve? Why is regression, often revealing itself almost immediately, the rule rather than the exception? ...

"It is precisely the conscious 'purchase' of many films and filmmakers on the deeper social processes that is far too slight. The works tend only to catch at certain elements, sensations, memories. By and large, they deliver merely glancing blows to reality. Filmmakers make a fetish out of rejecting an historical approach to any problem or situation. Everything is surface and immediacy ...

"The key, in my opinion, is the lack of ideas, and, in particular, the lack of historical understanding and socially critical consciousness. Most film artists at present are endowed with too narrow an intellectual base from which to persist in and widen their explorations. Hence their regression and the spectator's disappointment." [Toronto International Film Festival 2002: "Why are there so many disappointing films?" 23 September 2002][140]

At the same time, we witnessed the emergence of genuinely antisocial, malevolent trends: Quentin Tarantino and his imitators, from the mid-1990s onward. Indeed, we continue to see the flourishing of this sort of thing, in the raft of porno-sadistic horror films, and Tarantino's films themselves.

A number of interesting films came out in 2005, including *Syriana*, *Munich*, *Good Night, and Good Luck*, *Gunner Palace* (the documentary about the Iraq war) and *Brokeback Mountain*.

Clearly, a number of the films in mid-decade were associated with a growing horror over the Iraq war; the Bush administration and its open criminality, militarism and brutality; its contempt for democratic rights; its use of torture and secret prisons.

At the same time, we pointed to the real limitations of Hollywood's "new seriousness," that the filmmakers had far to go, and I think that warning has been confirmed. (The election of Barack Obama, in particular, has apparently occasioned a serious—and revealing—weakening of the critical faculties.)

If we turn to the films directly on the subject of the Iraq and Afghanistan wars (or that are intended to refer to them), or the Bush administration, we can see some of the problems.

There are numerous pointed works here (*In the Valley of Elah* [2007], *Rendition* [2007], *The Situation* [2006]; and *Death of a President* [2006] and *Battle for Haditha* [2007], which were made by British directors), as well as some generally lamentable ones (*Lions for Lambs* [2007], *W.* [2008], *The Hurt Locker* [2009] ...). Also, the documentaries by the team of Michael Tucker and Petra Epperlein, and James Longley's *Iraq in Fragments*.

---

[140] Available: http://www.wsws.org/en/articles/2002/09/tff2-s23.html

Numerous pointed films ... but if one may say it, these are primarily "small-bore" works, works that take up elements, specific aspects of the situation. If one compares them, as a body, with *Apocalypse Now*, or even *Platoon*, for all its histrionics—the latter were movies that attempted to make a broad statement about American involvement in Vietnam, to paint it as a crime, as an imperialist crime. This element is largely missing today.

The "nonpolitical" war film finds its apotheosis in *The Hurt Locker*, whose claim to fame is its "neutral" stance in relation to the conflict itself. It is no such thing. Director Kathryn Bigelow admits to being fascinated, mesmerized, by war and violence, and the film ends up glamorizing a new (or fantasized) kind of American hero. We called it part of a "deplorable trend" in our review last year, and we stand by that.

If we consider the films of the 1990s and 2000s as a whole, what overall picture could we draw? That a good number of colorful, lively, innovative and clever works were released, containing, in some cases, extraordinary moments. Today's films, and the better television programs (HBO series, even certain network situation comedies), contain many attractive features, including remarkable individual characterizations and recreations of specific social circumstances, and, on occasion, the representation of historical events that are spot on.

Numerous intriguing films and series, but none of them attempted to trace problems to the social order itself, none of them traced social and historical evolution. There is almost no universal critique. Again, these are essentially small pieces, small-bore. We have witnessed a tremendous weakening of the ability to confront society as a whole.

I want to point once more to the events of the last decade or so. Because we've lived through it, because it is already *our past*, there is something of a tendency to take for granted, to accept as inevitable, what has happened to and in American society.

But consider for a second what the population has experienced: a manipulated sex scandal and a near coup d'état in the late 1990s; the hijacking of a national election (or two) essentially unopposed by the liberal establishment; a massive terrorist attack that has never properly been investigated or explained to the American people; a neocolonial war in Afghanistan, now expanding to Pakistan; the invasion and occupation of Iraq justified by shameless lies, with the full collaboration of the media and both parties; endless threats against Iran and other regimes that are perceived to stand in the way of the US; the locking up of suspects in secret prisons and torture sites; a sustained attack on long-standing constitutional rights; the illegal doctrine of preemptive war; the massive corporate looting of the economy, to the tune of trillions of dollars; a devastating crash and subsequent bailout of the banks, also to the tune of trillions of dollars; the growth of immense social inequality and social misery in the US, with tens of millions of people unemployed or underemployed; major cities ravaged (the city of Detroit is suffering from a 50 percent unemployment-underemployment rate) ...

All this—and virtually none of it has been treated seriously in films (or novels or drama). From the point of view of formal logic, it's almost incomprehensible. As though you were a photojournalist standing at the window with a camera in your hand, an extraordinary uproar erupted in the street, and you deliberately turned away and took pictures instead of your children doing their homework. Some considerable countervailing pressure must be at work.

These are unprecedented events. They haven't gone entirely unnoticed or uncritiqued, but, one must say, in relation to the depth of the transformations, the artistic response has been entirely inadequate, statistically almost insignificant.

The power of money, extensive corporate control, and direct political pressure certainly play a role. However, there are also nominally independent film festivals. Individuals with video cameras and editing equipment can create their own works. There is very little of significance in this sphere, either. The only benefit of American "independent" cinema at the moment is that by and large it makes you long for Hollywood's products. I don't want to hurt anyone's feelings, but we are confronted for the most part with the self-involved, unenlightening products of 28- and 30-year-olds who have very little to say.

In our view, the artists have proven ill-equipped, unprepared intellectually for the developments.

The ideological pressures following upon the collapse of the Soviet Union and the other Stalinist regimes in 1989–91, all the blather about "the end of socialism," "the end of history," as well as the decay of the old labor movements in every country, and the social conditions that have emerged for masses of people bound up with these problems—all this has had consequences.

The reactionary climate of the past several decades in general has had an impact. The enrichment of sections of the upper middle class and their lurch to the right are facts of American social and political life. There has been a fantastic accumulation of wealth by a relative handful, including in the entertainment industry.

This is a very conspicuous process in New York City. Woody Allen and others have either made that same transition or succumbed, or been laid low, by its pressure.

That is part of the explanation, but it begs the question: why were the intellectuals so unprepared for those processes; why were they so vulnerable?

A fundamental theme of this presentation is the need for a *consciously socialist current* in filmmaking and among artists in general. We're not speaking of some sort of political litmus test; in other words, encouraging the emergence of artists who would win our ideological approval for some sort of short-term gain. That's not the issue at all. This is a practical, artistic and social necessity. We are inundated with films, novels and plays that go so far ... and no farther.

We have lived for decades in this country under conditions produced in part by official anticommunism, McCarthyism, the purges of left-wing forces from the unions, from film and television. Socialist thought was criminalized, marginalized, excluded. This is a central element in our current difficulties. And, it must be said, the radicalization of the 1960s did not make deep inroads here.

But art despises half-measures. It is untenable in the long run: making a half-critique, pointing to this or that surface development, this or that symptom.

Where is the artist today at total war with official society? Where is the artist who says: "I despise all this—patriotism, nationalism, war, the military, religion, the government, parliament, business, profits"? Who says, "I hate the hypocrisy, the criminality, the greed of the ruling classes. I want nothing to do with such people, I'll search out and align myself with their enemies." Artists have said and done this in the past; modern art is inconceivable without it.

The crimes of Stalinism threw an entire generation, or several generations, into crisis, from the mid-1930s onward. The terrible deeds carried out in the name of communism brought discredit on the noblest ideas in history. Stalinism itself, its twists and turns, its cynicism, its catastrophic policies, demoralized artists and intellectuals in the late 1930s and 1940s. Its crimes were then used by the witch-hunters and their liberal allies to justify the purges and the blacklist.

The artists are suffering from the combined effects of the traumatic events of the twentieth century. But these events and their consequences need to be studied, understood and overcome. Serious progress is impossible without that. It is simply not possible, in the first place, to represent truthfully the character of contemporary relations between people on this planet unless you understand the history of those relations as social phenomena.

What's needed? A number of things, in our view.

Greater artistry and intellectual effort. Art is exhausting, unsettling, difficult work. We have referred numerous times to the film school graduate with the unfurrowed brow. There is the problem of what the younger generation of filmmakers has been through, seen, experienced ...

People can't be blamed for what they haven't lived through, but we have to tell the truth. We say to the artists: what you know, what is in your head, is inadequate. You have to be oriented toward bigger questions, questions of society and history first and foremost. That doesn't have to be the substance of your work; it doesn't matter how intimate your immediate subject might be—another *War and Peace* or a love lyric—but there remains the need for the broadest thought and understanding, for presenting complex and difficult problems, all of which require real intellectual struggles.

Texture, complexity and depth come with knowledge, deep emotion, a deep understanding and feeling for the art form itself, its human and artistic possibilities, and not merely its technical capabilities, much less the desire to impress or to show off. Art is about showing life, not having a career.

As I've suggested, we need to revive protest, anger and outrage, the desire to see the world changed from top to bottom. It's hard to conceive of important work in our day without that. Absolutely critical, in our view: the artists must overcome the prejudice against socialism! Absolutely no major progress will occur without that.

If the artists brought together the technological innovations of the recent period—its freshness and cleverness, its color and rapid movement, and the ability to impart vast amounts of information quickly and clearly—with important ideas, artistic elegance and seriousness, and with a concern for humanity and its fate ... that would open the road to important work, in our view.

In 1928, Soviet literary critic Aleksandr Voronsky—Left Oppositionist, co-thinker of Trotsky, and eventual victim of Stalin in 1937—addressed this problem. It was part of his struggle for more seriousness about life and genuine engagement with the world in Soviet writing. He commented:

"We cannot simply 'wave aside' the sharpness of perception, the dynamics and the refinement of artistic devices, the rich impressionability, the new forms, the style and the 'shock effect' which were introduced into our literature by the impressionists, and by the individualistic schools in general on the eve of the revolution. That is not what is being discussed. Nor are we talking about a return to a Goncharovian realism ...

"The whole question for art right now is how, using the extremely sharp, individual and subjective devices developed earlier, to achieve the most objective portrayals of the world, i.e., portrayals in which its solid existence is most clearly palpable; so that at the same time these artistic discoveries of the world can be united with deliberate activity, with goal-directedness, with powerful, creative, social desires. In the end, desire is the mother of truth."[141]

I believe this is profoundly important. There is no going back to Ford or Welles. The greatest work, we have confidence, lies ahead. But the ingenuity of present-day filmmaking has to be combined with far deeper knowledge of the world, to bring out the true character of contemporary life, to enlighten and broaden the population, to appeal to what is best in it, to contribute to the cause of liberating global humanity from ignorance, exploitation and poverty.

A final point: what we have been discussing are objective problems, social problems, historical problems. We are farther than anyone from blaming individuals for the difficulties. We don't (or we try not to) heap abuse, on the pages of the WSWS, on the artists who fall short, even those who fall very far short. The problem lies outside them, in historical traumas and difficulties that have yet to be overcome, in new realities that have yet to be cognized. We fight with great urgency for a different perspective, a different orientation, but we also understand that big popular movements will play a critical role in dispersing the "clouds of skepticism and pessimism" (Trotsky).

As the working class begins to move, and it will, many of today's problems will seem trivial, or will disappear entirely. A new set of challenges and problems will arise, and we certainly welcome those. We will do everything in our power to assist the artists, the filmmakers, to arrive at a deeper understanding of the historical and social issues involved.

---

[141] Aleksandr Voronsky, "The Art of Seeing the World," *Art as the Cognition of Life* (Oak Park: Mehring Books, 1998), 391.

Index